SEX, LOVE, AND MIGRATION

SEX, LOVE, AND MIGRATION

Postsocialism, Modernity, and Intimacy
from Istanbul to the Arctic

Alexia Bloch

CORNELL UNIVERSITY PRESS   ITHACA AND LONDON

First published 2017 by Cornell University Press

Printed in the United States of America

Library of Congress Cataloging-in-Publication Data

Names: Bloch, Alexia, author.
Title: Sex, love, and migration : postsocialism, modernity, and intimacy from Istanbul to the Arctic / Alexia Bloch.
Description: Ithaca : Cornell University Press, 2017. | Includes bibliographical references and index.
Identifiers: LCCN 2017025809 (print) | LCCN 2017027191 (ebook) | ISBN 9781501712050 (epub/mobi) | ISBN 9781501709418 (pdf) | ISBN 9781501713149 (cloth : alk. paper) | ISBN 9781501713156 (pbk. : alk. paper)
Subjects: LCSH: Women foreign workers—Former Soviet republics. | Women foreign workers—Turkey. | Transnationalism—Former Soviet republics. | Transnationalism—Turkey. | Post-communism—Former Soviet republics.
Classification: LCC HD8528.5.A2 (ebook) | LCC HD8528.5.A2 B56 2017 (print) | DDC 331.4086/240947—dc23
LC record available at https://lccn.loc.gov/2017025809

To Milind

Contents

Illustrations

Acknowledgments

Writing a book is a unique labor of love. The labor for this book project has extended well over a decade, so the list of those to whom I am indebted is quite long and diverse. The project would never have come into being without the inspiring entrepreneurial spirit of central Siberian women I met in the early 1990s, who were traveling across borders to supply their communities with clothing. Likewise, my research benefited immensely from the generosity of numerous women involved in the shuttle trade or working as labor migrants from Russia, southern Moldova, Ukraine, and Belarus. I owe a special thanks to those identified here as Kara, Bella, Zina, Maria, Eva, and Nelli for introducing me to their circles, as well as for providing me with something equally precious, their friendship. Maria's, Zina's, and Nelli's families warmly welcomed me and my family in Istanbul, Moscow, and Moldova as this project extended through the years.

A number of sources of funding supported research and writing. The Humanities and Social Sciences (HSS) fund at the University of British Columbia (UBC), the Peter Wall Institute for Advanced Studies at UBC, and the International Research and Exchanges Board (IREX) provided support early on (2001–2003). The Social Science and Humanities Research Council (SSHRC) of Canada provided generous funding between 2002 and 2006, making it possible to conduct research spanning three countries, including by covering expenses to have my infant daughter accompany me. The UBC Killam Faculty Research Fellowship supported my sabbatical leave in Turkey (2007), and the UBC Arts Undergraduate Research Award (AURA) supported several undergraduate students to do library research. Finally, in 2016 I was fortunate to receive the UBC Dean of Arts Faculty Research Award, a form of support that could not have come at a better time; the award enabled me to set aside teaching and administrative duties for one term and focus on completing the manuscript.

Acknowledgements are due for portions of the book that have appeared previously, and for permissions granted for several images appearing in the book. Portions of chapter 2 were previously published in "Emotion Work, Shame, and Post-Soviet Women Entrepreneurs: Negotiating Ideals of Gender and Labor in a Global Economy," *Identities: Global Studies in Culture and Power* 18(4), and a version of chapter 6 was published as "'Other Mothers,' Migration, and a Transnational Nurturing Nexus," *Signs: Journal of Women in Society and Culture* 43(1).

I wish to acknowledge the Yapi Kredi Historical Archives in Istanbul for granting me permission to use an image from the Selahattin Giz Collection. Finally, I wish to thank Jared Bloch for allowing me to use three of his photographs, including for the book's cover.

I have benefited immeasurably from opportunities to try out ideas with a wide number of colleagues, and I especially wish to thank the following: the School for American Research and Carole Vance for organizing the workshop "Ethnography and Policy: What do we Know about Trafficking?" (2005); the Japanese National Museum of Ethnology (MINPAKU) and Yuki Konagaya for the "Narratives of Socialism" workshop in Osaka (2010); the Wellesley College Russian Area Studies Lecture Series and Philip Kohl for inviting me to speak at my alma mater (2012); and the Center for Semiotic Folklore Studies, Russian State University for the Humanities, and Sergey Nekliudov for so graciously hosting my participation in the seminar series "Folklore and Post-folklore" (2015). Early on in the project Marina Malysheva and Elena Tiuriukanova also encouraged me to pursue the research and facilitated access to the Moscow Center for Gender Studies. Nicole Constable deserves a separate note of appreciation for her long-term support and for inspiring me to think about gender and migration as an avenue for research. Finally, I am indebted to Bruce Grant for his warm collegiality over the years and for blazing a distinctive trail in the anthropology of the former Soviet Union.

Spaces for writing have also been essential for completing the book. I wish to thank the School of European Languages at the English and Foreign Languages University in Hyderabad, India, for arranging library access in the summer of 2006. Likewise, the Sociology Department at Boğaziçi University in Istanbul, and especially Faruk Birtek and Nükhet Sirman, kindly facilitated my research arrangements in the spring of 2007. The Department of Anthropology at the American Museum of Natural History afforded me a much appreciated, ongoing affiliation, including for a sabbatical year in New York (2012–2013). I am grateful to the Harriman Institute of Russian, Eurasian, and East European Studies at Columbia University for hosting me that same year as a Visiting Scholar; this enabled me to bring a complete draft of my manuscript into being in one of the most conducive spaces for writing that I could hope for, the library at the Union Theological Seminary. The coffee cart and its hardworking staff at the corner of 122nd Street and Broadway deserve a special acknowledgment for keeping me on track throughout 2012–2013.

I wish to thank those who contributed invaluable support and feedback at various stages of this project. Maria Believa, Dikmen Bezmez, Eda Cakmakci, Hansen Chou, Jenna Dur, Tatiana Gadjalova (Boya), Alexey Golubev, Oralia Gómez-Ramírez, Susan Hicks, Sungsook Lim, Anastasia Rogova, and Jayme Taylor assisted me in a multitude of ways. Joan Weeks, Head and Turkish Specialist at the Near East Section of the African and Middle East Division of the U.S. Library of Congress, advised me on spellings for Turkish names. Eda Cakmakci provided essential assistance for arranging image permissions with the Yapi Kredi Historical Archives, and she provided Turkish language expertise. Oralia Gómez-Ramírez ably carried out the time-consuming tasks of preparing images used in the book, including the formatting and copyright details, and creating the book's index. Jayme Taylor crafted the maps and Anastasia Rogova attentively corrected Russian translations and transliterations, as well as locating elusive sources. Under tight deadlines at the very end of the writing process Kathryn White and Susan Dwelle took on the job of editing the manuscript; Susan especially reminded me of the pitfalls of jargon and the joys of clear language. Office staff at the UBC Department of Anthropology cheerfully facilitated paperwork and grant administration throughout the project, and I especially owe gratitude to Radicy Braletic, Joyce Ma, and Eleanore Asuncion. Finally, at Cornell University Press I am indebted to James Lance for his timely enthusiasm for the project and for shepherding the book through its production. Three anonymous reviewers were immensely helpful as I revised and sharpened key arguments and Carolyn Pouncy turned a careful eye to copyediting. Any remaining errors are my own.

Friends and colleagues were essential to envisioning, carrying out, and completing the project. I am grateful to Julie Cruikshank for much-needed walks, gentle advice, and treasured discussions of writing and reading, including inspired new fiction. Laurel Kendall has been a mentor and friend, offering sage counsel and sharing her keen eye for textiles and love of fine vegetarian cuisine. Nina Diamond showed me the possible depths of friendship, and read and commented on an early draft of the manuscript, as well as lending her ear and sharp eye in the last stages of manuscript preparation. Early on Michael Hathaway provided frank assessments of key conceptual frameworks. Leslie Robertson offered regular reflection on the challenges of creating meaningful ethnography and she was a trusted sounding board for possible titles. Kyra Çubukçuoğlu has provided a thread of connection between Russia, Turkey, and New York that has stretched over three decades; I am also indebted to Kyra, her husband Ilhan, and their family for facilitating my research. Friends on the East and West coasts have provided welcome respite and perspective over the years; my thanks especially go to Gili Avrahami, Sumeet Gulati, Topher Jerome, Ashok Kotwal, Truus Kotwal, Nisha Malhotra, Terre Satterfield, and Homer Williams. A special note of thanks is due to Kate Swatek for the many sauna conversations and for nourishing my imagination through her love of stories that link us across wide expanses of time and place, from China to Pittsburgh to New York to Vancouver. Yael, Gideon, and Dror Lavi-Shelach knew just when and where to visit, as the project commenced in Istanbul and as it was wrapping up in Vancouver. In Russia the Savoskuls welcomed me in their home and provided me with an ideal location for initiating the project. Svetlana Savoskul aided me in making contact with shuttle traders and Oxana and Maria Savoskul consistently buoyed me with their interest in the book project. In Istanbul Thomas Bitner kindly allowed me to stay in his "tower" for research stays, short and long, Gaspard Biz shared his hearty laugh and his cosmopolitan outlook grounded in living for years in Russia and Turkey, and Gaelle Berthet shared her joie de vivre and knowledge of all the family friendly spaces one could imagine. Mostly, I was fortunate to meet Consuelo (Chelo) Echeverria early on in the research at her art installation at Istanbul's Galata Tower; her unfailing belief in the book and her generous spirit contributed immeasurably to the project.

In no small measure the book owes its existence to numerous instances of family support. Two women in particular made the research possible: my stepmother, Rebecca Sheppard, and my mother, Susan Dwelle. I am grateful to them for their unreserved willingness to care for their granddaughter, Mira, during extended fieldwork: in 2003 in Istanbul (both Rebecca and Susan), in Moldova (Rebecca), and Russia (Susan); in 2004 and 2005 in Moldova and Vermont (Rebecca); and in 2007 in Istanbul (both Rebecca and Susan). My father, John Bloch, inspired me with his deep commitment to challenging social inequality and his curiosity about rural spaces in the former Soviet Union, and he also assisted in essential care giving. My brother Jared's discriminating photographic eye gave me some fresh perspectives on the energy and allure of Istanbul. Finally, on numerous occasions my brother Tobias's expert logistical support in New York City considerably eased the difficulty of travel to and from Turkey with a small child.

Finally, my immediate family has made the book project possible to envision and, ultimately, to bring to fruition. Mira's life more or less spans the life of the research, and she has grown up knowing there are people across the world but especially in Istanbul, southern Moldova, and Russia who ask about her and revisit her infant pictures as they recall their own lives in the early years of the new millennium. Samir arrived as the research was wrapping up, reminding me of the pleasures of finding a fine balance between family and professional pursuits. I hope both Mira and Samir can ultimately see my efforts to forge a full, albeit sometimes harried, life as an example of one fulfilling way of being in the world. This way of being would not be possible to fathom without Milind Kandlikar. He unflinchingly single-parented during regular fieldwork stints, took on more than his fair share of household labor at crunch times, and reminded me to take time to laugh and enjoy a glass of wine. Mostly, he has steadfastly believed in the book.

In the following pages I have tried to bring to life the trials and tribulations, but also the hopes and dreams, of women on the move between the former Soviet Union and Istanbul. I can only hope that in some small part I have succeeded.

Note on Transliteration and Translation

The Modified Library of Congress system is used in transliterating Russian from the Cyrillic. Russian, Turkish, or Moldovan place names and spellings are retained, except when there is a commonly used English version. For instance, Bosphorus, not Boğaziçi, Moscow, not Moskva, and Gagauzia, not Gagauziia, are used in the text. Another challenge is posed by places that have more than one place name widely used in the present. For Chişinău or Vulcăneşti, in Moldovan, Kishinev and Vulkaneshty, respectively, in Russian, I have retained the word used by the speaker or source.

All personal names used in the text are pseudonyms, unless a person was acting in an official capacity. I have made an effort to use pseudonyms that were not uncommon names among women migrants I came to know from the former Soviet Union. For names in Russian I have followed the Modified Library of Congress system, except in the case of two names, where for the ease of the Anglophone reader I have used the more common English versions: Olga (instead of Ol'ga) and Maria (instead of Mariia). The spelling of authors' names appears, for the most part, as in the original sources.

When terms in Russian, Turkish, or Gagauz occur in the text, they are defined with the first usage. All translations from Russian to English or Turkish to English are my own unless otherwise indicated.

For those readers unfamiliar with Turkish or Moldovan spellings and pronunciation, a few guidelines may be of use. The *ă* appearing in Moldovan words is pronounced as "a" in *a*nnunciate. The *c, ç, ğ, ı, ö, ş, ü* found in Turkish words (and the *ç* and *ş* in Moldovan words) are pronounced as follows:

C, c   as "j" in *j*am
Ç, ç   as "ch" in *ch*uckle
Ğ, ğ   is usually silent, lengthens the preceding vowel
I, ı   a hard "i" as in fl*i*rt
Ö, ö   as in French eu, as in *deux*
Ş, ş   as "sh" in *sh*out
Ü, ü   as "u" in n*ew*

Unless otherwise indicated, monetary values are in US dollars.

Part I

MOBILITIES AND INTIMACIES

FROM THE ARCTIC TO ISTANBUL

In the spring of 1999 Zhenia and I sat by an apartment window in Tura, a central Siberian town in the Evenk District. In between tapping her ashes into the stove with her long fingernails painted in a deep red, Zhenia told me about her recent buying trips. Zhenia and I had come to know each other over seven years, since just before the end of the Soviet Union. As an indigenous Siberian, Zhenia had been the beneficiary of a number of affirmative action programs still in place in educational institutions in the 1990s; she had unsuccessfully trained to become a medical assistant and later a lawyer, before dedicating herself to educating special needs children and becoming a teacher. Zhenia felt stuck in this profession when I met her in 1992, and by 1993 she had endured months at a time without receiving a paycheck. Finally, in 1995 Zhenia looked to business as a profession, first working as an assistant for her older brother's grocery supply company and then in 1998 starting her own clothing import business.

Sitting in my second-story apartment we burned through a pack of Kosmos cigarettes and watched from the window as townspeople planted potatoes. Zhenia savored recounting the travails of her year. She declared that she would not return to Central Asia. On a trip earlier that year, while making a tiring journey by truck across Kazakhstan, Zhenia was mugged and lost the $1,000 she had brought along intending to purchase clothing for resale.[1] That was a hard way to make a living. She contrasted this with her satisfying and profitable trip to the United Arab Emirates (UAE). She felt lucky that she had managed to travel there, since soon after her trip the government ceased to issue visas to women under thirty unless a brother or husband accompanied them.[2] Zhenia brushed aside the UAE's concerns about young women taking up sex work; she remembered the Arab men's attention with fondness and recounted how she "felt like a queen" during her wholesale buying trip.[3] She had purchased several bundles of clothing for resale back in Siberia and described the thrill she felt in hiring men with trolleys to deposit her wares at her hotel. "I did not have to lift a finger!" She inspected her nails and reflected, "There, they really know how to treat a woman like a lady; they even kissed my hand in parting!" While Zhenia did not return to the UAE, her myriad subsequent trips to Turkey were as much about the new forms of intimacy that she and other women sometimes savored as transnational migrants as they were about supplying the growing demand for fashionable clothing in Siberia.

Zhenia is part of a global trend where women have become increasingly mobile since the 1970s. If until then men typically migrated, with women and children sometimes accompanying men as dependents, today about equal numbers of men and women are international migrants; of the 244 million people in the world today who live outside their country of origin (UNFPA 2015), half are women. People are on the move due to civil war, natural disasters, and unstable governments, but women's mobility, in particular, increased as of the 1970s with the global turn toward intensified economic restructuring that brought about the retraction of government services and new forms of precarity, along with an expansion of service economies and the demand for low-wage labor. As Zhenia's comments suggest, thinking about gender and migration in the former Soviet Union (FSU) can telescope our attention to how global economic crises and related neoliberal restructuring are integrally tied to what is often relegated to "emotional," "private," or "intimate" realms.[4] Once state socialism was, as one particularly apt analysis has noted, "no more" (Yurchak 2003), transnational mobility came to define lives on a scale not seen in this part of Eurasia since the end of the Second World War.

In the pages of this book I trace these linkages between transnational mobility, brought about by the end of socialism and the expansion of global capitalism, and the daily relationships that are often sidelined in accounts of migration. In so doing I show the radical ways that new mobility has shaped intimate practices or the emotional worlds and social ties of women, men, and children in Eurasia. A key trajectory of transnational migration out of the former Soviet Union has been to Turkey, and as post-Soviet women have engaged in circular migration between the former Soviet Union and Turkey, they have forged new forms of intimacy that are central to their transnational mobility. Post-Soviet women like Zhenia are not simply crossing physical borders. They are also part of renewed transnational flows between places that over much of the twentieth century were widely conceived of as East or West, capitalist or socialist, or modern or traditional, especially concerning questions of gender and sexuality. In moving between the lives of post-Soviet women employed in Istanbul in three distinct spheres—sex work, the garment trade, and domestic work—I consider how migrant women negotiate emotion, intimate relationships, and unpredictable state power shaping their labor. Moreover, in decoupling images of women on the move from simple assumptions about danger, victimization, and exploitation, I turn our attention to the intricate lives of people and the intimate ties, often based on love or commitment, that they foster in their transnational mobility.

Drawing on ethnographic fieldwork conducted over a decade (2001–2011) in Turkey, Moldova, and Russia, this book is grounded in the accounts of post-Soviet migrant women like Zina, Irina, and Olga, who all turned to transnational labor migration to Istanbul with the end of socialism in the region. In the mid-1990s Zina boarded a minibus in southern Moldova to seek work in Istanbul; in the wake of devastating economic restructuring, her job as a medical orderly had gone unpaid for months, and her husband had died while working on a temporary construction brigade in Moscow. Employed for over fifteen years in domestic work in Istanbul, Zina was able to earn a living; she renovated her home back in Moldova and supported two children through postsecondary education. Others—like Olga, a shuttle trader from Russia, and Irina, an exotic dancer from Ukraine—traveled as much out of a newfound sense of possibility as out of necessity. These sentiments, reflecting novel gender systems encountered by women border crossers, as well as excitement about unprecedented opportunities to travel, echo central themes in the many conversations I had with post-Soviet women moving between the former Soviet Union and Turkey. In portraying mobile post-Soviet women who are reweaving a social fabric frayed with the end of socialism, I aim to show in these pages how women are reworking intimacy in a time of widely atomized lives.

This is most definitely not a story of progression, of people mastering the ways of capitalism, and on the way jettisoning their "backward" socialist ways. Instead, this is a story of continuities and interweavings, of visions of modernity (failed, emerging, or contested), and ways that feminized mobility fits into a pattern of neoliberal restructuring that is increasingly defining Eurasia, including Turkey and the former Soviet Union. By focusing on women who struggle to maintain lives across recently porous transnational borders, this book provides a unique portal into reconfigurations of power and possibility in Eurasia. The new forms of mobility in the region have acted as a sort of handmaiden to reflections about "modernity," complicating liberal narratives that can assume a trajectory from an "oppressive" state socialism to the "opportunities" offered by global capitalism.

Socialist paradigms and forms of governance, however, were not immediately or evenly displaced, and people who lived under state socialism have widely continued to reflect on a sense of a derailed socialist modernity (Berdahl 1999; Yurchak 2003; Dunn 2004; Ghodsee 2009).

Many women I met, like Zhenia, recounted how they were initially dazzled by the possibilities created by border crossing and the intimate economies they encountered, but many also bitterly critiqued what they had lost with their insertion into circuits of global capitalism. Some scholars argue that with new forms of mobility, and the constriction of others, mobility itself has become a sign that is concomitant with modernity (see Chu 2010). Similarly, I see mobility as enabling us to understand shifting ideals associated with "modernity," something of a slippery category (see Cooper 2005, 113–49), but one often invoked by migrants I met in reference to gender ideals and intimate practices (see Abu-Lughod 1997). In writing about post-Soviet women who travel across wide expanses to work and live in Turkey for lengthy periods of time, I argue that intimate practices between men and women, mothers and children, grandmothers and children, and migrant women and Turkish men are a central part of the story of the massive mobility brought about by the intensifying forces of global capitalism and the waning power of state socialism. In presenting a portrait of intimate practices as at the crux of the experience of transnational border crossing, this book turns away from dominant discourses revolving around remittances, border regulation, and victimization and instead seeks to turn our attention to the experience of women migrants making lives for themselves in a newly transnational space.

Post-Soviet Subjects on the Move in Eurasia

Although the research for this book is largely based in Istanbul, Turkey, the focus is on post-Soviet migrants as people on the move, and less on the Turks with whom migrants interact. The migrants who are the subject of this book are diverse. Their time in Turkey can be sojourns of just a few days, but mostly it is years on end punctuated by variable "circular" patterns of short visits to home communities. A handful of migrants work with official contracts, but the vast majority arrive on tourist visas to work, and then overstay their visas, making them "undocumented"; they do not have the legal right to work, and having overstayed visas, they no longer have the legal right to be in Turkey. They come from a wide range of countries, including Belarus, Ukraine, Azerbaijan, Moldova, Kazakhstan, Armenia, Uzbekistan, Russia, and Georgia. Despite this diversity, labor migrants from the former Soviet Union are predominantly women and share a history of living in societies shaped by socialism, including a particular

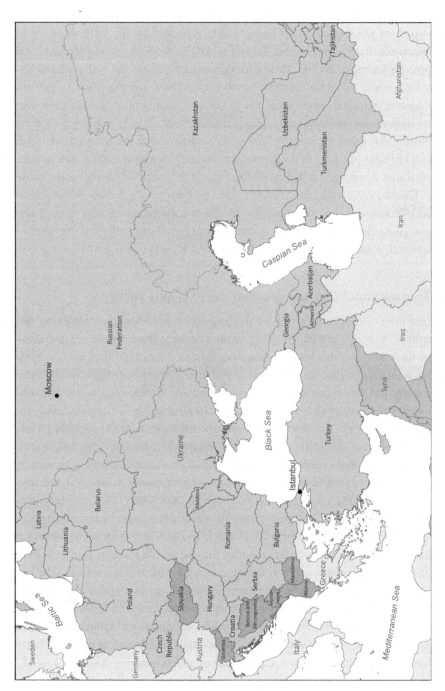

FIGURE 1. Map of Eurasia, focused on Turkey and the Black Sea Region. Created by Jayme Taylor.

ethic around the meanings of citizenship and a lingua franca of Russian. They also share the experience of being widely perceived by the Turkish public as hypersexualized (Gülçür and İlkkaracan 2000). Overall, the deeply gendered post-Soviet mobility into Turkey fundamentally defines the transnational circuits women maintain between Istanbul and home communities. Long-term migrants frequently foster close ties to transnational families, pursue their own aspirations for adventure and independence, and often establish emotionally meaningful ties with men in Turkey. In writing about the transnational lives and intimate practices of these newly mobile post-Soviet women, I seek to trace what one scholar has called the "routes" and the "roots" of people on the move (Clifford 1997); while the "routes" I trace are between the former Soviet Union and Turkey, and the "roots" are very much in a shared post-Soviet space, I also give particular emphasis to one community of post-Soviet migrants prevalent in Istanbul, women from southern Moldova.

Transnational Circuits between the FSU and Turkey

Like Roger Rouse, who writes of the "crisscrossed economies, intersecting systems of meaning, and fragmented identities brought about by a newly globalized world" (1991, 8), this book moves away from a more traditional ethnographic focus on a single place or ethnic group and instead revolves around transnational circuits and flows. Inspired by a vibrant body of scholarship on transnational migration (Basch et al. 1994; Glick Schiller 1999; Ong 1999), and particularly the gendered nature of this mobility (Morokvasic 1984; Pessar and Mahler 2003; Constable 2003; Hirsch 2003; Cheng 2010), I seek to show how mobility has become central to the daily lives of people in this part of Eurasia, as well as to portray the diverse ties post-Soviet labor migrants maintain both in Istanbul and with friends and family across the FSU and beyond. Post-Soviet labor migrants often aim to work in West European countries where pay is most lucrative (Ghençea and Gudumac 2004; Subbotina 2007), but in practice they go closer to home. For instance, Russia is the primary country for the shuttle trade in garments from Turkey, and it is also a major receiving country for labor migrants from the former Soviet Union, including from Central Asian countries, Ukraine, and Moldova (Bloch 2014; Reeves 2014, Demintseva and Kashnitsky 2016). In Russia migrant men and women find work in construction and apartment renovation, as well as in the service sector, with women increasingly in demand as domestic labor. Meanwhile in Turkey, women migrants are overwhelmingly in demand, especially in the service sectors of entertainment, domestic work, or sales (as shop assistants and interpreters), while there is far less demand for migrant men's labor.

Moldova, in particular, has a striking profile of labor migration, including into Turkey. Since the late 1990s almost 20 percent of working-age Moldovans have lived outside Moldova in a given year; in 2009 as much as 23 percent of the Moldovan GDP came from official remittances (Ghençea and Gudumac 2004, 41; Subbotina 2007; UNDP 2011, 129). Unofficial remittances and payments for goods, like the thousands of dollars that one of my interlocutors clandestinely strapped around her midriff on regular trips from Ukraine and Moldova as payment for goods bought in Turkey, also play a substantial role in this financial flow.[5] Similar to Rhacel Parreñas's (2001a) findings among Filipino transnational families, the remittance economy tying Moldovans to Turkey, and to Russia, is closely linked to an elaborate renegotiation of familial responsibilities and nurturing roles. Women's and men's long and/or frequent absences from home, their remittances, and their new spheres of work influence their roles as parents, spouses, and citizens in households and communities with which they maintain variable links.

The new social and economic roles that post-Soviet women, in particular, have come to occupy as they move goods, ideas, and remittances across post-Soviet borders are an important aspect of this expansive labor migration, which has received little attention. Women's accounts of their labor and their efforts to continue labor migration despite increased policing of borders tell a story that is too often overshadowed by accounts of victimization at the hands of criminal elements (e.g., Hughes 2000; Malarek 2003). In turning attention to the migrants and their intimate practices, we can understand the ways that post-Soviet women actively strategize to cross borders, including by remarrying so as to have passports reissued with new surnames, establishing long-term liaisons and marriage with Turkish men, and procuring work as entertainers in clubs. However, we can also think about how media and government structures inform intimate practices, and how not just individuals but also households are involved in intimate practices of nurturing those who are left behind in home communities. Overall, post-Soviet women's experiences of border crossing for labor migration fit within a global trend of gendered flexible labor that serves new forms of transnational capital and indelibly links intimate practices across wide expanses (Colen 1995; Ehrenreich and Hochschild 2002).

With tourist visas available on entry as of the early 1990s, women arrived in Turkey by the thousands just as tensions between secularist and Islamist visions of modernity were intensifying (see White 2002).[6] The ideals of the growing Turkish Islamist movement—defined by political and revivalist sentiments, including gendered codes of modesty—have particularly contrasted with visible markers of women's sexuality expressed by many secular urbanites in Turkey, including

Russian-speaking migrant women like Zhenia (Öncü 1999; White 1999).[7] Post-Soviet women have become the lightning rods for fraught discussions around gendered codes of modesty and expressions of women's sexuality (Hann and Béller-Hann 1998; Hacaoğlu 2002; Uygun 2004). The very ability to engage in transnational border crossing marks postsocialist women in Turkey as transgressive, something that contributes to their symbolic capital as embodying "modern" forms of intimacy (Giddens 1992; Parla 2009). Although Turkey is not the only destination for post-Soviet women labor migrants, it does seem to be the only one with such a high demand for feminized labor that for more than two decades consisted predominantly of migrant women from the former Soviet Union.[8]

From the early 1990s, as the former Soviet region's economies collapsed, the Turkish economy flourished. Turkey established an impressive civic infrastructure, expanded a solid professional middle class that was increasingly educated at prestigious overseas institutions, and built an economy based on agriculture, manufacturing, and textile production aimed at exporting to European and North American markets. Turkey was also fast becoming a popular destination for tourism, which from the late 1990s became one of the largest spheres of employment for Turks and non-Turks alike (İçöz et al. 1998; Gökovali 2010). Despite a major domestic economic crisis in 2000 and the global economic crisis in 2009, for nearly twenty years Turkey saw an overall steady rate of economic growth.[9] This growth has benefited from the extralegal flow of "irregular circular migrants" from the former Soviet Union, a large proportion of them coming from Moldova to fill the demand for low-paid, flexible, feminized labor in the growing service and informal manufacturing sectors (İçduygu and Yükseker 2012, 448; Keough 2015).[10] But an economic "pull" factor is not the only way to understand what compels post-Soviet women to look toward Istanbul as a place to transform their lives. Turning to the intimate practices of migrants in Istanbul draws us to consider how aspirations and imagination are at least as important as the pursuit of economic well-being.

Glamour-"scapes," Bollywood, and the Power of Imagination

In recent decades a plethora of work has turned to the imagination in examining exactly how aspirations become important for understanding the cultural dimensions of a recently intensified global economy. In particular, Arjun Appadurai's (1996) widely referenced work—pointing to global flows of images, people, money, and information via what he terms "-scapes"—has informed how scholars have sought to understand the gendered dimensions of global mobility. Studies of "sexscapes" of "sex tourism" in the Dominican Republic (Brennan 2004) and "marriagescapes" of so-called "mail order," or "correspondence," marriage in North America (Constable 2003) have evocatively explored the power of the imagination in propelling women's aspirations for transnational mobility. However, the relatively limited scholarship on shifting expressions of intimacy or sexuality in post-Soviet locations has tended to overlook the crucial role of the imagination and has focused instead on economic forces and "asocial" behavior brought about by the "chaos" of post-Soviet society (e.g., Nazpary 2001; Shlapentokh 2003). This approach downplays how diverse historical forces were shaping ideals of glamour, romance, and sexuality even in the late Soviet period and instead narrowly features the role of the state in regulating sexuality, with an emphasis on asocial sexuality as a symptom of the onslaught of Western capitalism. As elsewhere, in the Soviet Union there were multiple possibilities for how local practices might incorporate or refute global influences (see Larkin 1998).

A number of accounts of the history of sexuality in the former Soviet Union feature "the West" as a discursive force linked to mobility, especially for intellectuals (e.g., Shlapentokh 2003, 119), but even in a Soviet society where international travel was available only to a handful of elites, other foreign influences widely shaped aspirations, particularly among women. In the realm of emotions and intimacy, films produced in India were one of these important forces, as is evident in how often post-Soviet women I encountered in Istanbul referenced these films as sources of inspiration and relaxation in their lives. These reflections testify to how visual culture shapes imagination, and in this case the visual culture is a legacy of goodwill measures between India and the Soviet Union from the 1950s through the 1980s, when Soviet citizens were widely exposed to Indian film. The Soviet government purchased more than 190 popular Indian films and made Indian art films available at regular film festivals (Rajagopalan 2008, 8), as well as frequently broadcasting Indian films on television and featuring them in theaters and community centers in cities and small towns from Moscow to Moldova to Central Siberia.

Today people (mostly women) buy both classic Indian films and Bollywood blockbusters in the form of DVDs or eagerly turn to satellite television channels showing these films. The women I encountered in Istanbul watched these with friends on their days off and invoked favorite scenes and actors in casual conversation. Both younger and older women I met referenced Indian films as "romantic," depicting "true love," and portraying "beautiful, glamorous women" dressed in elegant, brilliant colored saris. Entertainers also spoke of drawing on Bollywood for inspiration for dance moves, and in several instances I joined entertainers in Istanbul when they shopped for performance outfits emulating styles they had observed in Bollywood films.[11] While none of the women I met sought to work in India, many cited Indian film as their key source for romantic ideals and images of glamorous women.[12] Their sentiments echoed those of men and women interviewed in Russia in the early 2000s who reflected on the appeal of Indian cinema as a "respite from a dull, unchanging and homogenous reality" (Rajagopalan 2008, 42). The typical genre of hyperemotional Indian cinema provided a window onto something exotic, but the popular romances especially validated women's desires to explore lives of passion, femininity, and glamour, states of being that were discouraged under late socialism and difficult to realize during the economic hardship following the end of socialism.

As Niki, a migrant from southern Moldova told me while we sipped our non-alcoholic beers in her apartment in Istanbul, "The beautiful Indian women in those films really know how to be feminine!" Imagining a glamorous life abroad played a part in compelling many women to seek work in Turkey, a destination more accessible to them than India and one with its own growing industry of melodramatic film. Moreover, once women became labor migrants, their ongoing consumption of such films served as one source for post-Soviet women migrants' reflections on love, romance, and more broadly, intimate economies in their daily lives.

Histories of Soviet and Post-Soviet Mobility

From the 1960s onward there was considerable contact between Soviet people and others from "socialist camp" countries in Eastern Europe and Asia, including India and Vietnam but also places like Cuba, Nicaragua, and Angola (Matusevich 2007).[13] However, only in the early 1970s were cultural exchanges between "the West" and the Soviet Union first established after decades of virtually impermeable borders (Gorsuch and Koenker 2006). These were soon followed by more widespread opportunities for student exchanges and cultural collaborations, albeit with carefully selected participants from the Soviet side, but only in the late 1980s did it become widely possible for Soviet citizens to provide a personal letter of invitation (*priglashenie*) and apply for an exit visa to travel as a tourist to "the West." After 1991, when the Soviet Union ended, it finally became possible for Soviet citizens to depart from their country even without exit visas.

At the same time, the state gradually ceased to supply many government-run stores, and shuttle traders like Zhenia began to fill a large gap in the demand for clothing (and other consumer goods) throughout this part of Eurasia. As a range of women recounted, throughout the 1990s they expanded their roles as small-scale traders to support themselves and their families, buying mostly clothing during short trips ranging from a few days to a few weeks in duration and reselling those wares in their home communities. Depending on the social networks they could draw on to borrow capital, traders typically invested from $100 to

$1,000 to purchase merchandise on each trip. In this way, the "shuttle traders" (*chelnoki*), or "suitcase" traders, most often women, literally transported goods back to community street markets in suitcases.[14] By 1996, however, government restrictions on imports into post-Soviet countries made the shuttle trade unprofitable for all but those with sufficient capital to pay for the services of shipping companies able to evade the high government import duties.[15] The more successful traders continued to move apparel from China, the United Arab Emirates, and especially Turkey, with the assistance of freight companies specializing in cargo delivery to their specific cities, including Moscow, Khabarovsk, Kishinev, or Almaty (Aktar and Ögelman 1994; Zhurzhenko 1999).

This history of post-Soviet mobility forms a critical part of the backdrop to the experience of many post-Soviet border crossers, including shuttle traders like Zhenia, whose mobility inserted them into a global economy and required them to engage with new intimate economies but also with rapidly shifting border regimes. Although this situation is not unlike those described by scholars writing about migrant women in Japan (Faier 2009) or South Korea (Cheng 2010), in the case of migrant women from the former Soviet Union, gender ideals, mobility, and intimate practices come together in distinctive ways.

FIGURE 2. In Laleli at stores catering to Russian speakers. Photograph by author, 2015.

GENDER AND MOBILITY

Official Soviet visions of modernity and related gender ideals and intimate practices were hardly monolithic and were being publicly contested by the late 1980s,
well before the actual end of the Soviet Union in December 1991 (e.g., Kunin
1991). However, the austerity measures and economic restructuring introduced
as central requirements of International Monetary Fund and World Bank provisions imposed on the region in the early 1990s accelerated the reworking of
gender ideals and intimacy. By 1996 the government had transferred more than
a hundred thousand commercial concerns to private ownership; with the privatization of more than fifteen thousand factories, more than 60 percent of the
industrial workforce was jobless (Stanley 1996; Grant 1999, 242). Women were
fired in disproportionate numbers, and by 1992 in some regions they accounted
for more than two-thirds of those registered as unemployed (Ashwin and Bowers
1997, 35).[16] With women's labor critical to the survival of households, women
turned to informal and semilegal forms of work, including the transnational
small-scale garment trade, domestic work, and sex work (Hann and Hann 1992;
Aktar and Ögelman 1994; Zhurzhenko 1999; Nazpary 2001; Akalin 2007), all part
of the increasingly global, and thriving, economy in nearby Turkey.

In considering the radical, and sometimes devastating, reworking of wom-
en's labor in the 1990s, I turn my attention to intimate economies to show what
the implications have been for individuals, households, and communities. In
grounding my analysis in the transnational encounters that have linked people
in this part of Eurasia for hundreds of years—from even before the Ottoman and
Russian Empires, to Russia as a current petro-power and Turkey as a major crossroads for people on the move—I hope to show continuities as well as more recent
ruptures brought about with global capitalism. Overall, while forces of global
capitalism shape practices of intimacy in the region today, historically specific
relations of power are also key to understanding the ways in which mobility and
intimacy are intertwined in this part of Eurasia.

Postsocialism, Transnational Mobility, Intimacy

An abundance of research on the former Soviet Union and Eastern Europe has
considered how the end of socialism brought about uniquely gendered transformations (Temkina and Rotkirch 1997; Gal and Kligman 2000; Pine 2002b;
Haney 2003), and social scientists have reflected on migration processes into
and out of the FSU (e.g., Malysheva and Tiuriukanova 2000; Tiuriukanova
2003; Ghençea and Gudumac 2004; Subbotina 2007; Reeves 2014; Marsden and
Ibanez-Tirado 2015). However, scholars have scarcely considered how legacies
of socialism, gender regimes, and new forms of mobility come together in the

region. In this book I bring these bodies of scholarship together with a focus on three intertwined themes: postsocialism, transnational mobility, and intimacy. The concept of "postsocialism" is closely linked to that of "modernity," something that has featured prominently in social science literature since the 1990s, including as something forged in conjunction with global capitalism (Harvey 1989; Giddens 1992; Appadurai 1996), as in tension with "tradition" (Huntington 1996), as taking multiple forms (Ong 1999; Rofel 1999), and as something that should be seen as a "claim-making" device that can be deployed strategically (Cooper 2005, 146).[17] The vibrant body of work on modernity cuts across scholarship on gendered mobility and migration, illustrating the ways in which aspirations to be "modern" also compel many people to seek opportunity far from home and from the demands of domestic life (Constable 2005; Faier 2009). Questions of modernity are also central in the literature on late socialism and postsocialism, with work examining questions of gender and intimacy (Berdahl 1999; Yang 2003), visions of modernity among non-Russians in the Soviet Union (Grant 1995; Bloch 2003a), and how people living in the former Soviet Union make sense of a supposedly invincible and "radiant" modern society that was "forever" until it was "no more" (Buck-Morss 2000; Yurchak 2003; Bloch and Kendall 2004).

Postsocialism and Eurasia

This ethnography is shaped by a rich literature on postsocialism in Eurasia (e.g., Burawoy and Verdery 1999; Hann et al. 2002; Humphrey and Mandel 2002; Buyandelgeriyn 2008; Rogers and Verdery 2013). While scholars have widely debated the utility of "postsocialism" as a concept, I argue that the term "postsocialism," and the closely related term "post-Soviet," serve important analytical purposes since they describe a common historical experience. As Hann explains, the term "postsocialism" can productively convey the common experience of "Marxist-Leninist socialism, the reproduction of a common layer of socialist institutions, [and] ideology and moral purpose over two generations or more" (Hann et al. 2002, 11).[18] Furthermore, the term "postsocialist" encapsulates the ways in which a Soviet past influenced and continues to influence specific ways of understanding gender, labor, and morality for those who lived under state socialism in the region.[19] By invoking postsocialist experience, these shared histories can be critically signaled. Following scholars who point out that the term "postsocialist" has utility as long as it is used to define specific contexts and practices (Humphrey and Mandel 2002, 3), here I use this term to underscore the ways in which a common experience of socialism has shaped intimate practices in a neocapitalist era defined by transnational migration.[20]

My analysis has a commonality with a number of works that consider how Soviet-era economic practices and exchange networks of favors have shaped social life and are now overshadowed by cash-based transactions and less clear social obligations and moral responsibilities (Humphrey and Mandel 2002; Wanner 2005; Patico 2008; Rogers 2009; Zigon 2011). In considering how a legacy of socialism shapes transnational mobile practices, I focus attention on the emotional and affective dimensions of intimate practices forged by "newly capitalist" transnational migrants.[21] Also, transformations of gender ideologies and related practices of intimacy under postsocialism inform my analysis. As in many locations where socialism defined daily practice over recent decades, the end of socialism in the region of the former Soviet Union brought about a radical shift in public discourses on gender (Posadskaia 1994; Gal and Kligman 2000; Pine 2002b; Hemment 2007), a subject I turn to in chapters 4 and 5. Although some might downplay a common experience of state socialism as an analytical framework for how people in Eurasia navigate the world (e.g., Barrera-González et al. 2013; Keough 2015), I argue that the legacy of state socialism significantly shapes how migrants from the FSU talk about their relationships, their work, and their daily lives, and therefore remains salient.

Transnational mobility, and the new social locations it requires women and men migrants to occupy, magnifies questions about gender and generation. This is particularly the case as socialist gender ideologies that emphasize women's "public" roles in society come up against more recent prevailing discourses in these neocapitalist societies, which associate women with domesticity and/or view them as sexual commodities (Einhorn 1993; Goscilo 1993; Rotkirch et al. 2007). My interviewees spoke about a Soviet era when many of the older labor migrants were factory workers or employed in agricultural spheres, but some were engineers, accountants, or hospital administrators; they recounted how they saw their labor as officially respected and rewarded. In interviews, many older women, regardless of professional background, lamented being inserted into a global service economy where ideals of socialist labor had no meaning, and they no longer had any social protections in the form of pensions, overtime, sick leave, or mechanisms for gender equity. In contrast, younger women tended to consider their work and life in Istanbul as exciting, urbane, and an escape from the confining socialist structures and gender ideals of the past. One of the key themes in the following pages is how, depending on their generation, women differentially evaluate the way mobility has shaped their lives and the lives of those close to them.

In thinking about transnational mobility, the term "Eurasia" also invites us to look beyond boundaries imposed by states, entities that do not last forever, and instead consider flows and exchanges transregionally. The concept of "Eurasia" usefully blurs boundaries, while also being elastic, something that has made the term appealing for many scholars writing about border-defying processes and experiences in the region (Von Hagen 2004). Moreover, as Jennifer Suchland has shown, the term "Eurasia" can productively decenter how Europe, Russia, and the United States are frequently seen as the implicit yardsticks by which social processes and gendered power are measured (2011, 838). Suchland usefully argues that the term challenges the too neatly defined boundaries of the nation-state and thereby further points us toward critically assessing the histories of diverse forms of power in the region (2011, 856). In its association with a broad, shifting expanse, "Eurasia" can simultaneously encompass places that are tightly linked by a shared history of state socialism and neighboring places with significant historical, trade, and cultural ties. The concept of Eurasia holds the analytical potential for allowing us to look beyond national borders and instead consider how large-scale transformations extend across borders as people come into contact with one another in an alternative global, or at least regional, system (Ong 1999; Sassen 2013). As Rogers and Verdery reflect on the term "postsocialism" (2013, 450), "Eurasia" can also be useful for continuing to examine the relationships between region and theory in anthropology. For the purposes of this book, I employ the term "Eurasia" in portraying the flows of ideas and images, trade goods, and people that for centuries have stretched between areas currently identified as part of the former Soviet Union and neighboring Turkey.

Transnational Mobility

Historically social scientists have studied migrants from the perspective of bounded communities and fixed nation-states, where a group was typically framed as moving from a "homeland" to a "host" or "settlement" country and largely severing, or at least attenuating, ties to home. In an effort to theorize the implications of globalization for our world, scholars have turned away from dominant models informed by modernization theory, defined by "peripheries" and a few key "centers," binary understandings of migrants and their milieus reflected in terms like "assimilation," "homeland," and "resettlement," and naturalized notions of the steady state of nation-states (Basch et al. 1994; Glick Schiller 1999; Brettell 2015). Instead, a rich realm of theory, sometimes animated by the place of aspiration and imagination in compelling mobility (Appadurai 1996) but widely focused on connections, flows, and multiple ties of belonging and allegiance, now resonates through scholarship concerned with mobility, diasporas, and transnational "social fields" and "circuits" expressed in the form of activist groups to transnational religious spaces to new migrant communities across the globe (e.g., Rouse 1992; Glick Schiller and Çağlar 2008; Abashin 2012). Notably, some have argued that globalization, including transnational border crossing, is not a new phenomenon (e.g., Ghosh 1992; Mintz 1998). However, the extensive scholarship in the 1990s and 2000s that took stock of how an increase in ease of travel, nearly instantaneous communication, global financial networks, and a burgeoning of media all intensified transnational ties has confirmed this to be an important area for research (Appadurai 1996; Hannerz 1996; Vertovec 1999; Constable 2003).

Although studies of globalization in terms of "transnationalism" have widely sought to position the nation-state as just one of many actors in transnational social fields, increasingly scholars have focused on states and state-like structures to critically examine how groups of people are differentially capable of pursuing transnational aspirations (Willen 2005; Mahdavi 2011; Ticktin 2011; Constable 2014). Furthermore, scholars are increasingly placing the very mechanisms of state border regulation at the center of their analyses (De Genova and Peutz 2010; Cabot 2014; Reeves 2014). Whether scholars focus on ongoing flows, diasporic sentiments, or state mechanisms for policing borders, an emphasis on transnational frameworks, "multi-sited" methodologies (Marcus 1995), and a recognition of the multiplicity of actors shaping border crossing, have all become foundational for studies of mobility.

Growing out of the broader critique of hegemonic categories deployed in social science research and writing (Behar and Gordon 1996; Lewin and Silverstein 2016), by the early 1980s feminist scholars began challenging pervasive assumptions that all people on the move would have similar experiences of migration and instead proposed a gendered analysis of migration (Morokvasic 1984). By the 1990s and early 2000s a rich literature examining the intersection of gender, power, and mobility had emerged (e.g., Massey 1994; Collier 1997; Parreñas 2001b; Pessar and Mahler 2003), including ethnographies dedicated to examining how gendered mobility shapes structures of intimacy (Constable 2003; Hirsch 2003; Brennan 2004). Scholars also began to examine how new structures of feeling—including new forms of romance, courtship, and "companionate" marriage—are accompanied by the global circulation of (and sometimes contestation of) what are perceived to be "modern" forms of intimacy (Rebhun 1999; Ahearn 2001; Hirsch and Wardlow 2006). Scholars have also turned their attention to the intersection of local, national, and global processes and histories that make cross-border marriages and other types of intimacies "imaginable" and where there are not always clear lines between relationships of love, obligation, and transaction (Constable 2005; Faier 2009; Cheng 2010). Finally, familial practices of intimacy within transnational households, including nurturing children and maintaining ties to parents from a distance, have also received considerable attention (Gamburd 2000; Parreñas 2001a, 2005; Leinaweaver 2010; Chamberlain 2013). I draw on this vibrant scholarship around gender and migration to show how mobile lives extending between Istanbul and the former Soviet Union are intertwined with new forms of "intimate practices," and sometimes reworked gender ideals, connecting parents, children, lovers, and households across this region of Eurasia.

Intimacy

I use the term "intimacy" as a nexus for several types of experience that are often elided in discussions of migration. The "intimate" is a realm broad enough to encompass relationships between parents and children, husbands and wives, temporary migrants and their close friends and boyfriends, the realm of domestic household space, and the sense of belonging that was lost with the end of the Soviet Union and the region's insertion into a global economy. I argue that the terms "intimacy" and "the intimate" helpfully demarcate an affective sense, one that is shaped by the forms of mobility men and women in this region have been engaging in since the end of the Soviet Union. The term "intimacy" is inclusive enough to help bridge structural shifts facing people like labor migrants out of the former Soviet Union *and also* the personal, often emotional negotiations these same people are caught up in. As Ara Wilson notes, "The turn to intimacy speaks to scholars' desire for a flexible term that allows new descriptions that do not reify nation, identity, family" (2012, 46). Like Wilson, I use the term "intimacy" because it allows us to avoid separating "the economy" from "the private"; thinking in terms of "intimate economies" emphasizes how the lines between market/public space and private space are intertwined. This emphasis on intimate practices allows me to portray the realm of emotion, a personally experienced state, in conjunction with affect, a collective state (Ahmed 2004; Berlant 2010; Pedwell and Whitehead 2012) that is shaped by and sometimes in tension with prevailing structural forces, such as neocapitalism or state socialism.[22] Moreover, thinking about emotion and affect together creates a productive analytical tension. After all, with transnational mobility as such a central aspect of social experience globally, individual people are confronting the ways their emotional selves do not always fit with the collective "structures of feeling" (Williams 1977) they encounter. This is especially the case for post-Soviet migrants as "people on the move" or mobile, transnational populations who have experienced a radical change in their intimate lives, where barely a generation ago they could rely on stable state structures to support public institutions, households, and some coherent sense of well-being.

STRUCTURES OF FEELING AND EMOTION WORK

There is relatively little written explicitly about the structures of feeling that defined individual experiences of state socialism (although see Paxson 2005; Yurchak 2003) or the new structures of feeling that are defining gendered practices in this region of Eurasia, and it is even more rare for scholarship to examine the intersection of emotions, intimacy, and mobility in the region. This is especially striking given the widespread personal trauma brought about by loss of employment, redrawn political borders, and related physical dislocation that the end of the Soviet Union caused for millions of people (IOM 2002). In thinking about emotions as defined in specific ways by political or cultural formations (Reddy 1999, 271), it is worth considering how people experience their insertion into a global economy, including as subjects of a new hegemonic project or as a form of liberation that they take part in crafting.

The concept of "emotional labor," what Arlie Hochschild has defined as "the management of feeling" (1983, 7), provides us with a way of reflecting on the experiences of post-Soviet migrant women in Turkey. Like other work on emotional labor, often focused on people who are disenfranchised or disempowered through capitalist processes, I consider post-Soviet women migrants as a group of people who are learning to "manage" their feelings to fit with the new realities of their labor. Nevertheless, I consider the ways in which emotional labor is not just required by new structures of global capitalism but also something migrants are actively participating in, and sometimes strategically making use of, as they rework gendered structures within households and sometimes mobilize intimacy to their advantage, as some entertainers I met did in capitalizing on perceptions of them as "without hang-ups" about sex. Overall, similar to a long tradition in anthropology, I argue that paying attention to emotions and emotion work can shed light on how people are experiencing shifting forms of power (Abu-Lughod and Lutz 1990, 2–3) under global capitalism in this region of Eurasia.[23]

SEX WORK AND INTIMACY: BEYOND TRAFFICKING

When discussing my project on post-Soviet women's labor migration, people inevitably asked me about the issue of trafficking. Scholarly work and popular media focused on women's mobility in this region of Eurasia have frequently equated it with trafficking. Even though international law defines trafficking as labor exploitation (not prostitution), based on force, fraud, or coercion of any person (and not just women), dominant discourses have tended to associate all women's migration with dangerous practices of "prostitution" and related sexual services and directly equate these with the trafficking in women.[24] Blanket assumptions of "exploitation" have come to define popular understandings of women's migration and drown out other forms of analysis, including around the emotion work of providing sexual services, intimate ties to households, or the structural inequalities in home communities that might compel women to become migrants. Portrayals of human trafficking, often focused exclusively on women and revolving around an opposition of "forced" versus "voluntary" migration, as well as a conflation of all forms of sex work with trafficking, have circulated widely since the early 2000s (IOM 2002; Angel Coalition 2009; CATW 2011).[25] These portrayals of trafficking often feature "rescue narratives" that would lead us to believe that there are tens of thousands of women from the FSU and Eastern Europe alone who are waiting to be "saved" from the deplorable conditions in which they find themselves as migrants engaged in sex work (see Soderlund 2005).[26] While such narratives slide over the fact that women do not necessarily seek to be "saved," nongovernmental organizations (NGOs) and international NGOs (INGOs), feature films and documentaries with titles like *The Price of Sex* (2011) and *Trafficking Cinderella* (2001) continue to perpetuate images of naive women victimized by criminals.[27] Without a doubt it is deplorable if even one person is trafficked, and these injustices deserve our outrage and efforts to address the problem.[28] Nevertheless, I am wary of how the idea of trafficking, and especially a focus on trafficking in women, can so easily dominate discussions of labor migration. As part of the growing concern for "security," discourses on trafficking both derail nuanced understandings of the links between global capitalism and women's and men's migration and justify increased policing of borders and expanding punitive powers of the state (Agustín 2006; Cheng and Kim 2014; Bernstein 2012).[29]

In some ways this situation is not all that different from the historical roots of the concept of "trafficking," generally located in the late Victorian era, when racial hierarchies paired with ideals of class and sexual propriety for women coincided with new forms of mobility. At the turn of the nineteenth to twentieth centuries, when there were widespread migrations of both men and women out of Europe, the mobility of phenotypically "white" women led to a concern around "white slavery," a concern that was rearticulated by the League of Nations in 1927 as "Trafficking in Women and Children" (Doezema 1999; Kempadoo 2005; Gorman 2008).[30] A number of academic and literary sources make reference to East European migrant women working as prostitutes, hostesses, and performers in the late nineteenth and early twentieth centuries, pointing to the transnational flow of "Russian" women, including to Turkey, Manchuria, and South America, but also to anxiety about their mobility (Guy 1991; Mansel 1995, 398–400; Murakami 1997, 136; King 2014, 148–50).[31] With the ultimate demise of the League of Nations and then the chaos of the Second World War, for decades the idea of "trafficking in women" became less urgent. It is striking how in the early 1990s, just as the Soviet Union was ending, economies across Eastern

Europe struggled to get reestablished, and a new wave of "white" women became mobile, a global discourse on "trafficking in women" reemerged.

Although Turkey's porous borders began to attract the attention of the European Union (EU) as early as the mid-1990s, with discussions around conditions to be met for EU accession (İçduygu and Yükseker 2012), only in 2002 and 2003 did Turkey come under pressure to recognize "trafficking in humans" as an issue within its borders. At that time Turkey received a "provisional 2," in the US State Department's annual Trafficking in Persons (TIP) report, a rating that threatened to affect Turkey's favored trade status with the United States.[32] Related to this assessment, in 2004 INGOs like the International Organization for Migration (IOM) began to turn increasing attention to women on the move in the region, including into Turkey.[33] One of IOM's key campaigns to bring awareness to trafficking involved a double-sided pocket brochure printed in Russian, English, Moldovan, and Turkish that was strategically placed at airport arrivals providing an emergency number to call in case someone was trafficked or suspected of being trafficked.[34] The entertainers I came to know were undaunted by the extensive media campaign that the IOM and other organizations were mounting to discourage young people from traveling to Turkey for work (Kirby 2004). They saw themselves as working hard under unfair conditions, but many spoke of preferring this kind of work to other options they had; moreover, most of the young women I met were completing second, third, or fourth contracts and were planning on returning to Turkey again soon, following a brief visit home.

Migrants I met aspired to traverse transnational borders, and sometimes intermediaries or employment brokers assisted them. Sometimes migrants were intercepted by state powers policing their entry into a country or looking to deport them for working illegally. These were all part of the stories they told about mobility and impediments to making a living. In writing about migrants' lives I aim to strike a balance between an overly celebratory portrait of globalization—with a focus on unprecedented possibilities for people, commodities, finances, and ideas to traverse wide distances—and an overly ominous one—with criminal figures orchestrating trafficking in women. Both approaches too easily overlook the complicated experiences of people trying to make their way in a world as they face increasingly policed borders. I seek to provide an alternative to the widespread discourses on "trafficking" in women that tend to drown out the enormity of transformations brought about by the newly porous borders in Eurasia. Ultimately, I trace a tangible sense of the complex, "crisscrossed" transnational lives many migrants have managed to orchestrate, maintaining friendships, relationships to men, and ties to home communities without losing sight of the structural forces working against them.

FIGURE 3. Information card with hotline number.

Origins of the Project and Mobile Methods

Like most ethnographic projects, this one gradually emerged out of a combination of serendipity and a desire to understand a broad phenomenon. In June 2000 I was attending a conference in Istanbul when I learned of the extent of post-Soviet migrant presence in the city. At first I was not surprised to hear a constant stream of Russian in the hallways and lobby of the small hotel where I was staying near Taksim Square, an upscale tourist area and one of the prime entertainment districts of Istanbul; after all, Russian speakers like Zhenia were on the move in this region of the world. I was surprised, however, when I realized that all the Russian speakers at the hotel over those several days were young, mostly blonde women in their early twenties, and they did not appear to be budget travelers or on short-term business trips, but instead worked as entertainers.

I had a glimpse of the wider phenomenon of Russian speakers in Istanbul during a brief visit to Laleli, the "Russian" neighborhood at the edge of Aksaray, the garment district on the other side of the Golden Horn. As they did with others perceived to be from the former Soviet Union, touts approached me on the narrow cobblestone streets, calling out in singsong voices in Russian, "*Devushki, dublenki*" (girls [look], fur coats) and "*Parikmakherskaia, manikiury!*" (beauty parlor, manicures!). These were their standard calls as they tried to lure the bustling, business-minded women traders from the former Soviet Union to pause and purchase a fur coat or update a hairstyle or manicure. These encounters sparked my thinking about the ways women from the FSU experienced being transnational labor migrants moving between a place of "failed" modernity (the former Soviet Union) and a place of increasingly contested modernity (Turkey), and more important, how these women migrants negotiated these lives stretching across transnational space.

In 2002 I was able to return to Istanbul to begin research among the Russian-speaking migrants traveling there. Olga, a shuttle trader I first met in 2001 at her boutique outside Moscow, introduced me to the intricacies of the Russian garment trade in Istanbul when she traveled there to purchase batches (*serii*) of dresses, pants, and shirts for resale back home.[35] As I detail in chapter 2, over the course of a week Olga showed me her way of doing business; she maintained long-term contacts with wholesalers, and while she looked for goods that would

FIGURE 4. At a shipping office. Photograph by author, 2006.

FIGURE 5.   At the "bus station." Photograph by author, 2004.

appeal to her Russian clients and negotiated deals with wholesalers, she also took time to drink tea they offered her and greet suppliers she had come to depend on. After Olga's goods were assembled, she directed the touts, who moved goods around the trade district by trolley or simply on their shoulders, to the cargo company she had selected for their reputation of delivering goods safely and with minimal import duty. At the cargo company office all the purchases for the day were amalgamated into large sacks and secured with heavy duty packing tape, each strip detached with a swift jab with a ballpoint pen.

One day, after taking a wrong turn from my hotel, I encountered a large group of animated Russian-speaking women who were congregated on a street corner. Despite shopkeepers' repeated attempts to prevent people from gathering, including by calling the police, this intersection of two city streets was the central gathering place for undocumented laborers from the former Soviet Union. Since the late 1990s the intersection, at the edge of Laleli, has emerged as the informal "bus station" (*avtopark* or *avtostantsiia*), as migrants referred to it, where minibuses come to drop off and pick up passengers destined for the FSU. The minibuses travel to the relatively nearby countries of Moldova and Ukraine (via Bulgaria and Romania), but migrants from other former Soviet regions also gather here, especially on Sundays when many people have the day off from their work as cleaners, caregivers, retail staff, and sometimes entertainers.

That first day at the bus station two sisters, Ruzhena and Udara, identifying as Tatar and recently arrived from Uzbekistan, struck up a conversation with me.[36] They told me of the hardships back home, of being swindled by a neighbor, and of being unable to support themselves as an engineer and physical therapist, respectively. Daily for two weeks I stood with these women and their fellow migrants from Belarus, Latvia, Moldova, and Kazakhstan, with whom they had loosely bonded, waiting for potential employers to approach with offers of work. I heard of challenges in forging new lives and hopes of breaking away from debt and many tragedies, while trying to maintain ties to children, parents, and sometimes husbands back home. Many migrants stayed in nearby women's-only hostels for weeks on end while they waited to secure work. In between long days of waiting on the sidewalk for what they considered acceptable offers of employment to work *na domu* (for "live-in" positions, paying at least $250 per month for six-day weeks), they grappled with deep moral quandaries over bodily integrity and self-respect. One day while taking a tea break in the garden of the nearby Şehzade Mosque, a group of women I sat with vehemently tried to convince a fellow migrant that it was not worth selling her kidney to pay a debt back home in Moldova.[37] On another occasion I joined one of my new acquaintances, who had not eaten a proper meal for two weeks, to take up the invitation for a modest lunch offered by one of the local shopkeepers. Afterwards I realized why my acquaintance had insisted that I join her; following our meal it was strongly intimated that we should sleep with our hosts, and my presence made it easier for my acquaintance to firmly decline.

These exchanges and interactions point to the sometimes desperate situations migrants confront in the face of dire poverty in the aftermath of the Soviet Union. These realities are, however, just one part of what migrants encounter. Migrant women introduced me to the novel cultural encounters produced when new forms of mobility bring together people whose imaginaries include the modernities defined by waning state socialism, on the one hand, and waning secular Kemalist principles, on the other. As relatively fluid borders bring about renewed interactions between people in this region, the emergence of an increasingly Islamist state in Turkey is often in tension with ideals of women's financial independence, sexual freedom, and gender equality—central tenets for post-Soviet women labor migrants. Post-Soviet women's presence in Turkey provides a window onto the implications of global capitalism for ideals about modernity, gender, and intimacy as former "empires" wane and new forms of global power emerge.

Mobile Methods Embodied

Research on migrants can be complicated to conduct, given the multitude of ties and structures influencing people on the move (Kearney 1995). Beginning in the 1990s scholars began pointing to the need to portray our newly mobile world by employing "multi-sited" methods (Marcus 1995), and in many ways this has become so widely practiced by ethnographers as to become a truism. The abundance of scholarship employing multi-sited methods has taken a multitude of forms, including work spanning dispersed layers of international scientific inquiry (Zabusky 2007); within different "scales" of global-local connection, as in the layers of actors key to the environmental devastation and concomitant activism around Indonesian rainforests (Tsing 2004); or tracing the shifting post-colonial and post-Soviet forms of governance in northeast Asia through the eyes of elderly Sakhalin Korean migrants moving between Sakhalin, Russia, and South Korea (Lim 2016). In the case of migrants from the former Soviet Union, they have become quintessentially multi-sited as opportunities for employment have all but disappeared in many communities, especially the more rural ones, and post-Soviet people often maintain connections with members of their house-holds, living and working long-term in two or more countries.

Even when a project is multi-sited, it is still grounded in specific *places* defined by indelible histories. The migrant women in this book came from a specific place, the FSU, inscribed with its own history, and they arrived in Turkey, and specifically Istanbul, with its own distinct history and cultural contours. Partly due to the concentration of southern Moldovan migrants working in Istanbul and partly due to ethnographic serendipity, two chapters (4 and 6) focus on southern Moldovans and the transnational ties they have maintained in Turkey and to relatives in Russia and back home in Moldova. The crux of the book is about migrants in Istanbul who, based on their lingua franca and shared his-tory, I call "Russian speakers" or "post-Soviet" migrants, although some migrants also referred to their compatriots from the former Soviet Union as "Soviets" (*sovetskie*) or "ours" (*svoi*). The majority of chapters (1, 2, 3, and 5) portray how transnational mobility has shaped intimate practices among a wide range of women moving between countries of the former Soviet Union and Turkey. As I explore in chapter 1, these migrants arrived in a place that was not a tabula rasa for links between Turkey and the regions of the former Soviet Union but a place steeped in a history of interactions in this part of Eurasia.

Within hours of my becoming acquainted with the migrants gathered at the minibus stop in Laleli, women were urging me to write about how the end of the Soviet Union had ruined their lives. Udara and Ruzhena, the two women I met from Uzbekistan, pressed me to get their words down in my notebook, saying, "We lived like people, and now we live like dogs." Others interjected, "The end of the Soviet Union was absolutely devastating! Look how we live now! What a tragedy!" Women frequently mistook me for a journalist, and although I cor-rected them, I did agree to their requests that I document something of their lives. I promised to tell the story of their hardships and how the end of the Soviet

Union meant a collapse of a secure life and a life now defined by precarity. In some ways women I met saw me as a resource, one that might help them to immigrate to Canada or deliver personal gifts to their families or friends. They also quickly assessed that my knowledge of English might be a valued commodity. A few times migrants referred affluent Turkish women to me when they came to the minibus stop seeking to employ domestic workers and then thought they might also secure a low-cost English tutor for their children; I politely declined these invitations.

Post-Soviet migrants were generally very willing to speak with me, but my research was sometimes hindered by other logistical matters. It was easy to make contact with migrants in the many wholesale garment businesses in Laleli, but maintaining ties could be challenging. Women frequently kept jobs for short periods of time, leaving when their employers proved to be abusive, when a better opportunity came along, or when they were needed at home, and this made it difficult to locate women at places of work. Furthermore, cell phone numbers changed regularly, especially after 2006 when Turkey began requiring official Turkish identification in order to register phones for service (Consulate General of Turkey 2012). Migrants themselves were aware of these difficulties in maintaining contact so they usually shared both their cell phone numbers in Turkey and their numbers and addresses back home, resources I have regularly turned to when seeking to locate a person I had originally met in Istanbul.

When I first began research in Istanbul in 2002, few migrants had cell phones and on their days off women would line up, phone cards in hand, at the banks of public payphones to make weekly calls home. Just two years later, cell phones had become ubiquitous. By 2011 the banks of phone booths occupying large spaces at the edges of public squares in Laleli, Taksim, and the pedestrian zone of Istaklal Caddesi were usually empty. Today low-cost international phone plans allow migrants to text family and friends many times a day, and since 2009 or so it has become common for migrants to maintain connections home via frequent Skype calls on their own or a friend's laptop. Although early in my research I sometimes corresponded with people by surface mail, in more recent years we have stayed in touch via e-mail, Skype, WhatsApp, or text messaging. Ultimately, for more than ten years I was generously folded into the lives of six households, primarily based in Moldova—with ties extending to Russia, Bulgaria, Romania, Great Britain, and Turkey. I also came to know a wide array of other migrant women during my fifteen months of fieldwork, each stint lasting from three weeks to six months and overall spanning more than a decade (2001 to 2011).

When the women I came to know at the bus station in 2002 gradually located work, I began spending more time in the wholesale apparel shops, meeting women who worked as translators and shop assistants for the almost exclusively male-owned and -operated businesses. These women—mostly from the former Soviet Union and especially Moldova, Ukraine, and Belarus—spent many hours with me over tea breaks speaking of their lives. Over the course of the research one woman in her late forties, Maria, frequently invited me and my daughter, and sometimes also my mother, home on her one day off each week for sumptuous meals that invariably included Maria's signature stuffed peppers; Maria's Turkish husband also enjoyed showcasing his collection of racing pigeons kept on his rooftop. Shop assistants like Maria taught me how women living as long-term labor migrants move fluidly between different spheres of work in Laleli and beyond, sometimes selling apparel to shuttle traders but at other times working as domestics, cleaning or providing child care, doing manicures and pedicures in the hair salons staffed by Turkish men, or selling gold jewelry at stores that were popular both with tourists from across the Middle East and with post-Soviet shuttle traders. Migrant women also taught me about the intimate ties they maintain with family, friends, and often with Turkish men.

Finally, I began learning about the lives of younger migrants following one of those moments of serendipity treasured in ethnographic research. In the hotel where I was staying I met Zina, a former movie projectionist and medical orderly from southern Moldova, who took time following her demanding work cleaning the hotel to share a cup of tea. Zina was enthusiastic about my project and in addition to the many introductions she later made for me to shops' assistants and her family and network in southern Moldova, she kindly agreed to introduce me to a number of dancers. As I explore in chapter 5, these women made a living as entertainers, something they widely embraced as glamorous, and they considered domestic work and jobs as shop assistants to be unappealing. Although the traders sometimes expressed a sense of shame about being involved in petty capitalist practices, a subject I explore in chapter 2, the entertainers did not express any such sense of shame. They dreamed of accumulating sufficient capital to become self-sufficient as entrepreneurs, with many of them aspiring to buy apartments back home and some aiming to become shuttle traders with their own boutiques supplied with apparel sourced in Istanbul.

On a steaming hot summer day in June 2002, when I first spent time in Laleli learning about shuttle traders from Olga, I also met Bella at the edge of the minibus lot. My first impression of Bella was that she was high energy and loquacious. Like most post-Soviet migrant women I met in Istanbul, Bella was woefully underemployed, with no job prospects, either in Moldova or Turkey, related to her degree in civil engineering. By keeping in touch and periodically meeting over the years, Bella's perspective on being a transnational migrant moving between Istanbul, southern Moldova, Romania, and Moscow has deeply informed this project.

In my fieldwork in the summer of 2003, one of my key aims was to trace the connections between those migrants I had met who were sending remittances home from Istanbul and their households in Moldova and Russia. Zina agreed with Bella that it was essential for me to travel to their hometown of Vulcăneşti, located in southern Moldova in the region of Gagauzia, to better understand what compelled women to leave for work in Istanbul. I was accompanied by my five-month-old daughter, as well as by my stepmother, who had generously offered to facilitate my research by caring for her granddaughter, and although we stayed with Bella, who was home briefly that summer, Zina insisted that we also meet her sister, Eva. Zina was sure that Eva would be very happy to discuss her experience of spending years raising her niece and nephew while their mother, Zina, was working in Istanbul. Within a few hours of arriving in Vulcăneşti we made arrangements to meet Eva at her small farm, just a twenty-minute walk from Bella's apartment, on the other side of the town center. As we made our way through the summer heat and dusty streets, my daughter began to fidget and squirm about in the Baby Bjorn strapped on to my torso. By the time we arrived she was shrieking, bringing to life my nightmare of what could happen during fieldwork with a child. I apologized profusely to Eva while my stepmother tried to console my daughter; Eva remained completely calm and, drawing on her knowledge as a midwife and herbalist, inquired what my daughter was eating. When Eva learned that we had recently tried feeding my daughter baby cereal, she pronounced gas as the culprit, and she gently massaged my daughter's abdomen, very quickly calming her.

During our stay in Vulcăneşti Bella also introduced me to Nelli, a woman in her early fifties who was caring for her granddaughter while Nelli's daughter, Niki, worked in Istanbul. The following year when I returned with my daughter and her grandmother to live for nearly two months with Eva and her family, I also spent considerable time with Nelli. Over several subsequent summers I returned to Vulcăneşti unaccompanied by family, but the first extended stay was especially important.

Conducting fieldwork with a young child had implications for the research in terms of how I was received, my attention to transnational nurturing practices, and the daily rhythm of doing fieldwork. Being immediately identified as a daughter as well as a mother significantly helped me to build rapport. I was often received with a widespread sense of empathy, with people helping with day-care arrangements, including obtaining the necessary vaccination records for enrollment, or in the first cold weeks of our late-spring stay in 2004, with finding warm clothing for my daughter. Instead of simply being a researcher of indeterminate standing who claimed to be a professor and married with a husband back home in Canada, I could be placed within a very familiar universe of middle-aged women drawing on family ties to provide for households; I could also be seen not just as a researcher but as a person with the same types of day-to-day responsibilities (such as cooking, cleaning, and caring for children) many of my interlocutors faced. "Old MacDonald Had a Farm" might not have contained the local *content* used to distract a child, but after weeks of hearing me desperately trying to sooth my tired daughter by singing this tune as I walked along the dusty (or muddy) road home, people could recognize the *form*. Also, having a young child who was still breastfeeding in the field meant that my schedule was not entirely my own. A "good" fieldworker tries to take up any and all opportunities to get to know their fieldsite, in this case by helping with agricultural labor, attending religious services, drinking tea with neighbors, taking part in cooking and general housework, going on local fishing trips with multigenerational groups, or stopping by the local pub. I did do a bit of all these, but my daily schedule—when I woke, when I left and returned home, whether I went out at night, and how much I slept—was circumscribed by my efforts to also be a mother, albeit with invaluable, caregiving support, what some scholars have called "othermothering" (Collins 1990, 119–23). As for all researchers, my data is shaped by my specific subjectivities.

After her sojourns with me in Moldova, at four years of age my daughter joined me again for nearly six months of fieldwork in Istanbul in 2007; on a daily basis she was lovingly cared for first by my mother and then by Turkish government preschool teachers and babysitters. I was fortunate to have such support, enabling me to spend long hours with migrant women after their work or sometimes to accompany them to the clubs, stores, or homes and establishments where they were employed. My daughter's constant presence opened many doors, including for priority line-ups at airports and unusually attentive service in cafes, but most important she interacted with my interlocutors and drew them to reflect on their own children or grandchildren. In some cases my daughter also provided a strong excuse for me to leave a nightclub research site before 1:00 a.m. (to relieve the babysitter). Mostly, having a child along during the research, and toward the end of the project having two children waiting for me at home, humanized me for the women with whom I interacted.

Other aspects of how I was perceived were also key in shaping this project. As a non-native Russian speaker who, nonetheless, has often passed as "Slavic" and has conducted research and lived among Russian speakers since just before the end of the Soviet Union, it was common for Russian speakers to mistake me for a fellow migrant. Most often, based on my accent in Russian, they mistook me as being from one of the Baltic states of Latvia or Estonia. Even when early on I made sure to correct the misrecognition, Russian speakers also generously took me to be one of their "own" (*svoi*), and for the most part they readily spoke with me.[38] Nevertheless, this misrecognition did not unequivocally work in my favor; even after explaining my research, women engaged in the garment trade sometimes viewed me as a possible competitor who might try to learn the best sources for garments and then undercut the retail prices in businesses back home. In these instances, understandably, women were less willing to be drawn into conversation.

Another instance of misrecognition, one tied to competition for souls instead of goods, occurred after I completed an interview with Polina, a woman from Ukraine, at the apartment she shared with her Turkish boyfriend in Istanbul. Polina suggested we exchange Skype IDs so we could keep in touch. When we turned on her laptop and opened Skype, her brother immediately Skyped in from the northern Russian city of Surgut, where he and his family were working on the then booming oil fields that were attracting migrants from across the former Soviet Union. Before Polina had a chance to explain my research, Polina's brother and his wife asked if I was on a "mission" (*missiia*). Such misrecognition of anthropologists as missionaries is itself not that uncommon (see Berlinski 2007); in this case the assumption was informed by the massive influx of missionaries into the FSU since the early 1990s, a subject I discuss in chapter 3.

In a less common instance of misrecognition, in particular neighborhoods I was perceived as a woman who might be offering sexual services. Several times when I was walking with one of the entertainers I came to know in Taksim, and other times in Eminönü, near the Galata Bridge, a cab driver called out aggressively to us, "Hey Aksaray!" referring to the garment district where Russian speakers and other migrants are especially visible. When I stayed in a favorite hotel in Laleli, right next to Aksaray, at different times during this research, it was common for hotel staff and shopkeepers to banter with me in a nonaggressive, flirtatious manner. In one unusual encounter at the minibus station, after I inquired in Russian about a minibus to Moldova, the Moldovan driver selling tickets glanced at my ringless hand and bluntly suggested that we go to a nearby hotel. As these experiences suggest, the idea of sexual availability was strongly associated with the "Russian" district, both by Turks and others in Istanbul.[39]

Receptions of me also depended to some degree on the class background of those whom I encountered. In initial interactions with well-educated Turks and post-Soviet professionals (not labor migrants), a different type of misreading sometimes occurred wherein they would assume that my aims as a researcher revolved around saving women from the dangers of trafficking. In contrast, a working-class neighbor in my apartment building in Istanbul or a teacher at my daughter's preschool was more likely to engage me in discussions about how sad it was for so many women to leave their families to work in Turkey. In social encounters when my research was not discussed, as in the thriving artistic scene in Beyoğlu along

Istaklal Caddesi or at the Şişli organic farmers market, I was most easily lumped together with the thousands of other expatriates living years on end in Istanbul, either for official work contracts or as foreign students.[40]

My research took place in three locations: Vulcăneşti, an agricultural town in the Gagauz region of southern Moldova and the site of severe out-migration to Turkey and Russia; Moscow, a destination for post-Soviet labor migration but also a primary departure point for small-scale traders in the garment business; and Istanbul. In Istanbul, the primary site for the project, I conducted research among two generations of post-Soviet women migrants (one cohort of women in their twenties and early thirties, and one in their early forties to late fifties). In addition to carrying out more than fifty semistructured interviews and doing participant observation at places of work, in public spaces, and at people's homes, I documented extensive life histories of twenty women working in different spheres, tracing their search for work, their efforts to support households, and their professional and personal aspirations.

To understand the transnational linkages migrants maintain and how labor migration shapes communities in Moldova and Russia, I drew on participant observation and semistructured interviews with family members of migrants working in Turkey, as well as with people considering migrating to Turkey or elsewhere. This part of the research focused on three households in Moldova, where women such as those I came to know in Istanbul are absent for years on end, and on three households in Russia, where women traders are frequently absent from home as well as being the primary breadwinners. In addition, in Moldova I met with migration scholars, spoke with staff in local libraries, museums, and vital statistics offices, and conducted formal interviews with school teachers and principals about the ways families are shaped by outmigration from southern Moldova.

The book weaves in and out of the lives and intimate relationships of five key women—Maria, Niki, Irina, Zina, and Bella—and their families. Two of the women worked closely with the garment trade for nearly twenty years, two have predominantly found employment as domestics, and one worked as an entertainer for nearly ten years. These women's accounts form the center of what follows, although the experiences of tens of other women—including Raia, Olga, Ania, Nelli, Eva, Kara, Nadia, Anna, and Polina—and their families also contribute to this story of how intimacy and mobility have intersected in the flow of migrants between the former Soviet Union and Turkey.

MAGNIFICENT CENTURIES AND ECONOMIES OF DESIRE

> In 2000 when we [post-Soviet migrants] came, here in Turkey they did not have cell phones or even washing machines. . . . They only just came down from the hills.
>
> —A Moldovan man speaking about his first impressions of Turkey, interview June 21, 2011

> When they first came here in the early 1990s, they were willing to do anything; they were hungry and came without fathers or brothers.
>
> —A Turkish shopkeeper speaking about post-Soviet women migrants, interview May 8, 2007

> My grandfather used to come here to trade back in his youth; I don't know what he traded exactly, but my grandmother told me he used to come here, back before the war.
>
> —A Gagauz woman speaking of pre-Second World War trade links to Turkey, interview June 25, 2005

> Turkey is quite pleased with the number of Russian tourists who visit, which exceeds three million a year, having Russian daughters-in-law, and trading with the Russians.
>
> —Hasan Kanbolat, columnist for *Today's Zaman*, 2012

The arrival of post-Soviet women in Turkey beginning in the early 1990s struck the Turkish public as a dramatic event, but the encounter of Turks and people from the former Soviet Union had significant historical precedent. Some historical ties were passed on via oral tradition, like the pre-Second World War trade ties mentioned in the epigraph above, but more recently popular media has fostered other senses of historical connection, particularly in regard to a glorious Ottoman past. In what is probably the most widely encountered example of "Ottomania," a laudatory portrayal of the Ottoman Empire that has swept Turkey, the telenovela *The Magnificent Century* (*Muhteşem Yüzyıl*) opens with the commanding, young Süleyman the Magnificent out on a hunting expedition. He receives news that his father has died, making him the next sultan of the Ottoman Empire. The series goes on to trace Süleyman's reign, which extended over forty-five years (1520–1565) and ultimately expanded the Ottoman Empire to encompass lands stretching from the Persian Gulf to the Danube River, bringing thirty to fifty million people under the direct control of the empire (Fromkin 1989, 34; Kaya and Tecmen 2011, 15–20).

Early in the series Süleyman is swept off his feet by the lively, fair Alexandra, a slave recently brought as a young adult from the outer regions of the Russian Empire. The series features palace intrigues and intimate lives, with a focus on Süleyman and Alexandra, who becomes Süleyman's wife, known as Hürrem and a powerful figure in her own right. This telenovela is just the latest of a now established Turkish media tradition, but this part historical drama, part soap opera is the first of its genre to focus on the intimate practices of a popular Ottoman ruler, and the first to feature his sometimes reviled, sometimes revered consort, Hürrem (Batuman 2014).[1] *The Magnificent Century* has also brought intimate ties between Turkey and Russia to the fore of public discourse.

As of January 2014 *The Magnificent Century* completed its fourth and final season, garnering record-breaking viewership, especially in Turkey but also throughout the Middle East, the former Soviet Union, and Eastern Europe.[2] In addition to causing a stir with its portrayal of a venerated sultan among libidinous women, the telenovela also embodies the intangible power of the imagination at play in the encounter of Turks and post-Soviet women in Turkey today. Although the series may not be the primary factor compelling women to migrate, it creates a sense of possibilities for them. For a Turkish viewership, the telenovela affirms a stereotype about "Russian" women as embodying dangerous sexuality, a quality that, according to the storyline of *The Magnificent Century*, had an integral role to play in the weakening of the Ottoman Empire.

The television series highlights a number of issues at stake since the early 2000s as Turkey has come to embrace Ottomania as portraying the height of political and cultural influence in the region (Potuoğlu-Cook 2006, 2008; Toksabay and Villelabeitia 2011; Batuman 2014). Despite the unprecedented popularity of *The Magnificent Century*, some found the telenovela's depiction of Süleyman to be in poor taste. As one commentator wrote on the intense debates about *The Magnificent Century*, "The Islamic World's version of America's culture wars is playing out in a lavishly recreated 16th century palace" (Rohde 2012a). Prime Minister Recep Tayyip Erdoğan and his Justice and Development Party (AKP) have widely sought to promote Turkey's "soft power" through the glorification of the Ottoman Empire, with the concomitant image of Turkey as its successor, a political aim that did not fit well with the racy soap opera/historical drama (Finkel 2012; Aydos 2013). In a speech in December 2012 Erdoğan called for federal judicial action against the show's producers. Erdoğan and his supporters saw the series as sullying the name of the most preeminent Ottoman ruler, known as Süleyman the Magnificent in European literature and Kanuni Sultan Süleyman, or "Süleyman the Lawgiver," in the Muslim world. As the tenth and longest reigning ruler of the Ottoman Empire, Süleyman is widely revered. He is noted for bringing about extensive reforms to the Ottoman legal system, substantially expanding the reach of the Ottoman Empire to encompass territory from the banks of the Danube River to nearly the entire Middle East, and for being an avid supporter of the arts and culture in his empire. He was also the first sultan in the Ottoman dynastic family that spanned thirty-seven generations to break with tradition and marry a woman from his harem (Peirce 1993, 61; 2015).

Erdoğan has pointed to *The Magnificent Century*'s rendering of Süleyman as cavorting with women and imbibing wine as outrageous. Erdoğan and his supporters insist the series is historically incorrect, casting Süleyman as an imperfect and morally corrupt ruler. In realpolitik terms, they are sensitive to anything that could potentially detract from Turkey's role as a pivotal player in the region (Akyol 2012; Kenyon 2013). In spite of considerable support for Erdoğan's position, and with more than seventy thousand complaints flooding into the television network's offices following the first airing of the series in January 2011, *The Magnificent Century* also earned the distinction of being avidly watched by over two hundred million viewers in as many as fifty-six countries, including Russia, Central Asian states, and elsewhere in the former Soviet Union (Rohde 2012b; Global Agency 2014).[3]

Mobility and Cartographies of Desire

In the twenty-first century, even prior to the debut of *The Magnificent Century*, the presence of Russian-speaking women in Ottoman harems occupied a visible place in the popular imagination of both Russian speakers and Turks. I first learned of Alexandra, or "Roxelana," as Russian-speaking migrants often referred to Süleyman's wife, Hürrem, in 2002, nearly nine years before *The Magnificent Century* first aired. As Irina, an exotic dancer from Ukraine who joined me in visiting several tourist sites during the early stages of my research, explained, Hürrem was born Alexandra Anastasia Lisowska.[4] She was of Ukrainian/Ruthenian/Polish extraction and the daughter of an Orthodox priest and was in Süleyman the Magnificent's harem before he chose to marry her in 1534 (Mansel 1995, 83; Peirce 1993, 2015).[5] Irina enthusiastically described Roxelana's significance for her peers and, she argued, for the Turkish men she encountered. She insisted that we visit the Süleymaniye Mosque, where Irina led me to Hürrem/Roxelana's tomb located next to the main mosque.[6] Irina recounted that women love to imagine themselves festooned with lavish clothing and commanding a sultan's attention, as Roxelana is widely imagined to have done. To emphasize her point Irina struck a come hither pose, elaborating that Russian women simply drive Turkish men crazy with their sex appeal.

FIGURE 6.   Hürrem's tomb beside the Süleymaniye Mosque. Photograph by author, 2003.

Like Irina, in conversation other people invoked the "long tradition" of concubinage and courtesans in the region, and they emphasized the way in which women could rise from such a station to one of power and influence in the Ottoman court.[7] Most often both Russian speakers and Turks I met referred to these women as being ethnically "Russians" (in Russian, *russkie*; in Turkish, *Rusça, Rusçalar*, pl.). In fact, however, women in the harem were from a range of backgrounds, even if traditionally women from Circassia, a region

FIGURE 7.   Haseki Hürrem Sultan or Roxelana. By Anonymous (www.topkapipalace.org).

on the border of southern Russia and Georgia, were preferred slaves among the elite of the Ottoman Empire (Erdem 1996, 61).[8] While the women sent to Istanbul did not all rise to positions of power like Hürrem, the presence of "Russian" women in the Ottoman harems was something that was historically well known throughout the region, even entering into oral tradition. As one historian writes, "For centuries in the Caucasus, mothers sang a lullaby over their daughters' cradles, beginning, 'Live among diamonds and splendor as the wife of a Sultan'" (Mansel 1995, 81).

Haseki Hürrem Sultan's life represents the most celebrated instance of a concubine rising to a position of power.[9] Hürrem went on to wield wide powers in the Ottoman court, including by maintaining diplomatic ties with heads of state such as the king of Poland and establishing massive mosque complexes across the Ottoman Empire in Mecca, Medina, and Jerusalem. Hürrem's important political role was virtually proclaimed by the enormous mosque complex that Sultan Süleyman had built in her name in Istanbul; it was the only such complex ever built by a sultan for his wife or concubine during his lifetime (Peirce 1993, 205).[10] The mosque complex remains today, with a functioning mosque and regional hospital in its place, and the neighborhood in which the complex is located is called "Haseki," in honor of Hürrem.[11] Hürrem's story is one both Turks and post-Soviet women often mentioned as an example of how Russians and Turks have a long history of erotic encounters, especially in Istanbul, a "site of desire" that *The Magnificent Century* has compellingly portrayed.

Istanbul as a Site of Desire

The Magnificent Century encapsulates a long-term configuration of "sites of desire," what Lenore Manderson and Margaret Jolly have called a "fluid terrain in the exchange of desires" (1997, 1); both migrant women and contemporary Turks widely imagine the Ottoman Empire as a once opulent, alluring center of global power, something to harken back to with nostalgia, and sometimes imbued with an aura of the erotic (Potuoğlu-Cook 2006). In a contemporary period marked by the hypermobility of post-Soviet women into Turkey, an affirmation of interethnic erotic ties, specifically between Turks and women from regions of the former Soviet Union, has seen a florescence. Cartographies of desire for some in Turkey are based in a specific historical trajectory that is, in part, exemplified by *The Magnificent Century* but also grounded in Turkey's place within a broad Eurasian imaginary.

A dramatic increase in mobility has been central to bringing post-Soviet women into the purview of a Turkish male gaze since the early 1990s, but the broader realm of the imagination is also key. As a number of scholars compellingly argue in their work on the intimate lives of transnational Filipinas, intimate encounters do not simply happen but are forged within concrete historical contexts where mutual imaginaries are constituted. In the case of the Philippines following the Second World War the presence of US military bases shaped intimate connections and brought about a history of "mail order" or "correspondence" marriage between men from North America and Filipinas; more recently, the geopolitical power of Japan and South Korea has brought about flows of gendered labor from the Philippines to those countries (Constable 2003; Faier 2009; Cheng 2010). Just as Filipinas are drawn to take up intimate ties with men from North America, South Korea, or Japan as part of a long-term political economy in which these countries represent sites of opportunity, I argue here that images of historical Ottoman economic power and opulence are part of what draws post-Soviet women into intimate ties with Turkish men. These historical images also come to be imbricated in intimate ties and ways of imagining the other, wherein Turkish men can imagine post-Soviet women through a prism of Süleyman's transgressive relationship to the exotic Hürrem, and post-Soviet women can romanticize the potential of relationships with Turkish men via a narrative of Hürrem's ultimate triumph as the wife of one of the most powerful and erudite sultans of the Ottoman Empire.

As a number of scholars have shown (Manderson and Jolly 1997; Stoler 2002), these "cartographies of desire," or the ways history, politics, and the imagination inform the shape desire takes in a given location, resonate throughout colonial relationships. The Turkish–post-Soviet matrix, however, highlights just how complicated and nonbinary cartographies of desire can be. A simple "white = power" and "black/brown = oppressed" does not work in this instance. Scholars have written extensively on the way Euro-American colonial histories play into the construction of racial categories, gendered intimate practices, and the shape power takes, including in North Africa, India, Southeast Asia, and China (Fanon 1963; Nandy 1983; Stoler 2002; Constable 2003). However, few scholars have considered how the politics of race and desire unfold when economic capital is held by racially "nonwhite" men and symbolic capital in the form of education and sex appeal is held by "white" women who are, nonetheless, economically unstable and therefore mobile.[12] The idea of intimate practices as interwoven with different types of power, and not just danger (Vance 1982), destabilizes simple binaries such as oppressed/oppressor, black/white, rich/poor, pleasure/danger, or European/non-European.

In featuring the relationship between Süleyman the Magnificent and Hürrem/Roxelana in the storyline of *The Magnificent Century*, the television series signals the long-term contested relationship between Russia and Turkey. The

Ruthenian woman in the historical figure of Hürrem takes a prominent place in the story portrayed in the series and in some ways could reflect the not uncommon long-term intimate ties between Turkish men and post-Soviet migrant women in urban Turkey today. The widespread viewership in Russia, as well as across the FSU and Eastern Europe, points to the ways that imagination is being commonly forged throughout this region of Eurasia, but possibly also to a fascination with an opulent Ottoman past that is intertwined with the history of a Russian empire. *The Magnificent Century* is part of a long history of encounters in the region, where borders, intimacy, and mobility have come together to forge a particular backdrop to the ties between Turkey and regions of the former Soviet Union. The encounters between contemporary migrant Russian speakers and Turks are informed by a cultural politics that has emerged over hundreds of years.

From Byzantium to the Jazz Age

The migrants and Turks I came to know in Istanbul did not always know the details of the centuries of interactions between peoples from the regions of present-day Turkey and the former Soviet Union, but they were aware that ties between the two regions extend back over a thousand years. Especially for people living near the border of Turkey and Georgia or Azerbaijan, the twentieth-century history of Russian (and then Soviet) dominance in the region loomed large, with Turkey caught between increasingly entrenched political camps (Reynolds 2011); when Turkey eventually became a member of NATO and a US ally after the Second World War, communities of coethnics and families were divided for several decades (Pelkmans 2006).[13] Even after the end of the Soviet Union in the early 1990s, the Turkish public tended to have a deep-rooted suspicion of all things "Russian" as being politically suspect (Keyder 1999), and former Soviet citizens could be quick to dismiss Turkey as a place lacking "culture" (*kul'tura*).[14] However, this simplification of the relationship between Russia and Turkey elides a varied history, even of the twentieth century, when some Turkish and Soviet allegiances emerged in the aftermath of the First World War (Kınıklıoğlu and Morkva 2007; Reynolds 2011) and when, in the 1920s, Turkey accepted refugees from the Soviet Union, before abruptly closing the border as the Cold War encroached.[15] With the warming of relations in the 1990s and early 2000s, made visible in the myriad border crossings, Turkey and the former Soviet Union, but especially Russia, have undergone a profound repositioning of cultural exchange and realignment of political power that in some ways echoes encounters from hundreds of years earlier.

"East," "West" and the Ottomans

Significant ties between Russian-speaking people and the region of present-day Turkey extend back at least as far as the fourth century, when Constantinople was founded as the capital of the Eastern Roman Empire and a schism between "East" and "West" first emerged. While the symbolic divide that is often invoked in bracketing the region of the former Soviet Union and Turkey apart from the "West" is not a fixed one (Tolz 2011), it could be seen in terms of age-old allegiances.[16] In the fifth century the Western Roman Empire became fractured and the Eastern Roman Empire, which by the late tenth century nominally included the kingdom of Kievan Rus', a federation of East Slavic tribes, solidified and thrived with Constantinople at its center until the fall of Constantinople to the Ottomans in 1453. Not infrequently migrants I came to know from Belarus, Ukraine, Moldova, or Russia referred to a celebrated Byzantine past as one to which they felt a connection; as one migrant told me, "Of course, we are drawn to more than just work here—after all, our people were here even before the Ottomans, our religious foundations are here." Eastern Orthodoxy is one of the many historical ties that especially non-Muslim Russian speakers invoke as connecting them to the region of present-day Turkey.

The origins of Kievan Rus', widely invoked as the precursor to the Russian Empire (but also claimed by Belarus and Ukraine as a geopolitical ancestor), are closely linked to Byzantium, and specifically Constantinople, as the seat of Eastern Christianity. With the consolidation of various Slavic tribes in the mid-ninth century, the state of Kievan Rus' emerged. The Rus' sought to secure trade partnerships and expand territory, and to this end over a span of barely two hundred years (860–1043), they sailed down the Bosphorus and attacked Byzantium multiple times (Bréhier 1977, 102, 176; Herrin 2007, 116). Byzantine coins excavated at what was the ancient city of Gorodishche (the present-day Russian city of Novgorod) attest to trade relations that were established dating back to the early tenth century (Herrin 2007, 137).[17]

By the time of these early cultural and economic exchanges, regular incursions by the Rus' against Constantinople resulted in a number of treaties granting Rus' merchants preferential access to trade with Byzantium (Bréhier 1977, 102). By 987 terms stipulated such details as how much silk Kievan Rus' could ask for in exchange for the slaves, wax, and honey it was offering, and how many Varangian warriors would be contributed to the Byzantine forces (Browning 1992, 101; Herrin 2007, 137).[18] Prince Vladimir was keen on allying his new state with the Byzantine Empire, and soon after his marriage in 987 to Anna Porphyrogenita (Anna Vizantiiskaia in Russian), he converted to Christianity and imposed the belief across his lands, calling for the destruction of "idols of paganism," widespread baptisms, and the construction in Kiev of two cathedrals ornately decorated with Byzantine inspired mosaics and icons (Bréhier 1977, 154; Herrin 2007, 114).[19] Byzantium became the preeminent seat of power that served to fortify the foundation of the Rus' as a Christian state. Nevertheless, prior to its eventual downfall under the onslaught of the Mongols (1237–1240), Kievan Rus' continued to orchestrate a number of attacks on the Byzantine Empire, seeking to extract favorable trade treaties and strategic positioning of Rus' warriors in Byzantine structures of power, and on occasion also creating alliances with the empire in its attempts to fend off the marauding forces of Bulgars from the north, Arabs from the south and east, and, ultimately, Turks. With the rise of Muscovy as a cultural center beginning in the thirteenth century, ties to Byzantium continued, but geopolitical circumstances compelled Muscovy and then the emerging Russian Empire to forge alliances with the Ottomans; in 1453 Mehmed II, also known as Mehmed the Conqueror or Fatih Sultan Mehmed, conquered Constantinople, bringing about the eventual end of the Byzantine Empire.[20]

The relationship between the Russian Empire and the Ottoman Empire was punctuated by conflict, with thirteen significant clashes between the two states over the course of just four hundred years, from the late seventeenth century to the early twentieth century (Kınıklıoğlu and Morkva 2007, 533); some of the bloodiest battles took place when the Ottoman and Russian Empires struggled for territory in eastern Anatolia leading up to and immediately following the First World War (Reynolds 2011). Prior to this period of emerging nationalism, however, distinctions between Muslims and Christians were not so clearly defined and people moved relatively freely between the empires. There were also various cross-border alliances and connections. For instance, from the mid-fifteenth to the mid-eighteenth century, Crimean Tatars, an offshoot of the Golden Horde, lived in the region of present-day Crimea (annexed/occupied by Russia in the spring of 2014) and pillaged surrounding regions to pay tribute to the Ottoman Empire.[21] This included provisioning the Ottoman Court with slaves, as the Crimean Tatars had done in bringing Alexandra Lisowska, Hürrem, to Süleyman's Court around 1520 (Peirce 1993, 58). For hundreds of years Russia also sought to maintain equilibrium with the Ottoman Empire so it could maintain strategic access to the Black Sea Straits, a trade route which one-quarter of Russia's total exports passed through by the early twentieth century (Reynolds 2011, 32–33).

Intimate Encounters and the End of Empires

Istanbul is a city steeped in histories of encounter, where trade, diplomacy, and empires have intersected, forging a cosmopolitan milieu. This was especially the case in the second half of the nineteenth century following the Crimean (1853–1856) and the Russo-Ottoman (1877–1878) Wars, when people came to the city in ever greater numbers; between 1829 and 1884 the population of the city more than doubled in size, from about 359,000 to 895,000 people (Woodall 2015, 20). Even as the Ottoman Empire began to lose power, in 1885 the city was seen as a destination where, irrespective of religious background, young men could seek their fortune; nearly 60 percent of the population was born elsewhere and included sizable numbers of Greeks and Armenians (Karpat 1985, 104).[22] However, by 1900, with increasing strife in the region as European powers competed over Ottoman territory and opportunities shrank within Ottoman structures, the city became less diverse and the majority of the city's inhabitants were Muslim, a striking change from just fifteen years earlier (Karpat 1985, 86).[23] The trend continued in the years leading up to and immediately following the First World War when an increasingly nationalist sentiment came to hinge on being Muslim. With atrocities against millions of Armenians and Greeks, as well as millions of Turks dying in the Allied onslaught on the Ottoman Empire, there was a subsequent massive population "exchange"; it is estimated that 1.2 million Christians departed Turkey for Greece and 400,000 Muslims left Greece for Turkey (Mansel 1985, 397; Reynolds 2011, 258).[24]

By 1918, when former Russian subjects first arrived in large numbers on the shores of Istanbul as refugees fleeing war and revolution, the population of the city had plummeted from nearly one million people prior to the First World War to about seven hundred thousand (King 2014, 113). The tens of thousands of Russian speakers who transited through and sometimes settled in the city were joined by the thousands of Allied troops overseeing the interwar period in Istanbul, as well as by refugees from Ottoman territories in the Balkans. This milieu was reminiscent of the second half of the nineteenth century, when waves of mobile populations brought diverse languages and a multitude of religious practices to punctuate public space. However, this time Russian speakers in particular shaped public space. In 1920, when Crimea was evacuated by the commanding general of the anti-Bolshevik White Army, General Wrangel, nearly 150,000 Russian speakers, many of them soldiers, arrived overnight on the shores of the Bosphorus.[25] One author describes how "the streets of Constantinople were crowded with Russian officers, with the hungry, drawn look of refugees driving cabs, or selling newspapers, shoe-laces or wooden dolls" and they were concentrated in the area of Beyoğlu, a region historically associated with foreigners and encompassing present-day Taksim square (Mansel 1995, 398).[26] In Galata, one of the long-standing enclaves of foreigners at one end of present-day Beyoğlu, a collection of small hotels became home to "Russian" prostitutes, and Russians dominated the entertainment of the city in a time that some have called the "Islamic jazz age" (King 2014, 7). Today Russian-speaking women entertainers like Irina are again visible in this part of the city in the side streets off present-day Istaklal Caddesi, the popular walking zone extending from Taksim Square to the Galata neighborhood featured in accounts of the 1920s.

In Pera, another Beyoğlu neighborhood along Istaklal Caddesi, which in the Ottoman era was host to foreign embassies and appealed to foreigners with its stylish establishments, Russian restaurants and clubs became synonymous with renegade nightlife. One entrepreneur, Frederick Bruce Thomas, an African American who had owned a series of jazz clubs in Petrograd, Russia, before the revolution, introduced the Charleston and the fox trot in his Istanbul club Maxim (Alexandrov 2013; King 2014, 138–42). In addition to the explosion of artistic productions and new forms of entertainment brought by those who arrived from Russia, there was the novelty of having wait staff who were women. According to one source, some Turkish men were reportedly "besotted" with Russian waitresses, who wore "high black boots, thin scarves . . . and heavy make-up," and others were appalled at what they saw as a bacchanalia (Mansel 1995, 339).

After the First World War Beyoğlu was widely associated with "decadent cosmopolitanism" in the form of social dancing, immoderate women's attire, and alcohol and drug use (Woodall 2015, 18). There were also a large number of

FIGURE 8.   Four women at the Turan Bar in Beyoğlu (Pera), 1930s. Courtesy of Yapi Kredi Selahattin Giz Collection.

Russian-speaking women, along with Greek and Armenian women, working as exotic dancers and in other forms of sex work (King 2014, 149).[27] Public outrage targeted Russian women in particular and wives and widows of prominent men were the most vociferous. In 1923, a group of these incensed women sent a petition to the governor of Constantinople demanding the "expulsion of these agents of 'vice and debauchery who are more dangerous and destructive than syphilis and alcohol'" (Mansel 1995, 400).[28] As Pelin Başcı writes, for Turkish readers of fiction in the 1920s, even invoking the name of the neighborhood "Beyoğlu" was sufficient to summon up images of immoral behavior on the part of the largely non-Muslim population that lived there (2003, 160).[29]

Public pressure let up as most Russians gradually emigrated abroad, and Russian women were no longer visible figures in leisure spaces of Istanbul. By 1934 the Turkish state had granted citizenship to just 986 remaining "White Russian" families.[30] While in this period the Turkish state especially favored the highly educated, aristocratic, so-called "White Russians" who were fleeing the Soviet Union, just a few years later anxiety over communism and suspected espionage led to a 1937 Turkish government order to refuse admission to nearly all refugees from the Soviet Union, and border crossing in the region was virtually curtailed, even for those with relatives just across the border in present-day Georgia (Pelkmans 2006).[31]

After the Cold War and the "Soft Power" of Turkey

For over fifty years there was minimal interaction between Turks and the former Soviet Union. Turkey was effectively on the front lines of the Cold War, with more than half of its national budget in the late 1940s and early 1950s spent on defense (Machado 2007, 94).[32] The Marshall Plan in Turkey brought about new agricultural technologies and road-building expertise, as well as educational training, all key in Cold War mandates to transform countries like Turkey that were thought to be vulnerable to the spread of communism. As then US Secretary of Commerce Averill Harriman emphasized, creating an economically prosperous Turkey was meant to be an "effective deterrent to Soviet aggression" (Machado 2007, 94). In fact, whether or not directly the result of the Marshall Plan, in the years following its implementation, the Turkish gross national product (GNP) surged, with a 40 percent increase from 1950 to 1952 alone, and the primary export shifted from tobacco to cotton, a product for which there was an enormous global demand (Machado 2007, 95). Unlike in some countries where the Marshall Plan was carried out, in Turkey the phenomenal economic transformation did not automatically predispose the country to embrace US policy initiatives or bring about a sense of economic and ideological direction in common with the United States.

Despite the Marshall Plan, for decades after the Second World War Turkey struggled economically and its growing population was underemployed, something that turned out to be a boon to postwar Germany.

In the aftermath of the sudden erection of the Berlin Wall in 1961, West Germany lost a key source of low-wage labor for its expanding economy, and Turkey became the new source. In the decade following the appearance of the wall, more than a million Turks traveled to Germany as "guestworkers," and fifty years later more than three million immigrants of Turkish heritage lived in Germany (Mandel 2008, 6). For decades Turkey was wary of becoming the source country for Europe's demands for human labor and raw materials. However, there was even more widespread wariness about Soviet power, on the one hand, and, on the other, about US desires for access to land for establishing military bases.

All this began to shift by the late 1980s for a number of reasons. First, as the Cold War let up and the Soviet Union's staunch political and economic positions began to waver, Turkey increasingly turned to Russia as a source of gas and oil. Nearly simultaneously, Turkey's domestic political and economic balances of power shifted, and like some other expanding economies of the 1980s (Bishop and Robinson 1998), Turkey fostered the service sector, and especially the tourism, hospitality, and entertainment industry while opening up its manufacturing to world markets (Tosun 2001).[33] These expanding sectors brought about an increased demand for low-wage labor, which drew rural Turks, predominantly men, into new economic spheres in urban locations but also made it profitable to hire undocumented foreign workers. By the early 1990s, for the second time in the course of a century, Russian speakers traversed borders into Turkey in large numbers, this time not as refugees, but in search of work. By the early 2000s not only labor migrants from across the former Soviet Union but also Russia's growing middle class was visible on the Turkish landscape as people flocked to Turkey as vacationers and basked in the flourishing tourism economy; in 2011 alone 3.5 million Russians entered Turkey on tourist visas (UNWTO 2012, 6–7).[34]

The arrival of such a large volume of relatively affluent Russian-speaking tourists created a whole new sphere of trade and cultural exchange, as well as exchange of services and goods.[35] In appealing to these tourists, the Turkish tourism industry created niches for low-wage post-Soviet migrants as well. It was not uncommon for migrants to combine selling luxury goods near the seaside with their own budget vacation with friends or family arriving from Belarus or Ukraine or Moldova. Antalya, a resort city on the Mediterranean Sea, became particularly popular with Russian speakers in the 1990s. As one woman, a shop assistant and sometime trader from Moldova, explained, each year she spent her vacation time in Antalya selling furs to Russian tourists; in 2011 she made $4,000 in two months, more than double what she calculated she could have made over the same period working as a shop assistant in Istanbul. For Turks as well, the expansion of the tourism economy shaped their professional lives, and during my research I frequently met Turkish men working as staff in hotels or as taxi drivers who told me in fully functional Russian that they chose to learn Russian as a way to improve their employment options in the tourism sector.

In addition to tourism, pilgrimage is a related area of increased interaction between Turks and Russian speakers. Pilgrimage from the former Soviet Union grew extensively in the early 2000s as Turkey sought to foster "faith tourism" by investing in restoring early Christian sites and enabling archaeological study of some of the oldest churches in the world (Güsten 2011).[36] Long-term labor migrants I came to know in Istanbul also sought out Eastern Orthodox ritual sites as part of their daily lives in the city. In particular, each April 23 several of my interviewees made a point of visiting Aya Yorgi Garibi (the Monastery of St. George) a popular pilgrimage site located high on the peak of Yücetepe on Büyükada, an island near Istanbul.[37] They joined tens of thousands of people traveling from a great number of places—including Turkey, Russia, Greece, and the Balkans—to take part in what is known as an ancient fertility ritual, but they also took part in rituals like unwinding a string along the steep path leading up to the monastery, just in case this might bring about better fortunes overall (Couroucli 2010; Schillinger 2011, TR1).[38] Even when migrants did not take part in this annual pilgrimage, many attended church at least on major holidays. Many middle-aged Moldovan Gagauz women I met made a point of going to church for Easter (*Paskha*) and Pentecost (*Troitsa*), usually at St. Pantaleimon, a small Russian Orthodox church that holds Sunday services on the sixth floor of a building in the harborside Istanbul neighborhood of Karaköy.[39]

Cultural and religious tourism have certainly forged renewed connections between Turkey and Russia. Nevertheless, perhaps the single largest link between the countries since the 1990s has been Turkey's reliance on Russia as a source of energy. By 2008 Turkey came to rely on Russia for nearly two-thirds of its gas supply and one-third of its oil needs (Ediger and Bağdadi 2010, 233).[40] Turkey continues to seek ways to attract Russian capital and create a more equal balance of trade.[41] As part of this effort, since the early 1990s Turkey has maintained a relatively open border with Russia and with other former Soviet states, making it fairly easy for temporary workers like Irina, the entertainer who first told me about Hürrem, and Zhenia, the shuttle trader traveling from central Siberia, to enter Turkey as tourists. For over twenty years Turkey granted mostly one-month tourist visas on entry to citizens of former Soviet countries, and as of 2013 state-to-state agreements extended visa-free entry into Turkey for two or three months for many citizens of countries of the former Soviet Union.[42] In turn, Russia also relaxed visa requirements for Turks, thus facilitating the growth of Turkish companies that have increasingly won tenders for major construction projects in Russia, as well as the mobility of the more than seventy-five thousand Turks who were employed as of 2012 in countries of the former Soviet Union (İçduygu and Biriz Karaçay 2012; İçduygu 2009, 282). With some variation from year to year, Russia has also tacitly agreed to overlook import duties on the "suitcase" or informal trade of apparel from Turkey into Russia, a topic to which I return in chapter 2. This particular configuration of a flexible border regime into Turkey is a critical aspect of the multibillion dollar bilateral investment of Turkey and Russia (Kınıklıoğlu and Morkva 2007), something that helps explain the existence of thousands of undocumented migrants from the former Soviet Union working long-term in Turkey.

Soft Power and the "Turkic Sphere"

The demise of socialist state infrastructures and the reworking of regional alliances created a fertile ground for Turkish influence in Eurasia. In the case of the Turkic-speaking Gagauz, for instance, as their status within Moldova became tenuous in the early 1990s, the then Turkish president, Süleyman Demirel, played an important role in positioning Turkey as a mediator in the arrangement that unfolded, and the Gagauz were ultimately granted significant administrative autonomy (Demirdirek 2008; Şenyuva 2012). In addition to such mediator roles in the 2000s, Turkish government aid packages and NGO and benevolent-association ventures continued to widely promote historical links with Turkey as part of Turkish "soft power" or indirect influence over states in Eurasia (Angey-Sentuc and Molho 2015; Kaya 2013, 68; Ghodsee 2009, 134, 140). Turkey has been careful to avoid creating tensions with neighboring governments, even as it has positioned itself as a political force. Established in 1992 to provide aid within the "Turkic sphere," encompassing southern Bulgaria and Central Asian states as well as southern Moldova, the Turkish Agency for International Development and Cooperation (TIKA) is one of the key actors overseeing the distribution of Turkish aid (Şenyuva 2012). In its work in southern Moldova the agency has sponsored a number of initiatives, including the training of Gagauz teachers in Turkey, the construction of sewage and water projects, and the reorganization and funding of a new health infrastructure.[43] Furthermore, as in Central Asia, Turkish government aid has also supported several schools in southern Moldova with an emphasis on Turkish language and culture. Alongside Turkish government aid efforts, the Fethullah Gulen movement has also had substantial influence in the region, namely through an extensive network of its own schools (Hudson 2008; Putz 2016).[44]

Turkey's effort to deploy soft power in the region could be seen as a form of exchange for the wide-ranging care work Moldovan women provide in Turkey, a situation many in Moldova consider to be to the detriment of women's own households (Keough 2015). Several people in southern Moldova told me they were cynical about Turkey's motivations, but they willingly accepted the assistance that arrived in the form of a newly constructed hospital, improved road system, and an expansion of educational opportunities; especially for Gagauz, as I discuss in chapter 3, the presence of the Turkish state provides them with forms of power vis-à-vis the Moldovan state. However, a critical assessment of Turkey's humanitarian projects suggests that they are integrally linked to Turkey's desire to showcase its ability to "help" Turkic brethren even as Turkey does little to create social protections for the thousands of migrant women laboring in Turkey without benefits and in fear of deportation, a dynamic described as "neohumanitarian" in other locations (Ticktin 2011). In this way, the poorly paid, largely female post-Soviet labor force in Turkey is a key part of the story of Turkey becoming a global force, capable of flexing its "soft" power, but also relying on newly mobile, flexible labor.

Politics of Gender and Intimacy in Turkey

In many ways, Turkey is a country of extreme dichotomies. It boasts an infrastructure on a par with that of many wealthy, industrialized countries in terms of financial institutions, road systems, and health care. Moreover, with 70 percent of the population urban-based, a growing middle class contributes to a cosmopolitan Turkey where men and women have access to higher education, urban fertility is considerably lower than the countrywide average, feminist organizations play an important role in public discourse, and women form a significant portion (34 percent) of all professionals in recent years (Sirman 1989; Countries 2002; Coşar and Gençoğlu Onbaşı 2008; Turkstat 2012).[45] However, in 2014 Turkey also had the highest level of gender inequality of all Organization for Economic Cooperation and Development (OECD) countries (UNDP 2016).[46] According to some metrics, in 2015 Turkey was poised to make significant improvements to gender inequality, but in the areas of women's economic and political participation this was not the case (World Economic Forum 2015).[47] In general, there is a dual reality in Turkey, where the politics of gender for an elite and growing urban middle class have been very different than for the rural, working-class, and poor populations.

Transformations in household forms of power in Turkey have occurred in diverse ways across the country over the twentieth century. However, these changes became most evident from the early 1970s as Turks became increasingly part of transnational circuits of migration into Germany (Mandel 2008), and then by the late 1970s as Turkey's government took on IMF loans and initiated neoliberal reforms, including curtailing public-sector spending, moving away from agricultural production, and putting resources into the export sector (Keyder 1999; Naylor 2004, 93–94).[48] By the 1980s Istanbul became the center for Turkey's intensive engagement with world markets (Öncü 1999, 104). Along with the rapid increase in foreign investment and sharp rise in exports from Turkey, the service sector suddenly grew. As in many other locations of rapid integration into world markets, by the early 1990s Turkey had opened its borders to new migrants who conveniently contributed to the supply of low-wage labor while also becoming a visible reminder of radical shifts in the Turkish economy and urban cultural landscape. Along with millions of households becoming transnational, millions of Turks have also moved into Turkey's urban centers, creating enclaves of rural migrants that have rapidly increased the populations of large cities such as Istanbul, Ankara, and Izmir (İçduygu et al. 2013, 16–17; Karpat 2004).[49] In sites like these Turkish women have widely become integral to home-based production, and especially piecework, where they produce textiles and engage in knitting or sewing (White 2004; Dedeoğlu 2008), and some women have also been employed as live-out domestic workers (Akalin 2007).[50] In 2012 the vast majority of women (more than 75 percent) were not employed outside their homes, and many scholars point to this to explain the unequal access to economic opportunities that remains a key issue for women in Turkey (Müftüler-Baç 2012; Hausmann et al. 2012, 15).[51]

Although profound transformations in legal provisions for gender equality accompanied the creation of the Turkish Republic in 1923, as Deniz Kandiyoti (1987) has written, women were "emancipated but unliberated." A wide range of legislation introduced in the early Republican era, as well as in more recent decades, brought about reforms, including expanding the right to education for girls and women and regulating when and where the veil could be worn. Nevertheless, family and household domains in Turkey have remained largely defined by patriarchal structures, with men's prerogatives governing decisions around fertility, education, and mobility; challenges to men's power may be one of the factors contributing to pervasive domestic abuse and disturbing levels of violence against women that appear to have escalated in the early 2000s (Koğacıoğlu 2004; Jones 2011).[52]

Ayşe Parla argues that the foundations for contemporary politics defining gender inequalities can be found in the 1920s, when "notions of being modern became articulated" in Turkey (2001, 70). As Parla notes, with the newly minted Constitution, the state was able to proclaim women to be equal citizens and thereby dispel concerns about the role gender and male privilege might play in perpetuating inequality (2001, 70–73).[53] For instance, in 1930 Turkish women gained the right to vote in municipal elections, and by 1934 in national elections, placing Turkey solidly within the trend for European countries of the time. However, in crafting women as new Turkish citizens, and creating the means for women to pursue careers in the realms of education, medicine, and beyond, the state simultaneously proclaimed it women's duty to be good wives and mothers; women were incorporated into the nation, but with the primary task of reproducing the family for the benefit of the state (Arat 1994; Koğacıoğlu 2004, 127–28). Thus, in Turkey today, in many ways men and women are fundamentally framed as having very different rights and being subject to different forms of social control, inequities that Turkish feminists have consistently challenged since the 1980s, and more recently sought to address as Turkey has aspired to EU accession.[54]

In addition to gender inequities written into the actual legal code, the way women's sexuality was framed by the 1923 Constitution also continues to have ramifications for women. With the establishment of the Turkish Republic, any idea of sexuality was purged from the way the new nation of Turkey positioned women. Women were to be "modern," both in appearance and in having access to formal education, but to be shielded from any associations with sexuality, a sign of a different, unwelcome version of modernity. Women were to be modern but modest, ideal citizen-mothers, a situation not unlike what Daphne Berdahl (1999) describes for late state socialism and "worker-mothers" in East Germany. As Berdahl notes, "the rights and privileges accorded to women under state socialism as well as its ideology of worker-mothers also served to reinforce as 'natural' women's traditional role in the home, thereby underscoring as well women's roles as biological regenerators of the socialist nation and as socializers of its citizens" (1999, 190). Likewise, as Kandiyoti writes about Turkey, "the national ideal was of a self-sacrificing comrade-woman [who was] also an asexual sister-in-arms" (1988a, 46).

Decades after the establishment of the Turkish Republic, women's modesty continues to be widely valued and signified in the form of virginity, something that resonates well beyond simply a sign. Until the early 2000s the Turkish state brandished the stick of "virginity" tests to discipline women and girls into conducting themselves "modestly" (Parla 2001; Frank et al. 1999).[55] While the 2004 Penal Code made virginity exams illegal, in the 2010s the state still reserved the right to require these in cases where moral questions were considered pertinent to legal proceedings. Related to this policing of women's sexuality, periodic exams intended to regulate moral conduct continued to be a part of the mandated monthly medical checkups for dancers I came to know in Istanbul in 2001–2011.[56]

Even if virginity exams are no longer legal, state regulation of women's sexuality remains firmly in place and is bluntly invoked as an issue of national debate. In comments made in May 2012 at the third annual congress of the women's branch of his party, Prime Minister Recep Tayyip Erdoğan declared that he would seek to outlaw abortions, except in the case of extreme medical conditions, and significantly curtail access to cesarean procedures.[57] Turkish feminists responded vehemently, opposing these attacks on women's control of their own bodies. One then MP of the main opposition party, the Republican People's Party (CHP), Aylin Nazlıaka, boldly stated, "The Prime Minister should stop standing guard over women's vaginas." Nazlıaka was in turn castigated by a number of politicians for using "vulgar" language and for daring to refer to women's sexuality (Sehlikoğlu 2013).

Turkish feminists argue that the struggle for gender equality in Turkey is a key part of the larger struggle for a more pluralist and inclusive democracy (İlkkaracan 2012). Some argue that, like Kurds who have demanded the use of their native Kurdish for the purposes of education, women should also be more extensively incorporated into the body politic as equals. Feminist scholars point to a range of ways in which male privilege defines public culture, including by making women feel like "interlopers in public spaces" (Kandiyoti 2011) but also by making it socially acceptable for men, but not women, to have lovers, as I discuss in chapters 4 and 5.

As I show in the following chapters, the politics of gender in Turkey, whether at the household level, enshrined in law, or embodied in telenovelas such as *The Magnificent Century*, are integrally tied to post-Soviet migrant women's long-term transnational circuits linking post-Soviet space to Istanbul.

Part 2

INTIMATE PRACTICES AND GLOBAL CIRCUITS

GENDER, LABOR, AND EMOTION IN A GLOBAL ECONOMY

As our bus pulled away from the curb at the Atatürk International Airport in Istanbul, Olga explained that PanUkraine was one of the largest companies arranging package tours for shuttle traders traveling from Moscow to Istanbul. Looking around I saw that aside from the Russian-speaking Turkish guide at the front, all others en route with us to the Hotel Prestige were women in their late thirties to late forties; Olga described the passengers as "prepared to begin trading as soon as we arrived," and she laughed at the Russian-speaking guide's mistaken suggestion that the "girls" (*devushki*) were naive and should be careful in their transactions. Most traders, she surmised, were like her, and after initially feeling ashamed to be involved in trade, for nearly ten years they had made the trek to Istanbul on a monthly basis. Beginning in the early 1990s, the journeys to and from Istanbul became part of a broader transformation of intimate practices and affective states brought about by new forms of gendered mobility in the newly capitalist region.

Focusing on women shuttle traders who make frequent trips between Moscow and Istanbul, in this chapter I examine discourses on one type of emotion, shame, as well as its link to ideal gender roles and intimate practices among Russian women entrepreneurs.[1] In a post-Soviet era increasingly shaped by transnational mobility, as well as by a persistent legacy of Soviet sensibilities and "emotion regimes" (Reddy 1999), women traders provide an ideal lens for thinking about what travels between eras marked by distinct ideologies, between nation-states, and between public and domestic spaces. Cultural practices, shared professional knowhow, and gender negotiations performed by this group of women are linked to a distinct postsocialist, and specifically post-Soviet, "transnational circuit" moving apparel into Russia, in this case from Turkey.[2] Russian women's insertion into a global economy beginning in the 1990s has required emotion work that is framed by Soviet-influenced reflections on labor and contemporary politics of gender in Russia. Despite this distinct cultural formation, ultimately there are many parallels with the way emotion work is required in other contexts where global capitalism has transformed work lives and required people to renegotiate intimate practices intertwining gender, labor, and expressions of power (Hochschild 1983; Colen 1995).

My point of departure is the emotion of "shame" and, to a lesser degree, its twin, "honor." A focus on this pair helps distill the contradictory ways in which women are positioned within both the intimate practices of newly capitalist Russia and a global economy in the 2000s. Ultimately, attention to emotions furthers our understanding of shifting structures of power in the region and beyond, but I also turn attention to how emotion, something often seen as a personal state, is linked to a collective, structurally inflected affect (Ahmed 2004). Women entrepreneurs' accounts highlight anxieties about proper forms of labor but also about gender sensibilities, which tend to elevate men's roles as breadwinners even when the facts are otherwise. These specific anxieties map onto the cultural and political context of the former Soviet Union, and they also resonate with the implications that women's intensified transnational mobility has for configurations of power globally. Women entrepreneurs' frequent accounts of the shame they felt at first getting involved in trade compelled me to think about postsocialism and emotions, along with reflections on gendered labor, as a portal onto shifting intimate practices of individuals vis-à-vis state power.

Traders' accounts reflect the ways that a wide range of people were formerly invested in state-defined moral frameworks that shaped belonging in a Soviet era (Grant 1995; Humphrey and Mandel 2002; Wanner 2005). As traders have learned to be good *capitalists*, they have had to unlearn, or at least disregard, the rules for being good *socialists*. The accounts of middle-aged Russian women traders reflect the sense of rupture many experienced as Soviet state hierarchies of value around work and education became meaningless, and new, often contested hierarchies emerged. This process has parallels elsewhere, including across the former Soviet Union and other countries where, until the early 1990s, state socialist ideals officially defined relationships between individuals, and the state above all other institutions shaped the forms power took (e.g., Berdahl 1999; Dunn 2004; Leshkowich 2006). Significantly, these renegotiations of relationships between individuals and state power are also characteristic of newly global capitalism; the focus on emotion and affective states provides a means for reflecting usefully on the ways that intimate practices may intersect with processes occurring on a global scale.

Drawing on the narratives of three women—Olga, Galina, and Ania—who all began working as small-scale traders in the early 1990s, in this chapter I examine

FIGURE 9. At a Moscow wholesale market. Photograph by author, 2002.

links between emotion regimes of late socialism and forms of gendered consciousness under emerging capitalism. In this economic landscape where the categories of capitalists and communists became blurred with the end of the Soviet
Union (see Grant 1999) I consider how emotion work mediates women's insertion into a global economy. These entrepreneurs each have a unique background,
including when and how they entered into trade, their levels of education, and
the composition of their households in Russia. Nevertheless, like the fifteen other
traders I formally interviewed and many I conversed with more informally from
former Soviet countries, these entrepreneurs are linked through their experience
of the shuttle trade, an artifact of the emerging post-Soviet market economy
and an active category of economic activity within post-Soviet public culture.[3]
Furthermore, these women from Russia entered into the realm of trade in an
era marked by abrupt ideological change; as Caroline Humphrey noted in the
early 2000s, Russia, like other postsocialist locations, was "inventing its own new
culture" (2002, 71).[4]

Shuttle Trade and New Forms of Labor

"Shuttle trade"—which draws its name from the Russian word *chelnok*, or the shuttle that a weaver moves to and fro as she creates a piece of cloth—describes the
small-scale business of moving consumer goods, and especially apparel, from

global textile manufacturing centers into the FSU. Shuttle trade officially debuted with the passage of the Law on the Customs Tariff of the USSR in April 1991 (Stanley 1996; Humphrey 2002, 73). While this form of "small-scale" trade was not unique to the FSU (for example, see Konstantinov 1996), the scale of it alone makes it an important area of inquiry. For instance, in the mid-1990s, at the height of the shuttle trade from Turkey to the former Soviet Union, exports ran to $10 billion annually (Yenal 2000, 3), a sum that was possibly nearly half of Turkey's total exports at the time.[5] By the end of the 1990s the shuttle trade had slowed, but it remained an important feature of mobility and trade in the region (Yükseker 2007; Weitz 2010).

From the perspective of the traders, the first years of international travel were imbued with novelty. Although people did travel extensively within the Soviet Union and some within the "socialist camp" of East European countries, the average person had never dreamt that it would become common to cross into Turkey or travel to Western Europe. My consultants fondly recalled their first journeys out of the former Soviet Union when they traveled to nearby Poland, Romania, or Hungary transporting household items, socialist-era lapel pins, or "cognac" (*koniak*) intended for resale (Hann and Béller-Hann 1998; Hohnen 2003).[6] One woman, a former employee in an electronics factory, who began trading in 1993, described her sense of amazement when she first traveled to Warsaw by bus; the second time she took her daughter for four days, and they spent half the time exploring the city, eating Chinese food, marveling at the well-kept, beautiful churches, and visiting museums. Drawing on the travel agency offers of *shoptur*, package tours with all-inclusive hotel and travel arrangements that catered to traders, people like her often combined a few days' vacation with wholesale clothing purchases for resale back home. In addition to the excitement about crossing long-closed borders, however, these journeys were being made out of necessity.[7]

As Humphrey notes, by the mid-1990s, "Around 30 million people (41 percent of Russia's working population) were engaged in the international trade in petty commodities and services tied to that trade" (Nikitina 1996, cited in Humphrey 2002, 73).[8] Women and other marginalized populations, in particular, frequently turned to the shuttle trade or to working as vendors for shuttle-traded goods (Zhurzhenko 1999; Humphrey 2002, 90–93; Werner 2004).[9] As the state abdicated its former role of maintaining government-run stores throughout the FSU, local "open-air" (*otkrytye*) markets expanded, with clothing imported by shuttle traders and other consumer goods, including tools and car parts, brought from Western Europe and Japan (via the Russian Far East).[10] Although China may have been the earliest destination for shuttle traders seeking to supply Russia with clothing (Zhao 1994, 401), by the mid-1990s Turkey became the primary source country. The trade in apparel can be seen as a tangible reflection of Russia and Turkey's newly intertwined relationship from the early 1990s onward. In 1996 alone more than two million people from the former Soviet Union and Eastern Europe entered Turkey as "tourists," and most likely many of these were making trips combined with the goal of shuttle trade (Tosun 2001, 299).[11]

With a number of urban centers serving as important loci for shuttle trade from Turkey, Istanbul is by far the most important nexus for a wide range of financial, political, and international transactions, including the thriving garment trade (Keyder 1999). The garment trade is concentrated in the neighborhood of Aksaray and adjoining Laleli, just one tram stop beyond the main tourist area of the historic Sultanahmet, where the Topkapi Palace and Hagia Sophia are located. Since the arrival of shuttle traders in the early 1990s, Aksaray and Laleli are conjoined in the popular Turkish imagination as the "Russian" area of town, with restaurants displaying menus in Russian and featuring borsht and "Russian salad," Turkish hoteliers and taxi drivers speaking conversational Russian, and neighborhood kiosks selling Russian-language newspapers and magazines.[12] Handwritten signs in Russian are taped to store windows and advertise for assistants who can "speak Russian and Turkish," or indicate especially for Russians, "We have large sizes."[13] In 2015 a prominently displayed digital sign in Russian offered migrants assistance in regularizing their status.

Like Olga, the woman I first accompanied from Moscow to Istanbul, shuttle traders arrive in Laleli on average bimonthly, staying for two or three days of intensive trade before returning with their merchandise to regions of the FSU. At hotels with names like Prestige and Paris, traders are met by staff who greet their return customers by name and remind them of the opportunities to take part in excursions around the city or to Black Sea beach resorts. Although Russian-speaking men from the FSU are sometimes encountered in this trade district, their sparse numbers make them conspicuous; moreover, it is women who seem to be most at ease in these trade spheres and who are obviously catered to by the overwhelmingly male, Turkish shopkeepers, tour operators, and restaurateurs (Yükseker 2004). As I discuss further in chapters 4 and 5, Turkish men and post-Soviet women are frequently drawn into each other's worlds, sometimes through work but sometimes also through a desire for intimacy.

Yulian Konstantinov et al. (1998) suggest that among traders who were traveling between Istanbul and Bulgaria, women predominated because the shuttle trade was seen as a low status sphere of work. Also, they argue that men were more selective about where they were willing to work, and the authors associate both the retail market settings in home communities and the profession of trade itself with low status (Konstantinov et al. 1998, 739). This may in part explain the gendered nature of the shuttle trade between Russia and Turkey. However, it is useful

FIGURE 10. "Legal assistance and advice, work visas." Photograph by author, 2015.

to take this further and to consider how women navigate these issues of status. As a number of scholars have suggested for other types of work globally where "service with a smile" or emotional labor is integral (Hochschild 1983; Ehrenreich and Hochschild 2002), women tend to predominate. As Arlie Hochschild (1983) argues, in sites of firmly entrenched capitalist work relations, emotional labor is integral to a patterned yet invisible emotion system that consists of "individual" emotion work as well as a range of interactions between people in both public and private life. In the case of post-Soviet women traders, they are adept at navigating an invisible system of emotion work in the public realm of their dealings in Istanbul, where their hard-nosed business dealings belie any sense of shame about being entrepreneurs. Back home in Russia they navigate a different system of emotion work, in particular to allay anxieties about two types of shame: one shaped by Soviet sensibilities of proper labor and another one linked to reified models of masculinity, men as household heads, and domesticity.

The women traders I came to know frequently treated their experiences in Turkey as a foil for framing their own lives as "liberated" from male dominance. For instance, while there is a wide range of clothing styles worn by Istanbullu women—including short skirts, jeans and T-shirts, and headscarves—given the location of Laleli, bordering Fatih, one of the more religiously conservative neighborhoods of the city, traders often encountered women who signaled their identification with a growing Islamist movement in Turkey through wearing hijab. Clothed in the *Tesettür* fashion, or "Istanbul chic," of long, black coats and colorful headscarves and often accessorized with stylish footwear (White 1999, 80; Navaro-Yashin 2002), these women personified for the traders the "oppressed" Turkish woman.[14] It was common to hear trader women murmur among themselves about how Turkish women are dominated by men, forced to "cover themselves entirely" (*polnost'iu zakryvat'sa*). At different times I heard trader women and entertainers invoke the same phrases—"It's not possible for them to breathe! There's religion for you!" (*Nevozmozhno im dyshat'—vot tebe religiia!*)—when encountering women possibly visiting from Saudi Arabia who were wearing full-face veils, such as burqua or niqab. Frequently post-Soviet women intoned that seeing Muslim women forced to wear such clothing proved that Turkey lacked "civilization" (*kul'tura*). Post-Soviet women's comments reflect both trader women's sense of cultural hierarchies and their lack of appreciation for how the widely circulating nationalist and Islamist discourses in Turkey, and elsewhere in the Middle East, get expressed through contests over women's proper gender comportment (Abu-Lughod 1997; Werbner and Yuval-Davis 1999; Parla 2001). Furthermore, however, post-Soviet women's comments foreground how trader women's own moral frameworks were forged through socialist ideals of modernity that hinged on their own distinct gender ideals, namely egalitarian gender relations and forms of labor.

Markets, Gender, and Labor

In their accounts of becoming traders, post-Soviet women entrepreneurs often articulated a sense of shame about the ways in which their new professions had forced them to make fundamental philosophical changes in their lives. In reflecting on their early years in the profession, they were keenly aware of moving away from a set of shared principles that grounded them as Soviet citizens; they frequently framed the newly capitalist society of Russia as one that was "degenerating." As in Nancy Ries's (2002) work focused on postsocialist narratives around money and morality, my respondents looked to the Soviet past to make sense of their experience of newly capitalist practices.

In interviews with traders they sometimes pointed to the years following the Second World War to explain the internalized idea of trade as a stigmatized profession in the Soviet Union. At that time, they told me, it was the women who often found themselves in such desperate straits that they were willing to risk fines and government sanctions just to provide for their families. With millions of men killed on the Western Front or imprisoned in the wake of Soviet repressions, women were left running households on their own. One woman told me how her mother was selling homemade quilts at a street market in the Russian Far East when she was arrested in 1946. She was accused of *spekuliatsiia*, or "profiteering," engaging in trade for private profit, and sentenced to three years in prison. Eventually the sentence was commuted and she lost one-half of her salary for three years instead of serving time. After that, my consultant recalled, her mother would always have to indicate on official forms, such as job applications, that she had a criminal record (*osuzhdennaia*).[15]

Experiences like these form the narrative backdrops for contemporary entrepreneurial activity, especially among an older generation of women traders. Women vividly recalled the dangers of trade in the past. Traders I interviewed expressed a range of reflections on their roles as "profiteers" (*spekulanty*), as they sometimes half-jokingly referred to themselves, thereby invoking a pervasive derogatory term from the Soviet era. Women traders' narratives on their new labor practices were interwoven with deep emotional reflections tied to the way in which work and proper forms of labor were understood. These cultural concerns are distinctively tied to the history of entrepreneurship (*predprinimatel'stvo*) in Russia (see Pesmen 2000, 126–45; Sasunkevich 2016). Grand narratives in the Soviet Union shifted over time and their weight differed depending on their location within the Soviet Union, but as Susan Buck-Morss (2000) and others (Bloch and Kendall 2004) have written, generally these grand narratives elevated the value of manual labor, the collective good created through socialism, and overcoming oppressive structures of capitalism. Traders' accounts turn our attention to how emotions around entrepreneurship were shaped by dominant structures of feeling defining Soviet and late Soviet society.

The scholarship on entrepreneurship widely focuses on an entrepreneurial ethic as something that is considered praiseworthy (for instance, see Weber 1958; Harrell 1985; Kapchan 1996; and Oxfeld 1999). However, turning to formerly socialist societies undergoing market reforms shifts this emphasis, underscoring the cultural contingency of the entrepreneurial ethic and the forms it takes. Entrepreneurship in the region of the former Soviet Union and Eastern and Central Europe has a particularly troubled history up until the late 1980s.[16] As the quotidian Russian saying, "Don't have 100 rubles, have instead a hundred friends," suggests, trade and making money have had a historically ambiguous, and sometimes negative, value in Russia (Brooks 1985, 269–94; Pesmen 2000, 126–45).[17] Still, some people did pursue private profit, even in the long period (late 1920s to late 1980s) when private enterprise was illegal and highly discouraged. Those who sought to profit from goods that were in short supply operated furtively with variable risk at different historic points (Sampson 1987; Humphrey and Mandel 2002).[18] Although in the past state socialist economic ideals did not match reality, and a parallel, albeit barely tolerated, economy existed, in Russia in the early to mid-2000s for people of an older generation a link between entrepreneurship and "exploitation" persisted. For many, entrepreneurship was tainted by a view of entrepreneurial activities as possibly related to the mafia or as "unproductive" compared to other "socially useful" forms of work, such as being a factory worker or teacher (Dunn 1999, 133; Kaneff 2002, 35; Pine 2002a; Patico 2008).[19]

Both men and women participated in the widespread parallel economy in Russia under late state socialism, but women were perhaps more attuned to this economy given their long-term role in organizing and provisioning the household with basic necessities like food, clothing, and medicine, items that were obtained through networks, informal exchange, and the semilegal street markets (*rynki*) at least as often as through government-run stores (Bruno 1997; Mukhina 2014; Sasunkevich 2016, 154–57).[20] In this sense, socialist ideals of labor, as something grounded in state production and fundamentally a part of nation-building and not related to a domestic sphere, were challenged on a daily basis by women. Nevertheless, as women traders' accounts in the next section indicate, they perceived their daily use of informal networks and exchange in their personal lives under late socialism as fundamentally different from what developed in the 1990s, when their professional lives became defined by involvement in trade. Under state socialism women were what Daphne Berdahl (1999) has called "worker-mothers"; they were officially defined in both a professional sense, as working for the state and building state socialism, and as shouldering the primary responsibility of caring for families. While state policy sought to mobilize women into the workforce and socialize the care of children and households, as I discuss further in chapter 6, this was far from fully realized during the nearly seventy years of Soviet power. Such official policies of gender equality were one of the first elements of socialism to come under attack in the popular culture of the late 1980s (Posadskaia 1994; Gal and Kligman 2000).[21]

By the early 1990s the gap between popular and official discourses around gender virtually disappeared. A new hegemonic discourse emerged with men's role as breadwinner elevated and women's ideal role situated firmly within the home. This discourse hinged on the idea that in empowering women with access to professional mobility, the socialist state had usurped male power (Kukhterin 2000; Kay 2006). Government policy that enshrines what some have called *domostroika* (Goscilo 1993), others the "new power of old men" (Thelen 2003), others the "retreat to the household" (Pine 2002b), and still others the "housewife gender contract" (Temkina and Rotkirch 1997) has emerged across former socialist regions, where women's space is now naturalized as a domestic one. In the first decade of the 2000s, the Russian government actively promoted this binary model of gender roles, most recently by instituting pronatalist policies meant to encourage women to have more children and to spend more years at home caring for them (Rotkirch et al. 2007; Rivkin-Fish 2010). It is in this context that women traders discussed the shame they experienced early in their careers, as well as the emotional labor they engaged in to maintain the semblance of "traditional" gendered divisions of labor in households, even as they sought to thrive in their work as entrepreneurs.

Traders' Narratives: Shame, Entrepreneurship, and Gendered Labor

Post-Soviet traders' accounts of entrepreneurship show how ideas of "shame" were often intertwined with negotiating new forms of labor and household gender roles.[22] As markers of a post-Soviet legacy, these ideas around shame cross class and family backgrounds, albeit in uneven ways. The traders I consulted had a range of professional experience, including in hospital administration, academic research, medicine, and factory work.[23] My consultants were women in their late thirties and early forties, with school-age children; in their reflections they tended to frame their households as important sites for providing emotional and material support for their children.[24] All three women whose accounts

I discuss here—Olga, Galina, and Ania—began their careers as independent vendors selling goods at open-air markets in hometowns of Russia. Although all the women's narratives featured some element of shame related to their entry into the world of entrepreneurship, their accounts also reflect the way a socialist ethic about productive work and meaningful labor was by no means uniformly shared by all small-scale entrepreneurs in a postsocialist era. Women were negotiating the "emotion work" required in their households around gender and labor on several levels.

Olga: Family Business and Preventing "Real Men's" Shame

Traders often told of their initial mortification at being associated with "trade" (*torgovlia*). However, traders' accounts also frequently incorporated reflection on the ways in which their new professions brought them great satisfaction. These feelings of pride had to be delicately managed so as not to add to the sense of shame that the men in their lives often expressed about being unemployed or employed within their wives' businesses. In many cases, women's work in trade brought together two discourses on shame: one grounded in Soviet sensibilities of proper labor, and a second one grounded in contemporary gender sensibilities that elevated men as breadwinners, something I first learned from Olga in 2002, when I accompanied her on the PanUkraine package tour for shuttle traders traveling to Istanbul.

Olga described her first months as a trader in the early 1990s, saying, "I was really ashamed" (*mne bylo tak stydno*), and she recounted how she figuratively just "hid under the stall" (*priatalas' pod prilavkom*) where she was selling clothes shuttled from Turkey. Being involved in trade was something she never dreamt she would do—it was simply beneath her stature as an educated woman, happily married with two children. Only after Olga waited for months to no avail to receive a paycheck for her work as a hospital administrator, and her husband lost his job as an engineer, did she turn to selling goods in an open-air market in her hometown about 60 miles south of Moscow. She started in 1993, just two years after the government began to permit transborder trade and license the open-air markets. Using small sums of money borrowed from friends and family, she began building up her business. She turned out to be an astute businesswoman. After seven years of shuttling low-end goods by train and bus from Poland and Ukraine for resale in the open-air market, she established a small boutique in the newly constructed mall located nearby.[25]

In our first conversation in her hometown in 2001, Olga described the "bustle" of being in business for herself as more interesting than her Soviet-era work as a hospital administrator. She also enjoyed meeting new people and being able to travel throughout Southeast Asia, Western Europe, and China. Most of all, however, she enjoyed what this business meant for her family. She was proud to have a "family business" (*semeinyi biznes*), and she was able to employ her whole family. Her husband took care of the transportation of goods, her teenage son was responsible for the bookkeeping, and her younger son in elementary school was learning the retail trade, as well as assisting with the store maintenance. Olga expressed her pride in being both a provider and a responsible, taxpaying citizen and explained, "I know that I create jobs and in this way I'm assisting the government, and on top of that I can help my family." Olga's justification of her profession in terms of "help" for her family (and country) perhaps points to her effort to downplay the pleasure she gained from succeeding in the very public realm of business. Also, by invoking help for family she was able to signify her connection to a domestic realm, an explanation similarly invoked by Russian women entrepreneurs in other contexts who also sought to justify their involvement in business (Bruno 1997, 63).

Olga's statements about her motivations to engage in entrepreneurship could be seen as interwoven with the status quo of power relations in her family; even if she was an entrepreneur, she was still signaling that the domestic realm was her primary responsibility. This form of negotiating on/around the domestic front was further substantiated in a conversation we had in 2002 after a day of wholesale purchases in Laleli. Olga and I sat in a restaurant at the Hotel Prestige and sipped mugs of beer as we took stock of what she considered an unusually fruitful trip. She had spent over $2,000 in just three days, and she was content; she had been able to find affordable suppliers for the wholesale polo shirts, dress pants, and shoes for her second, newly opened boutique specializing in men's clothing.

Despite her satisfaction with the purchases, Olga said that she had to quietly enjoy her business success when she was home; her husband had been unemployed since 1996, when his government engineering division shut down. Generally he was supportive of her business; nevertheless, Olga said she needed to protect his pride. She not only tried to downplay her triumphs in business, but she also tried to avoid asking him to assist too much around the house or with looking after their younger son; instead, she often called on her mother for help. Also, when possible, she actively played up her dependence on her husband, for instance, by remaining unable to drive. She explained that her husband's monopoly on the driving would help her husband feel like a "real man" (*nastoiashchii muzhchina*) when she called on him to drive her around town and transport the wares she sent home from Istanbul. We finished our beers and Olga sighed, saying not knowing how to drive was a small price to pay for mostly having a smooth marriage and adequate economic means for the family.

In a parallel way Carla Freeman (2007) argues that along with the new forms of labor people engage in as they are inserted into a global economy, they must also take on new forms of affective labor in domestic spheres. In her ethnography of women entrepreneurs in an increasingly neoliberal Barbados, Freeman shows that as new subjectivities around work emerge, these also shape the form "marriage partnerships" take. Like Olga, the Barbadian women entrepreneurs Freeman writes about sought to thrive in their business pursuits, in part, by drawing on relatively conservative and historically derived gender configurations. Women did not contest the forms of male power their husbands enjoyed, and they sometimes acquiesced to downplaying their own business successes in exchange for maintaining functional marriages which smoothed some of their business transactions.

Like the Barbadian women, Olga partly defined her successful entrepreneurship through the stable marriage partnership she was able to maintain with the emotion work she did to attend to her husband's need for validation as a household head. In this way, Olga's new form of labor was linked to affect that was forged by global economic shifts and new ideologies. Olga recalled her shame at taking on a profession colored by its vilification in the Soviet era but also expressed a sense of pride in having established her thriving business. This pride is then juxtaposed with her efforts to cope with her spouse's shame about being unemployed and more closely tied to a domestic sphere. While savoring her success as a transnational businesswoman, Olga safeguarded her husband from feelings of inadequacy by sheltering him from domestic responsibilities. This case provides a means for reconsidering the way moral frameworks, in this case around shameful labor, are negotiated when people are suddenly inserted into global capitalism; trade is no longer shameful, but long-standing codes of male honor, or definitions of masculinity, remain firmly in place, so in a post-Soviet context, new configurations of the relation between shame and trade emerge.

Post-Soviet women traders' concerns about shameful involvement in trade powerfully demonstrate the way discourses around emotion operate in a historically circumscribed way, a point scholars have made in other contexts as well (Wikan 1984, 648; Abu-Lughod and Lutz 1990, 5–6). In this case, attention to discourses on shame can teach us something about the way in which many people were defined by specific tenets of socialism. In traders' accounts the concept of "shame" is a productive category to explore since it puts individuals' relationship to an idealized Soviet citizen in relief. As Sara Ahmed writes, emotions themselves define boundaries of collectives (2004, 9–10, 108), but they also point to spaces of negotiation. Attention to discourses around shame both underscores a "post-Sovietness" that continues to define the region and points to how the gender politics of households are shaped as they are inserted into global economies.

Men like Olga's husband could feel shame about no longer enacting the role of provider as prescribed by dominant gender ideologies in late socialist and postsocialist Russia, and traders could feel shame as they entered a formerly illicit realm of labor because of how gender roles and the meaning around work shifted in late socialist society and later. The case of post-Soviet women traders vividly demonstrates how labor can be invested with particular affect and potentially experienced very differently by men and women, in part because they are unevenly inserted into a global economy. When traders' spouses feel shame because their ideal forms of masculinity are eclipsed by their wives' success, this is not simply a psychological process, but one reflecting how societal gender norms are being transgressed. Likewise, for women I interviewed the shame linked to entrepreneurship, exemplified by Olga's desire to "hide under the stall," was not merely due to a fall in social status. As demonstrated in the following account, social status was intertwined with the state ideologies marking trade as a suspect and morally tainted activity, but new forms of power (and powerlessness) were also refracted through the emerging emotion regimes.

Galina: Laboring for Socialism and the Shame of a "Social Parasite"

Unlike Olga—who after seven years of selling clothing in the open-air market garnered enough capital to rent space in the nearby indoor mall for her own boutique—most women working as vendors in the former Soviet Union in the 2000s did not have the financial means to rent retail space or make regular treks to Istanbul (or other centers of apparel production and distribution, such as Harbin, China). Instead they retailed goods sourced from established wholesalers within Russia. This was the case with Galina, a woman I met in 2001 who had shared a market stall with Olga during her early years of entrepreneurship in the same small city south of Moscow. Galina remained working as a vendor without much possibility of "classing up," but she shared some of Olga's sense of shame associated with her work as a trader.[26]

Until 1993 Galina worked full-time in a building materials factory in the section where two huge cauldrons were constantly fed to make steel. By 2000 the factory had shut down, and Galina had begun cobbling together income, in part through selling wares she purchased in Moscow. In 2003 Galina lived with her fifteen-year-old daughter, who was training to work as a technician in the dairy industry, and her ten-year-old son in a detached house on a small plot of land she had inherited from her parents. Her husband had died years earlier. She occasionally met with her lover, a construction worker on contract from Bulgaria, but he did not contribute to the household, and by 2003 she had supported her children single-handedly for nearly a decade.

Galina was significantly less successful at trade than her friend Olga. The main difference between the women was Galina's lack of capital. Although Olga was able to build her business through the social and financial capital of her friends, family, and professional network, Galina had no similar sources of support. She was forced to supplement her meager income, and in 2003 she first sold one of her goats and then began selling prepared lunches to the other vendors at the market. A passionate singer, Galina sometimes made extra cash by taking on jobs singing at wakes. Even after more than fifteen years of trade, however, she was not able to establish enough capital to move from the open-air market to a space in the nearby mall.

Despite their disparate social locations, Galina's narrative echoes some themes raised by Olga. Galina spoke vehemently about how difficult it was at first to trade at the market. She recalled how people would practically spit on vendors. The woman renting half of Galina's stall in 2001 was a teacher until the early 1990s, and she would hide when she saw former students or their parents approach her stall. Like the former teacher, Galina recalled how, when she began trading in the market, she also wanted to hide behind the stall, avoiding anyone who might recognize her. As she explained, "I felt like a *tuneiadets*." In invoking this Soviet-era term for a social parasite, or a person who does not engage in productive labor, Galina emphasized that to be a trader was to be a fallen socialist of sorts.[27]

Galina reflected on how life had changed since the end of the Soviet Union. She lamented that most people only had the markets as a source of income now and that this type of work and social milieu changed people. As she explained, "They become uncultured and lose sight of what matters—social interaction, music, and relaxation." Galina recalled how, as part of her benefits as a factory worker in the Soviet era, she could travel each year to vacation on the Black Sea for a month; since the late 1990s she could not save a penny, and a vacation of any length was not possible. She was barely able to pay for her household's food and clothing needs. There was little time, money, or energy left for what mattered in the past. As another woman at the market noted,

> [Under socialism] the system was really wrong; it made people fit all into one type. If you have a row of plants growing and some grow taller or fuller than others, these had to be trimmed; everyone had to be the same. We were limited by this system; we were confined to one way of seeing the world. . . . But then the system also looked after everyone; you didn't have to pay before being treated in the hospital; everyone had

access to the same day-care system; there was food and housing. True, some people got better things, but no one was left without.

Another woman standing at a nearby stall one day chimed in, "We worked hard in those days, but we were cared for . . . I gave my life to the factory and now they abandon us."

Comments like these reflect a widespread sense of how an allegiance to a social system with all its flaws was built up over time. Like any society, the Soviet Union had a set of grand narratives that were familiar to its citizens, and these included the common suffering during the Second World War, the way the state provided for all, and a clear common enemy—capitalism (Buck-Morss 2000). As a number of scholars have noted, among the less fortunate in a postsocialist era, these allegiances and deep-rooted nostalgia for socialist society tend to continue; in the first decade of the 2000s it was also not uncommon for a wide strata of the population, and especially older people, to wish for the stable lives they sometimes associated with Stalin's era.[28] The desire to hide beneath the market stalls was a by-product of a system that officially placed societal well-being above private profit. The fact that women entrepreneurs recounted these intense initial feelings with such vehemence even ten years after they entered the realm of trade demonstrates how they struggled to reconcile discourses of a market ethic that elevates entrepreneurship as socially desirable with deeply resonating discourses of a socialist era.

Ania: Capitalism and the "Devolution" of Society

Both Galina and Olga's accounts highlight a widespread sense of initial ambivalence or even antipathy toward the new market practices in which they became involved, but a few women expressed no such conflicted feelings. One woman I met in 2007 during her weekly buying trips to Istanbul described her decision to become a trader as a carefully calculated decision, largely tied to the need to find adequate housing. During a short break from her purchasing, Ania insisted on treating me to Turkish coffee, and she readily narrated how she came to be a trader. Until 1993 Ania had worked for ten years as a microbiologist for a research institute in Moscow. She emphasized that when she decided to leave the institute she was fairly established and had been publishing her work in well-regarded journals.

Ania described how in the early 1990s, as many people in Russia were being laid off, her husband quit his job at the microbiology institute and began engaging in the shuttle trade to Poland. Ania soon followed in his footsteps, leaving her job when it became obvious that the institute would not be arranging an apartment for her; the couple had lived in a two-bedroom apartment with her parents for nearly ten years. By 1994 Ania and her husband had established two stores in Moscow that Ania continued to supply in 2010 by traveling once a week from Moscow to Istanbul, often spending as much as $10,000 on wares in a single trip. She recounted that, despite her success at being a trader, the transition from being an academic was not easy; Ania said she had earned each dollar of her original start-up capital by standing in an open-air market selling her wares day after day, rain or snow.

The decision to leave her academic job was something Ania regretted in some ways and as she explained, "I left the world of ideas for the world of money." Ania described what she saw as the "slowing down" of human civilization; she equated the onset of a postsocialist, newly capitalist society with a sort of "devolution" of former socialist societies wherein education and learning had become relatively unimportant. In looking back at her decision to change professions in the early 1990s, Ania ruminated: "I'm not sure I would make the same choice again. When I ask myself from a philosophical and moral perspective—not from a market-driven one—this has been a very difficult life. . . . Something had to *break down in my consciousness* for this business life to work. In fact, for nearly five years my mother was ashamed of me because of my work."

Ania's parents were also academics, working in the same institute as she had, and Ania explained that her parents differed in their views on her new profession. Ania's mother was ashamed that her daughter would leave an academic life for one that had so much stigma attached to it, but she did agree to look after Ania's son during the regular trips Ania made to Istanbul. Like Galina, Ania sought out emotional support from her mother to smooth the regular operation of her business; neither of the traders' husbands was willing to take on the household work around caring for an elementary school-age child in their wives' absence. As Ania explained, without these care arrangements, her husband would never have agreed to her absence for days at a time each month.

Ania's mother only gradually changed her mind about her daughter's new profession as she saw how much better Ania could provide for the household through her business. Ania said that she herself had not felt any sense of shame when she began the shuttle trade. As she explained, "Money changes people, not [new types of] labor [*trud*]." Responding to my comment that a number of my consultants recounted feeling ashamed about entering the sphere of trade, Ania scoffed and then added,

> They were probably not entirely telling the truth; everyone likes money. Or else, maybe it is a matter of age, after all, my mom was also anxious about this business; . . . not everyone relates to money in the same way. When the iron curtain went up people scrambled to come here to buy

up goods . . . and it changed people. . . . Everyone thought the good life
had arrived; you could bring in just about anything [to Russia] and sell
it without taxation. Everyone fed at the trough [*obzhirali*].

Ania's reflections suggest that the early 1990s was a time of major ideational disjuncture for many, but particularly for people involved in entrepreneurship. Her
comments also emphasize the "emotional labor" that is particular to capitalism,
wherein "invisible" labor goes into the relations performed in work settings and
prospects of financial gain can change how people interact (Hochschild 1983).

Unlike Olga and Galina, Ania did not express any memory of her own shame
about her enterprise; she presented herself as having a no-nonsense, hard-headed
approach to her work. One might link this difference to the fact that Ania's business, primarily as a wholesaler of men's clothes manufactured in Turkey, was on
a decidedly different scale from Galina's work as a vendor in an open-air market
or Olga's boutique in a new mall. Ania's level of education, however, also sets her
apart. Her investment in the Soviet project was not the same as that of the average Soviet citizen, and one could argue that as an academic she entered the realm
of trade from a position that was more critical of the Soviet project.

Like many of the Russian intelligentsia Alexei Yurchak (2003) writes about,
Ania was able to leverage her social capital to successfully navigate through the
tumultuous end of the Soviet Union. Especially in contrast to Galina, Ania's
material circumstances improved significantly in the ten years after the end of the
Soviet Union, and this prosperity very likely overshadowed feelings of nostalgia
she might have had for socialism. Still, like the other two women, Ania reflected
on the fundamental changes she experienced in her sense of self in the newly capitalist Russia. In speaking of the "breakdown of consciousness" she underwent
in entering the world of trade, Ania signals how socialist structures of thought
shaped her inner world in the past, and how becoming a trader required a type
of emotion work.

In many ways Olga, Galina, and Ania share a common sphere of experience,
even an emerging consciousness of sorts. Their concerns, desires, and aspirations
intersect in significant ways. They continue to share a sense of place, including
sometimes a sense that they were betrayed by a system that they paid into. All
three of these women and their professions as traders are linked to a global economy, primarily through Turkish-produced apparel which they sell to Russian-
speaking populations with a history inflected by Soviet state ideologies. Finally,
as post-Soviet women in their forties at the time we met, all of them had their
sense of self as workers and members of society shaped by a Soviet legacy; they
are very much members of what Alexei Yurchak has called "the last Soviet generation" (2003, 486). This last Soviet generation is also the first newly transnational

generation of people on the move out of the former Soviet Union, and the first doing the emotion work in public and domestic spaces that is required to navigate their households' integration into a global economy.

Affective labor may be a key aspect of contemporary global capitalism, but it is not just managed by political or cultural formations; people like Ania or Olga or Galina also actively make decisions about how much to invest in it. The "managed emotions" of capitalism (or state socialism) are part of specific hegemonic projects, and people have variable degrees of desire to embrace or resist these, or simply ignore them. In paying attention to these emotions we can denaturalize any sort of "transition" or natural progression from socialist to capitalist forms of society and, instead, we can see continuities, frictions, and interconnections. Pointing to the role of emotion and affective states in Russian entrepreneurs' experiences of becoming traders destabilizes some commonsense ideas of capitalism as a liberating force in the region or socialism as simply oppressive, but most important, it creates openings for better understanding how gender, intimacy, and new forms of mobility come together in this area of Eurasia.

"WE ARE LIKE SLAVES—WHO NEEDS CAPITALISM?"

Intimate Economies and Marginal, Mobile Households

In June 2002 I first met Bella at the minibus lot, where she was hoping to locate her next employer for a domestic position. Bella heard about my research from other migrants and was eager to be interviewed and recount how she had been coming to Turkey off and on since 1996, most recently keeping house for two different families in "Smyrna [Izmir], Homer's homeland," as she described it. Like many of the women gathered at the minibus lot that day, Bella lamented missing the ceremony marking the end of school (*poslednii zvonok*) back in Moldova. Her eldest son was graduating from high school and would soon depart for Romania to take up a scholarship to study computer science, while her eight-year-old son was staying with his uncle, waiting for his mother and father to return from their months away as labor migrants. Bella insisted, "I would never have come here to be treated like a slave [*rab*], but I have to make a living!" Toward the end of our conversation, Bella said, "Make sure to get this down. I want to meet with Greenpeace and ask them who they think they are defending. What about us? Who will defend us [post-Soviet migrants]?" Just then Bella was approached about a possible job, and she quickly wrote down her phone number and address in Moldova and urged me to visit her so I could "really learn" what drove people to seek work in Turkey. The following summer I took Bella up on her invitation and traveled to southern Moldova, to the region of Gagauzia.

Arriving by air in the capital city of Chișinău one is struck by the expanse of rolling hills and clean air. Just over an hour's flight from Istanbul, relatively quiet and green Chișinău feels like another world. This impression solidifies as one takes the road south toward Gagauzia, and it quickly changes from a multilane highway into two lanes, then eventually into a gravel road; as vehicles slow down, the rolling hills come into focus. In the spring planting season, extending from mid-April to mid-May, driving this north-south road you see people busy working the land, hurrying to get seedlings of cabbage, tomatoes, or eggplants into the ground before Pentecost, one of the important Russian Orthodox holidays that continues to punctuate annual calendars for many people across the FSU.[1] On summer days one might catch sight of a stork nesting on a telephone pole, or a person bicycling along with a horse being led behind.

The country of Moldova, and the southern region of Gagauzia in particular, serves as a vivid example of the plight of relatively poor and recently impoverished regions in an era of global capitalism, where sovereign states are unable to create conditions for large sections of their population to achieve basic standards of living, and entire national economies come to depend on remittances sent from abroad (Basch et al. 1994; Hugo 2003; Ghençea and Gudumac 2004; Lucas 2005). In late Soviet times Moldova thrived on Soviet subsidies and on its own agricultural production of grains, sunflower oil, fruits and vegetables, and especially wine, with state farms as the site of this production employing a little over a third of the population; in 1993 Moldova had nearly a thousand collectively owned farms (Fedor 1995).[2] Moreover, for decades Moldova had been a vacation destination for those from northern urban centers in Russia who sought rest, relaxation, and a ready supply of fruits, vegetables, and wine. By the early 2000s, as in nearby Romania (Verdery 2003), agricultural production in the region had fallen into disarray, with the collectively operated farms largely dismantled and 82 percent of agricultural land privately allocated (FAO 2001).[3] Along with the return to farming for subsistence, remittances from abroad have become essential for most households, as reflected in the high level of labor migration.[4] Of the population of about 3.6 million people in 2010, as much as one quarter of working age adults was estimated to be absent from the country as labor migrants, and this trend has continued (National Bureau of Statistics 2016).[5]

In contrast to the media portrayal of Moldova as the "poorest country" in Europe, focused largely on the issue of "trafficking" or children "left behind" (e.g., Metaxa 2006; Coomes 2011), here I turn to how people *experienced* the dramatic shift from being the pride of the Soviet Union, as the agricultural site of plenty, to the poster child for what went wrong with structural readjustment policies in the former Soviet Union. In the early 2000s this historically marginal region of Gagauzia continued to be shaped by a lack of local opportunities but also by growing aspirations for a different life widely perceived to be possible via migration. Like some other locations of intense outmigration (Chu 2010), this community was also becoming strongly oriented around the idea of mobility as synonymous with realizing dreams, especially for young people. This chapter traces the implications gender, generation, and emerging class distinctions have for households as women and men are inserted into new transnational circuits of flexible, marginalized labor. Through this microcosm of one place closely linked to a circuit of mobility to Istanbul, the broader issues compelling migrants like Bella to leave Moldova are amplified, while the implications of this massive out-migration for home communities and for the reworkings of intimate economies within households in the region come into focus.

Transnational Moldova: A Portrait of Gagauzia

Outmigration from Moldova is especially stark at the southern end of Moldova, in Gagauzia, with one in every three families experiencing the absence of at least one household member (Subbotina 2007, 136). One day in 2004 as he stood gesturing out over former state farmland, Andrei, the brother-in-law of Zina, the former movie projectionist and medical orderly I met in Istanbul, shared his reflections on the massive outmigration from the regional center of Vulcăneşti.[6] As a former agronomist in one of the largest collective farms (*kolkhozy*) in southern Moldova in the late Soviet era, Andrei unequivocally declared that the dismantling of collectively run agriculture had a devastating effect in the region. As he explained, beginning in 1945 there were seven kolkhozes in Vulcăneşti, one of the three largest towns in the southern Gagauz region. In 1953 the seven collective farms were amalgamated into four, and in 1957 into two, Victory Collective (Kolkhoz Pobeda) and Karl Marx Collective (Kolkhoz imeni Karla Marksa).[7] In the early 1990s these two were joined in an effort to streamline costs, but in 1996 the remaining collective farm was privatized, with everyone employed there receiving a parcel of land. Andrei sighed and reflected that people were much worse off than when collective farms were thriving. Andrei would most certainly agree with Katherine Verdery, who writes about neighboring Romania that with the end of socialism, "the myth of property rights created great joyful expectations which the realities of risk bearing ownership would crush" (2004, 157).

In southern Moldova, people widely considered it a right to own a piece of land, but few people had the means to cultivate more than a small parcel. They lacked capital for purchasing a tractor or other machinery, not to mention expenses for seeds, fertilizer, or transporting their crop to market. Some people sold their land, but others simply rented much of their land back to a man who continued to manage the unallocated collective farm property; in return people received some of the crop production—mostly sunflower oil. In recent years people like Andrei have also spent a significant portion of their time working

FIGURE 11.   Farmland in Gagauzia. Photograph by author, 2011.

at least a small household parcel, something many households had not done to such a degree since before the Second World War. In 2011 it was common for households to combine small-scale agricultural production with short and long-term labor migration.[8]

At the intersection of contemporary Romania and Ukraine, the area of southern Moldova known as Gagauzia has had a wide-ranging history of governance inflected by the formation, downfall, and reformation of empires in the region over the past seven hundred years. For more than five hundred years, from the late fourteenth century until the late nineteenth century, the Ottoman Empire stretched into the region of what is present-day Moldova. Starting in the mid-eighteenth century, but most intensively in the mid-nineteenth century, as Gagauz fled Ottoman military power and sought refuge in the Russian Empire (Moshkov 1904; Ianyshev-Voloshin 1993, 37; King 2000, 211), they began to settle in what became known as Bessarabia, an historical region roughly contiguous with contemporary Moldova and a small part of Ukraine (located between the Prut and Dniester rivers). With the Russian defeat of the Ottomans in the Russo-Ottoman War (1877–1878), the Ottomans definitively lost control over vast territories, and Russia annexed southern Bessarabia (Reynolds 2011, 14).[9]

Subsequently Moldavia, and later Romania, vied for control of the region and between the two world wars a Union of Bessarabia under Romania was formed, although it was only recognized by a handful of countries, and notably not by the USSR. In 1940 the USSR annexed a region that included much of Bessarabia, as well as some adjoining areas, and named this new region the Moldovan Soviet Socialist Republic (Moldovan SSR). This history is particularly important in light of the strong allegiances Gagauz tend to have to Russia as the successor state to the Soviet Union.

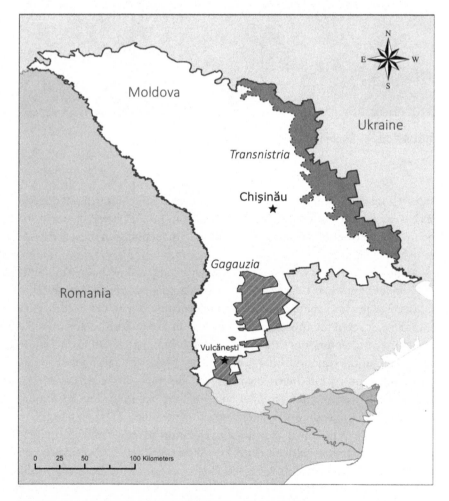

FIGURE 12.   Map of Moldova. Created by Jayme Taylor.

While the population of southern Moldova is diverse, including ethnic Bulgarians, Moldovans, Russians, and Ukrainians, the titular ethnic group is the Gagauz, who are Turkic-speaking and historically Christians.[10] By the early 2000s many Gagauz identified as Russian Orthodox, although growing numbers of people were increasingly drawn to Evangelical faiths (King 2000; Subbotina 2005, 22–23). Gagauz I met were fluent in Russian, but rarely in Moldovan, and those over about thirty spoke Gagauz, a language people described as close to "classical" Turkish, something they frequently mentioned as giving them an advantage in navigating the informal labor market in Turkey.[11]

Despite this advantage, overall the Gagauz have a long history of marginalization stretching back at least two centuries. With little access to schooling for most of the nineteenth century, and no systemic schooling in place in their communities for the first half of the twentieth century (Demirdirek 2008, 238), Gagauz had much to gain with the advent of Soviet power in Bessarabia after the Second World War.[12] With the establishment of the Moldovan Soviet Socialist Republic (1941), as a recognized minority, the Gagauz could aspire to benefit from Soviet-style affirmative action, including preferential access to higher education and some guarantees for representation within local- and republic-level governing bodies. As for many other minorities in the Soviet Union (Bloch and Kendall 2004; Bloch 2003a), from the late 1960s to the 1980s the Soviet state fostered a Gagauz intellectual class and also provided symbolic support for cultural revitalization, including in the form of Gagauz language supplements in local newspapers and the establishment of two museums dedicated to Gagauz history and culture (Demirdirek 2008, 240; see also Cash 2011). However, by the 1980s Gagauz activists voiced concern about a lack of more substantial commitments to developing Gagauz culture and language as vehicles for national consciousness, a challenge that became especially pressing with the rise of Moldovan nationalism.

With the turn toward Moldovan sovereignty in the late 1980s and early 1990s, Gagauz lost many benefits they had as a recognized minority and instead, like other minorities in Moldova, often became the target of nationalist sentiment. In August 1989, in the culmination of a Moldovan nationalist movement, a Moldovan language law was enacted that would impose sanctions on those who did not speak the state language, a situation Gagauz found intolerable (Demirdirek 2008, 236). Then in 1991, following the example of the breakaway republic of Transnistria, Gagauz voted almost unanimously for independence from Moldova, with some calling for Gagauzia to be recognized as a sixteenth Soviet republic, and others for Gagauzia to be recognized as an independent state (King 2000; Svanberg 2011, 161; Şenyuva 2012).[13] In response, citizen militias consisting of ethnic Moldovans gathered to storm Gagauzia and a violent confrontation was narrowly averted.

Although the crisis was eventually resolved, with Gagauz autonomy officially recognized on December 23, 1994, and the Gagauz remaining citizens of Moldova, the moderate local autonomy promised the Gagauz has only partially emerged (King 2000, 218–22; Demirdirek 2008; Plešinger 2014).[14] Realizing autonomy has been challenging, in part, because the Gagauz are concentrated in noncontiguous parcels of land situated in one of the most rural regions of the country. Moreover, the area has suffered from particularly harsh realities of unemployment, susceptibility to unpredictable crop yields, and massive outmigration that some Gagauz equate with making them a neocolony of Moldova.

In 2015 the Gagauz were by far the majority population in this southern region, accounting for 82 percent of the population of over 155,000 people calling Gagauzia home. There are also sizable numbers of people who identify with Bulgarian heritage, Moldovans (or those who identify with Romanian heritage), and people who are ethnically Ukrainian or Russian.[15] Over the past fifty years these ethnic communities have closely interacted, sometimes intermarrying and working side by side in the collective farming enterprises, local administration, and town institutions such as the hospital or schools. Irrespective of ethnic background, residents of this peripheral area of Moldova have all experienced marginalization as their region is no longer under the aegis of Soviet social policy, and their country has been (re)inserted into a global economy.

This is not the first time people in this part of the country have relied on outmigration to get by. In the late nineteenth century even relatively well-off families were known to send their children for apprenticeships in Germany to learn trades such as blacksmithing. Then during the interwar period of the 1920s and 1930s, when southern Moldova was on the periphery of the Romanian state, more than half the men were absent for portions of the year working on farms across the region, as well as in cities of Romania, where they worked as servants in the highly stratified society (Guboglo 2006, 379–80). In the decades after the Second World War, as part of the USSR, southern Moldova was also defined by seasonal outmigration. At that time men and women looked to the expanding agricultural spheres of Soviet Kazakhstan and the industrializing regions of Ukraine and Russia, as well as Latvia and Lithuania, where they often found work in the expanding forest industry (Subbotina 2005, 9–10). Between 1979 and 1989 the number of Gagauz in Russia more than doubled, while the number of people identifying as Gagauz in Lithuania increased more than sixfold. By the early 1990s, Gagauz were increasingly leaving their communities in southern Moldova and neighboring regions of Ukraine not for seasonal migration but for years on end (Subbotina 2005, 6). By the early 2000s tens of thousands of Gagauz had settled long-term in Russia and other states of the FSU, and thousands more worked as undocumented migrants in Turkey, as well as further afield, as they sought out ways to send remittances home.[16]

Like Bella, who stood at the microbus lot in Istanbul and urged me to visit her hometown of Vulcănești, people spoke passionately with me about the ways their lives have been affected by labor migration. They often pointed to health implications and the suffering of children and family members, but they also spoke about the range of ways they have developed for negotiating the border in pursuit of income that is critical to supporting their households, many of which survived on less than $45 a month in 2005.[17] Economically speaking, labor migration is a rational decision. For instance, in 2003 post-migration households increased their incomes four to thirteen times of their pre-migration levels, with the poorest households seeing the greatest benefits from migration (Ghençea and Gudumac 2004, 49).[18]

In addition to the economic logic of these border crossings, however, they have implications for social relationships both within households, and between those who stay and those who go. As Julie Chu (2010) shows for a community in southern China defined by massive outmigration, when more than half of a community aims to depart, for those who remain the very fabric of daily life changes, from the content of casual conversation to gendered social expectations in households to the realm of what are reasonable dreams for the future.[19] Outmigration of men and women from these communities radically reshapes intimate ties, from transforming how status is negotiated to recalibrating aspirations to reworking the very meaning of intimacy and nurturing of children.

It is widely assumed that women are the primary group leaving Moldova, and that their absence therefore creates a crisis of nurturing and overall family well-being (Keough 2015). However, it is striking that for years nearly twice as many Moldovan men have engaged in labor migration as women.[20] Popular discourses and media coverage of Moldova have tended to skim over men's migration and instead to focus on women's labor migration as a crisis, specifically one defined by the trafficking in women.[21] In a departure from the often sensationalist treatment of women's mobility out of the region, here I consider how outmigration shapes structures of power in home communities, how frameworks of intimacy have shifted as a result of outmigration, and how transnational mobility fosters aspirations for a different future.

A View from Vulcănești

Approaching the town of Vulcănești from the north, as far as the eye can see there are lush green fields of sunflowers, alfalfa, and wheat, with fields defined by long, low lines of grapevines popping up now and then. Occasional clusters of carefully tended wood-frame houses surrounded by green fences catch the eye, and after some distance down the road an apparently deserted three-story kolkhoz building appears and almost as quickly disappears as the bus ascends and then makes its way down a gentle hill, then briefly stops when a passenger calls out to be let off. At the crest of the last hill before the town center, the bus turns into the depot and Vulcănești appears below, with a gravel crossroads leading from the central road. On one axis the town center is demarcated at one end by a bus station located across the street from the relatively new Evangelical church, and at the other end by the town museum, library, town hall, and a Voxtel outlet (one of the two mobile phone companies in the country in 2004). The two blocks between these ends are lined with several cafes with plastic chairs set out on the sidewalk, an Internet gaming salon where young boys sit glued to computer screens most days during the summer and after school, a stationery store, a secondhand clothing outlet (the "*gumanitarka*") run by the Baptist church since the mid-1990s, a post office, a bank, a newspaper kiosk, and small grocery stores, one of which also houses a currency exchange.

Along the opposite axis of the town, in one direction there is a two-story commercial building mostly organized into small, one-room stores that sell women's clothing shuttled from Turkey, as well as a Seventh-Day Adventist church, a dimly lit Internet salon, the "House of Culture"—a sort of community center—and several small grocery stores.[22] In the other direction there is a bank, a bakery, a drugstore, the town clinic, and a set of market stalls that were formally used by the kolkhoz to sell its products but in 2004 were rented out. On a Saturday afternoon when the market is full of vendors selling flour from Kazakhstan or "Amerika" (the United States), whole grains, dried apricots, sunflower oil, Moldovan wines, local eggs, DVDs of Bollywood films, and various items of clothing imported from Turkey, the town seems bustling. Even then, however, the town feels like a hamlet of no more than a few thousand people, not the official number of nearly seventeen thousand residents.

During the months I spent in Vulcănești, each day I would walk the half-mile or so from the house where I was staying to the town center. By late fall the route would be blanketed with snow, and in spring the muddy roads and sidewalks required one to step gingerly, but by late May the way was dry and dusty and easily traversed on foot. The traffic—a few decrepit cars, a horse-drawn cart, or a rare Land Rover—was light, except on the weekend market days. Along the route bright yellow pipes were suspended in the air, stretching from block to block and house to house, carrying gas used for heating and kitchen stoves when households could afford this. Most of the houses along this route were wooden, with their large yards/garden areas surrounded by six-foot-high, mostly green, wooden fences; many had a bench positioned just outside the gate. Older women

FIGURE 13. A street in Vulcănești. Photograph by author, 2011.

FIGURE 14. At the town crossroads. Photograph by author, 2011.

frequently rested on these benches enjoying the interaction with passersby that this afforded. Walking along the street I learned that grandchildren were coming to stay for the summer, or that children had been off working for years on end without being able to make it home for a visit from Russia or Turkey or, less often, America. Other days I would meet a neighbor returning from her shift at the bakery, and she would insist on giving me fresh rolls. Sometimes she took the opportunity to share news, like about her sister's brief visit from Turkey, timed to deliver much needed money to a relative just released from jail.

Walking a bit farther out of the town center, evidence of the many transnational connections became even more apparent. Smart-looking tin roofs glistened in the sun on the newest houses, made of large and fortress-like brick construction standing out among the many older wood-frame houses, with nearly each one sporting some sort of home renovation, from fresh paint to entire additions. Bricks piled beside driveways and a few dish antennas also reminded passersby of the steady flow of remittances coming into the town, a phenomenon common to communities of outmigration worldwide (see Chu 2010). The prospect of remittances and their actual flow punctuated daily interactions, one of several ways radical mobility was remaking lives in the town.

Absence and Mobility

In the spring of 2007 I was in Vulcănești just after Easter. One Sunday evening my hosts, Zina's sister Eva and her husband, Andrei, invited me to join them to visit with Andrei's sister on the other side of town. To get there, we walked the two miles or so, since the two sons in the family who kept the ramshackle car running were in Russia; one had married there and settled in Siberia, and the other had found undocumented work in a restaurant in Moscow. As we walked, a small tremor shook the earth, reminding me of Gagauzia's location in an area prone to regular, minor earthquakes; my hosts barely noticed the event. The holiday meal, featuring our hosts' homemade baked red peppers stuffed with ground meat and accompanied by the locally produced Isabella red wine that I had brought, was enjoyed by all. As nearly always in this town, talk turned to the members of the family away earning money; in this case Andrei's sister's husband was away in Russia for six months, working on a construction brigade, and the older daughter was in Turkey, cleaning houses. Andrei's sister gestured to her newly renovated living room and noted that her husband's work over the past six months had paid for the recent home improvements. They were now saving to pay for their younger daughter to attend college, and accumulating the necessary money would be difficult.

The theme of absence and mobility out of this community loomed large in daily conversations. Many households had at least one adult member away working for a minimum of several months of the year, and usually longer, in Italy, Spain, Portugal, Ukraine, and, mostly, Russia or Turkey.[23] It was also not uncommon for the children and grandchildren of a household to have immigrated permanently to Russia and less commonly to another country. Turkey was widely invoked when people spoke of their mothers, sisters, aunts, and other female relatives and friends working abroad. High-school students, especially girls, often looked to Turkey as a place they could most easily establish their independence, and young people with newly minted undergraduate degrees, but few professional opportunities in Moldova, debated whether to seek prospects for work in Istanbul. Zina's daughter, who had immigrated to Russia with her husband, told me that of the twenty students in her graduating class, just five (two girls and three boys) remained in Moldova studying and working. The fifteen other students (nine girls and six boys), all worked outside Moldova; aside from Zina's daughter and one other young man in Russia and one young man in Romania, the others were all in Turkey. Likewise, nearly all the middle-aged women I came to know in Vulcănești had either spent time in Turkey working, mostly as domestics in Turkish households and in restaurants, or spoke wistfully of not being able to seek work abroad for a variety of reasons.

GENDER, LABOR, GENERATION

Women occupying prominent positions in town, such as the directors of local high schools, the head of the Vital Statistics Office, and the town museum director, all spoke of looking for work abroad. In 2004, when I first met Elena Maximovna, the director of the Vulcănești local history museum, she recounted that she earned less than $20 a month and had worked in her job for twenty-five years. Like many others, she explained that she would have liked to leave for work in Turkey, but she was held back by her passion for her work at the museum, like the curation of an exhibit based on oral histories with veterans of the Second World War that she was then preparing. Still, at times when Elena Maximovna was unable to financially help out her son, a student at the local technical college, she seriously thought about leaving for Turkey. She often considered securing work there and then seeking out something for her husband, who would also like to go, but in the end her "favorite work" (*liubimaia rabota*) kept her in the museum.

Generally, women in less prominent positions or those who were unemployed found it easier to become migrants, although frequently they faced resistant husbands and children. One woman who had spent several years working as a domestic in Istanbul told me that her husband in Vulcănești "did not permit" (*ne razreshaet*) her to go to Turkey; he argued that he made enough building houses for the newly prosperous households in town that she did not need to work at all. Another woman who recounted working for eight years for a wealthy Turkish man, overseeing his frequent parties on his personal yacht, also said her husband would not allow her to return to Turkey and preferred that she spend her energies as a housewife. In this case, the woman also explained that her mother was too busy professionally to care for her granddaughter, and it was out of the question for her husband to be in charge of caring for their child. Women who had sometimes spent a decade or more working in Turkey often described how in returning to Vulcăneşti they were chafing under their husbands' desires for them to stay home and be housewives.

This politics of gendered labor in households was closely interwoven with elements of class distinction, as illustrated by the case of Rosa. She had worked as a librarian and her husband formally occupied a prominent position in the collective farm administration. In 2003 Rosa left for Turkey to work in a restaurant. She returned home six months later, as soon as she had earned enough to pay her son's university tuition, and after her husband begged her not to leave him alone any longer. In 2010 Rosa again left to work as a labor migrant, this time as a domestic in Moscow. Her close friends were surprised that they were not part of a festive sendoff for Rosa, the common event organized by friends and family when someone decides to spend months away as a labor migrant. Rosa's friends learned about her departure much later and suspected that Rosa was hoping to hide the fact that she needed to seek work as a domestic; from their perspective, she sought to maintain the modicum of distinction she and her husband had enjoyed, with a solid, well-maintained house and a son who had recently migrated permanently to the United States, having won the "Green Card Lottery."[24]

In addition to the widespread labor migration into Turkey and Russia, irregular migration to Western Europe was sometimes discussed. This option was not very common, and it was reportedly pursued more by men than women. As one man explained in 2007:

> There are all kinds of ways to get to Poland's border with Germany and simply swim across the river where there are no border guards. Or you could try the method a friend of mine used where he paid $100 to a border guard who let him into a neutral zone near Yugoslavia, and he went through a bathroom where he exited into Europe. It used to cost $40–$50 to get a person to ferry you into Europe, but now it is $150–$200. This is a lot of money, and people are afraid; there could be maniacs working as middlemen; it is better to try legal migration.

For the most part, migrants sought to cross borders into Russia, Turkey, or Ukraine, where they could cross legally, even if once there, they might overstay their visas. Although the prospects of earning larger salaries in West European countries appealed to some, until well into the 2000s traveling there legally was virtually impossible for rural migrants; they usually lacked the thousands of dollars that countries like Italy demanded be placed in escrow as insurance that people would return home at the end of any contract. In contrast, since the early 1990s entry into Turkey had been simply a matter of receiving a tourist visa on arrival, and entry to Russia merely required a valid passport. Those of Romanian heritage, like one of the high-school principals I interviewed, could easily enter Romania on a visitor's pass, recognized at the border for short-term journeys, or even obtain a Romanian passport. Likewise, until spring 2014 and the Russian military intervention in Ukraine, southern Moldovans with a car who were seeking to save on staples made daytrips to Bolhrad, Ukraine, just over the other nearby border.[25]

Although Turkey was the most prominent destination discussed by potential women migrants, Russia and sometimes Romania were also important destinations, depending on ethnic background and educational accomplishment or professional spheres. For instance, those with Romanian ethnic origins reflected on the possibilities of finding work in Romania, and many had applied for Romanian citizenship. In 2006 the Romanian government announced that all residents of Moldova who lived in the Moldavian territory from 1918 to 1940, when the area was part of Romania, as well as their immediate relatives, would be eligible for citizenship. By 2010, 120,000 of the nearly 3.6 million Moldovans had Romanian passports, with 800,000 applications pending (Bidder 2010; Dimulescu and Avram 2011).[26] Likewise, when Bulgaria joined the EU in 2007, those Moldovans who could claim Bulgarian ethnic background were eligible to apply for Bulgarian citizenship, although there were fewer such people than could apply for Romanian citizenship.[27]

Just because someone applied for and received Romanian (or Bulgarian) citizenship did not mean they were immigrating. For instance, in 2004 the director of the Vulcăneşti Romanian lycée, a high school created with the establishment of an independent Moldova, told me that although she would soon get Romanian citizenship, she would go to Romania only if she failed to get the school to increase her pay. For people without professional training, or for young people, immigrating to Romania was considered an option only if they were academically inclined. Even then, like Bella's son, whose mother first suggested I travel from Istanbul to Gagauzia, local high-school students wishing to study in Romania could realize this dream only if they qualified for a Romanian government scholarship. Even as a recent addition to the EU, Romania's economy was not growing significantly, and unskilled employment was notoriously difficult to secure; Russia and Turkey were often more viable options for those without academic or professional prospects.

Since the mid-1990s Turkey has been the most accessible destination for those seeking to become labor migrants, although by 2010 there was a shift toward Russia as a preferred destination, as it revised policies regarding temporary migrants and began streamlining processes for becoming a permanent resident (Bloch 2014). In particular, young men I met in Vulcănești who had worked in Turkey began to look to Russia as a place where they might have a future. Like Turkey, Russia also provided academic scholarships, especially to Gagauz, and it was common for those young people who won scholarships to remain in Russia after their studies. In contrast to Turkey, young families were also drawn to Russia, since both men and women easily located employment, especially in Moscow's expanding service sectors and construction. A lingua franca of Russian, greater opportunities to permanently settle, and sometimes historical or family ties, make Russia desirable as a destination. However, by 2015 Turkey was again appealing to migrants as a viable option (Chernozub 2015). The falling price of oil, and the concomitant economic crisis and sanctions imposed by the United States and Western Europe in retaliation for Russia's military intervention in Ukraine, had led to significant job losses, making it difficult for migrants to find and maintain work in Russia. For some Moldovans, there were also other destinations enabled by religious affiliation.

RELIGION AND MOBILITY

In the first decade of the 2000s the Evangelical church in Vulcănești occupied a key place in how people envisioned mobility and provided one of the three primary routes—along with labor migration and marriage migration—constantly featured in daily discourse. Religiously motivated migration was significant as Moldova became increasingly drawn into transnational networks of Evangelical religions (see also Glick Schiller and Çağlar 2008), but also as new religious movements have promised to link people to modernity and a "morally empowering" way forward (Pelkmans 2009, 8). These Christian transnational networks have a long history in the region dating back to as early as the mid-1800s when present-day Moldova and bordering Ukraine were sites of rapidly expanding religious movements (Camfield 1990, 693–94; Hardwick 1993). At that time Evangelical beliefs were brought to the region by German colonists, who encountered the already existing Molokans and Dukhobors, as well as other "Spiritual Christians." Spiritual Christians shared a rejection of outward observances of ritual, embracing instead the direct revelation of God, and emphasizing the equality of all humans as part of a vision of a more just society. Along with the expansion of Spiritual Christianity, by the second half of the nineteenth century the Baptist church was firmly established in the area and increasingly drew converts (Hardwick 1993, 32), with some sources estimating 100,000 Baptists and 250,000 total evangelical Christians by the time of the Russian Revolution (Swatsky 1981, 29; Hardwick 1993, 33).[28]

In 2010 nearly 97 percent of the population of Moldova identified as Orthodox—either Moldovan Orthodox (allied with the Russian Orthodox

FIGURE 15.   View of the Seventh-Day Adventist Church in Vulcăneşti. Photograph by author, 2007.

Church, 86 percent) or Bessarabian Orthodox (allied with the Romanian Ortho-dox Church, 11 percent). A growing number of people also sought to identify with other religious communities, including Old Believers (Old Rite Russian Orthodox), Roman Catholics, Baptists, Pentecostals, Lutherans, Presbyterians, Seventh-Day Adventists, Jehovah's Witnesses, Baha'is, Jews, Molokans, Falun Gong, and Muslims (US Department of State 2010, 2012b). As elsewhere in the world, the Evangelical movement is especially gaining adherents in Moldova, and as of 2012 the Union of Evangelical Christian Baptists of Moldova had 482 churches, with nearly 20,000 confirmed congregants (Baptist World Alliance 2011; EBF 2012), or double what it was just twenty years earlier.[29] Moldovan-based Evangelical missionaries also have a broad transnational influence, with representatives "planting churches" from Chukotka, Russia, to Dushanbe, Tajiki-stan, to Turkey (Sprinchana 2011).

The growth of the Evangelical church in Vulcăneşti, and Moldova broadly, has largely relied on resources provided by the Southern Baptist Convention (SBC), the largest Protestant group in North America. To a lesser extent the European Baptist Federation (EBF) is also a force in the expansion of Evangelical churches in Moldova (Sprinchana 2011; EBF 2012). The SBC connection—along with a longer-term history dating from the late 1970s, when the United States began granting asylum to those from the Soviet Union who were identified as suffering religious persecution—has created avenues for migration to the United States via family class migration and church-sponsored migration. In Vulcăneşti, one of the most visible ties to the United States was through Evangelical churches in Sacramento, California. Members of Sacramento congregations have visited Vulcăneşti each summer since the early 1990s, thereby maintaining an active missionizing role and, as several younger people told me, bringing gifts, teaching English, and espousing humanitarian values; aside from support for the local church, they also established a secondhand clothing store, which Zina's sister Eva and others I met called the gumanitarka.[30] Believers from Vulcăneşti migrated to cities other than Sacramento as well, but the Sacramento link was one I heard about frequently as I waited in line to purchase eggs, or when I chatted with one of the elderly women sitting on a bench outside her house, or when I spoke with an older woman about her desire to spend more than the month each year she was permitted on a tourist visa to see her grandchildren in the United States. Relatives of those who had immigrated spoke of these migrations in dreamy terms, reflecting on how fast people settled into their new lives, sponsored by Baptist communities that enabled them to buy homes and find work.

When people became "born again" (*priniali veru*), this was a cause for much discussion. At the market or during tea at the Vital Statistics Office, or on bus rides from the Chişinău airport south to Gagauzia, people would exchange news about who had converted. It was common for people to reflect on whether conversions were genuine or simply orchestrated with emigration in mind. Several times when I found myself in discussion with recent converts, they took the opportunity to ask for advice about emigrating to Canada, a topic that highlighted a sharp ideological divide in the community. When I happened to mention the conversations with converts to my host, Andrei, the former kolkhoz agronomist, he vehemently said: "I would never beg to go to Canada! How can they simply 'find' God as a route to migration! It is all a sham!" However, the converts I met seemed sincere about their newfound faith; the fact that it was linked to a key path to migration may or may not have deepened their sense of commitment to the Evangelical Church.

MARRIAGE MIGRATION AND THE INTERNET

As the third predominant means of migration that defined daily life in Vulcăneşti, marriage migration was the least visible. I knew from some of the labor migrants I met in Istanbul that they had first considered marriage migration before turning to labor migration, and when I stayed with Bella briefly in Vulcăneşti in 2003, I learned that one of her neighbors was considering marriage migration to Russia, an

FIGURE 16. *Sekond khend* store with *"gumanitarka"* handwritten on the door. Photograph by author, 2011.

arrangement being made through an acquaintance. More often I heard about transnational marriage migration from young women I met at the Vulcănești MoldTel office, located next to the post office and diagonally across from the gumanitarka. Young women I met were regularly paying to use the computers so they could access international marriage websites in their search for foreign marriage prospects.

One twenty-four-year-old woman, Lena, whom I met while we were wait-ing in line to pay for our Internet time, told me she had known great hardship in recent years. While Lena was in university, her father was struck down by a drunk driver. After graduating, she sought happiness in marriage but ended up divorcing and moving back in with her mother. Lena told me, "I've known what it means to be hungry, what it means to not even have a piece of bread; I wouldn't wish that even on my worst enemies." With her degree in accounting Lena was able to make sure they had food at home, but she also wanted to find a "soulmate," so she spent months corresponding with different men, including one from Canada and one from Italy. Ultimately, none of them seemed serious enough for her, so she was thinking about other options for marriage and was considering approaching a marriage agency, a strategy common in urban cen-ters across the former Soviet Union (Luehrmann 2004; Patico 2010). Although Lena was raised as a Baptist, she had no immediate plans to emigrate. She was also adamant that it was impossible for her to become a labor migrant, since it would require her to leave her mother alone in Moldova. But she concluded, "If the right man were to come along . . . ," she would consider leaving Moldova with her mother to start a family, in a form of migration that is apparently not uncommon for marriages secured between North American men and post-Soviet women (Johnson 2007).

Young women I met sometimes explored the three types of migration—labor, religious, and marriage—simultaneously, but more often young women, just out of high school or recently having completed a university degree, tried out the labor and marriage migration options serially, turning to labor migra-tion if marriage migration did not seem realistic. Religious migration was most often an option for younger families, who were sponsored to become members of a Baptist Church community in the United States. These various possibilities for migration were frequently the subject of heated conversations, with anger directed at the workings of capitalism in the region and how the end of the Soviet Union had made it necessary for people to seek lives abroad.

Capitalism, "Slavery," and "Dirty Work"

Donna Hughes, one of the primary proponents of an abolitionist stance in regard to sex work in the former Soviet Union and Eastern Europe, writes, "There can be no true democracy in any country if half the population can be viewed as potential commodities to be recruited, bought, sold and enslaved" (2000, 650). Activist scholars like Hughes ardently campaign against sex work, or what they often elide with "sex trafficking," but people I met in southern Moldova were mostly concerned with the everyday oppressions of capitalist work relations. They invoked slavery-like conditions when they assessed the options for employment in their town and greater region of Gagauzia and when they reflected on how their families felt driven to become transnational labor migrants. Capitalism as a coercive force loomed large, even for those with more social and economic capital than others.

Almost daily, acquaintances in Vulcănești reflected on how their labor was no longer valued in the ways it had been in a socialist era. Migrants home for brief visits frequently commented that their roles in a Turkish or Russian service economy situated them in a rigid social hierarchy, while the same processes were evident in the emergent capitalist economy in Moldova. They spoke of being treated no better than "slaves" (*raby*), or "dogs" (*sobaki*). Such refrains entered into lamentations about how the past had been so much better; for instance, when Zina's sister Eva flipped through her photo album and pointed to images of people taking part in an International Workers' Day (May 1) parade, she sighed, saying, "We were proud to be Soviet and our work mattered; not like now." Frequently women and men contrasted their situations with their lives during the Soviet era when menial labor would not have been grounds for them to be considered subhuman. In the Soviet period, as the shuttle traders I came to know reflected, such disdain was reserved for those engaged in trade or in accumulating capital for personal gain.

Strikingly, the narratives of especially older Vulkaneshtians I met, were dominated by themes of anger about low wages and poor working conditions, and anxiety about changing household configurations and the increasingly difficult return trips between southern Moldova and Turkey and Russia. Since the mid-1990s the only possibility for steady paid labor in Gagauzia was in one of the three wine bottling plants (*vinzavody*) that, like nearly all former state-run factories and even public utilities, had been transferred to private ownership in recent years. In 2005 all three of the plants were at least in part foreign-owned, with one entirely Russian-owned, one a joint American-Moldovan venture, and one a Russian-Moldovan venture.[31]

Despite the lack of other options in Vulcănești, people were not keen to take up jobs at these wine bottling plants, even though they paid better than most other options in town. The work required long hours, sometimes as much as sixteen to eighteen-hour shifts, and garnered just 700 lei per month, less than $50 in 2004. The plants initially hired "young" people because managers believed they would not make demands, based on their lack of work experience in the socialist system of labor relations. Until 2003 the companies only employed people younger than thirty-five, but with the lack of applicants in 2004 they extended the maximum age to forty-five. As Eva quipped, "When you get hired there they write up two pieces of paper, one formalizing your employment and the other preparing for your termination." The revolving door Eva referred to shows how workers felt not only poorly paid but also entirely expendable. Understandably, entry-level jobs at the bottling plants appealed to few townspeople, except as a desperate measure. In conversation they especially referred to these jobs as akin to "slavery" (*rabstvo*).

In the Kaloglo household, Eva and her husband, Andrei, forbade their teenage son, who was anxious to earn spending money, to work in the bottling plants; they insisted the work was dehumanizing and that their son's labor was worth more than $50/month. Like many others, Eva assessed the growth of the wine plants and the expansion of capitalist processes generally. She described Gagauzia as a "colony" (*koloniia*) for Moldova, bitterly saying: "The Moldovan government basically sold off the electric utilities to the Spanish without any fair return for the Gagauz region, and the government has also happily sold off the wine bottling plants to private interests. The workers get paid poorly and they work like dogs. And look at the profits for the company! . . . Moldova uses Gagauzia as its colony—it is cheap labor for the capitalists. We are like slaves! Who needs capitalism? We were happy in Soviet times."

Others who worked for some time at the wine bottling plant were no more happy with the employment. Again the phrase "we are like slaves" (*my kak raby*) was frequently invoked. One young woman, Yana, told me that as a computer programmer working at one of the wine plants she was often there for twelve hours, but not infrequently for more than twenty-four hours nonstop. She said: "They treat us like slaves, making us work as much as they want without any overtime. After all, there are no jobs here in Vulcăneşti. They can simply fire you and hire another batch of workers."

In applying age discrimination in their hiring practices, in one sense the wine bottling plants had assessed the situation correctly; younger people were more willing to take on jobs that did not guarantee them any rights and had few benefits, and like Yana, they were more pliable, acquiescing to long hours of work without overtime so as to keep their jobs. Although social scientists are increasingly documenting the effects of outmigration on communities left behind (e.g., Gamburd 2000; Chu 2010; Åkesson 2011), there has been little work on how a shift toward employment in global service economies shapes aspirations of youth. In the case of southern Moldova, this is one of the striking aspects of the hypermobility in the region. One of my consultants noted how the ten-year-old granddaughter she was raising thought of Turkey as her ideal destination for when she finished high school. In 2005 her mother had been in Istanbul for eight years, sending home remittances that kept her daughter fashionably dressed, well fed, and attending the local music school. As one school principal told me, a whole generation was being raised with the understanding that the most dependable way for them to attain a modicum of material comfort was to become labor migrants; after all 30 percent of students had both parents working abroad.[32] For young people in southern Moldova mobility came to be a sign closely linked to aspirations for material well-being, rather than one linked to the ambivalence that global capitalism invoked for their parents' generation.

Generational and Gender Aspirations

Like Mary Beth Mills (1999), who identifies important ways in which the rural to urban migrations in Thailand are shaped by cultural logics of young women supporting elders, I see important ways that southern Moldovan migration patterns for young people fit with shifting intimate household economies. In tracing those economies, or linkages between rural spaces and urban ones, Mills shows how realms as disparate as affect and filial piety can be allied with material realms of capital accumulation, or at least aspirations for this, as young women pursue their dreams. Likewise, in the town of Vulcăneşti, while growing up has become synonymous with seeking possibilities abroad, young women, in particular, are also closely tied to a sense of obligation to, but also responsibility for, their natal families. In a shift from past household practices, young women's earnings, in this case as migrants, are a key component of household economic well-being. Young women balanced this knowledge with a desire for independence and mobility.

Several of the eight young women (ages nineteen to twenty-nine) I became acquainted with in 2004 had close family or relatives in Turkey who had offered to arrange work for them. Once they saved or borrowed the money required to process a passport and cover transportation (about $50 in 2004), it was simple to make the trip, either by minibus via Romania and Bulgaria, if they had a Romanian passport, or by ferry via Ukraine.[33] However, the young people I met in Vulcăneşti were also considering other foreign employment. One young woman, Mila, explained how her brother had found work in Ukraine at a Turkish-run factory producing canned goods; one of Mila's sisters was planning to join her brother, and Mila was also considering this, but only as a last resort. She wanted to go to Istanbul.

Young women were not unaware of the hardship of being an undocumented worker in Istanbul. Several spoke of how their mothers had worked for periods of time in Istanbul but returned when they became ill, were worn out by the long hours and poor pay, or family members could no longer manage without them. Mila told me that her mother had been in Istanbul for one year cleaning houses but returned because Mila's father could not manage the seven children on his own. Mila explained that her mother had been anxious to return to Vulcăneşti since her husband was a hard drinker. However, there were few opportunities for supporting the household in Vulcăneşti.

Like Mila, many young women spoke with excitement about the prospect of traveling abroad, and mostly to Istanbul, a major metropolitan center with job opportunities of a less manual sort than those available at home or in nearby and accessible Ukraine. Mila, for instance, reflected on how one of her sisters was already employed in Istanbul as a nanny and could easily make arrangements for her as well. Mila hoped that option worked out because she considered the work in Ukraine at the canning factory to be "dirty" (*griaznaia*). Some young people resorted to local agricultural labor or work in the wine bottling plants, but most agreed working abroad was preferable. The socialist discourses of older people who lamented the loss of systems of social value that rewarded manual labor, and labor linked to social productivity and recognition (see Keough 2015), were notably absent among young people.

In weighing her options, Yana, the computer programmer working at the wine bottling plant was also anxious to leave Gagauzia. In the summer of 2004 she was considering marrying a young man she had met over the Internet who had emigrated from Moldova to Israel; Yana's parents were wary of this option and did not want Yana to go so far away. Yana had corresponded with her prospective husband for over a year, but she was not too keen on his proposal; she was unsure what her employment options would be in Israel, and she did not want to waste her recently earned university degree and be dependent on someone, especially in a foreign land. Another possibility was to join her friend in Istanbul in a job as a shop assistant. In reflecting on her life in Vulcănești Yana explained: "It is not really life here to just go to work every day for twelve or more hours; there are no young people here [to meet up with]. My friends in Turkey keep calling and asking me to go there. They have apartments and jobs and could find me work too." Still, Yana was torn about leaving for Turkey. She knew that most employment options in Istanbul would be in sales, entertainment, or as domestic help; it was unlikely she would be able to work in her area of expertise. Moreover, if she were to take a position in Istanbul, or leave for Israel, she would have to leave her parents' household in Vulcănești and consider how to maintain support for them while pursuing her own dreams.

Intimate Economies of Households: "Working the Land" and "Apartment Dwelling"

Young people like Yana aspired to leave southern Moldova, but they were, nonetheless, integrally connected to households. Young women, and less often young men, sent remittances home on a regular basis. Parents and other relatives often looked after grandchildren and sometimes anxiously awaited finances that could cover essential food and utilities. In other cases, such as the account of the Kaloglo household that follows, women left children with sisters or other relatives and sent earnings home. Reflecting on the intimate economies of two specific households highlights how transnational mobility forges new understandings of status, generational obligations, and gender ideals.[34]

The Kaloglo Household

In many ways the Kaloglo household is a typical one, in that since the late 1990s household members have been labor migrants to Russia and Turkey, and the household continues to rely on labor migration for remittances. It is also typical of households allying with a Gagauz community (rather than an ethnic Moldovan one) in terms of its multigenerational connection to household production based on agriculture, and its bilingualism in Russian and Gagauz, with no one in the household fluent in Moldovan.

Like many families identifying as Gagauz, the Kaloglos have extended family ties linking them to their household plots owned over several generations.[35] This is evident even in the built structures belonging to Gagauz-identified families. Most houses dating from the mid-twentieth century or earlier were built with a smaller dwelling typically located across from the main house; this was where the youngest son and his family would live, and eventually where the older male head of household and his wife would live once a youngest son inherited the responsibility of running the farm (Kuroglo 1980). Such an arrangement has historically allowed for a built-in multigenerational working of subsistence plots, and this often extends into the present.

In 2004 the extended household of the Kaloglos consisted of: Eva and Andrei, the former kolkhoz agronomist; their teenage son, Viktor; their older son who had received a scholarship to study in Russia; Zina, who was mostly in Istanbul; and Zina's two grown children, who were studying in Chişinău and sometimes visited. Also, Zina and Eva's elderly mother did not live with them, but she frequented the household in what amounted to a virtual extended family arrangement, with many common meals and household labor divided among the three adults and the son, Viktor. The Kaloglos were intensively running a small-scale farm—raising chickens and geese, as well as growing a wide range of vegetables and fruits and producing their own wine—all of which provided for their own household consumption. However, this type of household economy was relatively new for them. Until the early 1990s, the Kaloglos had supported their extended household based on salaries received from Andrei's administrative work in the kolkhoz, Eva's and Zina's work at the local hospital, and Zina and Eva's parents' pensions.[36]

With the tailspin in the local economy in the early to mid-1990s, and the dissolution of the state farm system as landholdings were widely privatized, the Kaloglo household was forced to reconfigure. In 1996, when paychecks barely covered even expenses for food, Zina's husband was a labor migrant on a construction site in Moscow and had been working there for two years. Zina described how at first they thought her husband had simply disappeared, but later it was confirmed that he had been discovered dead at his worksite in Russia. Soon after hearing of her husband's death, Zina closed up her house, left her work as a medical orderly and occasional movie projectionist, and departed for Istanbul, leaving her ten-year-old and twelve-year-old children in the care of her sister, Eva. In Istanbul Zina quickly located what she considered to be a lucrative position as a shop assistant. This enabled her to earn money for raising her children and to visit home at least once per year for several weeks. Zina was able to send regular remittances via the minibuses traveling from Istanbul, as well as periodically transporting money herself, and these funds went toward the children's education, some upkeep of her house, utility bills for her house and Eva's, and basic household necessities.

The extended Kaloglo household weathered the late 1990s and up until 2004 by relying on Zina's remittances and on their small-scale farm, as well as on income from Eva's job as a nurse and from Andrei's itinerant construction jobs in Russia. From 1997 to 2000 Andrei traveled for months at a time to work as part of a Gagauz construction team outside Moscow; nearly the entire $10,000 he was able to earn went toward sending his older son to university. Despite pooling household incomes and remittances, times were difficult in 2004. In their frequent telephone calls and during Zina's visits, conversations often vacillated between the desperate need for money and the price one had to pay for earning it. Repeatedly Eva told me, "I'm tired of being poor." Zina consistently sent money from Turkey, but she also told her sister Eva how Turkey was dehumanizing; she insisted that she did not want her children to be exposed to that life in a foreign, uninviting land, a *chuzhbina*, as she called it. As Eva said: "Making 200 lei [about $20/month, the average pay for people in Vulcăneşti in 2004] is also dehumanizing. Why not make some money and see something of the world?"

Over the years Eva often told me she was anxious to go to Turkey herself, but there were "big politics" (*bol'shaia politika*) preventing her from making the trip. She suspected that her husband and son resisted her seeking work in Turkey because she did the brunt of the work around the house: "Of course, they are happy that I cook, clean, feed the animals, tend the gardens, et cetera." Eva complained that while she never left the house except to go to her work at the hospital, the men in the family were far more mobile and had ample free time to spend drinking with friends or go fishing. Like the Sri Lankan women Gamburd (2000) writes about, these Moldovan women seemed keenly aware of the irony that they could stay home and perform domestic work without pay or migrate and do the same work for a wage. However, unlike the Sri Lankan women in Gamburd's study, few middle-aged women I met thought of the domestic labor in which they engaged as "biological destiny" or "sacred calling" (Gamburd 2000, 195) performed for family. Instead, women I met in southern Moldova saw demands for their domestic labor as a recent shift from a time when they were able to dedicate themselves more fully to their professions, without the necessity of also maintaining homesteads where they had to grow food and raise chickens and geese to feed their families. Although younger women typically pointed to migration as a means to adventure, older women like Eva sometimes reflected that migration was appealing both for the possibility to "see the world" *and* for the chance to earn a wage for domestic/household labor she had to do anyway.

Nevertheless, Eva repeatedly told me how proud her family was to live their lives *na zemle*, or working the land, something that connected them to long family histories of farming. Both Eva and Andrei's families had farmed to one degree or another, and they saw themselves as drawing on this traditional subsistence knowledge; in fact, in a pattern of ultimogeniture common among Gagauz, as the youngest son Andrei had inherited his father's assets and a plot of land.[37] Even as members of the kolkhoz, Andrei's family had kept a hundred sheep as part of its private farmstead, and Andrei's father was well regarded as a shepherd. Eva's natal family also worked its own household land, even while her father was a manager on the kolkhoz. Eva reflected that she could never imagine herself living in an apartment (*na etazhakh*); she would not know how to use her time.

In 2004 when I first became acquainted with the Kaloglo household they were struggling to pay basic bills, but over the years migration was critical in contributing to their relative prosperity. By 2011 Eva and Andrei's combined income was still barely $120 a month, more than half of which they spent on utilities, but they were also substantially supported by their sons, who had settled in Russia with their families. With the regular remittances the Kaloglos received they had renovated a part of their house, insulating the walls, installing running water, and repairing an aging roof, as well as updating furnishings; they marveled that their sons' remittances had paid for all the work on their home. Furthermore, as the younger son proudly told me, he had purchased a good-quality used car for his father. Remittances also made it possible for the Kaloglos to invest much less of their own labor in maintaining their house and caring for their small farm. In 2011 they were able to hire itinerant laborers from a nearby village to beat rugs, plow and weed the garden, and help with harvests.

Over the course of the early 2000s Zina's situation also changed, so she was no longer economically integral to the Kaloglo household but still maintained close ties. By 2010 Zina's two children had completed their studies and established their own families and Zina did not feel compelled to remain in Istanbul. For many reasons Zina also did not feel drawn to returning to Vulcănești. In 2010 her mother died and Zina's children lived in Chișinaŭ and Moscow, so only Zina's sister, Eva, and Eva's husband, Andrei, remained in Vulcănești. After fifteen years of living in Istanbul, Zina was used to living in the city, and when she was ready to leave Turkey, she decided to move to Moscow to live with her daughter and son-in-law and help care for her granddaughter. Still, transnational networks of care and intimacy remained important, and Zina's granddaughter frequently spent her three-month-long summer vacation living with her great-aunt Eva and great-uncle Andrei.

While the Kaloglo household portrait reflects how migration has played a critical role in the lives of families in southern Moldova since the 1990s, turning to a household with fewer forms of capital further highlights the differential ways mobility is shaping the region, including at the intimate level of the household.

The Milshniaga Household

When I arrived in Vulcănești with my infant daughter and stepmother and stayed with Bella in the summer of 2003, we went across the street to meet Bella's friend Nelli. Nelli was in her small yard in the midst of weeding vegetables, surrounded by her peonies about to burst open and grapevines growing up and around the windows of her apartment. She ushered us into her home on the ground floor of the concrete apartment building and offered us tea, cookies, bread and butter, fried eggs, and slices of sausage. In this first conversation and in many subsequent ones over the years, Nelli narrated aspects of her life and introduced me to her wide network of friends, as well as to her own close family members.

Unlike the Kaloglos, the Milshniagas had not lived in southern Moldova for generations. Nelli had arrived with her husband in the 1970s from a town to the north, whose inhabitants, like herself, predominantly identified as ethnically Moldovan. In her youth Nelli worked a range of jobs, but never pursued post-secondary education, despite her keen sense of critical reflection and intellectual curiosity. In the late Soviet era Nelli had worked in a state-run cafeteria, as a bus conductor, and as a seamstress. Her husband, an ethnic Bulgarian, left her when her two children were young, so she had raised them on her own, without nearby family; her own natal family was several hours away, and more distant relatives lived about an hour away to the west, across the border in Romania.

As it had for most people who had migrated to Vulcănești to take up jobs in the late Soviet years, the local government had allocated Nelli an apartment in the five-story cement apartment blocks located a ten-minute walk beyond the center of town. These apartment dwellers were sometimes spoken of as living *na etazhakh*, in contrast to living *na zemle*, as many longer-term residents of

Vulcăneşti did. The apartment blocks were largely inhabited by those who had either moved to the area within the last generation or had moved away from the household production of their parents and extended family.[38] After the end of the Soviet Union, those who had not had access to higher education, or even to plots of land for maintaining subsistence agriculture, found that their work in low-level, often menial positions in state-run organizations, like schools or the local hospital, was no longer sufficient for supporting their households. Nelli's household was, like many in these apartment blocks, dependent on remittances from abroad, with only a few subsistence foods, like potatoes and cabbage, being grown in a small kitchen garden beside the apartment building.

It had not always been like this. In raising her two children, Nelli had worked long hours and thought about how her daughter, with an exquisite voice and a flair for performing, could ultimately excel in the music or entertainment sphere. She dreamed of her son becoming part of the managerial staff in the kolkhoz. When the Soviet Union ended in the early 1990s, Nelli lost her job and briefly shuttled goods—such as Lenin memorabilia and cognac—to a border town in Romania, located just twenty minutes away by car. Nelli's daughter, Niki, was just completing high school. She hoped to enroll in a music institute, but the timing was bad; the institute in Chişinău turned her away, saying that those from Gagauzia, which at the time had sought to secede from Moldova, were not welcome there. Niki returned home, found work in a beauty salon, soon after married her high-school sweetheart, and then gave birth to a daughter. Just a few years later Niki decided to leave her turbulent marriage and have her mother stay with the child while she traveled to Turkey in search of work.

Just after the end of the Soviet Union, Nelli herself had spent nearly two years cleaning houses in Turkey. Nelli's poor health ultimately meant that she had to return to Moldova. In the early 1990s she could find few work opportunities, so it was a relief when her daughter, and soon afterward her son, found a sales position in Istanbul. When I met them in 2004, Nelli struggled to provide for herself and her granddaughter, but the monies Nelli's son and daughter sent from Turkey made it possible to purchase food and clothing and pay for utilities, as well as pay the extra fees required for Nelli's granddaughter to attend music school. Every few years Nelli and her granddaughter had been able to travel to Turkey and enjoy time visiting with Niki, and Niki made an annual trip home, sometimes also coming home for important ritual events. For instance, in 2004 Nelli excitedly showed me home videos of Niki accompanied by her boyfriend, Ali, attending a friend's wedding in Vulcăneşti. Nelli was hopeful that her daughter's long-term boyfriend might eventually become her son-in-law.

By 2011 Nelli was less optimistic about her family's prospects. Niki had broken up with her boyfriend and returned for an extended stay with Nelli while she considered what she would do next. Nelli's granddaughter was finishing high school and aspired to study at a music conservatory in Chişinău, but there was little hope of finding the means to pay for this. Despite material circumstances, Nelli continued to manage on a small pension and intermittent remittances from her son, who had returned to Turkey. In the summer of 2011 times were especially tough, with Nelli's son sending the majority of his earnings to support a young daughter being raised by his ex-wife. Still, Nelli and Niki decided to repaint their bedroom a light violet and remodel with a full set of furniture, a purchase they made for $1,000 across the border in Romania.

Nelli and Niki had begun to make use of the easily obtainable Romanian "short stay" visas and travel regularly to Romania for trade, and by 2013 their Romanian passports allowed them to stay for longer in Romania and beyond. This also meant that they were again in frequent touch with relatives in Galaţi, just on the other side of the border, although those kin were in similar straits, with most young people away as labor migrants and few household resources (Weber 2014). Most often Nelli and Niki transported vegetables, like potatoes from Romania, and resold these out of their garage space across from the apartment block, but sometimes they also took special orders for car parts or tires. As Nelli explained with resignation, this was little different from what they were doing to survive in the early 1990s, only now there was no demand for cognac or Lenin memorabilia in Romania, so they were only moving goods from Romania into Moldova. Nelli reflected that while they were able to make relatively large sums through the shuttle trade in the early 1990s, now the profit margins were much smaller; after paying for gas and any customs duties or bribes, on most trips they were lucky to break even.

In many ways the Kaloglo and Milshniaga households differ in terms of their ability to thrive in a neocapitalist Moldova. However, since the end of the Soviet Union they have both relied on labor migration. In both households men set out for Russia to work on construction, and in both, women went to Istanbul to work as domestic laborers or shop assistants. Remittances sent home went toward paying utilities, buying groceries, and paying for education. Still, the portraits of these two households reflect the degree to which household circumstances prior to the end of the Soviet Union shape the options today. Everyone suffered when the stable, Soviet system came apart, but those with greater social capital—such as an education or strong ties to structures of power and ongoing social services (e.g., the kolkhoz administration and the town hospital)—and economic capital (land) were better able to support their families. Furthermore, those households that could rely on more than one or two sources of income fared better. People like Eva and Andrei were well positioned in times of crisis to rely on their land holdings and long-term knowledge of animal husbandry, as well as formal paychecks, even if they were meager. In addition, they were able to pool resources with Eva's sister, Zina, and with a member of an older generation (Eva and Zina's mother) so as to aggregate available capital, eventually supporting their sons enough that they were able to carry on providing significantly for the household.

In contrast, people like Nelli faced the challenge of raising a family without nearby kin. With the end of the Soviet Union, Nelli's household also lacked critical landholdings and knowhow for farming, as well as a specialized education— the social capital that could have insured a stable, if poorly paid, job and better pension. There is a wide spectrum of material well-being for households, even when they share a reliance on labor migration.

Remittances, Distinction, and Burning Books

Recent scholarship on remittance economies in Eurasia has reflected on some of the implications of the transnational flow of labor and finances for whole communities (see Reeves 2014). However, relatively little work has focused on the meanings attributed to the relational aspect of remittance economies, or *who* is sending money or goods and *to whom*. As Åkesson (2011) shows in her research among Cape Verdeans, remittances are inherently bound up in kinship ties; it matters immensely the degree to which kin ties are maintained, disregarded, or thwarted, and by whom. Furthermore, remittance relationships are linked to shifting systems of value among those who stay behind and benefit directly from remittances. As Wanner (2005) argues for Ukraine, the infusion of cash-based forms of exchange in Moldova has redefined social obligations and challenged systems of value.

In discussing remittance arrangements, some residents pondered what they saw as related dependencies and growing consumer desires. Some asked what motivation people could have to make a living locally if they could depend on funds coming from abroad. Those able to provide for most of their household needs by working their land tended to be especially critical of those living in apartments, but also of others not working the land. As one subsistence farmer who was also working in the town health care system commented: "They are just living off their children's remittances; they do not work and they don't plant anything. They buy everything, even potatoes!"

It was not uncommon for those households taking care of migrants' young children to rely heavily on remittances.[39] For instance, in 2004 one woman I met recounted, as she bounced my toddler daughter on her knee, how she cared for her five-year-old grandchild and received remittances from her daughter, and less frequently from her son-in-law. The son-in-law had not seen his daughter since she was five months old, and the daughter had not seen the child since she was eight months old. The woman explained that she was struggling on the remittances she received to heat and light her home, as well as keep her grandchild fed and clothed. She no longer worked in a job receiving a paycheck and said she could not find time to tend a garden.

Such women were subject to quiet but strong disapproval by those working their land and continuing to work in wage labor positions. The view that receiving remittances can lead to a lack of initiative in households is not unique to Moldova (see Åkesson 2011, 254). However, the ways people reflected on the transformation of social relations is specific to the postsocialist setting of southern Moldova, where reworkings of class, ethnic and national belonging, and gender ideals come together in specific ways. During my research judgments about people being unwilling to work hard were often wrapped up in the ways people in Vulcănești variously framed modernity through a socialist lens of *trud*, or labor—the sense of something having value for being produced through one's efforts (Wanner 2005). In valorizing work that required what they saw as genuine labor, some older people in Vulcănești implicitly judged those who were able to survive primarily on remittances. As Leyla Keough has noted elsewhere in southern Moldova, distinction is attained through manual labor and by working the land, even if labor migration is crucial for households (2015, 146).

In my research I found a class dynamic wherein those who were landless and living in apartment blocks were especially criticized by those working the land, including for their patterns of consumption. The apartment dwellers' strategies for improving their lives focused more on their ability to cross borders for economic opportunity and less on symbolic capital garnered during the Soviet era or, in more recent years, on education. As Wanner (2005) found in Ukraine, in a post-Soviet era conspicuous consumption in the form of major renovations, clothes, jewelry, used cars, or furniture is often a form of distinction that contrasts with that still relied on by landholding households. In general, the landholding households calibrated distinction in regard to education and professional stature, while deemphasizing the importance of consumer goods and a set of social relations defined by money. However, as in neighboring Ukraine, and as the household portraits above suggest, these boundaries between forms of distinction have been increasingly blurred. This situation is illustrated by the following account.

One day in 2011 I accompanied Andrei to pick up some money Zina sent from Istanbul via a minibus service doubling as an unofficial money transfer company. I was reminded of how access to social and economic capital tends to shape the ways households use remittances, but also how they experience transactions around remittances. Andrei was not sure where exactly to pick up the money, and he was a little sheepish about asking for directions, since this made it public knowledge that he was receiving a remittance. We had to ask at several shops before we found the money transfer company that had set up temporarily around the back of a building. In the awkwardness of receiving a money transfer, Andrei asked if he could have "the parcel" that had arrived in his name. The clerk answered, "Do you really think we would have the actual money sent in *a parcel*?" The clerk then asked Andrei to sign his name before she counted out the US dollars. Andrei confided that he usually picked up money directly from an acquaintance carrying it for Zina, and he was a bit embarrassed by having to deal with a company to do the transaction. Dealing so directly with money in a public setting detracted from the distinction Andrei still had as someone who had occupied a prominent position within the collective farm system. Having to sign for the money and attest to receiving it from a sister-in-law made this awkward transaction more visible, and so even more difficult.

Another instance in the Kaloglo household underscored how questions of distinction, household gender roles, and shifting systems of value collided as labor migration resulted in remittances in various forms. In 2007, when I arrived at the Kaloglo household, a washing machine still in its cardboard box was in the middle of the hallway.[40] When I asked about the machine, Eva scoffed and told me, "Zina sent it from Istanbul to show off." Andrei grumbled that they did not want the unnecessary washing machine and would get rid of it. Given the long hours each week that most people spend washing clothes by hand, I was surprised by their comments and gathered that the washing machine embodied several issues for the Kaloglos. First, the lavish expense of a washing machine reflected Zina's ability to afford such a gift, and this uncomfortably highlighted new relations of power within the household. Second, it mattered that it was a widowed sister-in-law who was giving this to a family that had raised her two children. Zina proudly told me the machine was meant as a sincere sign of her appreciation for her sister and brother-in-law's support in raising her children, but the Kaloglo household saw it as a sort of crass expression of Zina's economic achievements, and one that marked them as morally implicated in the questionable pursuit of conspicuous consumption (see Wanner 2005). Even more than this, however, it mattered who sent remittances and for what purpose. It was fine when Zina sent money specifically to support her children in the care of the Kaloglo household, but her primary status as a sister-in-law in the Kaloglo household made it awkward for her to give what was seen as a major luxury item after the children had established their own households. The lavish gift highlighted the fundamental reorganization of economic power even while local gender hierarchies continued to position men as household heads.

While remittances are tied to shifts in how distinction plays out for households, neocapitalism in the region also changed hierarchies of value more broadly. In the past, access to formal learning, and especially to higher education, was an important form of distinction across the FSU. Formal education set kolkhoz agronomists apart from kolkhoz workers, nurses apart from orderlies, and teachers apart from those working as illicit entrepreneurs. As Jennifer Patico (2008) traces elsewhere in the former Soviet Union, in southern Moldova the hierarchy of value that placed knowledge gained through formal training at the pinnacle of achievement had eroded by the early 2000s, and money and the ability to be financially stable became primary. However, those raised in a different era retained some sense of another system of value, where a widespread, deep veneration of formal learning and books defined public culture, even in rural areas.

In a striking illustration of the generational differences between those raised under socialism and those coming of age in a neocapitalist era, Eva recounted a story about her younger son who, partly due to financial constraints, had not been able to continue on for postsecondary education. In the late 1990s the family had been struggling to pay for utilities and had discussed burning old furniture in their cook stove instead of paying for gas to heat their home. Eva recalled coming home to find her teenage son burning books as a fuel source. Eva exclaimed: "Can you imagine, burning books! And in this house where books and ideas have meant so much to us! Young people just do not have the appreciation we have for learning and education!" The end of the Soviet Union has meant radical reworkings of a wide range of cultural values and ideas about distinction, yet another way that the retraction of the state is felt at the intimate level of the household.

Gendered Border Crossings: Health Care, Passports, and Names

One could see southern Moldovan households as fixtures on the social landscape, while the women moving across national boundaries are creating new types of connections, even as they shuttle back to these ongoing household units. Unlike Claude Lévi-Strauss's (1969) idea of women as a unit of exchange linking different groups and perpetuating these groups' internal arrangements and hierarchies, here I see women as actively forging new types of power as they take part in remaking the intimate economies of households. This was especially evident in discussions with migrants about the common practice that numerous women had engaged in until 2004 of outmaneuvering customs and border control officers.

Throughout the 1990s and into the early 2000s women could make relatively frequent sojourns home from Istanbul with few restrictions, except for paying $30–$50 for the bus via Bulgaria and Romania back to Gagauzia. Customs and passport control points usually required migrants to pay modest fees for overstaying their one-month tourist visas, but a small bribe or good fortune in encountering a sympathetic border official often meant minimal problems, and women were not too concerned about being deported since they could get new passports reissued and return easily. Women repeatedly told me that they were in demand in those years; they had no problem locating work again in Istanbul if they lost a position after a visit home.

Women recounted how in their first years of coming to Turkey they did not hesitate to travel home for major life cycle events, such as christenings and weddings. In some cases, the need for medical care brought migrants home when they could not afford necessary health care in Turkey. Beginning in the early 2000s medical care in the town hospital in Vulcănești was increasingly provided on a fee-for-service basis, and while it was considered costly by local standards, migrants returning home from Istanbul or Moscow considered it relatively affordable.[41] Staff at the hospital noted that women migrants tended to return to Vulcănești when they needed abortions or other gynecological care.

In addition to negotiating the border to access reproductive health care, women's border-crossing strategies included those around being deported. On deportation from Turkey they would receive a prominent "deport" stamp in their passports, and this would make it impossible for women to return to Turkey, at least on that passport. However, throughout the 1990s and into the early 2000s, deported women frequently had passports reissued in Moldova with different names. They did this by establishing new official identities through mechanisms of divorce and marriage.

From the early 1990s to the early 2000s the Vulcănești region saw the number of divorces more than double, even as the population of Moldova dropped.[42] This occurred at a time of severe outmigration and a wide range of social and economic stresses for households, so it is improbable that the increase in divorces was simply a matter of women seeking to reissue passports. Still, given what I heard from women like Zina and Bella, this is very likely one of the significant factors. Like several other women, Zina told me that she had her passport reissued four times with four different surnames after each subsequent marriage (or divorce) in Moldova: the first time she married in the late Soviet Union and had children with her husband, whose surname she took; then in the late 1990s she married two separate acquaintances, paying $50 each time, once reestablishing her maiden name, and once taking her new "husband's" surname; and the last time she married, she took her mother's maiden name as her surname.

These practices point to the ways Moldovan women literally (re)crafted their sense of self, or at least their official identities, as a mechanism for border crossing. In (re)naming themselves, women renegotiated their mobility. As Rubie Watson (1986) has written about historical naming practices in rural China, multiple names conferred status on men, and throughout life men gained additional names as they moved through their life cycles. In contrast, rural Chinese women remained "unnamed," often with only nicknames at birth, and not gaining new names as they moved through life; in a society that placed great value on male status embodied in names, rural Chinese women's "nameless" state was indicative of their lack of significant status. In contrast, Moldovan women have had a fundamental freedom to take on new names and to wield forms of power associated with the ability to be mobile. Moreover, like the men Watson describes, Moldovan women's life stages were often marked by new surnames and linked to the coming-of-age experience of labor migration.

Moldovan men's and women's ability to take on new names, and therefore to have passports reissued, also varies in a culturally specific way. Women can simply take on a new name as a result of registering a marriage. Men in Moldova can on marriage technically take on a new legal surname as well, but this is a less normative change in identity than it is for a woman to change her surname upon marriage or divorce.[43] During my research women tended to adopt the surname of their spouse on marriage, and as in many locations in the former Soviet Union, divorce was relatively easy to process, with little stigma associated with it.

By 2004, with the onset of new security measures—including biometric passports and databases tracing the histories of passports held by an individual, and requirements that on deportation migrants had to remain out of the country for the corresponding amount of time they had overstayed their visas in Turkey—women no longer employed the practice of serial marriages in Moldova to negotiate the border. This again changed mobility patterns; with migrants unable to depend on being able to return to Turkey once they had left, many migrants I met chose to remain in Turkey for years on end without returning home. These strategies are part of the story of how intimate practices have been shaped by new mobilities in the region as women and men have sought ways to maneuver within the constraints of growing precarity that came to define their lives with the end of the Soviet Union.

Since the late 1990s people in Gagauzia, like the Kaloglos and Milshniagas, have become a source of flexible, marginalized labor both for local forms of neocapitalism, such as the wine bottling plants, and for centers of global capitalism, like Istanbul, Turkey. As middle-aged women such as Zina, Nelli, and Eva navigated their limited options for households based in Moldova, they looked to prospects for labor migration for themselves but also for younger household members. Younger women like Lena, Yana, Mila, and Niki sometimes looked to transnational marriage, religious communities, and, on occasion, to educational opportunities as forms of mobility, but labor migration is an option that cuts across generations and defines intimate economies of households, as well as intimate practices around marriage, irrespective of social status. Mobility itself becomes a way of negotiating distinction and status within households and between households, as well as being key in how intimate economies of care, aspiration, and distinction get realized. The next chapter turns from the intimate economies of households in Moldova to consider the transnational circuits of intimacy that migrant women engage as they negotiate intimate relationships with men in Istanbul.

Part III

SEX, LOVE, AND UNPROMISING STATES

STRATEGIC INTIMACY, "REAL LOVE," AND MARRIAGE

I was visiting with several women from Moldova who were living in Fatih, a neighborhood bordering Laleli, when the fourth woman staying in the one-bedroom apartment returned from her work as a cutter in a garment factory. Raia, a pleasant looking, blonde-haired woman with a strong and compact build, wanted to smoke, and she invited me to join her on a park bench outside the apartment building. Unlike most of her friends, Raia could sit in parks without fear of being spotted by police and threatened with deportation. Raia had a valid visa since her Turkish boyfriend, Ahmet, sponsored the cost of her travel home every month; each time she returned on a one-month tourist visa issued at the airport.

I first met Raia in 2006 when she had been traveling to Turkey for two years, and her son was three years old. After leaving an abusive husband in 2004, Raia departed for Turkey in search of a means to support herself, her son, and her aging parents. It was not hard to find work, and her cousin, who was already in Istanbul, acted as a reference. Raia had been working in a small wholesale clothing store selling women's suits for about a year when she met Ahmet. As a friend of the owner's he dropped by frequently, and it became apparent that he was drawn to her.

When they finally went out together, Raia said she cried; she felt conflicted and did not really want to date Ahmet. He asked her, "Don't you feel it in your heart, that we are meant to be close?" She told him no, she did not feel anything in her heart, but perhaps that would change. When she traveled home and consulted with her mother, Raia began to reconsider. Even though Ahmet was married and had two children in their twenties, Raia's mother—who used to work in the Soviet state farm system until it collapsed in the early 1990s and then briefly worked in Istanbul cleaning houses—encouraged her to take Ahmet's interest seriously. She said, "Well, maybe it is your fate; why don't you try it out and see how it goes?"

Raia recounted how Ahmet was really good to her, and she said, "He is like my brother, father, and boyfriend, all in one; this is much more than I could ever have imagined, and it is what I needed living in this foreign country, all alone with no family or anything." Like Raia, many women I met reflected on their attachment to boyfriends and on their boyfriends' support, which supplemented remittances home. Many others also recounted how they had contracted marriages of convenience or, as post-Soviet women migrants call these arrangements, "fake" marriage (*fiktivnyi brak*) to secure their status.

In this chapter I draw on multiple conversations, as well as formal interviews, with post-Soviet women primarily working long-term as sales assistants, exotic dancers, and domestic workers. I consider the central role that intimate ties with Turkish men play for migrants' efforts to maintain transnational circuits of intimacy between Turkey, Moldova and sometimes Russia.[1] I came to know a wide range of women (and sometimes members of their families) from Moldova, Russia, Belarus, and Ukraine who had worked for one to fifteen years in different neighborhoods of Istanbul, including Aksaray, Laleli, Zetinburnu, Şişli, and Taksim.[2] Although the women were employed in diverse spheres and were not always from the same post-Soviet countries, they had much in common, including their knowledge of Russian, the intimate ties they fostered transnationally, and frequently, the liaisons they negotiated with Turkish men.

In examining post-Soviet women's negotiations around various forms of intimacy they engage in as labor migrants in Istanbul, I explore the implicit line between "real" and "fake" or performed intimacy (see Brennan 2004). Women's deployments of intimacy could be seen as simply strategic, but women's narratives and diverse experiences provide evidence that complicates a simple binary of "true" intimacy and instrumental forms of intimacy. I also seek to show how the structural constraints under which women migrate from places like Moldova, Ukraine, and Belarus to Turkey shape decisions they make about intimate practices, including when and with whom to forge liaisons and whether to marry. Ultimately, I argue that the women I came to know are weighing emotional, material, and practical concerns around intimacy and negotiating their options within the confines of shifting Turkish border regimes and ideals about gender.

Marriage, Love, Migration

Popular estimates of the number of marriages between post-Soviet women and Turks tend to be vague, with numbers ranging from fifty thousand marriages contracted in one year to three hundred thousand "Turkish-Russian" marriages overall, but with no reference to the specific countries of origin for the women marrying Turkish men.[3] For a number of reasons it is difficult to know what it means for women from the former Soviet Union to be married to Turks. Among the many issues, women could be married and then emigrate from Turkey, be married and then soon after divorced, or get married to a Turk working outside Turkey (e.g., in Russia). Nevertheless, data pertaining to marriage between foreigners and Turks, including that regarding post-Soviet women and Turks, suggest that from the mid-1990s to early 2000s marriage was an important avenue for securing citizenship (İçduygu 2009, 289).

While I met dozens of post-Soviet women migrants who had married in Turkey, and I heard about a number who had met and married their Turkish husbands for "true love" and settled in Turkey, only a few women I met claimed to have married in Turkey for "true love" (*nastoiashchaia liubov'*). Significantly, as of 2016 there were two avenues to gain citizenship in Turkey: (1) demonstrate Turkish "descent or culture" to be naturalized; or (2) marry a citizen.[4] At least until the early 2000s, post-Soviet women appear to have widely turned to marriage as one way of securing their status to remain in Turkey long-term. Of the more than seven thousand women from the former Soviet Union who gained Turkish citizenship between 1995 and 2000, almost all of them did this through marriage to a Turkish citizen (İçduygu 2009, 289).[5] After 2004, when borders and marriages became more thoroughly policed, women looked to this strategy for mobility less often.

Nevertheless, for many post-Soviet migrant women their lives were significantly shaped by intimate ties with Turkish men. As a number of scholars have noted for other locations (Constable 2003; Brennan 2004; Cheng 2007; Carrier-Moisan 2012), marginalized women's negotiations around romantic liaisons and relationships defined by intimacy challenge assumptions of how "love" as an emotion might be experienced—namely, not always as separate from strategic concerns as some might imagine. Building on these insights in analyzing post-Soviet migrant women's intimate practices, I seek also to show how the diverse types of liaisons women invested in during their long-term stays in Istanbul are part of transnational circuits of intimacy linking women's lives in Istanbul with their home communities.

Intimacy and Mobility

As cross-border marriages, virtual communities, and intimate service economies have become commonplace globally, new ways of forging intimacy have become widely imaginable; at the same time, mobile women like Raia are reconfiguring meanings they attach to relationships of love, obligation, and transaction, often finding these to be blurred (Constable 2003, 2005; Cheng 2007; Faier 2009). Like other scholars thinking about "intimacy" and its reworkings in a newly global era (Rebhun 1999; Hirsch and Wardlow 2006; Bernstein 2007a; Freeman 2007; Padilla et al. 2007; Constable 2009), I draw on this concept as a way of bridging the domestic, personal realm and related inward-looking tendencies with a more public and often politicized realm recognized as being shaped by global forces. "Intimacy" and "the intimate" may at first seem to fall into the realm of psychology and/or emotional terrain, a designation that would invoke universals, unmarred by larger social forces. However, as a number of scholars have shown, intimacy is also a space of negotiation where individuals face structural and geopolitical constraints tempered by a sense of possibility (Hirsch 2003; Constable 2003; Faier 2009), something that can be heightened by mobility. In thinking about forms of intimacy forged by people on the move, a dialectic of aspirations for personal transformation, on the one hand, and stark realities of structural constraints imposed by border regimes, on the other, create a productive space for reflecting on the ways that intimacy is shaped as much through emotion and the imagination as by material concerns and state power. Even as I show how impediments posed by border regimes shape the forms that intimacy takes, I also point to the complexity of motivations, structures of feeling, and emotional attachments that define women's migration experience.

Intimate Economies in Shops and Homes

The portrait of Raia's life traces details that parallel many of the relationships women forged with Turkish men. Moreover, Raia's experience also parallels a global trend of millions of people who have become labor migrants as local economies have faltered and demands for low-wage employment have expanded in more prosperous countries. Although transnational transfers of remittances are not unique to women migrants from the FSU, the ways in which post-Soviet women have widely engaged in intimate practices in Turkey are distinctive. Most ethnographic research among migrants in Turkey from the former Soviet Union and other former socialist countries has not focused on intimacy (e.g., Akalin 2007; Parla 2009; Keough 2015), and the scholarship that has considered intimacy emphasizes economic transactions (Yükseker 2004). Here I argue that negotiations around intimacy are not just about transactions, integral to the maintenance of the transnational circuits women maintain between Turkey and former Soviet countries, but are also about emotional ties and intersecting desires between Turkish men and post-Soviet women.

Although some of the women I came to know in Istanbul were working as exotic dancers, and others more directly in sex work, many were employed in less stigmatized forms of labor as domestic workers, sales assistants, and, less commonly, in the garment industry. Almost all the women were widowed, divorced, or separated from husbands and fathers of their children, although some younger women had never been married or had children. Critically, post-Soviet migrant women's sensibilities about intimacy frequently fit with Turkish men's emerging desires to situate themselves as modern and cosmopolitan. This situation is reminiscent of what Leiba Faier writes about Filipinas traveling to Japan to work in politically and economically marginalized towns, where they were in demand as entertainers and often wives; as she suggests, in these spaces of working-class Japanese men's interactions with Filipinas, men could feel worldly, important, and superior when they "helped" Filipinas (2009, 37, 75).

Like Japanese men, Turkish men also voiced a desire to "help" migrant women they dated (and less often married). However, in contrast to what Faier outlines, with local Japanese hierarchies positioning Filipinas as culturally inferior to Japanese, Turkish men's desires for liaisons with post-Soviet women have pivoted around an opposite sense, that post-Soviet women are especially "cultured" and embody qualities men have sought to emulate and gain prestige from; by helping post-Soviet women, Turkish men could vicariously gain a sense of being modern and in some way upstanding as they maintained liaisons with the women. Just as intimate economies are defined and sustained within specific imaginaries and structures of power elsewhere in the world (Wilson 2004; Cheng 2007), in Istanbul waning socialist ideals, cultural imaginaries of secularism and Islam in Turkey, and new configurations of class mobility have come together to shape intimate economies.

These intimate economies were formed in two primary spaces, that of trade and the domestic realm. Postsocialist shuttle traders initially came to Laleli and encountered shopkeepers, sometimes Kurds who had relocated their trade as a result of Turkish state counterterrorism in eastern Turkey and later, in 1995, the first Iraq War (Shankland 2003; Yükseker 2004).[6] As members of a marginalized and politicized minority group, Kurdish men I met described being drawn to post-Soviet women for their beauty and education but also for their origins in the FSU, a place where a sizable Kurdish diaspora resides, and a place historically sympathetic to Kurdish diasporas.[7] One of my interlocutors even pointed to what she saw as a common political sensibility between herself and her Kurdish boyfriend, explaining, "He is a former socialist."

Within spaces of domestic employment middle- and upper-class Turks, most likely not identifying as Kurdish, also encounter post-Soviet women migrants. Turks have come to desire "Moldovans" as, irrespective of ethnicity, they tend to refer to Russian-speaking women who are employed in domestic labor (Keough 2015). As Leyla Keough explains, Moldovans working as domestics in Istanbul, many of whom identify as Gagauz, are valued for being "European, professional, educated, modern, clean, cultured and hard workers ... visible markers of a modern home" (2015, 123). Keough shows how women employed in domestic work evoke in Turks "cultural ideas based on their views of modernity" (2015, 99), views which simultaneously frame Moldovans as "white" and "Westernized" and, therefore, very likely "over sexed." This tension between being considered ideal workers and being feared, and sometimes desired, for embodying expressions of sexuality associated with Westernized, modern ideals encapsulates how Russian-speaking migrant women were widely perceived in Turkey during my research. While stereotypes would position these women as if their gender ideals and sentiments about sexuality were static, in fact, they have been forged over time.

Sex/Gender Systems: Masculinity, Femininity, Sexuality

The post-Soviet setting from which many women are migrating has seen radical shifts in what Gayle Rubin termed the "sex/gender system" (1975), or the way in which biological selves fit with social systems and gender expectations. As in other East European countries defined by state socialism, in the Soviet Union women were defined in a professional sense as working for the state and building state socialism, while still shouldering the primary responsibility of caring for families (Ashwin 2000; Gal and Kligman 2000). In part due to the disjuncture between ideology and reality, official policies of gender equality were one of the first tenets of an earlier era to come under attack in the popular culture of the late 1980s and early 1990s (Posadskaia 1994; Kay 2006; Hemment 2007). Likewise, by the late 1980s the decades of socialist discourse that sought to contain public discussion of eroticism and of the aesthetics of everyday life was also widely being critiqued. It became commonplace to encounter "erotica" (especially featuring women) in the media and public space and for men and women to freely reflect on sexuality (Attwood 1990; Kon 1995; Goscilo and Lanoux 2006); one of the most referenced examples of this new ethic was the blockbuster film *Interdevushka*, that portrays the life of a nurse turned foreign-currency sex worker (Kunin 1991).[8] By the late 1990s counterdiscourses across the region emerged, emphasizing that women should aspire to their "natural" roles and domestic spaces (Pine 2002b; Thelen 2003). This went along with a sharp binary gender model in which women were to be protected, appreciated, and supported by men and no longer defined by their roles in socially productive work (Temkina and Rotkirch 1997).

Likewise, the prevailing sex/gender system within urban Turkey has undergone dramatic change since the 1980s. A range of feminist scholars have reflected on the ways patriarchy has shaped the society (e.g., Kandiyoti 1988b; Ozyegin 2015), including how queer and trans communities have experienced a dominant sex/gender system (e.g., Zengin 2013, 2016). Gul Ozyegin's work is especially useful in thinking about the relationships of urban Turkish men to post-Soviet women. Based on research among upwardly mobile young adults who were born in the 1980s, Ozyegin writes of how in the first part of the 2000s youth struggled to "renounce the [dominant] model of selfless femininity and protective masculinity," while remaining connected to the "social relations, identities, and histories"—what she calls "connectedness"—that defined their lives (2015, 3). Ozyegin notes major trends shaping how gender and sexuality were experienced in Turkey in the early 2000s, namely by: the diminishing power of a paternalistic state governing economic and civic life; the growing Islamization of the public sphere; and Turkey's bid to become part of the European Union (2015, 4). Within the context of these three broad trends, Ozyegin examines how upwardly mobile young men were renegotiating the relationship between selfhood and masculinity.

Ozyegin outlines forms of masculinity her consultants inherited from their fathers, which she calls "protective masculinity," and considers how the majority

FIGURE 17.   Women fishing off the Galata Bridge. Photograph by Jared Bloch, 2009.

of men she interviewed resisted this form of masculinity, instead looking to other ways of shaping a masculine self. Nevertheless, she argues that "facades" make it possible for upwardly mobile young men to appear to refute "patriarchal constructions of masculinity as controlling and dominant while [in fact, still] exercising gender domination" (2015, 5). Based on interviews with twenty-two men, Ozyegin traces the feminine ideals that upwardly mobile men held, which revolved around a dichotomy. On the one hand, men identified potential girl-friends as "ambitious," "charismatic," and what they called, "selfless" women who were willing to support men's egos and the development of their selfhood and ambitions. On the other hand, they also identified potential girlfriends as being "selfish" women who were independent and focused on realizing their own ambi-tions (2015, 109). Ozyegin convincingly shows how heterosexual young men in her study were drawn to both types of women. "Selfish" women who are per-ceived as modern, affirm men's need for recognition, attesting that the men are progressive and able to refute ideas of "protective," dominating masculinity, while "selfless" or positive women encourage men, support them, and reinscribe ties to social norms, including around gender and dominant masculinity (2015, 120). Ozyegin found that while men overwhelmingly voiced a *desire* for partners who were independent and pursued their own needs, men were mostly *in* relationships with women who affirmed their egos, acting with "maternal selflessness."

As Turkish men are negotiating what forms of masculinity to embrace in their lives, post-Soviet women have been widely faced with what some scholars have called "a crisis of masculinity" in their home communities. This is thought to be one of the key reasons that Russian-speaking women engage in transnational marriage migration (Luehrmann 2004; Patico 2010). Jennifer Patico examines how a crisis of masculinity compels Russian-speaking women to seek out mar-riage especially with North American and West European men in an effort to become "more positively valued and evaluated" (2010, 19).[9] Patico notes that women turned to international marriage services to look for husbands because they had struggled in home communities of Belarus and Russia to find husbands who would be financially stable, sober, and not abusive, but also to find hus-bands who would provide for them both materially *and* emotionally (2010, 25). Some women also recounted that they found the more gender-egalitarian atti-tudes in the domestic realm, especially among American and Canadian men, to be appealing. Patico points to the need to consider the intertwining of eco-nomic and emotional concerns that contribute to the appeal of foreign spouses for Russian-speaking women (2010, 32). Significantly, Patico goes on to examine how a certain "crisis of masculinity" in the United States is another crucial part of the story explaining why American men and Russian-speaking women find each other appealing; the American men perceive an erasure of gender differences as central to contemporary calls for gender equality in North America, and they see American women as too often lacking femininity and "family orientation" but also too materially concerned and self-centered (2010, 38). Russian-speaking women, who often find normative family arrangements unattainable in the conditions of economic strain in the former Soviet Union, look to marriages with Western men to fulfill aspirations for attaining their ideal families. As Patico concludes, both Western men and post-Soviet women are looking to be "differently valued, differently desirable, and differently competitive" (2010, 40).

The intersecting sex/gender systems Patico examines as key in drawing Russian-speaking women and North American men to one another, significantly resonate with the relationships I observed between Russian-speaking migrant women and Turkish men. These relationships seem to enact a "protective masculinity" enabled by a certain interlocking of Turkish men's desires for women they can care for, with post-Soviet women's search for men who can provide materially and emotionally for them. The particular configurations of Turkish masculinity, shaped by what Ozyegin sketches as ideal female partners being either "selfless" or "selfish," also seem to temper how Turkish men widely encounter Russian-speaking women migrants. Post-Soviet women labor migrants embody an ideal combination of characteristics; they seem to appeal to some Turkish men in combining features of "selfless" and "selfish" women. Post-Soviet women migrants are desired for being educated, savvy in wielding their sexuality, and independent but could also be seen to simultaneously massage male egos and fulfill what Ozyegin describes as men's need to affirm dominance through performing roles as providers.

Many post-Soviet women migrants I came to know in Istanbul drew on their intimate relationships with Turkish men to help them sustain their social ties with their children, grandchildren, and parents (and more rarely spouses) across time and space, as well as sometimes to sustain themselves emotionally. And while some women relied on men to smooth their residency status by arranging marriages of convenience, a practice that could provide financial security, women's relationships with Turkish men were also part of their place-making efforts in Istanbul. Thus distinct intimate practices permeated the transnational circuits maintained by post-Soviet women labor migrants.

Secularism, Islamists, and Signs of Modernity

In the "market war over identities" that emerged as the moderate Islamist Justice and Development Party (AKP) came to power in 2002, secularist and Islamist-identified Turks reaffirmed their deeply held beliefs; in some ways commodities signified modernity for both groups. For years the portrait of Mustafa Kemal

Atatürk, the founder of the Turkish Republic, acted as a "secularist" commodity, where not only in government spaces but also in households and commercial sites images of the former leader were prominently displayed.[10] These images were meant to showcase allegiance to ideals of "militant" secularism that were enshrined in public discourse and institutions by the founder of the Turkish Republic; the images also heralded Turkey's transformation into a modern, secular society, proclaiming itself as no longer impeded by religion (Reynolds 2011, 260).[11] In a similar manner, the *türban*, or newly fashioned bright headscarf worn by an increasing number of Turkish women since the 1990s, has signaled a religious modernity for many Islamists, where women's modesty is key (Navaro-Yashin 2002, 229–38). These signifiers of very different modernities have remained salient as the tension between secular and Islamist allied segments of society has intensified along with the steadily increasing support for the Justice and Development Party.

The AKP's support since the early 2000s springs, in part, from being the first Islamist party in the history of the Turkish state to become a ruling party and to address recurrent concerns of marginalization raised by religious proponents and more economically marginalized segments of the population. However, the AKP has also gained popularity because of Prime Minister Erdoğan's ability to rally populist sentiment that castigates "secularists," as well as a wide array of others who do not support the AKP (e.g., Kurds, atheists, Alevis, feminists, leftists, etc.) (Hansen 2017).[12] The AKP positions itself as religiously moderate but nevertheless in opposition to the paradigm of Kemalist secularism that has defined the country since the establishment of the Republic in 1923. The AKP has embraced ideals of a free market economy and, intermittently, accession to the EU, along with firm renegotiation of the relationship of the secular state to religious practice, including in regard to gender ideals. For instance, in 2011 the AKP prevailed in passing legislation making it legal for women to wear headscarves in most state institutions, such as universities, except not as employees in government offices; in 2013 this "democratization package" legislation was extended to encompass nearly all state institutions, and in 2016 it was extended to the police force (Taşpınar 2012; Turkey Allows 2016).

Expressions of support for Islamist ideals in the form of gendered codes of modesty contrast starkly with the increasingly visible markers of liberal ideals around sexuality and desire that widely defined secular urbanite Turkish women's sensibilities in the early 2000s (Öncü 1999; Potuoğlu-Cook 2006), as well as Russian-speaking migrant women's sensibilities.[13] The context of Turkey, specifically Istanbul, is a reminder that the politics of place critically shape how people envision possible gender roles and ideals, and how they understand sexuality and desire (White 1999; Öncü 2002, 171). With the influx of migrants in the late 1990s, Turkish men and Russian-speaking women began to forge distinctive structures of intimacy revolving around perceptions of each other's sexuality. Women in the shuttle trade and those living and working for years in Istanbul encountered the logics of intimacy defining them as potentially sexually available. Deniz Yükseker (2004) argues that post-Soviet wholesale buyers made the most of these logics and drew on forms of "strategic intimacy," including a wide array of flirtatious interactions, to secure favorable prices on the merchandise they exported home.

During my research marginalized, low-wage labor migrants also engaged in forms of strategic intimacy, albeit with more long-term aims that went well beyond securing favorable pricing for merchandise. Unlike for the traders, the ability of women labor migrants to work beyond the term of their one- or two-month tourist visa was tied to their ability to negotiate intimacy. While skills in negotiating sexual innuendo grease the business exchanges Yükseker (2004) describes and are generally a form of reciprocal exchange, the forms of intimacy that my interviewees sought out were fundamental to their long-term well-being and often blurred the divide between emotional and instrumental ties or between love and transaction. These intimacies could lead to secure housing, permanent residency, and substantial benefits for dependents, including those back home or those now making a living in Russia, but they could also lead to lasting relationships. These forms of intimacy emerged in a context of marginalization, where a large group of women turned to strategic intimacy to garner some security for their dispersed families. These strategies became especially important as Turkey began more systematic policing of migrant women from the former Soviet Union.

Of Marriage and Mobility

In 2004, after more than a decade of relatively open borders for citizens arriving from the former Soviet Union, the Turkish state began to tighten border controls. This followed on the heels of 2003 legislation that imposed restrictive measures on marriages between Turks and foreigners. With the passage of the law foreigners marrying Turkish citizens now had to endure a three-year waiting period before they were allowed to apply for citizenship, a process that included a rigorous in-person interview and, frequently, a visit to applicants' residences. The introduction of this legislation was widely viewed as "protecting" innocent Turkish men from Russian women who sought marriages of convenience (Hacaoğlu 2002). The wording of the law does not identify specific ethnic groups, but it appears to have emerged in response to public opinion vilifying women labor migrants from the former Soviet Union as "Natashas," or possible "prostitutes," often suspected of being "disease spreaders" who were scheming to gain Turkish citizenship (Béller-Hann 1995, 231–32; Hacaoğlu 2002).[14]

Just as prior to 2003 it was common for women migrants who were deported from Turkey to remarry in their home communities and thereby receive new passports issued with new surnames, it was also common for women migrants from the former Soviet Union to arrange a marriage of convenience to a Turkish citizen. As Polina, a woman working as a shop assistant told me: "In those days it was really simple and it cost nothing; I paid about $5 to a coworker in the late 1990s, and we got married. I did not see him again for twenty years, and I was able to get my residency and citizenship really quickly. These days it has become impossible!"[15] Nadia, who had worked as an entertainer told me, "I was lucky because I did my fake marriage at the right time and got my citizenship easily; that's why I could get my [property management] business established and even build a house for my mother back home." Unlike Polina, Nadia, and other women who arrived in the 1990s and early 2000s, those who arrived later could not rely on simply conducting an inexpensive business transaction to secure their legal status in Turkey. They had even more reasons to seek out long-term intimate relationships with Turkish men.

The marriages I heard about that women had contracted more recently often involved considerable sums and a boyfriend paying a third party for the arrangement. If in the past women could easily afford to pay for these arrangements themselves, with the increased policing of marriages between Turks and foreign women the costs rose. Because my consultants were usually romantically involved with married Turkish men, the arrangements for marriages of convenience typically involved financial compensation to a third party, often a student. The marriages I heard about in the mid-2000s involved women's lovers making payments of as much as $500 per year to "husbands" until women obtained their citizenship. Women relied on assistance from their romantic partners to facilitate their legal status; they first became temporary residents and, after three years and the requisite interview, if all went well they could become citizens (and get divorced).

Marriage and Intimate Liaisons through Time

Over the past 150 years, marriage as an institution has undergone significant transformations in Europe and North America and has shifted from an institution based on financial or familial obligation to one based on "companionate marriage" or marriage based on love (Hirsch and Wardlow 2006).[16] In late nineteenth-century Constantinople the same ideals became popular among elite segments of the population, and by the 1920s they circulated more widely (Başcı 2003).[17] Although marriages meant primarily to secure ties between families were commonplace in this period, discourses of "love" and "choice" had taken hold in relation to marriage (Duben and Behar 1991, 96–97). A dual standard, however, remained in which "decent women" could not have love affairs, while it was widely understood that men could have liaisons with concubines (*cariyes*) or prostitutes and have co-wives (Vergin 1985, 573; Duben and Behar 1991, 96; Başcı 2003). Concubines were often Circassians (from southern Russia) who worked as indentured servants in Constantinople homes, and some Ottoman men considered them desirable marriage partners and mistresses (Duben and Behar 1991, 145).[18] In the late nineteenth and early twentieth centuries, possibly in imitation of the Ottoman sovereign's prerogatives, high-ranking government officials sometimes had multiple wives. Even after Turkey instituted the 1925 marriage code, which legally enforced monogamous marriage, well into the 1960s, at least in Istanbul, it was not unheard of for more established men to have more than one wife (Duben and Behar 1991, 156).[19] Halide Edib, considered part of the Turkish literary canon, commented at the turn of the nineteenth and twentieth centuries that such arrangements reflected how "'modern' men of wealth, power, and status were not quite modern" (Başcı 2003, 156–57). It appears that with the heightened mobility of post-Soviet women, the practice of multiple marriages, or at least the desire to "keep" a woman, again raises questions about how ideals of modernity and intimacy relate to one another.

Post-Soviet women's mobility and the associated liaisons women form with Turkish men highlight how closely linked transnational border crossing is with shifting structures of intimacy in Turkey and, as a few scholars have argued, with shifting structures of intimacy in the former Soviet Union (Bloch 2003b; Luehrmann 2004; Patico 2010). According to Béller-Hann (1995), the arrival of Russian-speaking migrant women in northeastern Turkey in the 1990s evoked public concern about the degree of financial and emotional investment men made in these women and prompted the circulation of discourses on how post-Soviet women were destroying Turkish families. In the name of families, local feminist organizations called on government authorities to make it more difficult for post-Soviet women to cross into Turkey; according to these narratives Turkish men were drawn helplessly into the alluring arms of migrant women. From another perspective, however, these cross border liaisons echo what Nicole Constable has written about transnational intimacies as building on men's and women's "contradictory transnational fantasies, desires, and imaginings of marriage, tradition, and modernity" (2005, 3).

"Kept" Woman, Mistress, and Wife

While post-Soviet women migrants I met widely sought liaisons with Turkish men, these arrangements ranged from being "kept" women to wives to mistresses. The ways in which women positioned their relationships were closely linked to options back home, their visa status—that is, whether they were on temporary work visas, had overstayed a one- or two-month tourist visa, or had ever been deported—and their keen perception of themselves as sexualized bodies within Turkey. As Anna, a twenty-three-year-old exotic dancer from Ukraine who worked in Turkey on multiple contracts in nightclubs explained: "I agreed to being a 'kept' woman for my boyfriend once, but only for two months, not a day longer. I was bored stiff! He paid for my apartment, bought me clothes, everything, including $100/week spending money, but he expected me to be home all the time except when I went out for aerobics. It was unbearable!" This perspective on being "kept" was less typical for older women.

Being a "kept" woman was a status sought out by many women I met in their thirties and forties, who were often employed as sales assistants or domestic workers. For instance, Alexandra, a forty-two-year-old woman from Moldova who was employed as a domestic worker, told me that she wished her boyfriend (*drug*) would be willing to "keep" her. He did rent a modest apartment where they met once a week on her days off, but Alexandra lamented that her boyfriend was "afraid" of his wife so would not agree to fully support her. Other women, like Inna, a thirty-one-year-old woman from Belarus, described how she enjoyed being "kept" as a better alternative to unemployment at home or the low-paid, unglamorous employment as a domestic worker that could require travel to distant suburbs like Beykoz, or the exhausting job of a sales assistant in Aksaray or Laleli. Inna described how she was happy when she met her boyfriend Hassan and he courted her with presents of jewelry and nights on the town. When he offered to rent an apartment and provide spending money to cover her needs, Inna quit her job and took up the offer.

Negotiating Terms of Intimacy

In contrast to the Filipinas and Chinese Constable (2005, 169) writes about, or the marriages Patico (2010) discusses, where women sought to marry North American men in part as a means to "more egalitarian" relationships, the post-Soviet women I came to know generally saw their lives with Turkish men differently. They rarely spoke of their relationships in terms of equality but instead in terms of economic and legal stability, and sometimes romance. As Alexandra explained to me, "You can get by on just a job, but life is much easier with a man around; just about everyone I know has a Turkish boyfriend." Inna said, "All women like these nice things, a little perfume, a new dress, and some romance; we have a hard time getting these things at home where our men are often drinking, earn little money, and have forgotten about how to please women." Often a relationship with a Turkish man permitted women to send home larger remittances; bring mothers, children, or grandchildren for summer vacations to Turkey; and expand employment opportunities. Overall, women emphasized the idea of legal stability and financial support created through these ties, but emotional considerations factored in as well.

Although women spoke of the financial concerns that had driven them to seek work in Istanbul, discursively they often deemphasized a simple material exchange with men. They invoked the idea that men "help" (*pomogaiut*) them and their families and thereby pointed to the complexity of their relationships with Turkish men. One might argue that this could be a linguistic ploy by the women to make their situations feel more acceptable, but it was also common for Turkish men to be entangled in women's family obligations. For instance, in the role of "boyfriend," several men took part in attending and financing wedding celebrations for women's family members back home or working in Russia, while others, like Niki's boyfriend Ali, sponsored summer visits to Istanbul for women's mothers or children or traveled to Moldova and Russia for New Years' celebrations with women's families. In this way, many women described their boyfriends as fulfilling provider roles but also filling emotional, companionate, and sometimes physical needs. As one woman told me, "No one can live for years on end without human warmth; of course many of us seek out Turkish boyfriends."

Women's accounts often featured their mothers encouraging them to consider the benefits of living as Turkish men's mistresses. Raia, the woman whose portrait opened this chapter, explained that her mother back in Moldova advised her to pursue a relationship, saying, "Your heart might not feel anything now, but that can come with time." Raia reasoned that her decision must have been right; her boyfriend turned out to really care about her young son back home in Moldova and often gave her money to help Raia's mother care for him. Women and their families, or at least their mothers, were carefully weighing how ties to Turkish men could help ease the desperate material circumstances back home.

The forms of intimacy migrant women forge in their adopted countries, where they often work for years on end, are both strategic and potentially fostered by mutually appealing concerns where "love," "romance," and material benefit merge. Like other scholars blurring this line between "real" marriage practices and marriages of convenience and questioning the divide between "love" and instrumentality (Freeman 2007; Faier 2009), in the following portraits of post-Soviet women maintaining transnational circuits between Turkey and their homelands I consider how mobility, love, and intimacy intersect.

NIKI

When I was departing from Moldova in 2005, Nelli urged me to be in touch with her daughter, Niki, in Istanbul. When I phoned her, Niki invited me to visit her and explained how to take the suburban train from Aksaray out to her area. I exited the station and was met by an elegant young woman dressed in a crisp powder-blue linen suit. We went to sit in a park near Niki's apartment where young children played soccer and elderly couples were vigorously walking.

Niki recounted how she had come up against the Turkish state's restrictions on undocumented migrants. She arrived in Istanbul in 1996, when the economic devastation following the end of the Soviet Union made it impossible for her to make a living as a hairdresser. This, in addition to a failed marriage, gave her few means to support her five-year-old daughter. Leaving her daughter with her mother, Nelli, Niki drew on a contact in Vulcăneşti to find a job in a drugstore in Istanbul. After working there for less than a year, one of the male employees began sexually harassing her, and Niki left. Niki eventually secured work in a clothing store as a sales assistant, where she worked for over a decade but with significant effort on her part.

As Niki explained, in addition to employing her in 1997, the owner of the store, Ali, soon hired her brother. After nearly three years of working as a sales assistant, primarily serving as an interpreter for the Russian-speaking wholesalers shopping at the store, one day the police apprehended Niki and her brother and took them into custody. In court Niki and her brother pleaded that they were not working for the store but simply engaged in wholesale transactions of clothing to resell back in Moldova. The judge pressed them to explain why they were at the store on overstayed tourist visas. They said it was expensive for them to go back and forth, and they had combined a holiday with their business trip. In short, they testified that it was a mistake, but that they were not working for the store.[20] Partly because of Niki and her brother's loyalty and willingness to protect him, Ali was able to influence an official and avoid a hefty fine for hiring undocumented workers.[21] Niki and her brother were ultimately deported, and Ali paid for their way home to Moldova.

They had been home less than a month when Ali called to invite them back. Niki's brother did not want to return—he preferred instead to travel to Moscow for work—but Niki returned to Turkey, using a new passport issued in her maiden name. Niki resumed her old job and moved into an apartment that Ali had rented for her. Several years later, Ali arranged a marriage of convenience for Niki with a student he knew, and Ali and Niki waited for Niki's permanent residency to be processed.[22] In subsequent years Niki returned to Moldova almost yearly, and Ali accompanied her; he even attended Niki's brother's wedding. By 2009 Niki decided to quit her job at the store and remain at home in the apartment, explaining that while she could not be married to her "lover," she had converted to Islam as a sign of her devotion to him. (Notably, that same year, with Niki's residency application denied, it became dangerous for her to be visibly present at her former workplace.) The way that Niki spoke of her relationship over the years shifted between the terms "boss" (*khoziain*, in Russian or *patron*, in Turkish), "boyfriend" (in English), and "lover" (*liubovnik*, in Russian), suggesting the fluid nature of the relationship. Where initially Ali was simply an employer, over time he became a lover.

As with Niki's relationship, the long-term relationships many women have with Turkish men often involve reciprocal forms of care, emotional support, and leisure time spent together; not infrequently, women convert to Islam as a sign of their sincerity, and men take part in key ritual events in women's home communities. However, since the women rely so much on patronage in the form of financial support and sponsorship for fictive marriage arrangements, some troubling power imbalances also define these relationships. As in the narrative that follows, women rely on different logics at different points during their stay in Istanbul and women sometimes weigh the costs of contracting marriages, especially a "love" marriage.

MARIA: GAMBLING WITH "REAL" MARRIAGE

When Zina first introduced me to her friend in 2003, Maria was dressed in a leopard-skin patterned synthetic shirt, tightly fitting tan pants, and low pumps; this chic and rather sexily clad woman turned out to be a grandmother, sales assistant, and former radio technician, among other things. By 2009 Maria had worked in Istanbul for over fifteen years. She established herself as a sales assistant, helping wealthy Russian-speaking clients, like Ania, the successful shuttle trader, select clothing for resale in high-end boutiques back home. In 2003 Maria earned about $400 a month in salary, and by 2009 she earned about $800 per month.[23] In addition to this, each month she could count on several hundred dollars in tips and gifts from clients who appreciated her skill in selecting models of clothing that were in demand back in Russia. Maria considered herself lucky, but she struggled to cover expenses, including $150/month for rent, and regular remittances for her two young adult sons in Moldova, as well as for her daughter and two grandchildren living in Moscow.

In 2005 Maria decided to marry a man who was sixty-five, fifteen years her senior; soon after the marriage Maria moved in with her new husband, a retired shoemaker with a small pension that barely covered their rent. Maria explained to me, she had "fallen in love"; the marriage was not fake, but "real" (*nastoiashchii*), although Maria also later told me she left a younger lover for her future husband who was more likely to provide her with long-term material security. Several of

Maria's friends were skeptical of her motivations for marrying. Her close friend Zina, whose sister Eva had hosted me in Moldova, and who had worked as a domestic in Istanbul for fifteen years, reflected, "Everyone is anxious about securing housing and avoiding deportation, but Maria has *sold herself*!" (*prodalas'*). From Zina's perspective, Maria was forcing herself to ignore the boorish nature of her retired husband just to secure Turkish citizenship.

After several months Maria's friend Zina became even more outraged by the marriage, explaining: "He is home all day and does nothing! He has a miserly income. Maria is at work all day and comes home to a pile of dishes, to cooking, and cleaning. . . . Excuse me, but I would never agree to lie with that living corpse [*zhivoi trup*] in one bed! . . . how can Maria bear it, living with someone who does not respect her? He treats her like a servant!" Zina's critique hinged on her perception of the lack of real benefits to the marriage, either in material form or in the form of "true love" or even romance. However, Maria insisted she was "in love," and besides, she saved on rent, and this money could be sent to her daughter in Moscow and her sons in Moldova or saved for the house she was renovating back home in Moldova.

Zina simply refused to call this a "real marriage" (*nastoiashchii brak*). From her perspective, "a man should respect and pay attention to his wife; it is not simply that they are living together or sharing a bed, they should have basic human interactions, not like a living corpse, simply existing." She intoned that it was poor judgment for Maria to marry and wondered, "Why not simply work hard, and deal with the fines on exiting the country? What does she really get out of it?"[24]

As evident from this narrative, not all women agreed about the benefits of becoming involved with Turkish men. In castigating Maria for "selling herself" by contracting a "real marriage," Zina's commentary emphasizes the conundrum in which women find themselves. Older women especially have fewer men seeking to maintain them as "kept" women or mistresses, so contracting "fake" marriages paid for by boyfriends is difficult to arrange. Moreover, as reflected in Niki's narrative, since the mid-2000s marriages of convenience between Turks and post-Soviet women are stringently policed for what the state perceives as fraud. Securing residency status, and thereby the long-term possibility to work in Turkey, has become more difficult. In these circumstances, Zina judged Maria for getting married "for real" and dedicating her life to caring for someone just to secure her residency status.

Women frequently spoke of having more power from a position of an illicit relationship than they would in a "real marriage." The exchange they demanded for maintaining relationships was for Turkish men to contribute to their material well-being. Remittances, goods, and better earning power are all part of the intimate circuits women seek to foster through the relationships with Turkish men. "Real" marriage curtails this form of power since women are no longer bargaining with men; once married, women tend to find themselves constrained by the rules of relationships that position them as providing domestic labor—cooking, cleaning, and washing—without remuneration and potentially without meaningful intimacy. As Alexandra quipped when I asked if she would ever consider marrying her Turkish boyfriend, "Well, like them all, he's already married. Besides, he makes a much better lover than a husband."

A focus on intimacy as central to transnational migration highlights how gender matters to the study of migration. First of all, sex/gender systems shape the intimate practices of migrants. In the case of post-Soviet women migrants, they depart from countries where public discourse is widely defined by post-Soviet gender ideals positioning women as in need of men's protection and sponsorship. Once in Turkey, post-Soviet women encounter the widespread public imagination of "Russian" women in the region as sexualized others who live physically distant from close family members for months on end. Women like Raia, Niki, and Maria find themselves turning to relationships with Turkish men both as a means of seeking out "human warmth" while they live long-term in Istanbul, as one consultant explained, and as the only tangible means of potentially securing residency in Turkey. Thus in this case gender matters, as women are keenly aware of how their prospects for safeguarding long-term transnational mobility are very much defined by intimate relationships with Turkish men.

Migrants enmeshed in shifting structures of feeling and constrained by immigration and citizenship regimes in receiving countries draw on intimate relationships to enable their roles as providers for households back home, but also sometimes to fulfill their own needs for meaningful relationships. By considering intimate practices of migration both in material terms and in terms of reciprocal emotional exchange, perhaps we come closer to portraying migrants' experiences. Post-Soviet migrant women engage in intimacy with Turkish men in a context defined by the Turkish state but also by shifting gender ideals in Turkish society. In a way, migrant women are engaged in a set of nested intimacies where many women draw on relationships to better funnel remittances to loved ones in home communities, but like Niki they also sometimes fall in love in Turkey. Not unlike other cases of "love," here the line between "love," or emotional ties, and material security is one that blurs and shifts over time, but especially when women spend years on end without legal status in Turkey.

Public policy in Turkey continues to define migrant women's intimate practices. As of 2017 the Justice and Development Party was firmly entrenched as the ruling party in Turkey, and it has continued measures to circumscribe migrants' options by stepping up police raids on clubs, where some undocumented post-Soviet women work, and increasing sweeps of public spaces where post-Soviet migrant workers from diverse backgrounds gather after work and on their days off. With few other means of regularizing their status, the state continues to indirectly push women to seek increased economic security in the form of intimate relationships. While undocumented post-Soviet migrants continue to work and live in Istanbul, as in other metropoles of the EU, Asia, and North America, their lack of avenues to a regularized, if not permanent, status significantly shapes the ways they forge intimacies in a precarious world.

INTIMATE CURRENCIES

Love, Romance, and Sex "without Hang-ups"

In 2000, when I was staying in a hotel in Istanbul at the edge of Taksim Square one evening I was in the lobby just before 7 p.m. I was surprised to encounter two separate groups of young women who appeared to be from the former Soviet Union; they were joking with one another in Russian and touching up makeup, apparently waiting for their friends to join them. When they departed, I asked the hotel clerk if they got many Russian customers, and he laughed disparagingly, saying, "Those girls, they are just dancers!" As I learned the following day, from one of the dancers in the "Ukrainian" group, the young women gathered nightly just before departing for the nightclub around the corner so they could arrive at the club as a unified entertainment troupe. Far from being "just dancers," these women provide a portal onto how intimate economies are being remade in Eurasia as women differentially capitalize on their sexuality "without hang-ups" (*bez kompleksov*) and also activate intimate currencies of love and romance.

The entertainment industry, in which young women from the former Soviet Union readily find employment in Turkey, is at the crux of this chapter, along with young women's accounts of their experience working as entertainers in Istanbul in the early 2000s. Here I refer to the women interchangeably as "dancers" (*tantsory*), the term women used to refer to themselves, and "entertainers," a term widely found in literature examining similar types of work revolving around women employed in nightclubs with male clienteles (Tyner 1996; Cheng 2010). In portraying the lives of the post-Soviet dancers I met between 2000 and 2007, I show how they negotiate their insertion into one sphere of global capitalism, where their aspirations for mobility are tightly entwined with a shifting politics of sexuality, as well as constrained by states' border regimes. Even as dancers maintain close transnational ties with home, they strive to realize cosmopolitan selves. In contrast to a literature that frames women working as exotic dancers and in other forms of sexualized labor as uniquely victimized by this form of labor (Erokhina 2000; Hughes 2000; Malarek 2003), I draw on feminist scholars writing about the "intimate services economy" and sex work (Agustín 2006; Bernstein 2007a; Cheng and Kim 2014) to consider how post-Soviet women draw on intimate currencies of love, romance, and sex "without hang-ups" as one means of realizing transnational mobility.

Intimate Currencies and Club Life

One afternoon in 2002 Kara, an entertainer who was halfway through her six-month contract, was interested in practicing her English and invited me for tea. I walked up the several flights of stairs to her room and found Kara painting her nails in preparation for her evening's work; she motioned for me to take a seat on one of the three single beds. She had taped handwritten notes with conversational English and Turkish phrases to the wall next to her bed; she laughed and said these were study aids for her work since the more she could converse with clients, the better chance she had of increasing her nightly pay. As clients' bar tabs grew, her cut increased.

Kara explained that she was on her first contract as an entertainer and had sought out this work in frustration over the low pay available back home in Ukraine. In her first job as a telephone operator, a month's work resulted in no more than $20. In the other jobs she had attempted—for instance, in a local market, where she would freeze standing outside in winter selling clothing shuttled by her boss from Turkey—she could earn only $1/day.[1] At the end of the six-month stint in Turkey, Kara was planning on renewing her contract; she was saving money to help send her eighteen-year-old brother to college and to get her mother a visa to work in Italy.

Like several other entertainers, Kara had tried to arrange a marriage through an Internet matchmaking service before seeking work abroad. She corresponded with three men for several months, and for a brief period she dreamed of marrying a man from "that place where a lot of automobiles are made": Detroit, Michigan. In the end, having her letters translated and constantly updating her file with the marriage service was too expensive to keep up; besides, she explained, "It was a silly dream to think that someone else would solve my problems."

In 2001 Kara turned to possibilities for working abroad and visited every European consulate in Kiev to learn about temporary work visa requirements.

Everywhere she checked required fluency in English or a local language to issue a visa. Kara also looked into arranging work in Italy through a semiofficial network of friends and acquaintances, but she learned that this would cost a minimum of $350, and she did not have the money. Turkey was the last resort, a place where everyone knew you could arrange a visa to work in a club without any significant expense, and without knowing Turkish or any other foreign languages.

When I visited with Kara that afternoon, she brought out her photo album, filled with snapshots taken during her time in Turkey. The post-Soviet entertainers I met often flipped through their photo albums full of images taken during expeditions to the beach, birthday celebrations, and special evenings, like New Year's at the club. Similar to Filipinas working as entertainers in South Korea (Cheng 2010, appendix), many post-Soviet entertainers documented their time abroad through the photo albums; these served as a testament to their adventures and allowed women to demonstrate to friends and family their ability to take part in a more cosmopolitan world of Istanbul. Although this could be tricky, as Kara noted, because not everyone knew she was working as a dancer, and in sharing her photographs, she would have to admit to them that she had not been in Italy cleaning houses. Kara's album contained many images of her and other dancers at the *kazino*, as she referred to the club where they performed nightly.[2] Kara flipped through images of a day at the beach, dinner out with her most recent Turkish boyfriend, and a New Year's celebration at the club where she was pictured in a white, sequin-laden costume. Here she paused and noted that her costume was wearing out after months of performances, and besides she had gained nearly ten pounds since she arrived in December, so her costume no longer fit as her mother had designed it. Kara laughed with self-deprecation, "*Tantsory!* [Dancers!] We're supposed to be dancers, but look at us trying to be glamorous!" She added, "But this work is okay; compared to the dreariness of home, it is like a vacation [*otpusk*]."

In embracing new ways of expressing and performing sexuality, including through pursuit of glamour and related currencies of intimacy, entertainers like Kara sought financial independence and a claim to being modern, mobile subjects (Chu 2010). Unlike post-Soviet shuttle traders or domestic workers and shop assistants in Istanbul, entertainers—who were generally women migrants in their twenties—were largely unconflicted about embodying a sexual persona, putting this to use in their repertoire of "mobility capital" (Dahinden 2010, 330). Post-Soviet women are situated within a long history of "Russian" women as cultural others in Turkey, but they are also products of a particular cultural formation, a socialist one, with resonances in a contemporary time.

In contrast to a much more familiar narrative of women's experiences of mobility in this part of Eurasia as one of victimization at the hand of traffickers (e.g., Malarek 2003), I trace instead how women like Kara often saw their aspira-tions for mobility as impeded by states. Women, and especially younger women, have become subject to forms of control that intensified as states sought to respond to a concern with trafficking in humans. In the case of Turkey, when the US Department of State rated Turkey as a "3" (2002) and then a "Provisional 2" (2003) in the annual Trafficking in Persons (TIP) report, and as Turkey was assessed for potential accession to the EU in the early 2000s, there were significant implica-tions for migrants. The Turkish government was pressured to intensify policing of its borders and turn attention to any women who could have been trafficked, including by conducting bar raids and detaining suspected sex workers.[3] More-over, long before these international pressures to increase the policing of borders and public space, for decades Turkey had regulated those it perceived as pos-ing a public health danger (Şimşek et al. 2004).[4] In this chapter I examine how entertainers negotiate various mechanisms of control, as they capitalize on intimate currencies to pursue their aspirations in Turkey.

In invoking a focus on "intimacy," I aim to portray something of how daily experience, interpersonal exchanges, and larger social structures are shaped by forces of global capitalism. As Ara Wilson (2012) has argued, drawing on a concept of "intimacy" enables us to address shifts in both "domestic" spheres and "public" spaces that are linked to the forms agency can take. The story of post-Soviet women working in Istanbul nightclubs is, in part, the story of some Turkish men's desires for what they imagine to be cosmopolitan forms of sexuality meeting up with post-Soviet women's desires to engage with cos-mopolitan spaces. As I show, women seek out work as entertainers, in part, to pursue dreams of modernity, and Turkish men frequent the clubs where these women work in an effort to feed desires for sexual (or at least sexualized) encounters with "modern," exotic women. Similar to Leiba Faier's (2009) work on Filipinas and their relationships with rural men in Japan, my focus is on an "encounter" that in many ways hinges on aspirations for and understand-ings of modernity. Post-Soviet women entertainers wield what they call their sexuality "without hang-ups" (*bez kompleksov*) as a sign of their modernity but also as a sort of intimate currency that facilitates their mobility. Women seek to benefit from men's financial expenditures, and women make strategic use of the forms of power they embody by presenting themselves as sexually "lib-erated," relatively well educated, and phenotypically "white" in urban centers where these qualities are in demand.

Overall, this chapter examines the prevailing tensions entertainers face around expressions of sexuality and intimacy, and I consider how women think about their work in the entertainment industry as linked to independence, romance, and being worldly, three things they often see as impossible in their home countries.

Socialism, Sexuality, and Intimacy

While mobility is central in bringing post-Soviet women into the purview of a Turkish male gaze, as Nicole Constable compellingly argues in her work on correspondence marriage between North American men and Filipinas and Chinese women, such encounters do not simply happen but are forged within concrete historical contexts, or "sites of desire," that are shaped by "personal circumstances, personality, imagination, [and] serendipity," but also by distinct histories (2003, 28). Post-Soviet women's imaginaries of Turkey and Turkish men are shaped, on the one hand, by popular narratives, such as those featured prominently in telenovelas such as *The Magnificent Century*, and by contemporary debates around gender, sexuality, and secularism in Turkey. On the other hand, they are also shaped by Soviet discourses around modernity involving sexuality, gender, and intimate encounters.

As labor migrants, post-Soviet women encounter a Turkish public sphere tempered by Turkish models of modernity as well as reactions to secular Turks' efforts to transform society since the early twentieth century. When the women I met commented on the headscarves Istanbullu women sometimes wore or conversions to Islam among their post-Soviet acquaintances, they rarely registered the ways their observations were grounded in a particular historical moment in Turkey where Islamist concerns have increasingly shaped public culture. Instead, they often framed themselves in contrast to Islamist women, implicitly categorizing themselves as "modern" or "civilized" people, different from the dominant population of Turks. Less often women had a more nuanced understanding of the politics involved. For instance, Polina, a woman from Ukraine who worked as a shop assistant, made reference to the legacy of socialism as shaping the performance of gender and related ideals; when I asked her about veiling and how her Turkish boyfriend viewed this, she said: "He would not agree with this; he certainly would not want me to be veiled. He is not like the rest, he is Alevi and a former socialist." In this way, Polina signaled her understanding of the diversity of Turkish communities, including how Kurdish, and specifically Alevi Kurdish, community ideals might differ from dominant ones and the ways that veiling fits within broader political debates.[5] Whether or not women explicitly discussed the history of socialism and its positioning around gender and sexuality, a common legacy informs the collective identity of postsocialist women migrants.

Sexuality and Intimacy: From the Revolution to Domostroika

The first years after the Russian Revolution promised a radical departure from the gender regimes that prevailed in Europe in the early twentieth century—a departure that envisioned a society where women would be freed from the demands of domestic space, so they could become citizens on par with men. Social theo-rists and political strategists debated how women's insertion into wage labor and the "withering" of the family would enable women to contribute to a socialist, and ultimately communist, society of equals. This vision of a radically differ-ent gender order—sometimes including an ideal of "free love," where sexuality would not be constrained by the institution of marriage—was widely discussed by key social theorists of the time, such as Alexandra Kollontai (2008).[6] With the revolution in 1917 the Bolsheviks took the first steps to bringing about their radical social vision of gender equality; they established civil marriage and made it possible for either spouse to initiate divorce, and soon afterward they legalized abortion and did away with the idea of "illegitimate" children. The enactment of the 1918 Code on Marriage, the Family, and Guardianship forged the pos-sibility for fundamental change by sweeping away "centuries of patriarchal and ecclesiastical power" and bringing about a new era focused on individual rights and gender equality (Goldman 1993, 49). Organizations such as the *Zhenotdel* (Women's Department of the Bolshevik Party), which Kollontai cofounded and headed for two years (1920–1921), aimed to educate women in the new laws gov-erning marriage, divorce, and work and to create the conditions where men and women would contribute to and rely on society, instead of the family, including for raising children (Goldman 1993, 2–10; Kirschenbaum 2001).

In the wake of the utopian gender ideals of the 1920s, a much more conserva-tive set of ideals became enshrined in law by the 1930s. As the number of street children and levels of social chaos grew in the aftermath of economic restructur-ing in the 1920s, the family became a key part of the state's efforts to control its citizenry. In one scholar's words, the state focused on a "repressive strengthening of the family unit" (Goldman 1993, 327) as intrinsic to a new era of social reform. The pendulum swung back toward conservative understandings of marriage, the family, and sexuality and the "withering away" of the family doctrine of an earlier era was negated; as a culmination of the gradual reorientation of dominant poli-cies throughout the 1920s, in 1930 the Zhenotdel was disbanded. As pronatalism and profamily discourses permeated society, in 1936 abortion was once again made illegal, and the idea of "illegitimate" children was again enshrined in law. The Soviet state offered women a "bargain," whereby men would be compelled to support families (including in the form of alimony), but women would need to both take part in the labor force and continue to produce future workers, with-out an option of abortion and with significantly less provision for state support than early visionaries had imagined (Goldman 1993, 336). As Wendy Goldman evocatively writes, "Stalinist policy toward the family was a grotesque hybrid: rooted in the original socialist vision, starved in the depleted soil of pov-erty, and ultimately deformed by the state's increasing reliance on repression"

(1993, 342). Marxist revolutionary ideals maintained a focus on drawing women into the workforce, but this was now seen as crucial for the rapid industrialization of the Soviet Union and no longer linked to ideals of women's "liberation" or the radical vision of "free love."

Depending on the source, very different portraits of Soviet sexuality emerge. According to Anna Rotkirch, the "repressive" period in regard to family and sexuality extended from the 1930s to the 1960s, followed by a period of what she calls "domestication" (1960s through the late 1980s) (2004a, 96). Drawing on autobiographies of people defined by key turning points in sexual culture in Russia, Rotkirch writes of three "sexual generations": those born prior to the Second World War, those born after the war and up to the early 1970s, and those born after the early 1970s. Rotkirch defines the pre-Second World War generation as being defined by "sexual silence" (2004a, 96) and "repression," when there was no accepted space for public discourse on sexuality, abortion was illegal (1936–1955), divorce became difficult, and children born out of wedlock were again stigmatized. Although marriage was not widely seen as a prerequisite to sexual liaisons, sexuality was something to be contained within the private space of a heterosexual, committed relationship.

Rotkirch describes the next sexual generation as the generation of "learned ignorance," and she describes people of this generation as being relatively uninformed about sexuality (2004a, 103). As she explains, the term "sex" (*seks*) entered popular and more official language, but there was still limited information about sex circulating in Soviet society, and most of it was prescriptive in nature: for instance, focused on proper "sex roles" for boys and girls, or warning teenagers of the supposedly unhealthy effects of masturbation. Rotkirch emphasizes the lack of "sexual revolution" in this period, but others describe this generation as treating sex as a site of resistance to, or at least avoidance of, Soviet power. For instance, Dmitry Shlapentokh writes, "[In the 1970s] sexuality was still one of the few activities in which one could engage without direct supervision of the state and this could explain why Soviet citizens of Brezhnev's era engaged in uninhibited sexual practices" (2003, 120). Vladimir Shlapentokh writes how under Stalin, love was a "refuge," but how especially post-Stalin people could "let themselves go emotionally" with love and sex (1989, 177). The very different analytical approaches of these scholars, with one focused on lack of information about sex and the others pointing to "uninhibited sexuality" defining a 1970s generation, suggests that even within generations there were divergent experiences of sexuality, including those based on gender, geography, social hierarchy, and probably moral community (e.g., Muslim, Christian, or secular).

By the late 1980s in the Soviet Union public culture around intimate practices was rapidly changing and people much less frequently associated sex with marriage or long-term relationships. The popular press and media provided strong evidence of this shift as it began to openly criticize the poor availability of birth control and the presence of street prostitution (Gessen 1995). An "unbridled" sexual economy following the end of the Soviet Union is pegged by some as being a reaction to the pervasive ethic in grandparents' and parents' generations, where there was a clear separation between, on the one hand, state-enforced "family values," and on the other, the realm of the erotic (Kon 1993, 24; Shlapentokh 1989, 177). In this new milieu a language of sexuality became increasingly commonplace, with a plethora of sources ranging from families as sources of information to self-help books to psychotherapy to media portrayals to a federal sex education program instituted countrywide in high schools by the late 1990s (Gessen 1995; Rotkirch 2004a, 108). The overall result was a widespread ease in discussing sexuality, as well as a sense of sexual knowledge, and the ability for youth, albeit more often in urban settings, to articulate reflections on sexuality.

"Sexuality without Hang-ups"

Indeed, many young women migrants I met in Istanbul who came of age in the late 1990s and in the early 2000s expressed a sense of sexuality as something to be embraced, as an integral aspect of what made them modern young people. Young women frequently spoke of their lives in a positive light as embodying an ideal of "unrepressed" sexuality or sexuality without "hang-ups." One telling exchange between roommates—Zina, who was no longer cleaning the hotel but working as a domestic in three different houses, and Raia, the Moldovan migrant whose mother encouraged her to accept her boyfriend's advances—reflects this sexual ethic inflected by generation:

> ZINA: Do you really want to wear those short shorts out on the street [on the way to work as a shop assistant in Istanbul]? I bet you would not even wear them at home to go shopping!
> RAIA: I'll wear a long jacket when I go out for work, but actually, at home [in Gagauzia] I have no problem wearing these shorts [amused laugh].
> ZINA: Even to pick up your son at day care?
> RAIA: I don't really think anything of it; I don't have any hang-ups.

Unlike the older women in their forties and fifties who were working as shuttle traders, shop assistants, or domestics, the younger women, sometimes working as entertainers but also in the same spheres as older women, were explicit about their ease with sexuality. Sometimes young women also emphasized how their sense of sexuality set them apart from both older post-Soviet women and Turkish women. This widespread view among younger women migrants of ideal sexuality as being "without hang-ups" was reinforced by common Turkish stereotypes of Russian-speaking women in general. When women travel to Istanbul for work, usually living without family, husbands, or children for months on end, they can appear untethered from kinship networks and the demands of households and family and therefore be seen as sexually available. In her research among Gagauz domestics, Leyla Keough also notes how women from the former Soviet Union and Eastern Europe "transgress traditional Turkish codes of class and gender" and that they are perceived as "ambitious and driven women" and "morally loose or overly sexual" (2015, 106). Keough indicates that this perception is heightened by the association of Orthodox Christians with more overt sexuality than is assumed for other women in Turkey. Strikingly, popular Turkish sentiment and young post-Soviet women's sentiments converged on this idea that post-Soviet women embody sexual selves, something they both associate with a form of modernity. While Keough briefly analyzes sexualized selves as a double-edged sword, with some Turks finding it alluring and others repelled by it, younger post-Soviet women migrants I met also sought to capitalize on what they considered a sort of intimate currency.

Younger post-Soviet women especially perceived their ability to display what Anthony Giddens has called a "plastic sexuality," a critical element of their allure for Turkish men. Indeed, in public discourses in urban Turkey, post-Soviet women as a group are imagined as having the ultimate plastic sexuality, something that is enticing for some and imminently threatening to others. However, Giddens's definition of "plastic sexuality" as "decentered sexuality, freed from the needs of reproduction" (1992, 2) only describes sexuality as a fixed sociological phenomenon. The critical component of how women understand the power of their sexuality and the intimate practices in which they engage requires attention to the ways they foster intimacy over time but also in particular interactions.

Intimate Currencies in the Clubs

As early as the 1920s Turks and tourists seeking a night on the town have flocked to the central district of Taksim, where there is a concentration of "exotic," relatively upscale nightclubs. This region of the city is viewed as quintessentially modern Istanbul with shopping, high end hotels, chic cafes, and popular restaurants extending from the edge of Gezi Park and Taksim Square along the pedestrian zone of Istaklal Caddesi for nearly a mile to Tünel, where a historical funicular trundles down the steep incline to the mouth of the Golden Horn, just before it spills into the Bosphorus. The post-Soviet migrants I came to know did not generally spend time at the Tünel end of Istaklal Caddesi, but they often spent leisure time in and around Gezi Park, the site of the massive protests in 2013, which were set off by the city's plans to develop the park into a shopping mall.[7]

FIGURE 18. On Istaklal Caddesi, near Taksim Square. Photograph by Jared Bloch, 2009.

FIGURE 19. On the Golden Horn, looking toward Süleymaniye Mosque. Photograph by Jared Bloch, 2009.

This relatively rare green space in the densely populated Taksim district is also where I frequently brought my daughter to play in the spring of 2007, when we lived in the neighborhood, and where I sometimes arranged to meet entertainers for interviews at the tea garden, just minutes away from the nightclubs where they worked.

The nightclubs in this region generally cater to high-end guests, including foreign tourists, and they are known for featuring alluring dance numbers (Potuoğlu-Cook 2008). In the mid-1990s several became known for hiring post-Soviet women, who often performed in troupes of four to eight people, sometimes including men and women; women told me in 2007 that there were eleven similar night clubs along Istaklal that were hiring post-Soviet entertainers at the time. The owner of the hotel where the entertainers I came to know stayed told me that prior to the post-Soviet dancers, Polish women were hired, and before that, young British women. The entertainers frequently gossiped about the hotel owner's wife, a Polish woman who reportedly first arrived in Istanbul to work as an entertainer and then married one of her customers, the wealthy Turkish man who in 2011 continued to take part in the day-to-day business of the hotel. Similar to the "fairy tale" endings others have written about (Constable 2003; Cheng 2010), on almost a daily basis the dancers were faced with a living testament to the fact that one could work one's way up from a dancer to become an established, and perhaps even wealthy, businesswoman.

With entertainers living in the same hotel as I did, I was able to engage in ongoing discussions with them. Our interactions were sometimes casual—often while the women were preparing for work, applying makeup, fitting bras, or ironing costumes—but I also conducted twelve more formal interviews, as well as maintaining contact with three women, including Kara, for more than a decade. Over research visits spanning several years, I had multiple informal interactions with different groups of entertainers while we relaxed in the hotel lobby watching television, or while they practiced their dance routines, or while they tried out conversational English with me. In addition, by joining in on a number of outings, including on a weekend beach trip and shopping along Istaklal, and attending shows at two of the clubs where women danced, I learned something of their working lives and aspirations.

In many clubs, like the one where the women I met were employed, entertainers both danced and cajoled men to spend as much money as possible. Although some women purportedly engaged in selling sex, in the club context this was not their primary means of making a living. Instead, their pay consisted of a set minimum for each night, with additional pay earned for each "consummation" (*konsumatsiia*), a term entertainers widely used to refer to securing a customer to join them at a table. Furthermore, a "good" customer bought as many as ten (extremely overpriced) drinks, and women received a commission for each drink purchased. In 2007 one club manager explained that entertainers where he worked received $50 per night, as well as about $1.50 (2 lira) for each drink a customer bought; although this manager thought most dancers made at least an extra $100 in tips each night, none of the women I came to know had such earnings.[8] Entertainers recounted that their success on a given night depended on the effort they made with customers, but also on whether the show was adequately professional in its execution to appeal to customers and whether their managers directed potential customers to their tables.

The dancers I met in Istanbul did not speak of being coerced or deceived into taking on their work, although they did feel that they were paying unfair fees to the agencies that had arranged their visas and working contracts. Due to their contacts with previous migrants, women were mostly aware of the conditions they were to encounter on arriving in Istanbul, and many were on repeat contracts as entertainers or previously had worked abroad elsewhere. Ten of the fifteen entertainers I met in 2002 and 2005 were on their second and third six-month contracts as dancers in Turkey; at least two of the women had worked in Poland and the Czech Republic as seamstresses, and one woman had also worked as an entertainer in Greece and Lebanon, where she hoped to return soon because she could renew her tourist visa for up to four months at a time. None of the women had worked as shuttle traders, since they lacked the capital to initiate such a business, although some of them, like Kara, had worked as sales staff, selling wares at open-air markets for an employer. The entertainers generally spoke with disdain about working as vendors back home or domestics in Istanbul; such labor was viewed as far less glamorous and less lucrative than entertainment. Women aspired to upward mobility, which most of them equated with saving enough money to run their own garment import businesses and opening boutiques in their home communities.

For most women, this dream was a distant one. Their work involved long and odd hours—beginning around 7:00 p.m. and sometimes extending until 5:00 a.m.; in 2002 for their labor they typically earned around $450/month. However, after expenses, they could save barely $200/month. Still, this was significantly more than the $20–$50/month women could hope for back home working the unskilled jobs available at the time. After paying the monthly fees for accommodation, and the fee to their "manager" (*menedzher*) in home countries for arranging the contracts and travel expenses—about $400, paid over three months—they could count on a steady monthly income.[9] They had ongoing daily expenses—including for their costumes and makeup, not to mention food—however, based on their paychecks and tips from fans, several women I knew in 2005 claimed to have sent home $1,000 in remittances by the end of their six-month contracts. Those with additional sponsors or wealthy Turkish boyfriends were rumored to be sending $5,000 home in the same period.

FIGURE 20. Promotional flyer for a Taksim nightclub.

By 2007 average monthly pay had increased to nearly \$700/month and, while many aspects of the work had not changed, it is significant that dancers began to have more bargaining power.[10]

At least since the 1990s clubs have played a significant role as hosts to the flow of temporary migrant women from the FSU working in the entertainment sector in Turkey. An intermediary, who the entertainers called a "manager," was typically based in women's home countries of Ukraine, Belarus, or Russia and worked for a company that recruited women, made travel and visa arrangements, and, prior to women's departure, often ran basic training around routines women could potentially do together as a performance troupe (Bloch 2009). In 2002 a few women showed me their six-month work visas where type of employment was indicated as "ballerina"; they scoffed at the designation. Some of the entertainers did have training in ballet and other forms of dance, but they viewed themselves more as performers than ballerinas, something they tended to associate with high culture of the Soviet era.[11] Until 2005 the Turkish clubs arranged with the Turkish Ministry of Labor, and possibly the Ministry of Tourism, to issue six-month visas, and the clubs were also responsible for women obtaining the mandatory monthly medical exams, which included screening for sexually transmitted infections (STIs) and AIDS.[12] Several women I spoke with were especially outraged by these practices of policing their bodies, since they saw this as equating their work with that of "prostitutes" (*prostitutki*).

After 2005, when the six-month contracts were no longer available for dancers, clubs increasingly employed women on tourist visas who arrived without any intermediary making prior arrangements and without any performance troupe or "collective" (*kollektiv*). Women tried to establish performance troupes onsite, but this was difficult, especially as women had different levels of training in dance, and different tourist visa periods, for example, some for one month, some for two months.[13] As one entertainer explained, clubs also tried to avoid employing the same women for consecutive contracts; the club management said their clientele would get bored if women stayed too long at a club. However, entertainers suspected the constant shift of dancers was an arrangement between the clubs and the police, in part meant to prevent dancers from organizing and demanding better work conditions and pay. In interviews club managers affirmed that they had some arrangements with police; when police were paid off adequately and clubs operated according to parameters set out by them, raids were less frequent. Also, if there were raids, instead of sending post-Soviet women off to the Istanbul detention center for foreigners ("*yabancı şube*"), police were more likely to demand a modest "fine" and release the women. With bribes, fines, and a frequent rotation of dancers, the police were willing to view dancers as simply "tourists" on overstayed visas who just happened to be in a club. Without the payments, entertainers risked being detained or even deported. This is what dancers feared in the spring of 2007, when several clubs in the Taksim district of Istanbul were unwilling to pay what they saw as unreasonable sums to the local police precinct; raids were temporarily stepped up and clubs suffered almost immediately. When for several weeks women who had tourist visas refused to go to work, the club owners eventually paid off the police, and dancers returned to the clubs. Both according to dancers I met and to club owners, police raids were clearly linked to whether or not club owners had fallen behind in paying off the police.

Increasingly, by 2007 entertainers most often located work via their own friendship and kinship networks. In the same year the Turkish Ministry of Labor also began issuing a limited number of entertainer visas for women to work for one year. Most clubs found the process of applying for these work papers onerous, and they continued to risk employing women on tourist visas. In 2007 a club manager told me that about half of the dancers in his Taksim club were on a one-year work permit, while the others were on tourist visas.[14] Dancers would stay for the duration of their two-month visas before briefly returning home; they then returned repeatedly for two-month stints at different clubs.

By 2010 dancers also located work via the websites that particularly hotels in southern Turkey began to rely on for recruitment to fill positions during the busy summer season when British, German, and Russian guests arrive in large numbers.[15] In 2013 some hotels or Turkish companies recruiting for hotels explicitly sought Russian speakers, noting that their clients were predominantly Russian.[16] The Titanic Deluxe Bilek Hotel posted an advertisement noting that speaking Russian and English was "a must" for the position, with knowledge of Turkish a "plus." The duties for the position included providing parties and concerts for Russian guests (Learn4Good 2013b). Some 2013 advertisements also explicitly sought women who were "attractive" to fill positions as entertainers in nightclubs.[17] The malleability of the concept of "attractive" is evident, with at least one 2016 advertisement on the same website calling for only "British" and "Scandinavian" men and women to apply for positions as "host/hostess/entertainer," but with a stipulation "no work permit provided, however, very safe working environment is assured" (Learn4Good 2016).[18] These shifts and pledges of "safe" work conditions may be linked to Turkish government efforts to safeguard mobile, transnational labor, and thereby signal goodwill in addressing concerns raised by anti-trafficking campaigns on the part of INGOs like the International Organization of Migration.

While the entertainers I met rarely mentioned NGOs' anti-trafficking efforts, and they had not taken note of the IOM anti-trafficking pocket brochures being handed out at the airport, they frequently reflected on how their countries of origin sought to control their movement through borders. This was particularly pronounced for those coming from Belarus, as reflected in my conversation with two dancers packing to depart when their two-month tourist visa had come to an end in 2007. Aksana and her friend spoke about their means and routes of travel from Belarus, and how with President Lukashenko's then recent legislation, formal government permission was required to leave the country on anything but a tourist visa.[19] Even on tourist visas, the easiest way to travel was via Moscow. When Aksana and her friend traveled to Turkey in 2005, they went via Moscow and returned retracing their route, flying from Istanbul to Moscow, traveling by overnight train from Moscow to Vitebsk, Belarus, and finally by bus for several hours to their hometown. Aksana explained that the Russian authorities were much less rigorous than the Belarus ones in policing entries into and exits from the country. Even so, Aksana explained, women generally knew that they must travel *na bak*, or "with bucks," carrying at least $300. Border guards frequently hassled women traveling without a male partner or family member, often demanding evidence, such as a significant sum of money, as proof of women's claims that they were traveling for vacation (not illegal employment). Aksana recalled that during their last trip her friend had been turned back at the border because she did not have the unofficially required $300 to show the Russian customs and immigration officials.

These state interventions into intimate spheres of personal finances and autonomy hinder women's mobility and mirror other emerging deportation regimes globally (De Genova and Peutz 2010). Border regimes and policing that target women's mobility are often shaped by states' efforts to demonstrate willingness to combat the trafficking in women. Especially for states marked by a poor rating in the annual US State Department TIP report, as in the case of Belarus (2016), without demonstrable efforts to address concerns about trafficking, they risk losing most favored nation trading status with the United States or at least castigation in the international community. Women's mobility is hindered by the focus on trafficking, but equally important, such a focus has also detracted from finding durable solutions for addressing the working conditions under which undocumented migrants labor. Unlike the situation for some other migrant worker populations, such as Filipinas in Hong Kong (Constable 2007), as of 2011 post-Soviet migrant workers in Istanbul did not have their own dedicated advocacy groups to represent their interests. Instead, international discourses on trafficking continued to emphasize the dangers of women's mobility, framing women as victims of potential traffickers, while disregarding the diverse realities of women's undocumented labor.[20] In contrast, as the narratives of post-Soviet women in the next section suggest, women's aspirations, desires for glamour, and strategies around making a living as entertainers show them to be far more than victims. Moreover, their accounts reflect how mobility and the transformations of intimate economies in Eurasia are interwoven.

Desiring Glamour and Mobilizing Romance: Women's Accounts

One day when we were looking at Kara's photo album, Zoia, one of Kara's roommates, commented on the shifting reception of Russian-speaking entertainers in Turkey. Zoia, a young woman from southern Ukraine, explained that it was a decent living now, but nothing like ten years ago, as she had heard from older entertainers. At nineteen Zoia was on her second contract, having worked in 2001 in Izmir, a city to the southwest of Istanbul. Zoia lamented that ten years ago the "Russian" women were considered really exotic: "The Turkish men were *astonished* [her emphasis] by Russian women and they were giving gifts of diamonds and gold. Now they give nothing much." It was not uncommon for such a discourse of glamorous possibilities to be invoked to explain what drew women to seek out work as entertainers in Turkey.

I also heard from Nadia, a young woman from central Moldova, about how the glamour of exotic dancing had changed over time; as the novelty of post-Soviet women dancing in clubs wore off, dancing also became less lucrative. As we sat in a tea garden in Gezi Park, Nadia explained how she arrived in Istanbul in 1998 when she was twenty-three. She was immediately drawn to exotic dance both for its glamour and because she could make "good money." Nadia described how at that time work as an exotic dancer was especially well paid, and she found it easy to travel back and forth to Moldova to renew her visa. By the early 2000s, however, these jobs no longer appealed to her since after expenses Nadia could barely take home $25 for one night of performing in a club. She turned to other options to pursue her economic aspirations.

When we left the park and walked to her nearby apartment, Nadia told me she was unlikely to return to Moldova any time soon; by staying in Turkey and working as an apartment rental agent, she could finance the construction of a house for her mother and brother back home and support herself. As she pointed to certificates displayed on the wall attesting to her completion of a series of Turkish courses, Nadia relayed that she considered herself "lucky" to have a legal status in Turkey and to be able to pursue various business interests. In 2001, in partnership with her Turkish boyfriend, she opened a property management company and, like thousands of other post-Soviet women, arranged her citizenship through a fictive marriage. Nadia described herself as a shrewd businesswoman who had never risked being "derailed" by romance (see Holland and Eisenhart 1990).

However, as entertainers often recounted, negotiating the tensions between "love" or romance and money was not always easy. Not all the women I met were as successful as Nadia, but to varying degrees they also sought to mobilize intimate currency in Istanbul as a part of their trajectory for mobility.

The Luxury of Love: Muzhateers, Boyfriends, Friends

Entertainers frequently saw their time as Kara did, as "a vacation" from dreary hometowns, but like Nadia, they were also focused on economic goals, and fostering intimacy was key to attaining them. Many women sought to maintain a clean division between true intimacy and love versus economic rationality and money. True love became a dangerous luxury when it threatened to derail their primary aim of improving their material circumstances, but it could be a windfall if one could "play" the situation and foster intimacy with those who were adequately prepared to provide financial support. Similar to the Filipina entertainers in South Korea who Sealing Cheng (2007) writes about, the post-Soviet entertainers I met tended to view "true love" as problematic and, at best, fleeting. It was not simple to be immersed in a currency of intimacy and yet retain rigid boundaries between what was genuine and what was strategically enacted emotion; these seemed to blur together often. Women's narratives were saturated with reflections on relationships, and they frequently discussed the tensions between "falling in love," romance, and their material goals.

At the bare minimum women sought to maintain at least one steady relationship with a man who would occasionally take them to dinner and supply them with a cell phone. These relationships were not always viewed as simple commercial exchanges, however, and were sometimes intertwined with emotional ties. Depending on the intensity of these ties and on the level of financial support being provided, the entertainers distinguished between sponsor (*muzhateer*), boyfriend (*blizkii drug*), and simply friend (*drug*).[21] Women usually only had one sponsor, while they would have several boyfriends and friends. In their free time outside of working hours, women often met with men fitting in all these categories for meals, trips to the beach, or shopping. They cautioned one another, though, that it was not worth "falling in love" with any of these men, who were unlikely to reciprocate and whose material support could be short-lived.

The categories of "sponsor" and "boyfriend" were somewhat fluid, but women especially sought to establish a sponsor. A sponsor might not see them every week but would provide them with substantial material support, such as return tickets home, regular monetary gifts, and occasional weekend vacations. Boyfriends could be upgraded to sponsors if their investment shifted from occasional meals and gifts to more substantial displays of material wealth, and for this reason women often fostered relationships with both a sponsor and at least one boyfriend simultaneously.

These relationships punctuated women's time, whenever they were not at the club dancing, and women assiduously kept track of their schedules so that they could be available when men sought to meet up. Frequently I would agree to go with a dancer to the *steklari*, as the dancers called the long stretch of Istaklal Caddesi with cafes, movie theaters, bookstores, and storefront after storefront featuring alluring clothing, shoes, or jewelry in their shop windows; and just as we began our window shopping, a cell phone would ring. "Oh, sorry, that was my boyfriend, and he wants to meet up," was something dancers often told me; spending time with an anthropologist posing constant questions rated well below the option of seeing a boyfriend. On other occasions when women had assessed that a boyfriend was not really providing material benefits and just taking up their emotional energy, they would use our outings as an excuse to give a boyfriend a cold shoulder.

All the entertainers also maintained ties with "friends." As Kara explained after one of her daily flirtations with a local fruit seller, and another time when she got a favorable price on a pair of shoes after flirting for several days with the shop assistant, "You just never know—it could be useful in the future—so why not flirt?" It was always possible that friends could be upgraded to become boyfriends, although less likely sponsors. Entertainers had a keen sense of the material circumstances of the men in whom they took an interest, and only those with considerable means would be seen as potential sponsors.[22]

DARIA

Women rarely claimed to be "in love" with the men they became involved with, and in cases where they did, it was considered unfortunate. This was the case with Kara's second roommate, Daria. She was on her third contract in Turkey and was thinking of how to negotiate her fourth. Daria often spoke of her eight-year-old daughter back home in southern Ukraine, who was being cared for by Daria's sister and was attending a private school funded by Daria's earnings. One afternoon Daria told me, "I'm just so tired, eight years without a break" (*Ia tak ustala, 8 let rabotaiu bez pereryva*). She flipped through some photographs she had just had developed and changed the subject, pointing to an image of a young Turkish man embracing her on a beach. She reflected that she felt lucky to have a boyfriend, someone who genuinely cared for her, but she worried about the relationship if she couldn't arrange work in Istanbul at the end of her club contract. Daria's roommates expressed concern, saying Daria was in trouble—she had fallen in love with this man, and it was not bound to work out.

Instead of relationships premised on love, more often romance was mobilized in less permanent forms. Women were keenly aware that the relationships with men could be fleeting, and so they were careful to cultivate Turkish men they met who might potentially become sponsors, or at least boyfriends. One Sunday afternoon in 2002 when I accompanied nine of the dancers on an outing to the beach I observed how dancers went about this. At the beach I soon noticed that Kara and another entertainer were not swimming so much as flirting with several young Turkish men. They eventually exchanged phone numbers, and Kara later quipped that one could always use another boyfriend who could take you out or buy gifts, or even possibly become a sponsor who might lavish more significant resources on you. The man she often referred to as her sponsor had disappointed her recently; he had not called for two weeks, and Kara surmised he was trying to avoid feeling pressured to provide the money sponsors customarily gave to the entertainers for their return tickets home.

In other cases, like Daria's, Turkish men fell in love with entertainers, and this created its own problems in an intimate economy where love and money fit uneasily together. In an interview with Can, a Turkish club manager, he had been telling me about the workings of his club when he commented on how his former girlfriend performed there. Can said he missed his girlfriend terribly, but they could no longer be together. She insisted on continuing to work in the club even though he pleaded with her to just let him support her. As he said with exasperation, "I would have given her money! How can I be with her if she is dancing!" Can said he was simply perplexed as to why his ex-girlfriend would want to continue in such a profession, especially when he was sure she cared deeply for him. As the next portrait suggests, women's forthright accounts about their efforts to privilege economic stability over emotional concerns point to a disconnection between what men and women sought in intimate relationships.

IRINA

Irina, the woman who first introduced me to the figure of Hürrem/Roxelana, worked in a number of jobs back home in Ukraine—including as a baker, bookkeeper, and market vendor—before deciding to go to Turkey. As she explained, at home she had a great set of friends, her parents, her eight-year-old daughter, and some work. Things were more or less okay with her husband too; she noted: "Everyone said he was absolutely beautiful, and in bed he was fantastic! But he just did not want to work; there was no money in the household." Irina said she got tired of him and decided to move back in with her parents. Then in 2001 she left home for Turkey, leaving her daughter to be cared for by her parents.

One day after Irina and I visited the Kariye Museum, the Byzantine Chora church with its interior walls covered in stunning mosaics depicting biblical scenes, over tea Irina told me about the men who were her friends (*druz'ia*) in Istanbul. She said she was selective and had no need for men who did not have any money. "Why would I hang out with them? It is fine if they are nice guys, et cetera, but in Ukraine I had tons of such friends." As she explained, she left home "to find the guys with money ... why would I seek out the losers once again? ... All I want from life is a big kitchen and a chance to prepare food for a husband. I can't really *afford to love anyone*; no, I need to find a husband who can provide for me, but meanwhile I am here earning a living."

Autonomy and the "Girlfriend Experience"

While most of my interviewees were not as blunt as Irina about the need to find "the guys with money," a theme of avoiding the potential constraints of "love" in favor of economic stability and independence permeated their accounts. Some of them spoke of this in terms of autonomy they sought to establish—sometimes from former husbands, often from parents, and sometimes from boyfriends or sponsors. For the most part, women's concerns revolved around housing, wanting an apartment of their own, and the desire to live separately from their natal families on their return to former Soviet locations. In some ways this need for personal autonomy echoes the desires expressed by women migrants portrayed in other locations. In the case of Filipina domestic workers in Hong Kong, Constable (1999) writes about "ambivalent returns" to households in the Philippines, where women typically lacked the autonomy they had come to appreciate in Hong Kong. In Marie-Eve Carrier-Moisan's (2012) study of Brazilian women migrating to larger cities and engaging in intimate encounters with European men, she also found women frequently preferred the relative autonomy they could enjoy away from the demands of their natal families. Likewise, post-Soviet entertainers did not long for the demands of their households back in Ukraine, Moldova, Russia, and Belarus. Just like Filipina domestics in Hong Kong and women immersed in the sexscapes of eastern Brazil, many of the post-Soviet entertainers first left home for economic reasons but then found that they relished the individual freedoms they could enjoy as well. Working and living in Turkey provided women with a degree of control over their lives and a sense of independence, ideals they associated with being modern, fully realized adults, as reflected in the following two portraits.

AKSANA

As we sat in her room, Aksana arranged her clothing and cosmetics in a suitcase and spoke about her family. She recounted how her twenty-one-year-old sister lived with her infant son at her parent's home in Belarus; her older sister, in her thirties, lived with her son not far from their parents. Aksana said her parents knew she was in Turkey dancing, although they did not know that she danced topless. She did not seem too concerned about this and turned to laugh at her roommate's attempt to hide some condoms that had been left lying on the bed. At the time of our conversation Aksana was twenty-four and could not wait to get an apartment of her own; as she insisted, "I am not going to do this forever, [I will] just get established and get my apartment." Other entertainers had similar plans. For instance, Rita, an entertainer from a small town in Ukraine who dropped by during our conversation, chimed in: "I need a two-bedroom apartment in case I get married and things don't work out; I would rather be throwing out my husband than be on the street myself. If I need to, I would just get a roommate."

Prior to coming to Turkey, Aksana was employed as a seamstress for three years, but this paid poorly. She knew she would never be able to afford an apartment on that pay. Before that she worked abroad in Poland, where she picked fruit and tended gardens for three months. That was hard work, and she didn't want to work so hard for so little pay—just $250/month. When we met in 2007, after just six weeks in Istanbul, she had been able to save $1,000.

Although Aksana missed her family, she worried that if she went home she could fall into a standard life of marriage, kids, and low-paid job, a reality she found unappealing. Aksana was dismissive of marriage, saying perhaps in her thirties she would consider it. As she explained, "I don't want to be controlled by someone; I want to be independent" (*Ne khochu byt' pod kontrolem; khochu byt' nezavisimoi*). She saw her time in Turkey as a means to achieve her goal. She laughed, telling me she kept information from her boyfriend as a way of retaining control over her situation. For instance, she arrived to work in Turkey in 2006 and did not even tell him. He was in Ankara and thought she was in Belarus. She recalled the time before that, right when she was departing from Belarus, and he called on her cell. He pleaded with her to just come as a tourist to Turkey, just to visit him and not work. She brushed him off, pretending she needed to be home with her family, but in fact she was off for her next contract in Istanbul.

Despite the desire for personal autonomy that most of the entertainers expressed, like them Aksana also sought out the financial support of sponsors. As she explained, it was a delicate balance of maintaining control while still benefiting from the attention of a sponsor. Aksana's friend, a tall woman with big, dark eyes and long eyelashes, who was studying economics as a distance education student in Belarus, came by one afternoon as we were wrapping up our conversation. She and Aksana were planning their departure for Antalya, a trip that Aksana's Istanbul sponsor was paying for. The two women lamented that they would be missing the opportunity to earn at least another week's worth of pay at the club, but they were also glad to have a paid vacation in Antalya, and they were excited to see the beaches and to live in a nice hotel before returning to Belarus. Aksana reasoned that the trip also made sense because it might prevent one of her Istanbul boyfriends (not a sponsor) from getting the idea that she was too attached to him.

IULIA

Most women I met did not envision working as a dancer for more than a few years; however, dancing in Turkey was viewed by many as giving them more economic and sexual independence than other options they had. Women like Aksana spoke unflinchingly of Turkish men in terms of what could be gained from being in relationships with them—sometimes misleading them, always maintaining several boyfriends, and moving from one sponsor to the next. This was also the case with Iulia, a twenty-one-year-old woman from a small city south of Moscow who, over tea one summer afternoon in 2005 in Gezi Park, told me that she had dreamed of becoming a theater actress. Her parents had insisted she go into law, but six months short of completing her law degree in Moscow, Iulia decided she was tired of studying; she left university but was unable to find work. By chance she met a German tourist on the subway, and she ended up showing him around and then sleeping with him. At first she found the relationship exciting; they kept in touch over e-mail and she missed him when he was back in Germany. The German man visited her family several times, and Iulia described how, when he would call, her parents would begin using sugary language to greet him. Iulia mocked their tone, saying "my darling" (*golubchik moi*). With a look of disgust and a flick of her cigarette Iulia recalled that when the German man invited her to be with him in Germany, her parents urged her to go. Ultimately, she did travel there but, as she explained: "It just did not work . . . and I had to force myself. I just didn't feel for him in my soul." She returned home but again could not find work, so set out for Turkey.

At this point Iulia rearranged her long legs and the waiters at the Gezi Park tea garden quickly responded as she waved her arm for her cigarette to be lit. She ruminated, "The Turkish guys just get lonely since their religion does not allow them to really spend time with women." She added that it was much better to be in Turkey with these men than in Germany. In Germany she could not wait to leave. Her boyfriend wanted sex all the time, and there was no question of holding back. In contrast, Iulia viewed Turkish men as a sort of eager and polite audience for whom she could perform her sexuality but remain in control of it, without having to engage in sexual intercourse. As she explained: "Here I can go to restaurants, be gifted clothing and flowers, and be desired, but they will not do anything. . . . I can easily play this out for another six months (*Mozhno eto vse rastianut' na shest' mesiatsev*)."

Iulia's account underscores the instrumentality of many dancers but also the ways in which women see themselves as having a certain form of power unavailable to them in their daily lives back home or elsewhere. Like the women Elizabeth Bernstein (2007a) writes about working in northern California's intimate services economy, these post-Soviet women often emphasized how their work was about engaging in performances of intimacy. In Bernstein's analysis, she develops a useful concept of "bounded authenticity" to explore how escorts, and the men who sought their company, were involved in an intimate economy of the "sale and purchase of authentic emotional and physical connection" (2007b, 192). Bernstein describes how North American men seek out the "girlfriend experience" (GFE) because it is an efficient way to engage in intimacy, albeit in a commodified form; she argues that this makes sense in a neoliberal setting where men feel they cannot afford to take time away from work to nurture authentic relationships. In a sort of twist on Bernstein's formulation, the post-Soviet dancers in Istanbul were also concerned with time, money, and autonomy. Like the men seeking escorts in Bernstein's study, post-Soviet entertainers understood the GFE, or the BFE (boyfriend experience), as an efficient, relatively safe exchange, where women performed forms of intimacy that a girlfriend might provide, only without the burden and demands of a long-term relationship.

Iulia's account especially illustrates a situation I heard about frequently, where entertainers saw their work in contrast to the possibility of feeling powerless and trapped in a relationship. Iulia explicitly discussed capitalizing on sexualized intimacy that she could engage in on her own terms. She fled from a relationship where she did not "feel it in her soul," and where "true love" and her dependence on her boyfriend required her to be available for sex on demand, to a situation where she felt more in control of her body and her economic well-being. In Istanbul she was taking part in an economy of desire where being capable of *performing* intimacy was key. This was paired with a wide range of options for Iulia to deploy as she engaged men who were prepared to spend money on her. Iulia and other dancers I met were trying to capitalize on the perception of them as embodying sexuality "without hang-ups," even as they sought to maintain their own terms on how they would play out the girlfriend experience with men.

Learning to Labor "without Hang-ups"

Another significant aspect of dancers' narratives concerned the performance of sex work as a form of labor they had to learn. Some embraced the work, and others spoke of it like any other job, involving terms they agreed to in exchange for a paycheck. For most, learning to dance was an extension of other experiences away from home; for a few, the work was too alienating and they did not stay in the job.

One afternoon in 2005 over tea and a few cigarettes in the hotel lobby, Anna and Sonia reflected on their first days in their jobs as entertainers. Anna, who was twenty-five at the time, recounted how she first began dancing a year earlier; her friend Sonia, who was twenty-one, started two years earlier. They spoke of the demands of the work as something they had adapted to, but recalled one dancer who had recently returned home to Ukraine. She was nineteen, "but acted like she was ten when she arrived," said Sonia, who described how the woman was disdainful of the work. During their shifts, when customers were seated at entertainers' tables, this woman refused to capitalize on the possibility of creating a girlfriend experience with clients. She also did not want to make small talk with men, and she could not bring herself to take part in coaxing clients to spend endlessly on overpriced drinks, one of the basic requirements of the job. Anna and Sonia concurred that the work was not for everyone.

In contrast, Sonia said she did not feel any anxiety about taking up this work, possibly because she learned to be on her own early on. As she explained, as a child in Ukraine every summer she went off to Pioneer camp, where she got used to living alone and fending for herself.[23] She added that she knew what she was getting into and said, "It is not such a big deal, it's just dancing after all." Anna agreed that after their first week in the club in Ankara (where she and Sonia had their first contract), she also came to think of the dancing as no big deal. She added: "It is just a matter of perspective. If you relax and just see this as being at a disco, then it is fine. You can just go to work and enjoy dancing, and recall that this is just a job, at the end of which you get a paycheck; that's what made it okay for me, even though it was tough the first week." Anna described how in her first days in the job she called her mother in Ukraine for comfort. Her mother intoned, "It's not such a big deal. This is just a job and there is no need to be getting upset." Anna leaned close to me and added, "It is not as if we are having sex or anything; we just try to be *bez kompleksov*," once again invoking the expression often used by dancers to indicate a sense of unrepressed sexuality, or sexuality without "hang-ups." This ideal of sexuality without hang-ups could be seen as a global mantra for a generation of young people but especially young women seeking to capitalize on a demand for a particular type of authentic intimacy, possibly a key hallmark of global industrial capitalism, where service work, mobile populations, and postmodern family forms come together (Hochschild 1983; Bernstein 2007a; Cheng and Kim 2014).

Performing Sexuality

In addition to engaging in a global intimate services economy, however, these post-Soviet dancers shared some common history. They could be seen as taking part in a post-Soviet sexual revolution where, according to Igor Kon, "sexual freedom became one of the most important aspects and symbols of social liberation" (1995, 3). Although only a subsection of young people from former Soviet regions were labor migrants in Istanbul, these entertainers were very much part of a post-Soviet generational gestalt where there was a distinctive relationship to media and the benefits of money, as well as a positive association with the idea of sexuality "without hang-ups."[24] In contrast to their parents' generation, sexuality was seen as fundamental to their subjectivity and something to be consciously performed and capitalized on.

Nearly all the women I interviewed reflected on the element of performance that came with their work. For instance, Aksana ruminated one afternoon, "All of life is one big game, a game about sex." She added, "All that matters in life is how good you are at this game." Other women spoke explicitly about enjoying the performance of sexuality and the relative respect they received from Turkish men. Irina, the woman from Ukraine who said she could not "afford" to love anyone, told me that she was not fazed by dancing in the club; in fact, unlike some dancers, she often enjoyed dancing topless. She described how in school she had been very shy, "like a mouse"; and she beamed as she recounted that on her first trip home from Turkey, she projected such a sense of confidence that one of her former teachers did not recognize her. One of Irina's favorite phrases, "These days you have to know how to work the situation" (*Segodnia nado znat' kak podygryvat' situatsii*), reflected her thinking about a sense of adaptable or even fluid identity. Irina also happened to identify as a devout Christian; the evening after we visited the Byzantine Chora church, she dropped by my hotel room with her Bible, thinking I might like to borrow it to peruse passages related to some of the iconography we had seen that day.

Other dancers never mentioned religious sentiments to me, but, like Irina, they were well aware of the way they consciously embodied a certain type of sexuality. This was a topic they especially linked to their choice of clothing. As Rita, the woman who planned to buy a two-bedroom apartment in case she had to throw out her husband, told me, she restricted her movements beyond the hotel and the club, and when she did go out in her free time, she avoided wearing provocative clothing in an effort to blend in. She explained that she avoided wearing even T-shirts that were too tight, since, "Why would I want extra attention anyway? I can meet men at the club." Other women reflected on how they changed their daily presentation of self when they arrived in Istanbul. Irina said that during the day she stopped wearing makeup, like the eye shadow and mascara that she had worn on a daily basis in Ukraine, because she got tired of the attention she attracted. Men were incessantly poking and pinching her, so when she had time off she decided to change her appearance, including wearing jeans instead of skin-tight stretch pants. These efforts to fit more seamlessly into Istanbul youth culture were echoed by women who were not working as entertainers; many domestic workers and shop assistants, like Raia, pointed to their efforts to downplay what they described as the "sexiness" (*sexual'nost'*) of their outfits (e.g., short shorts, tight jeans, or low-cut blouses), at least during the day when they were traveling to work. Thus post-Soviet women migrants in Istanbul were constantly assessing how they were being received by Turkish society at large, and how signaling variable degrees of "sexiness" could work to their benefit.

In focusing here on post-Soviet entertainers and the intimate economies at work in their sojourns in Istanbul, I have sought to add a layer of nuance to how sex, mobility, and intimacy are frequently discussed. As I have argued, entertainers' lives were not simply about being underpaid, overworked, and victimized but were at least as much about women's aspirations and their efforts to realize their goals. The narratives of romance, love, and longing for independence invoked by women tell us about the emotional lives of migrants and, as with negotiations around intimacy, point to how private lives are being reshaped in a global economy.

Like women migrants in Hong Kong, Japan, and South Korea (Faier 2009; Cheng 2010; Constable 2014), post-Soviet entertainers forged distinctive intimate practices as mobile subjects. Often post-Soviet entertainers I met were like Aksana, excited to be relatively independent, earning their own disposable incomes; sometimes they were happily pursuing their own aspirations separate from families, boyfriends, and household responsibilities and commitments back in Ukraine, Belarus, Russia, Moldova, or even elsewhere in Turkey. Many young post-Soviet women I met discussed ways to make their sexuality "without hang-ups" work to their benefit. They spoke of their ability to navigate intimacy as a skill they had learned and as a currency they could deploy. Like Iulia, women were well-aware of how they provided a sort of girlfriend experience for their Turkish sponsors and boyfriends. The dancers I came to know were pursuing their own projects, often seeking by means of their mobility to take part in what they saw as a more modern, cosmopolitan way of being, albeit within the constraints of the service economy in which they found themselves.

Like Cheng, who found Filipina entertainers in South Korea to be employing "strategic intimacy" within unequal structures of power (2010), here I also see women's agency playing a key role in their encounters as entertainers whose options are, nevertheless, constrained by both post-Soviet and Turkish states. States make fundamental decisions about how to structure their economies, as well as how to regulate borders and bodies, and they also determine how difficult it will be to maintain documented and undocumented work. Women's work as entertainers depends on the mercurial Turkish state not policing entertainers' visa statuses too closely but also on their countries of departure not preventing them from traveling abroad. Moreover, states remain culpable for not providing the economic means for young women to work closer to home. Young women did not speak of youthful aspirations to work within the intimate services economy; instead many young women, like Kara, Iulia, and Daria, spoke of unrealized aspirations for careers in medicine, theater, or teaching, and they explicitly linked their migration to unsuccessful efforts to support themselves in their home countries' fledgling market economies. After finishing high school, they had sought work as secretaries, telephone operators, or vendors before turning to mobile strategies and strategic intimacy as a dependable source of income.

The history of Soviet sexual politics significantly informed how young women thought about their intimate practices, but they were also shaped by the flows of global capitalism. In a parallel way, Bernstein powerfully shows how, in the early 2000s, a quotidian erotic sphere more or less permeated public culture in the United States, albeit in tension with "traditional" ideas about sexuality and family (2007b). In setting the stage for her analysis of sexual economies in the United States, Bernstein writes that "the proliferation of forms of service work, the new global information economy, and 'post-modern' families peopled by insoluble individuals have produced another profound transformation in the erotic sphere" (2007a, 6). Like Bernstein, I link forces of global capitalism to shifts in intimate cultural practices; however, I do not see entertainers as "insoluble individuals." Entertainers I met were crafting selves that were deeply defined by prevailing global forces shaping intimate practices, but many entertainers' accounts reflect how performing the intimate "girlfriend" self in demand in Istanbul in the early 2000s *also* coexisted with other subjectivities. Although these women resourcefully sought out spaces for pursuing their projects of modernity, many were also deeply tied to their commitments in home communities. Like Daria and Irina, who were sending some of their earnings home to family members who were caring for their school-age daughters, or Kara and Nadia, who were supporting their mothers and brothers, many dancers I met were pursuing their own aspirations as well as providing for economic needs of family members. Dancers had realized a cherished dream of mobility, which they frequently saw as a first step to modern subjectivities, but nevertheless the women I met had traveled distinct routes deeply rooted in home communities.

"OTHER MOTHERS," GRANDMOTHERS, AND THE STATE

As a passenger on a small minibus making its way north to the capital of Moldova in the summer of 2004, I was accompanied by my toddler daughter and stepmother, along with eight other passengers packed in elbow to elbow. One young woman sitting next to me was departing for a housekeeping job in Moscow. She was leaving her ten-month-old daughter in the care of her husband and mother for the second time since the child was born. After the three-hour bus journey Sveta would continue her trek from Chișinău via an overnight train to Moscow. She sighed with resignation that she didn't know exactly when she would be seeing her daughter again. Sveta's daughter, like nearly one-quarter of children in Moldova, was growing up with at least one parent away as a labor migrant (UNICEF 2009).

When our planeload of passengers bound for Chișinău was significantly delayed at Istanbul's Atatürk International Airport in 2011 I heard yet another account of how a family was raising a child through a transnational nurturing arrangement. Tania, a friendly woman with long blonde hair and bright blue eyes who was returning to her family in a small town in Gagauzia, told me that since 1997 she had traveled to Istanbul for regular stints working as a domestic for six months at a time. She and her husband rented an apartment and took turns traveling for short visits home to Moldova. Tania's sixteen-year-old son was barely two years old when she and her husband began leaving him with his grandparents; as she told me, "I thought a long time about leaving my son, but in the end it really helped when I told myself that lots of women have done this, and it is really necessary for me to raise him this way; he is a smart boy and wants to go on to study mathematics."

I encountered many young women like Sveta and Tania reflecting on their negotiations around mothering from a distance, arrangements that often extended from their children's infancy well into early adulthood. In many instances, as children grew they were cared for by a close relative who oversaw daily needs, while mothers', and less often fathers', remittances financed basic necessities and educational opportunities, like private school or music lessons, as Daria and Niki had done for their daughters. In interacting even briefly with migrant women, I would hear about the decisions women were making regarding their children and implicitly about what I call a "transnational nurturing nexus," or the complex ways that families and households were providing for children by combining historical caregiving practices with investment in transnational circuits of mobility (Rouse 1992; Hewlett 2013) extending primarily between Istanbul and southern Moldova but also to Russia, Romania, and sometimes even farther from home. In this chapter I explore the idea of a transnational nurturing nexus involving "other mothers," as well as state-funded institutions such as day cares, in an effort to move beyond a focus on mother-centered care as a cultural universal (Glenn 1994) and, instead, to direct attention to the diverse, historically situated practices that shape nurturing.[1]

As women migrants like Sveta and Tania shared their reasoning with me about having others care for their children, I wondered about these decisions and the specific contours of this transnational nurturing nexus. I learned that children left for years in the care of their grandmothers or aunts sometimes referred to *them* as "mama," and when called to the phone or to a Skype conversation to speak with long absent biological mothers, children would be called to speak with their "other mother," in Russian *drugaia mama*. Children's separations from parents were not always easy, sometimes requiring reconfigurations of households or creating strains for parent-child relationships, but such caregiving practices were common, and nurturing by "other mothers" has a long history in the region, dating to well before Moldova's incorporation into the Soviet Union. Overall, I trace my argument about other mothers in Moldova in connection with a tradition of feminist scholarship on nurturing, mothering, and "othermothering." I argue for thinking about the transnational nurturing nexus many southern Moldovan women are part of as shaped by global economic restructuring and demands for gendered labor but also as rooted in local histories of nurturing practices. In the pages that follow I consider the local histories of "other mothering" in southern Moldova, but first I turn to some ways scholars have theorized about motherhood.

Other Mothers and Shifting the Center

Beginning in the 1970s feminist scholars looked to find universal frameworks for understanding gender inequality (Lewin and Silverstein 2016, 10–12). Around the same time influential theories examining mothering as a social practice emerged (Glenn 1994, 4–5), and these prompted an abundance of research and debate dedicated to the diverse forms nurturing can take and the relative weight of biological and cultural factors (Stack 1974; Collier et al. 1982; Moore 1988; Scheper-Hughes 1989; Collins 1990, 1994). Black feminist scholars posed one of the strongest critiques of universalizing theories, with Patricia Hill Collins (1994) arguing that feminist theorizing paid scant attention to particular ideas about motherhood and the contexts in which they were generated. Collins writes, "Black women's experiences as bloodmothers, othermothers, and community othermothers reveal that the mythical norm of heterosexual, married couple, nuclear family with a nonworking spouse and a husband earning a 'family wage' is far from being natural, universal and preferred, but instead is deeply embedded in specific race and class formations" (1990, 222–23). Collins urges us to be attentive to the diverse experiences of motherhood and, instead of pursuing generalizable theories, to "shift the center" of analysis to provide a more rich understanding of human experience (1994, 61–62).

Like Collins, a number of feminist anthropologists have critically assessed how motherhood, class, and assumptions about divisions between public and private spheres play out in different locations (Clark 1999; Berdahl 1999; Freeman 2007). In her study of market women in Ghana, Gracia Clark found that middle-class, Western ideals of "self-effacing, homebound wife and mother" that were on the rise from the 1980s into the 1990s (1999, 719) did not map easily across cultural contexts and time. Instead she documented the way women's paid work among market women in Ghana was seen as an integral part of motherhood. Likewise, Daphne Berdahl (1999) demonstrated how, following the fall of the Berlin Wall, socialist frameworks combining positive valuations of work and motherhood collided with discourses placing women firmly in the home; East German women were no longer meant to be "worker-mothers," with women's paid labor highly valued along with their reproductive roles, and instead they became simply "mother-consumers" (Berdahl 1999).

More than twenty years earlier, in what remains a touchstone for scholars interested in a critical analysis of mothering, Carol Stack (1974) authored an ethnography of a community of midwestern African Americans living in the "flats." Stack's work contested deeply held assumptions about the forms mothering and nurturing could take in North America and showed how kin and those providing nurturing are "those you can count on." Stack's important study was one of the first to powerfully point to the central role of kin and networks—what some scholars, like Collins (1990), would later call "othermothers," rather than biological mothers—as a basis for nurturing and community, especially for people on the margins.

In thinking about nurturing practices in southern Moldova I draw on the rich scholarship around mothering and motherhood as I reflect on "othermothers"—the various people, not always biologically related to children, doing caregiving in southern Moldova—and "other mothers," the relationship that Nelli's granddaughter and others sometimes invoked in referring to their often physically absent biological mothers. While the former emphasizes the mothering practices of those other than a biological mother, the latter focuses on "other" or "different" ways of being a (biological) mother, including by providing material and emotional support from a distance. The phrase "other mothers" preserves how this idea was expressed in southern Moldova, emphasizing biological mothers as the "other mothers"—not the primary caregivers but still taking part in a transnational nurturing nexus in a different, or "other," way that involved channeling resources in the form of remittances without being physically present. Although my emphasis is on "other mothering," namely how biological mothers who are not physically present but nevertheless take part in mothering practices, both processes, "other mothering" by transnational migrant mothers and "othermothering" by a wide network of people, are at work in southern Moldova.

Scholars have shown how "othermothering," "child shifting," and child fosterage are critical for communities throughout the world, especially as heightened precarity brought about by an intensified global economy compels family members to be absent as transnational labor migrants from months to years on end (Ehrenreich and Hochschild 2002; Schmalzbauer 2004; Leinaweaver 2010; Bledsoe and Sow 2011; Chamberlain 2013). Based on her ethnographic research among British-Caribbean families, Mary Chamberlain argues that child fostering or "child shifting"—with grandmothers raising grandchildren in Jamaica, Barbados, and Trinidad while their parents migrate for work in Britain—is a practice that has emerged over hundreds of years (2013, 305). In dispelling dominant theories focused on an idea of adaptation to economic circumstance, Chamberlain instead shows how such a family formation preceded even migration movements in the late nineteenth and early twentieth centuries and can be seen as *enabling* migration, rather than being a consequence of it (2013, 305). Likewise, Jessaca Leinaweiver (2010) shows how historically grounded practices of child fosterage in Peru insure companionship for aging parents, even while children are provided for, thereby enabling parents to engage in transnational migration to Spain.

Southern Moldovan women's experience of other mothering has parallels with experiences portrayed both in the rich literature on African American mothering practices and in the emerging literature on transnational nurturing practices being forged by diverse migrants. While I did not encounter the phenomenon of "community othermothers" that Leah Schmalzbauer (2004), Chamberlain (2013), and Collins (1990) describe, where a nonbiological mother takes it on herself to serve as a community resource and support for a wide number of nonkin children, nurturing of children by "othermothers," and most often grandmothers or aunts, was common among the households I came to know. Most significantly, southern Moldovan women's experiences of arranging for othermothering for children, like that described by Chamberlain (2013) for the Caribbean and Leinaweaver (2010) for Peru, demonstrate that this type of family formation is not just a desperate attempt to provide care for children. Instead it is a dynamic, historically based practice that enables women to become long-term labor migrants and provide substantially for their households. Nevertheless, migrant mothers' transnational mobility has also brought about a specific form of "other mothering" that is defined by nurturing from a distance. Migrant mothers have widely become the primary providers for households and thereby brought about changes in the long-term nurturing nexus in the region.

Nurturing from a Distance

A growing scholarship on transnational parenting examines so-called nurturing from a distance, an experience increasingly common for migrant men and women who are forced to leave children in the care of others for long periods of time. In particular, recent work on transnational parenting has asked how children fare under such arrangements. Overall, the absence of parents who nevertheless send remittances means improved material circumstances for children left behind, and while generally children initially express some degree of emotional distress, many are genuinely loved and provided for by caregivers (Gamburd 2000, 199; Mazzucato and Schans 2011, 705). A number of studies have argued that children left behind may benefit materially while suffering at an emotional level (Schmalzbauer 2004; Parreñas 2005; UNICEF 2009). However, other studies have found the situation to be more complicated (see Carling 2012; Vanore et al. 2015). One study of well-being among children of migrant men in Southeast Asia suggests that the experience of transnational caregiving may be significantly shaped by cultural and historical factors (Graham and Jordan 2011). The researchers found that in two countries, Thailand and Indonesia, children expressed a sense of poor psychological well-being when their fathers were migrants, compared to children whose fathers were not migrants. In two other countries, Vietnam and the Philippines, there was no difference noted for children of migrant and nonmigrant fathers. Likewise, in a survey focused on the psychosocial well-being of Moldovan children aged four to seventeen with and without migrant parents, contrary to widespread assumptions, Michaella Vanore et al. (2015) found that children's psychosocial health was not directly determined by whether they had migrant parents. However, they did find that the gender of a child—overall, boys tended to fare worse than girls, especially if the father was absent—the gender of the migrant parent, and the caregiving arrangement all affected if and to what extent parents' migration corresponded to a decrease in a child's psychosocial health (2015, 258). All these studies provide a valuable perspective on how children fare, but they do not substantially consider the cultural practices and larger "nurturing nexus" that also shapes the experience of transnational nurturing.

In a few contexts, especially in Southeast Asia (Parreñas 2005; Graham and Jordan 2011) and Latin America (Schmalzbauer 2004; Leinaweaver 2010), the challenges of transnational nurturing are increasingly the focus of scholarly attention. In other locations, like the former Soviet Union, despite the widespread practice of women's transnational labor migration, local nurturing practices have not been widely researched in light of this mobility (however, see Keough 2006; Leifsen and Tymczuk 2012). The few references to transnational parenting in this region tend to make generalizations about contemporary migration as causing a deterioration of the "traditional family" and about what form nurturing practices take (e.g., nuclear families raising children) (Elrick 2008, 1513). Instead, I turn attention to what one scholar (Carsten 1995) has called "indigenous ways of acting out and conceptualizing connections between people," or "relatedness," to emphasize how nurturing practices are understood locally. As transnational mobility has recently come to define a life stage of young people in a number of locations, these conditions may forge new ways of connecting between parents and children, but they also build on practices that were already in circulation prior to the escalation in mobility brought about by weakened states and an intensified global economy. In focusing on the transnational nurturing nexus, or various elements contributing locally and across borders to realize caregiving in southern Moldova, we can gain a sense of local forms of relatedness without resorting to models of cultural practices that would frame these as dysfunctional.

Mother Love and "Not Enough" Care

The stories I came to hear over and over in Moldova point to the personal costs of "mothering from a distance" but not necessarily to a sense of "abandonment" and "not enough" care that Rhacel Parreñas, for instance, traces for Filipino children left behind by migrating mothers (2005, 125–30). Parreñas details the ways in which the media and the Philippine government perpetuate a prevalent public sentiment that mothers "should" be providing intensive daily care for their children. This public sentiment, in turn, vilifies absent transnational mothers (but not fathers) for being insufficient nurturers, a refrain some of the youth in Parreñas's study also voiced. Parreñas's analysis revolves tightly around gender discourses that frame women as needing to be "martyr moms" (2005, 109), performing intensive nurturing practices even at a distance, in their efforts to avoid castigation. Parreñas emphasizes an untroubled link between dominant discourses and internalized gender ideals in the Philippines but leaves local histories, class inflections, and cultural practices around nurturing relatively unexplored.

Despite significant work on the implications of transnational parenting, within this literature there is little focus on variation across space and time in regard to nurturing practices. The important critique of "natural" bonds of "attachment" and "mother love" between children and parents, especially mothers (e.g., Scheper-Hughes 1989; Franzblau 2002), tends to get lost in writings on transnational mobility, as does the vibrant literature on "othermothers" and diverse forms of kinship (e.g., Stack 1974; Collins 1990). Instead, idealized middle-class forms of mother love and universal emotions are too easily reinscribed in portrayals of the pain of separation for women migrants and their children, leaving little room for thinking about diverse nurturing practices.

In taking a different approach, my portrayal of Moldovan migrants and their families parallels the work of scholars writing ethnography of the "particular" (Abu-Lughod 1991; Gamburd 2000; Constable 2003), which emphasizes stories, local practices, and history with the aim of avoiding the homogenization of difference. I show how the other mothering I encountered in Moldova and Istanbul does not simply reflect ruptures in care brought about by transnational mobility and pressures of global capitalism. Instead, it is part of a nurturing nexus of multiple layers of care. This nurturing nexus includes parents, grandparents, and extended kin but also state-sponsored spaces like day-care centers and residential schools. Intimate practices of child rearing were reconfigured with the end of the Soviet Union and the subsequent economic pressures placed on households. In addition, there are continuities in the logics of nurturing drawn from an earlier era of caregiving. I argue that the prevalent practice of children being raised by "othermothers" with "other mothers" (biological mothers who are physically absent) taking part to various degrees, is integrally tied to the "other" forms of nurturing that have defined this region over the past century, including as state structures sought to transform how women balanced their lives as workers and mothers.

Mothercraft and Maternalist Policies from the Soviet to the Post-Soviet Eras

From the beginning of the Soviet era, motherhood posed an ideological challenge for the state. The state sought to transform women into productive citizens who could be worker-mothers, contributing to building the new socialist society

through their role in the workforce and through their education of new generations. Nevertheless, in the early 1920s to 1930s, as urban migration flourished
and at least twenty-three million men and women moved from rural areas into
urban centers to take up work, children were not welcome and were generally
seen as a "burden" preventing women from being productive workers (Denisova
2010, 56).[2] Motherhood and traditional child-rearing practices were frequently
framed as standing in the way of forging a new, industrialized society; and
new forms of "mothercraft," or means of caring for and educating young children, were introduced to address this problem (Waters 1992, 123; Ransel 2000;
Kirschenbaum 2001).

Within months of the 1917 Revolution, village women especially, seen to
be steeped in religious and "backward" ideas, became the primary subjects of
efforts to transform childbearing and child-rearing practices.[3] Without any tsar-
ist network of public kindergartens or day-care centers in place, educators had
a daunting task; even in Moscow in 1917 only 2 percent of the preschool-age
children attended any form of kindergarten (Kirschenbaum 2001, 37). As part of
their vision of "social upbringing" (*vospitanie*), the Bolsheviks planned to establish nearly five thousand preschools across the Soviet Union by the early 1920s.
These goals were not easily met in the conditions of civil war that extended for
more than three years after the Bolsheviks came to power, and by 1919 even in
urban centers, only 5–12 percent of all preschool-age children were served by
these newly imagined educational institutions (Kirschenbaum 2001, 38).[4] More
than a decade later, even though there was a significant increase in preschool
institutions, the majority of children did not attend them and, in fact, fewer children attended them in 1931 than in 1921.[5]

This gradual reduction in preschool programs between 1921 and 1931 was
partly due to the economic constraints faced by the Soviet Union but more
to a shift in political aims. The retrenchment in social policy embodied in the
new family code of 1926 not only reinscribed conservative social mores around
marriage and sexuality but also reinstituted the family as critical to forging new
socialist citizens (Goldman 1993). The state's prior commitment to the "withering away" of the family and supplanting parents with preschool institutions
gradually waned. Instead, "small comrades" were to be forged though the joint
efforts of newly "socialist" families and preschools (Kirschenbaum 2001).[6]

Along with what Lisa Kirschenbaum calls the "unabashed sentimentalization
of motherhood" that emerged by the mid-1930s (2001, 133), child-care programs
were once again officially expanded, including with plans to extend into rural areas.
New family code legislation in 1936 also introduced a range of maternity benefits,
including monetary payments for low-income mothers and mothers with "many"
children, repercussions for fathers shirking alimony payments, and more prenatal

and postnatal medical care (Denisova 2010, 73–74). However, due to inadequate staffing, lack of political will at local levels, and unequal access to social benefits for urban and rural dwellers, many of the legislated changes remained only on paper, especially in rural areas, until after the Second World War.

The most significant components of the campaigns to transform mothercraft involved establishing rural health care centers and child-care facilities, both of which were ultimately important for women's participation in the newly collectivized agriculture (Kuroglo and Filimonova 1976; Ransel 2000, 44–79). The Soviet government was especially anxious to expand the availability of child care, both to induce women to have more children and to incorporate more women into the paid workforce; between 1928 and 1940 the number of day-care centers across the Soviet Union increased more than tenfold, with collective farms often providing child care in some form (Denisova 2010, 165).[7] Still, these efforts remained particularly fraught with internal tensions around pronatalist policies, on the one hand, and prolabor policies with insubstantial social support for families, on the other (Kirschenbaum 2001).[8] As an illustration of this situation, Eva, the woman whose household hosted me during extended stays in southern Moldova, recounted how stressful it was for her to get to work on time when her son was in preschool in the mid-1980s. Having her son in preschool made it possible for her to take on a position of responsibility at the hospital, but because the preschool opened at the same time she had to be at work, and she absolutely could not be late for work, she had frequently had to leave off her five-year-old to wait ten minutes outside the gate while she rushed off.

As late as the 1970s, child care was still not plentiful, especially in rural areas. For children under two years old there were widespread shortages, but also for three- to five-year-olds day-care shortages were widely recognized (Madison 1972, 831–32). In urban areas fewer than 50 percent of all eligible children attended day care, and in rural areas only 30 percent. In the early 1970s in the Vulcăneşti region, there were reportedly twenty day-care centers, as well as some "seasonal" ones, established under the aegis of collective farms (Kuroglo and Filimonova 1976, 30), yet a shortage of adequate child care persisted. This meant that in most rural areas, like the majority of Moldova, through the 1970s young children were being cared for primarily by family members, often by grandmothers who were retired from wage work.

In rural areas the crisis around child care was exacerbated by the lack of provision for maternity leaves. Under Soviet law all able-bodied people of working age were required to work (outside their homes). However, until the late 1960s only urban women had access to maternity leave and child care (Denisova 2010, 78–80). (Two to four months' maternity leave was granted to urban women as early as the 1930s.) Only in 1965 were rural women who were employed in collective farms granted maternity leaves of two-and-a-half months, and only in 1968–1969 were rural dwellers granted the same pensions, sick leaves, and maternity leaves as urban dwellers (Ransel 2000, 131; Denisova 2010, 73–80). Furthermore, in many rural areas, like southern Moldova, women waited well into the late 1970s to gain access to post- and prenatal care (Ransel 2000, 239). The biggest changes to the provision of social support for women and children were felt in the 1980s, when financing for children's hospitals, maternity wards, and prenatal centers significantly increased (Denisova 2010, 172).[9]

Despite the long-term rural crisis around health care and child care, even as early as the 1920s the Soviet state established boarding schools or residential schools (*shkoly internaty*) to educate school-age children and support women balancing the demands of motherhood and work (Makarenko 1973; Waters 1992, 128; Bloch 2003a).[10] Initially these schools were also envisioned as places for children to gain access to a specialized education, for young street children to learn technical skills, or for indigenous Siberians to be inculcated with Soviet state-defined values. After the Second World War, when mother-headed households were common and the Soviet Union was extremely short on people of working age to join the labor force, residential schools of various types expanded countrywide to train students in vocational skills and make it possible for parents to work long hours (Ambler 1961; Ipsa 1994). In Moscow shuttle traders (and other Muscovites) told me that in the 1940s and 1950s, when their parents had long factory shifts, it was not uncommon for children to be left during the week at a residential school and only go home to parents on their day off. This system functioned into the post-Soviet era as well. For instance, in central Siberia in the early 1990s a number of indigenous Siberian women educators told me they were able to complete their professional training by periodically leaving their children in the local residential school while they traveled, sometimes over two thousand miles, to attend professional meetings or meet the biannual in-person exam requirements of distance education programs based in Leningrad (St. Petersburg).

Likewise, in southern Moldova people recounted how in the difficult post-Second World War years, as well as more recently, residential schools played an important role in cases when parents had no relatives with whom to leave children or grandparents were not capable of taking on the responsibility of caring for children. As in the case of an elderly woman I met in Vulcănești in 2004, who was petitioning to care for her grandson over the summer when he was not in school and his parents were still away as labor migrants, sometimes the residential schools worked in conjunction with parents or other relatives to care for children. Today there is a move away from any form of institutional care as Moldova undergoes a reform of its educational and child welfare systems and seeks out ways, including new forms of social support and financial payments, to have children remain in households, if not with parents or close family members (Kaufman 2009; UNICEF 2009). As I explore below, not only the systems of child care, but also public culture around parenting, and especially mothercraft, is again shifting in southern Moldova, as it is across many parts of the former Soviet Union.

Postsocialist Nurturing and "Maternalist" Ideals

Over the 1990s and early 2000s in Russia and neighboring formerly socialist states, legislation emerged that reflects shifting ideals around motherhood and a turn toward increasingly "maternalist" or "familialist" policies. While recognizing the benefits of these policies, scholars have critiqued them for elevating motherhood to a sacred role to which women should aspire above all else and for contributing to growing gender inequality (Temkina and Rotkirch 1997; Rivkin-Fish 2010; Fodor and Kispeter 2014).[11] In the case of Russia, in the first decade of the 2000s new policy measures significantly expanded socialist-era concerns with the "protection" of motherhood and children and instituted substantial financial benefits. For instance, in the last years of the Soviet era legislation was put in place that increased maternity pay and leave until a child turned three and also created a one-time payment to mothers at the time of a child's birth. Subsequent revisions to legislation in a post-Soviet era further inscribed maternalist ideals in a number of ways, including by extending maternity leave benefits to those adopting children, by guaranteeing full wages paid to mothers for up to eighteen months' leave, and by creating a provision for single mothers to receive child benefits until their child turned sixteen (Rotkirch et al. 2007; Denisova 2010, 168). Further legislation supported by President Vladimir Putin promoted an explicit pronatalist policy, where a one-time "maternity capital" payment of $10,000 would be paid to each family that had a second child.[12]

In Moldova, as of 2016 there was no substantial "maternity capital" payment, but the state has nevertheless invested in maternalist policies that are meant to maintain the well-being of women and children. In 2014 benefits related to children were composed of three parts: maternity benefits, a "child-raising" allowance paid for up to three years, and a one-time birth payment. For maternity benefits, in theory women could receive 100 percent of their average earnings from the thirtieth week of pregnancy, for a total of 126 days. The child-raising allowance could be paid for up to three years and was calculated as 30 percent of a mother's average income for the six months preceding the birth. The one-time birth payment was 2,600 lei (about $177 in 2016) for a first child and 2,900 lei (about $190) for each additional child (US Social Security Administration 2014, 208–12).

I met several women who returned from their work in Turkey or Russia to give birth and take maternity leave, but this was not simple. Although they could receive the one-time birth payment, because they worked outside Moldova and they had not paid into the social security system, they were only eligible to receive the child-raising allowance for eighteen months, at a fixed amount of 300 lei per month (less than $15 in 2016). Furthermore, if they returned to their work abroad, they became ineligible to receive the monthly maternity benefit.[13] Given the relatively meager material benefit, many women, like Sveta, the woman I met on the bus who was leaving her ten-month-old for the second time to return to work in Moscow, curtailed their maternity leaves. Instead they sought alternative care for their children so they could return to work within months of the birth of a child.

In addition to the various ways that post-Soviet states have sought to define how children are cared for, households have developed their own ways of providing for children, often drawing on historical patterns of care. In the late Soviet period it was common for children in urban households to spend long summer vacations with grandparents, and even to be primarily cared for by a maternal grandmother until they went to school at age seven, thereby freeing mothers and fathers to fully devote themselves to full-time study or work. While scholars have documented the long history of "extended mothering" in Russia (Rotkirch 2004, 160), wherein mothers, and especially grandmothers and less often a network of family and friends, take on parts of caregiving for children, the practice seems to be transforming. In Tatiana Tianynen-Qadir's (2016) study among border-crossing Russian-Finnish grandmothers she shows how parenting in western Russia was rarely concentrated just within a tight nuclear household of mother-father-children, and today grandmothers also incorporate border crossing as a key nurturing practice in households. In urban Russia Jennifer Utrata (2011) writes about a striking increase in recent years of mother-grandmother-children households, what she calls "co-mothering," with little or no involvement of fathers (Utrata 2011). The extent of grandparent involvement is reflected in survey research among young adults in Moscow who were born in Russia in the 1990s. Of those surveyed, one-third had a grandparent (usually a grandmother) as a member of their immediate household, and three-quarters said that they had at least weekly contact with a grandparent. Most said they had a more intimate relationship with their grandmother than with either of their parents (Semenova and Thompson 2004, 126–27).[14] In southern Moldova households have also historically employed their own versions of "co-mothering" and "extended mothering" to raise children, a pattern of care that women migrants described as intensifying as they were drawn into transnational labor migration with the end of the Soviet Union.

Nurturing from a Distance: Five Women's Narratives

The forms of intimacy maintained with children and the role of caregivers were woven into wider narratives of women's efforts to migrate to Istanbul. Women recounted extended family support for children and often took for granted the historical practices of parents being separated from children for long periods of time. Frequently narratives pointed to domestic abuse, alcoholism, or the death of a partner during his stint as a labor migrant in Moscow as triggering women's own journeys as labor migrants. Even when male relatives were alive and active members of a household, they frequently had secondary responsibility for children, with children living instead with a female relative or close friend of the family.

Caregivers were not left entirely on their own to care for children, and younger children up to the age of seven often attended one of the six town-administered day-care centers for part of the day, while children from the age of seven attended one of the town's several schools.[15] I had an opportunity to meet some of the primary caregivers bringing children to day care in 2004 when my daughter attended day care in Vulcănești. I learned that of the twenty-two children in my daughter's group, nearly half of them were living with a grandmother. I also learned from grandmothers that they considered their daughters to be too tough on their kids. The grandmothers complained that children found it hard when their mothers occasionally visited, especially since mothers were inconsistent with disciplining children and rarely adhered to the schedule the grandmothers had established for their grandchildren. Much like the caregivers for children of transnational migrants in Honduras (Schmalzbauer 2004, 1325), grandmothers I spoke to confided that they were ultimately relieved each time the parents' visits were over and they traveled back to work, because the children could finally resume their familiar routines. The fact that grandmothers were caring for grandchildren while daughters were away working was not viewed as a tragedy, just the most recent wrinkle in a long history of caregiving practices in the region.

As the following portraits of Raia, Maria, Niki, Polina, and Bella show, women negotiate a wide range of nurturing arrangements and in this way are deeply enmeshed in a transnational nurturing nexus.

Extended Nurturing: Raia

Raia, the woman who took her mother's advice to become Ahmet's girlfriend, is in many ways typical of women from multigenerational, extended families in southern Moldova (Kuroglo and Filimonova 1976; Guboglo 2006). In 2005 of her four siblings only Raia was in Istanbul, while one of her three brothers was working in St. Petersburg and the other two remained at home in Gagauzia. The brother working in St. Petersburg was married to a seventeen-year-old girl who lived with Raia's parents, waiting for her young husband to return and meanwhile completing high school. The other two brothers at home were teenagers and still in school but in some ways considered to be adults. One of them had a girlfriend, a teenage girl who had also come to live with Raia's parents. Given their professions—Raia's father was a carpenter and her mother a former state farm laborer—they could barely support themselves and their five dependents (the two sons and daughters-in-law, plus Raia's young son). Raia's economic contributions to the household were critical and followed the pattern established by her mother who, prior to being diagnosed with cancer, also briefly sent remittances home from Istanbul when she worked as a live-in domestic looking after children and cleaning.

Raia first decided to depart for Turkey after she left her husband; he used to beat her and lock her in the cellar when he got drunk. She was relieved to escape that situation. In 2006 Raia showed me a picture of her then five-year-old son dressed in a cowboy outfit she had sent from Istanbul. Raia moved her finger over his image and gave him an air kiss. She explained that while leaving her son with her parents for several years in a row was not easy, it was preferable to being home with no money. In the summer of 2006 Raia was especially proud of being able to send a red bicycle home for her son.

In some ways Raia's transnational nurturing practices, like those of many migrant mothers I met, fit with Anna Rotkirch's (2004b) description of "extended mothering," as involving mothers, grandmothers, and a network of family and friends, and linking rural and urban spaces. In a similar way, the transnational circuits of post-Soviet women's migration into Turkey are partly defined by the nurturing of children. In sending regular remittances and material goods home, Raia was enmeshed in a nurturing nexus involving aunts, uncles, and grandparents who cared for her son at home; the extended family enabled her to pursue work in Turkey and to maintain the transnational flow of resources.

Grandmothering from Afar: Maria

Unlike Raia, Maria, the woman who married a retired shoemaker in Turkey, did not have the benefit of a large extended household. Maria was compelled to leave Moldova in part because, like so many middle-aged migrant men who worked in Russia in the early 1990s, Maria's husband died in a work-related accident in Moscow while employed at a poorly regulated construction brigade (Reeves 2013; Bloch 2014). Shortly after this tragedy, Maria left for Turkey, sending a teenage daughter to live with her aunt and study in Moscow and leaving two sons, aged ten and twelve at the time, with a close friend's family in Moldova.

Maria recalled how the friend who first convinced her to travel to Istanbul had a husband who was willing to stay home with their children, his daughter and Maria's two sons. Only later did Maria convince her own sister to look after the sons, but that did not work out either since the remittances she sent home were, in Maria's words, "drunk and squandered." Maria described how in her absence her sons ran around town "hungry" (*golodnye*) and were always on the streets playing without supervision. With her husband's family estranged, and her natal family back in Latvia, it was a constant struggle for Maria to arrange adequate caregiving for the children.[16]

Maria's sons did not finish high school, and although this was a disappointment for Maria, she was initially happy when they came to live with her in Istanbul. Soon after, however, supporting them became difficult. The sons made more than $100/week working in a wholesale garment storefront, but they spent all their income on drinking and socializing, leaving their mother to pay the rent and cover food expenses for the household. When, in 2004, Maria fell in love with her future husband and soon married him, Maria was faced with a difficult decision; her husband did not smoke or drink, and although he was generally calm, Maria feared that he would be unwilling to live long with her rather wild sons. Coming to Turkey had been about supporting her sons' future, but now they had chosen their own paths and Maria was hesitant to allow her sons to ruin her chance to be happy.

Despite resolving to pursue some of her own aspirations, however, Maria's case also reflects a situation faced by a number of middle-aged women migrants I met who arrived in Istanbul in the mid-1990s to support young children or to help their older children pay for the cost of higher education. Once these children had grown, they sometimes continued to rely on their parents. As Maria said, "I am so tired; when will it stop? Each month I send off money to my children but it is time for them to work!" In 2013 Maria continued to send money, especially to aid her sons but also for her grandchildren in Moscow and Moldova.

When Maria's sons were deported from Turkey in 2007 and returned to live again in Moldova, one of them fathered a child. Although Maria's son did not play a role in his daughter's life, Maria felt compelled to provide some support for the mother of her grandchild. In this way, too, Maria was not unlike many mothers I met who were sending money and clothing to their grown children and grandchildren located both in Moldova and Moscow. In some cases this was in the form of a gift, not critical to the monthly household operations. However, as Tianynen-Qadir (2016) shows for transnational grandmothers moving between Russia and Finland, migrant grandmothers in Turkey were often an important source of support for young families, especially when the men were unable to work, had abandoned their families, or had become casualties of industrial

accidents. In some ways this was a permutation of widespread nurturing practices in southern Moldova, just on a transnational scale. While transnational
grandmothers' support was not automatic, more often than not grandmothers
remained central to household incomes or, as in the following case, to caregiving
for grandchildren.

Other Mothering and Cell Phones: Niki and Nelli

As women work abroad to provide for children, often sending substantial remittances home to finance their care and education, they participate in caregiving
to varying degrees that can shift over time. Numerous factors influence their
caregiving, including the amount of remittances they send and the degree to
which caregivers depend on these remittances, the levels of intimacy between
women and other caregivers, and the access mothers, children, and caregivers
have to communication technologies. In contrast to those like Maria, whose children came of age in the early 2000s, for migrants arriving in Istanbul even just
a few years later, the possibilities for communication had radically changed how
women maintained ties with children and caregivers. If in 2002 one domestic
worker in Turkey told me she felt fortunate to have found a relatively well-paying
job where her employers would pay for her to make two phone calls home each
month, by 2004 cell phone access had made such a benefit all but obsolete. Cell
phone calls from Turkey to Moldova had become relatively inexpensive, and text
messaging had become part of daily interaction. This technology was also key to
my introduction to Niki; I first spoke to Niki in 2003 during one of her phone
calls to her mother, Nelli, in Vulcăneşti.

In 2007 in Istanbul my daughter and I frequently met Niki when she would
invite us to the wholesale clothing store where she worked as a shop assistant.
One afternoon over tea at the store and later at her apartment around the corner
where we enjoyed nonalcoholic beer as we watched a Bollywood film dubbed in
Turkish, Niki spoke about her attempts to provide for her teenage daughter back
home in Moldova. Like many men in the years immediately following the end of
the Soviet Union, Niki's husband went looking for work in Moscow in the early
1990s. The first few years he was away, he returned home every few months, but
by the mid-1990s his visits were more sporadic. Niki lived with her mother and
her infant daughter, and they struggled to get by, given the small maternity benefit Niki received and the long stretches when her mother's salary as a bus driver
went unpaid. Ultimately, Niki and her husband were separated, and Niki decided
to go to Turkey.

Niki's mother, Nelli, had just returned from a stint in Turkey, so she was able to
advise Niki on the best way to find work and how to avoid trouble with the local

police. Like the mothers of many of Niki's friends and classmates, Nelli agreed to become the primary caregiver for her five-year-old granddaughter. Niki's daughter eventually got to know her father, but for nearly seven years she did not see him, and she came to think of her mother, who visited for several weeks once or twice a year, as her "other mother," and her grandmother as "mama." Nelli was proud of this relationship, and in recounting her granddaughter's early years said: "I was the one who always bathed her, even when her mother was home. . . . I took care of her."

Niki tried hard to be in frequent communication with her mother and daughter. For the first several years it was expensive to call, but the advent of widely available and affordable cellular phone service by 2004 radically changed the intensity of contact migrants could maintain with home. Calling became affordable, and texting and Skype opened up a world of frequent instant contact. Both when I met Niki in 2005 and in subsequent years when I visited her in Istanbul, she maintained close ties with her mother and daughter by calling or texting with them several times a day. Niki worried about her daughter's exam results in math, Moldovan, and English, all of which would determine her further academic opportunities. She also firmly supported her daughter's desire to play the flute, and Niki made sure that her mother had the necessary money for tuition. Niki was not physically present on a daily basis. However, her daily conversations with her daughter insured that she weighed in on important decisions and was well informed about her daughter's general well-being. She also invested her energy in encouraging her daughter and reminding her regularly that she had ambitions for her.

In some ways Niki's nurturing from a distance reflects family forms and practices described for Russia (Rotkirch 2004; Utrata 2011), where daily care of a child is often shared by a mother and a grandmother. However, even though the close communication that Niki maintained with her mother and daughter mirrored such physical proximity, the nurturing practices Niki and Nelli engaged in were more akin to what Collins portrays for "othermothers" (1990, 119–22) among African Americans. In the case of othermothering, mothering is a matter of a relationship built around nurturing and not grounded in direct biology; in fact, when Niki's daughter referred to her grandmother as "mama" and her mother as "other mother" (*drugaia mama*), this reflected the degree of relatedness she had with each of them, not the degree of biological closeness. Furthermore, the transnational space through which Niki nurtured, and the importance of communication technologies, introduces another nuance, namely how "othermothering," where biological mothers take part in mothering but not as a primary, physically present figure, was facilitated. As part of a transnational nurturing nexus of the early twenty-first century, cell phones and Internet technology have facilitated family forms that enable migrant worker-mothers to maintain meaningful channels of intimacy with their children and other members of their households, while also pursuing their own aspirations for work and travel.

Othermothering as Enabling Migration: Polina

The distinction between "othermothering" and "other mothering" is especially vivid where, for various reasons, women removed themselves from an active role in raising their children. This was the case for Polina, a coworker of Niki's brother to whom he first introduced me in the summer of 2011 in Istanbul. When we met, Polina was dressed in a black T-shirt and black stretch pants shot through with sparkles and was carrying an array of parcels as gifts for her upcoming visit to her hometown, a Gagauz village in a region of Ukraine bordering Moldova. Later that week Polina invited me to her apartment and over tea told me about her life in Turkey. She explained that she had first come to Istanbul in 1997, when her pay of $60 a week as a shop assistant was more than ten times what she could make at home. She came to Istanbul to escape her abusive husband, whom she had struggled to make peace with for more than ten years.

Polina's departure was not a sudden one. Each time she clashed with her husband, she took refuge with her sister who advised her to leave for Turkey and promised to help look after Polina's son. However, Polina was anxious about leaving her fourteen-year-old son of a previous marriage, so she persevered in the relationship. Polina finally decided to take action, applying for and receiving a passport. Her neighbor, who had worked in Turkey for years, offered to help her find work and a place to live, and most important, she promised not to tell her husband where to find her. Polina borrowed money from her sister and traveled by bus from Vulcănești, via Romania and Bulgaria, to Istanbul.

Polina was afraid to return to southern Moldova, but she missed her son, and after eight months she decided to try to work out the relationship with her husband. Although Polina found her son doing well living with her husband— apparently her husband had formed a strong bond with her son from a very young age—she was unable to smooth over her own relationship with her husband. In fact, they fought fiercely soon after her return, and her husband took the opportunity to condemn Polina, calling her a "Turkish whore" (*Turetskaia shliukha*). Polina said she did not hesitate to pack her bags and return to Turkey, and she did not make another trip home for several years. Her son finished high school but to her disappointment did not go on to higher education. He got married in his early twenties and had two children, but the marriage did not last. At the time of our conversation Polina sent monthly remittances to her ex-daughter-in-law to help support her grandchildren.

Polina's narrative highlights how othermothering and kinship networks are key to enabling women to become transnational migrants. Polina was able to draw solace from her sister's promise to look out for her son, and this helped her make a definitive decision to leave for Istanbul. In addition, the fact that her ex-husband got along well with her son made it easier for her to make a new life in Istanbul; in effect, even though Polina could no longer live with her husband, as a dependable caregiver for her son Polina's ex-husband was also part of a nurturing nexus that made it easier for Polina to pursue migration and remake her life, a life that did not include an active part as an "other mother" raising her teenage son. After working as a shop assistant for a number of years, Polina ultimately fell in love with a Kurdish man with whom she had lived for ten years when I met her.

Histories of Othermothering: Bella

In 2003, shortly after my daughter, stepmother, and I stayed briefly with Bella in her apartment in Vulcănești, Bella departed for work in Russia. I did not see Bella again until 2007, when we sat over dinner in the apartment I was renting in Moscow, and Bella spoke of her life. She shared a vivid and historically grounded account of othermothering as a cultural practice that had long shaped southern Moldova, and she also traced her experience of being a transnational other mother. Bella anchored her account of her family in histories of mobility stretching back more than a century. She described how, in 1880, at the age of five, her Albanian grandmother arrived in the region of contemporary Gagauzia (then Bessarabia) as a refugee fleeing the latest series of wars between the Ottoman and the Russian Empires; since she was without parents, she was taken in by a wealthy merchant family.[17] She was well cared for and ultimately, at the time of her marriage, given land and even a small house. After marrying a local sheepherder, she gave birth to seven children—including Bella's father, who was born in 1912. Bella's father remained in the region and after going to Albania to earn a degree in Tiraspol, he returned to Bessarabia to become a much-loved teacher of physics and mathematics in the local school. The respect local people had for Bella's father was significant enough, even as late as the early 1980s, that Bella was given priority over others in the town administration's allocation of government-owned apartments in the city center of Vulcănești.

The lineage Bella recounted was recognized even though she was, in fact, raised in a different household from her father's. In a pattern of adoption common to the region but not for girls, at the age of five Bella was sent by her parents to live with one of her father's brothers. As Elizaveta Kvilinkova writes, historically when a family adopted a child from relatives, the child was most often male and usually ten to twelve years old; frequently children were legally adopted and would become an heir to the family property, as well as having the responsibility to look after adopted parents in their old age (2007, 221).[18] Bella explained her relatively unusual situation, telling how in her family there were very few children in her generation; three of her father's sisters did not have any children, while another had a daughter, but she died when an unexploded bomb from the Second World War detonated in the field where she was playing. Her father's brother, who inherited the family house and the family-run mill from Bella's grandfather, did not have any children. Bella's parents tried to send one of their sons to live at the family house and ultimately become the heir to the property. However, the son shied away from the hard work demanded of him and would not stay with Bella's aunt and uncle. Ultimately, Bella was sent and she settled in, enjoying the love her aunt and uncle lavished upon her.

There were few relatives around the large stone house until the 1970s. Of her father's siblings, his older brother and sister left for Romania in the brief window of time between the Soviet Union taking over power in the region (1941) and closing the border (1944). Another brother was sent off to Siberia in the late 1930s as the representative of what was viewed as this "kulak" family, considered relatively rich since it owned the single flour mill in the area. Bella's much older siblings, twins, were toddlers at the time, and they were being cared for by Bella's mother's aunt because Bella's parents were studying in Kishinev. When they heard of the efforts to collectivize property in the region, Bella's parents traveled home to their village and found their twins in the arms of the aunt, who was sitting at the train station. According to Bella's account, their house had been taken by the local authorities, and the aunt and children turned out into the street; ultimately, Bella's aunt and all of her mother's family were "sent off to Siberia" for being wealthy landowners.[19] Bella's parents made arrangements for the twins to live with Bella's father's family, and then they returned to their studies in Kishinev.

As Bella recounted a life punctuated by the fall and rise of empires, she also portrayed a local pattern of othermothering, wherein it was commonplace for family members other than parents to care for children. Bella told how, after two years of studying engineering (1978–1980), she got pregnant and, after giving birth and taking maternity leave, left her son with her aunt. The same woman who had raised Bella looked after her son so Bella could complete her education. Bella's aunt was alive until 1991, when she lost her battle with kidney disease, or she might have also cared for Bella's second son when Bella became a labor migrant several years after his birth.

In 1996 Bella was taking maternity leave from her job to raise her second child. Once her son began day care at two years old, she fully expected to return to her job as an engineer. However, although in the early post-Soviet period some former Soviet maternity benefits continued, by the mid-1990s these benefits had eroded, and one of the provisions that changed was a guarantee that mothers could return to their jobs after maternity leave. Bella learned that, contrary to her expectations, her job had not been held for her. As she described it:

> This was a time of extreme economic hardship, with all kinds of people getting laid off, and it was clear that my only option was to go to Turkey to look for work. I left my sons with my husband and headed for Istanbul. . . . It was easy to find good work; before everyone was going there, you could even choose between jobs. I found work with a family looking after two children for \$400/month, and I kept that job, happily working for nine months. I wanted to stay in Istanbul and see the flowers in the spring. I told my husband over the phone and he said, "I'll give you flowers . . . you better get home!" so I ended up going home. I didn't really want to leave; that woman was really nice to me, and I got along so well with the kids. The woman was sad to see me leave since she was only able to get out with her husband when I was there to stay with the kids.

In the end, Bella worked in Istanbul off and on for nearly seven years. In 2002 her older son departed from home on a scholarship to study computer programming in Romania, while her younger son went to live with Bella's brother's family on the other side of town in Vulcănești; they had two small children, and it was less lonely for Bella's son than staying alone with his father. As Bella described it, her husband, a local policeman who worked long hours, began drinking in her absence, which made it more difficult for him to provide adequate supervision for their son. Bella returned annually for brief visits to southern Moldova, and in 2003 she left for Moscow. There she worked long days on an apartment renovation crew, and she looked forward to summers when her younger son would travel to Moscow to spend his vacations with her; in this way Bella was also engaging in "other mothering," while her relatives back in Moldova continued to provide the primary care for her son during the year. After living in Moscow for more than twelve years, in 2016 Bella moved back to Moldova.

Other Mothers and a Transnational Nurturing Nexus

A number of themes weave through the attempts by Raia, Niki, Maria, Polina, and Bella to nurture across borders. The mid- to late 1990s emerge as a traumatic time for families in the region. As the foundations of social stability disappeared almost overnight with the collapse of Soviet state supports, households faced financial crisis. Men were often the first to migrate in search of work on construction brigades in Russia. As in the case of Maria's first husband, many of these men did not return, and only after months of receiving no remittances did women learn that their husbands had died in work-related accidents or possibly found lovers. When men were present, like Raia's and Bella's husbands, they often sank into heavy alcoholism, and households struggled to stay intact.

In addition to household earnings suffering in this period, the state role in a nurturing nexus also diminished. The maternity benefits that had been in place in most former Soviet and East European countries dwindled in Moldova to levels that were no longer significant to households.[20] As well, the maternity leave benefit, which had ensured one's place of work would be retained for two to three years (in the 1980s and into the 1990s) was no longer guaranteed in southern Moldova by the late 1990s. Moreover, by the 2000s benefits were paid according to one's last place of work, with women receiving their full pay for up to four months. However, if there was no last place of work, or if one had been self-employed, women were often ineligible for maternity benefits (Stewart and Huerta 2009, 162).[21]

Othermothering as a local nurturing formation enabling mobility also emerges from these accounts. As Kvilinkova writes about the late nineteenth and early twentieth centuries, "If a child was adopted at an early age by her aunt, then both women (the [biological] mother and the aunt) were called mother" (2007, 221).[22] Like the linguistic practices Collins (1990) alludes to (e.g., "bloodmother" and "othermother") for diverse African American approaches to nurturing, linguistic practices in Moldova also reflect the othermothering vividly portrayed in women's accounts. Versions of these practices continue today as transnational worker-mothers, who were often raised by extended families themselves, now arrange for their own children to be cared for by grandmothers, aunts, and close friends.

Particularly Bella's account—but also Polina's, Niki's, Maria's and Raia's—reflects how the historical practices of othermothering in southern Moldova made it possible for women to imagine becoming transnational labor migrants. Turning to kin or friends was not framed as a desperate measure but as one that fit within a familiar cultural repertoire. As in Maria's and Polina's accounts, when parents or siblings could not care for children, it was not uncommon for women to turn to friends as either primary or assistant caregivers, and grandmothers often readily embraced caregiving as a normal part of the nurturing nexus defining their households. As Eva, who raised her sister Zina's children in the 1990s, said about her own and Zina's grandchildren in 2010, "Of course the grandchildren should stay with me so their parents can work more." In a way, this mirrors a pattern of what Rotkirch has called an "urban-rural nexus" around child care (2004b) that has typified family structures in Russia over the past hundred years, where children are often cared for by grandparents and older relatives in a rural setting, especially over the summer months, while a younger generation works or studies in cities. Likewise, similar to what Leinaweaver (2010) describes for Peruvian migrants and Chamberlain (2013) for Caribbean-British families, othermothering acts as a distinct caregiving form that is crucial to enabling transnational circuits of mobility between Turkey and Moldova, and sometimes Russia.

The distinctive nurturing nexus of care in southern Moldova goes beyond just familial support and instead consists of historically grounded practices and knowledge (e.g., adoption and expectations of state social support), as well as rapidly changing practices of what some in southern Moldova called "other mothering." This form of mothering, or nurturing from a distance provided by biological mothers, requires some form of othermothering or daily care and nurturing provided by grandmothers, aunts, and close friends, as well as some government institutions such as day-care centers, but it also increasingly involves biological mothers maintaining close and frequent emotional connections home via phone and Internet technology.

As for African American communities engaged in othermothering, in an era of a devastated local economy and an ineffective state, marginalized southern Moldovan communities have increasingly had to turn to "those you can count on" and rely on networks of kin and friends (Stack 1974, 90–107). Nevertheless, as Nelli's granddaughter emphasized in calling her mother Niki her "other mother," in analyzing the shape othermothering takes in Moldova, it is important not to elide the ongoing, nurturing from a distance that "other mothers," or migrant mothers, also frequently provide.

Local Patterns of Nurturing or Universal Motherhood?

Forms of mothering in Moldova raise important theoretical questions about how families negotiate support for one another, how transnational mobility may shape the ways caregiving is practiced, and how children experience being raised as part of a transnational nurturing nexus. Assumptions around an inalienable mother-child bond and mothering as innate have received extensive critique in recent decades, especially in the wake of Nancy Scheper-Hughes's (1989) work in shantytowns in Brazil, which destabilized prevalent assumptions about universal forms of "mother love." However, the phenomenon of migrant mothers prompts a renewed discussion of these ideas. As scholarship critically examines the implications of a globally feminized migrant labor force (Ehrenreich and Hochschild 2002), a growing volume of research, as well as popular news coverage, has emerged around the way children "left behind" especially suffer (Parreñas 2005; Coomes 2011). Framing analyses in this way reanimates Euro-American popular discourses of the 1970s and 1980s (Glenn 1994) situating biological mothers, rather than anyone else, as inherently better suited to nurture. The case of southern Moldovan othermothering and transnational nurturing suggests otherwise.

As Henrietta Moore writes, "The concept of 'mother' is not merely given in natural processes (pregnancy, birth, lactation, nurturance), but is a cultural construction which different societies build up and elaborate in different ways" (1988, 25). Moore goes on to state that the idea of "mother" is not only established through "maternal love, daily childcare or physical proximity" (1988, 26) but also through long-term material support, frequent communication, and sometimes more infrequent physical proximity but no less significant ties. From the perspective of North America, where the "cult of motherhood" took on new forms in the 1980s (Sanger 1996; Clark 1999), southern Moldovan women's relative ease with leaving their children for extensive periods might be seen as a conundrum.

It is striking that unlike many of Parreñas's Filipina respondents, who "sobbed" (2005, 115) during interviews, post-Soviet women did not exhibit this type of affect. Over the many conversations we had about transnational nurturing, unless I specifically prompted Moldovan women migrants, they rarely mentioned that they "missed" (*skuchat'*) their children or felt guilty about leaving them back home. In reflecting on their migration, older women did tend to emphasize the need to educate their children, and younger mothers would often recount their migration histories and hardships with reference to those who were othermothering children back home. There are several factors that would seem to contribute to the differences in affect that Parreñas and I observed among transnational migrant-mothers. First, young people I met rarely had independent households, and when young women like Niki or Raia gave birth, they most often lived with their mothers. Given that young women's material and emotional lives were usually closely intertwined with those of their extended family, it makes sense that care for their offspring was also incorporated into this web of relationships and that othermothering became part of the nurturing nexus defining transnational migration. Second, and particularly key to my argument, is the distinctive nurturing nexus in southern Moldova that is inflected by histories of state support, or at least expectations of it, for worker-mothers and historical knowledge of how mothers, grandmothers, and othermothers balanced work and household tasks. In this way, both public discourse and social practice shape how women experience having children raised with othermothers but also the affect women express about others caring for their children. These transnational migrant mothers are "other mothers" who do not necessarily see an inherent conflict between mothering and (transnational) work (see Glenn 1994, 14–16).

Although histories of state support and practices of othermothering mitigate the ways in which women experience these migrations, they do not negate the widespread human suffering brought about by men's and women's large-scale outmigration from home communities. The stories of women labor migrants remind us of the social costs to structural readjustment in marginalized regions like southern Moldova. Especially when households are engaged in a transnational nurturing nexus in raising children, the lack of government support for households places an incredible strain on those upholding the various parts of the caregiving—financial, real time, and virtual. Even in these conditions of material hardship, it is important to avoid assuming universal frameworks around the experience of motherhood and the practices of nurturing and instead to look to the particular contours of transnational nurturing practices. As Raia's, Maria's, Niki's, Polina's, and Bella's accounts show, an analysis privileging biological mothers as primary caregivers would misrepresent the diverse other mothering practices interwoven with their transnational mobility. In thinking about the experiences of transnational migrants and their households seeking to forge multilayered forms of care for their children, ideally we can "shift the center," as Collins writes (1994, 61–62), and be cognizant of the historical continuities and creative measures shaping mobile mothers' nurturing practices in a world of growing precarity, shrinking government assurances, and increase in women's transnational mobility.

ON THE MOVE

The world has radically changed since this research concluded and tensions over borders, mobility, and people on the move are more extreme both globally and in Eurasia than they have been in decades. More than four million Syrians have been displaced by civil war since 2011, with more than three million registered as refugees in Turkey, and many also seeking to transit through Turkey in search of refuge in Europe. Escalating violence and government repression have defined the public sphere in Turkey, with a failed coup in July 2016 and a subsequent political purge of more than 130,000 people (Kingsley 2017).[1] In late November 2016 Prime Minister Erdoğan threatened to open the "border gates" and permit the predominantly Syrian refugees residing in Turkey to access the EU, a move that reflects Erdoğan's confidence in Turkey's essential role in policing mobility for Europe at a time when the EU's future is tenuous. These events highlight how geopolitical balances of power have significant consequences for refugees and migrants.[2]

Whereas the end of the Soviet Union was marked by the easing of border restrictions and hypermobility in Eurasia, the current global order is defined by popular calls for securitization and border regulation. If in the two decades following the end of the Soviet Union labor migrants and well-heeled flexible citizens traversed relatively permeable borders, we are now in a different era, one of global anxiety. Under the leadership of President Vladimir Putin Russia has intensified policing of the relatively open borders that citizens of the former Soviet Union have crossed since 1991, and anti-migrant sentiment has become commonplace.[3] The sentiment shared by many in this part of Eurasia is reflective of a global shift away from an era defined by globalization and a move toward isolationism. Since the end of the Soviet Union people have come to rely on their ability to engage in a myriad of border crossings for trade and circuits of labor migration, as well as to provide for households and pursue personal aspirations, but this era appears to be ending.

Empires and Circuits

Less than a decade following the end of the Soviet Union and the fall of the Berlin Wall Daphne Berdahl wrote, "Tensions between East and West, as well as the tension produced by each system's contrasting ideologies of gender and womanhood, continue to be assimilated and negotiated in multiple and diverse ways" (1999, 205). In Berdahl's formulation "East" and "West" referenced political formations of "capitalism" and "state socialism" and suggested a sharp divide between them. Such an "East"-"West" binary seems less salient now than it did two decades ago. As migrant women have spent time outside the borders of the former Soviet Union, become immersed in new forms of labor, and negotiated intimate practices at home and abroad, they have become similar to other marginalized women on the move globally (Colen 1995; Ehrenreich and Hochschild 2002). Moreover, as the memory of state socialism fades, it is likely to become just one of the many historical forces shaping the region, with the binary of capitalism and state socialism becoming less important.

Nevertheless, one must also carefully take into account local histories to identify the forms that power and disempowerment take. In the first decade of the new millennium, the meanings people attached to socialist and postsocialist frames of reference continued to have salience for them. The ways that migrants have imagined intimate ties across borders have been fundamentally shaped by generations of socialist ideology and social practice that were informed by ideals of gender equality, meaningful labor, and expectations of a state that would provide for the needs of its citizens. For the immediate future this frame continues to be critical for understanding the shifting gender systems, structures of feeling, and processes of mobility that define the region. When Kara, the entertainer from Ukraine who was saving money to help her brother pay for school and her mother migrate to Italy, rhetorically asked me, "How can a government stand by while its population is forced to flee abroad to make a living?" she was not asking this in the abstract. Kara was angrily reacting to the abrogation of a historically specific social contract. For Kara and others, the legacy of a socialist state continues to be substantial, with an expectation that states should provide for their citizens, so men and women would not have to pursue their aspirations beyond their homelands.

The transnational flows discussed in these pages have multiple origins and destinations, with the primary flow I have traced moving between north and south, from Russia to Moldova to Turkey. Other flows are also part of the story, as when southern Moldovans like Bella, with ethnic ties to Romania or Bulgaria, are drawn into additional transnational circuits, and when thousands of Turkish male contract workers live long-term doing construction in Russia and Kazakhstan. Critically thinking about these transnational flows reorients unidirectional arrows suggested by models of modernization. Instead, attention can turn to the circuits where people, money, and imagery, such as that circulated by *The Magnificent Century*, move along conduits often forged by trade but also built on long histories of cultural and political connection. In all these flows, to some degree, people are pursuing aspirations for a newly radiant future inherently linked to the very act of mobility. In this way the post-Soviet story of labor migration into Turkey provides a portal onto how people fare as empires wax and wane.

Intimacy

In focusing my attention on intimacy in multiple forms, I have sought to trace both the "costs" of global capitalism for women and their households and the possibilities created by mobility. While intimate practices in multiple registers—for example, sexuality without hang-ups, strategic romance and marriage, and other mothering—were recognizable forms, I also hope to have humanized people by showing the diverse types of relationships women are managing and by enmeshing women within relationships with each other, as well as with lovers, families, and communities. The sudden ability to cross borders in the early 1990s was a sort of revelation for many women. In conversation, women periodically reminded me that labor migration was not just about earning a living or suffering without one's family. In one memorable instance, one afternoon in Istanbul Zina recalled the 1990s as an exhilarating time to be employed in Turkey, and she confided, smiling slyly, "My dear, I did not always clean houses . . . I had other work too." She went on to describe with relish how when she worked as a sales assistant she would travel regularly between Ukraine and Turkey, carrying up to $50,000 strapped to her body for payment on goods that had been sent from Turkey to Ukraine. The routes south to Istanbul opened up possibilities for a sense of exhilaration, as well as for the prospect of providing for households back in home communities. These stories of a sense of expanding horizons, along with the ability to maintain intimate ties both locally in Istanbul and transnationally—through a nurturing nexus with children, parents, and other relatives back home—have proven to be a central element of these gendered transnational circuits.

States and the Future

By virtue of being engaged in transnational circuits, moving between marginal hometowns and cosmopolitan centers like Istanbul, the women I came to know negotiated the barriers of multiple states and gained immeasurable expertise. Women became experts in import/export operations, with specialized knowledge of how much could be packed of what to cross which borders. They also became local immigration consultants with insider knowledge of what it takes to obtain visas and renew passports, what would be sure to create impediments at the border, and what alternative travel routes could be taken. And they often became savvy capitalists, whether or not they embraced this development. With the end of the Soviet Union, which women often told me emphatically was a "tragedy" (*tragediia*) for them and their families, people became a new type of neoliberal subject, seeking out opportunities and shouldering responsibility for services the state provided in the past. As Zina explained in Istanbul one afternoon, "We have had to learn how to play the system; we had to learn that no one will look out for us." More than anything else, in a short period of time the women I came to know had remade themselves to make a living, while continuing to dream of better lives.

In a Skype call with Bella as the final pages of this book were coming together, she reflected on what years of labor migration have meant for her. "I worked for more than ten years in Russia and nearly seven years in Istanbul, and what do I have to show for it? I did put my sons through postsecondary education in Romania; oi, that involved a lot of running around! But what is left?" At age fifty-two Bella had just returned to Moldova to live, and she reflected on her job search. She told me she had recently been turned down for a position in a call center where, as she described, "you would have to sell people things they don't want." She was back to hanging wallpaper in apartment renovations, work she had been doing when she first arrived in Moscow in 2003 but also work that did not provide for her pension or health insurance. She had gone off into a transnational migration circuit and returned, but she faced the same indifferent state that she had left behind when she departed in search of something better nearly twenty years earlier. In an era of transnational flows, including of migrants and refugees, in many places states have become even less accountable to their growing number of absent citizens, and destination states have felt little obligation to safeguard rights or well-being for non-citizens, people on the move.

As this generation of post-Soviet migrants ages, and many of the next generation also become labor migrants, what will the future bring as a global underclass continues to travel long distances to labor in the households and intimate service sectors of more wealthy, privileged global centers? Will the next generation—migrants' children—come up with a way to pressure their governments to address their plight as marginalized citizens in the world? Will international efforts coalesce around guaranteed basic rights for people on the move? It is possible that outrage like Eva's about southern Moldova being a "colony" of "slaves" laboring for global capitalism could bring about an effective solidarity movement among post-Soviet labor migrants. Even without such a movement, in recognizing the myriad ways that labor migrants manage to forge meaningful lives we can begin to appreciate their negotiations with shifting forms of power. The potent combination of transnational circuits, shifting ideals about gender and intimacy, and intimate bonds between Turkish men and Russian-speaking women is part of the unfolding story of how new configurations of global capital shape personal lives but also the story of how migrants make lives for themselves despite the injustices of this newly precarious world.

PEOPLE FEATURED

AKSANA Worked as an exotic dancer in Istanbul for short contracts over nearly five years; returned home to Belarus, and dreams of realizing aspirations of her youth to become a classical dancer.

ANDREI Looking toward retirement, Andrei continues to work for the Vulcănești municipality.

ANIA Became a significant player in the import business from the garment district in Istanbul, regularly expending up to $10,000 in purchases.

BELLA After moving to Moscow she ran a thriving business renovating apartments and enjoyed annual visits to her sons and grandson in Romania. In 2016 she decided not to pursue permanent residency in Russia, and instead moved to Romania to live with her sons.

EVA Nearing retirement from her work at the town hospital in Vulcănești, she now travels twice a year to spend several months with her grandchildren in Russia.

GALINA Ran a stall selling clothing at a market in a city to the south of Moscow; she continues to sing and sell food at the market.

IRINA Worked as an exotic dancer in Istanbul for two years and ultimately married a German she met in one of the clubs. Moved to Germany with her daughter and became a housewife.

IULIA After dropping out of law school in Russia, worked as an exotic dancer in Istanbul for a short contract; returned to Russia where she still dreams of pursuing a career in acting.

KARA   Worked as an exotic dancer in Istanbul for several years, supporting her mother and brother at home in Ukraine. She married and moved to Bulgaria where she works in a grocery store while raising her school-age son.

MARIA   For more than twenty years she worked as a shop assistant and later sales manager in Laleli; in 2014 her husband passed away, and Maria decided to move to Moscow to live with her daughter and grandchildren.

NADIA   Arrived in Istanbul in the late 1990s and was able to capitalize on the relatively well-paid work as an entertainer; in the early 2000s she opened her own property management company with her boyfriend as a business partner.

NELLI   Raised her granddaughter while her daughter, Niki, was in Turkey, and now enjoys periodic visits from her granddaughter who studies in Romania.

NIKI   After years of living in Turkey in 2011 Niki returned briefly to Moldova and eked out a living shuttling goods from Romania into Moldova. After receiving her Bulgarian citizenship in 2013, she left to work in Great Britain.

OLGA   After starting a small shuttle trading business, she prospered. She expanded her boutique and now has a chain of men's clothing stores in the suburbs of Moscow.

POLINA   Works in Laleli as a shop assistant as she has since the late 1990s; she lives happily with her Turkish boyfriend and makes yearly visits to her grandchildren in Ukraine.

RAIA   Worked as a sales assistant in Istanbul for two years and hoped to marry her boyfriend. She has returned to live with her parents and son in Moldova.

ZHENIA   Central Siberian shuttle trader and former teacher. Passed away in the early 2000s.

ZINA   Worked as an itinerant domestic worker and shop assistant in Istanbul and as a projectionist and medical orderly in Moldova. She now works as a domestic in Moscow, where she often cares for her granddaughter. She dreams of finding an Indian husband.

Notes

INTRODUCTION: FROM THE ARCTIC TO ISTANBUL

1. Especially following the 1998 economic crisis, when the ruble was volatile for a number of years, it was common for people to conduct business and refer to large expenses in US dollars.

2. Nasra Shah and Indu Menon (1997) detail some of the policies receiving countries in the Middle East, and particularly Kuwait, had toward women migrant workers in the 1990s. See Mahdavi 2011 for an account of the conditions faced by both women and men labor migrants in Dubai.

3. As a number of shuttle traders recounted, even if women traveled with husbands, if they had different last names they would very likely be denied entry to the UAE. As of 2015 the UAE Embassy indicated on its website (Embassy of the UAE 2015) that those holding passports from fifty-two listed countries were eligible for visas on arrival. Russian citizens (among others) were required to arrange visas in advance of arriving in the UAE, and there were no different policies for men and women or any age restrictions indicated.

4. Throughout the text I refer to the former Soviet Union and the FSU interchangeably.

5. Judging from how often migrants asked me to deliver funds or expensive gold jewelry to relatives, themselves brought funds home, or sent money via other informal channels, it is easy to imagine that as much as half of the total remittances were being transferred informally.

6. By the early 1990s most post-Soviet citizens could enter Turkey on a one- or two-month tourist visa issued on arrival. Turkey's relatively permeable border policy, beginning in the 1990s, is linked to Turkey's status as one of the signatories of the Black Sea Economic Co-operation agreement meant to facilitate trade and border crossing in the region; Albania, Armenia, Azerbaijan, Bulgaria, Georgia, Greece, Moldova, Romania, Russia, and Ukraine are also signatories to this agreement (Aktar and Ögelman 1994, 344).

7. "Islamist" is a broad term generally referring to the politicization of Islam, but understood variously. Malise Ruthven writes of "Islamism" as the "ideologization" of Islam in terms of politics, where some symbols from the "historical repertoire of Islam" get deployed, "just as communism ideologizes the reality of the commune, socialism the social, and fascism the ancient symbol of Roman consular authority. Islamism is not Islam . . . it is important to distinguish between them" (2012, 26). In Turkey since the late 1990s a growing number of people have come to equate the term "Islamist" with a "revival of civic life, incorporating into the political process conservative women" and with a "challenge to the monopoly on urbanism and modernism" held for decades by Turks defining themselves as secular, Westernized, and urban (White 2004, 149; see also White 2002; Vojdik 2010).

8. Post-Soviet labor migration in the twenty-first century spans a large number of countries, with significant concentrations of people in Israel and Western Europe, especially Spain and Italy (Golden 2003; Solari 2014), and across Asia, including in India and South Korea. It became popular in the early 2000s for women from the Russian Far East (e.g., Vladivostok and Khabarovsk) to seek work in South Korea, Japan, and China, and these destinations have also appealed to women labor migrants from Moldova

(Subbotina 2005, 179; Bloch 2009). In addition to low-paid labor migrants, from the 1990s onward there has been a steady stream of highly skilled migrants securing work in their fields of expertise and leaving the region of the FSU (Kuznetsov 1995).

9. Dramatic inflation and a fall in the Turkish lira accompanied the economic crisis of 2000; the Turkish lira was devalued from 680,000 lira to $1 to 1,200,000 lira to $1. However, from 2002 to 2011 Turkey's economy grew about 7.5 percent annually (Taşpınar 2012).

10. In the absence of reliable data on undocumented migrants, police apprehensions reflect something of the diversity of the migrants coming from the former Soviet Union and Eastern Europe. Between 1996 and 2006, Moldovans were apprehended more than any other group of migrants from the former Soviet Union; Ahmet İçduygu and Deniz Yükseker (2012, 443–48) provide approximate numbers for the countries with the highest level of apprehensions as follows: Moldova (53,000), Romania (23,000), Georgia (18,000), Ukraine (18,000), and the Russian Federation (18,000).

For the almost 620,000 irregular migrants apprehended in Turkey in this period, İçduygu and Yükseker (2012, 444) distinguish between two categories of transit migrants, those they call "irregular circular labor migrants," which they identify as coming from the former Soviet Union and Eastern Europe, and asylum seekers, coming from a wide range of countries and making up 52 percent of the total transit migrants (2012, 443, 448). With the escalation of civil war in Syria since 2014, asylum seekers in Turkey have been overwelmingly from Syria; as of April 2017, of the more than 5 million people registered as refugees fleeing Syria, nearly 3 million were registered in Turkey (UNHCR 2017).

11. Bollywood is only the latest version of popular Indian film in the former Soviet Union, but classic Indian film also continues to resonate with many people in the FSU. For instance, see Bollywood's Raj 2013.

12. A growing number of women from former Soviet states have found work as entertainers in India. According to Indian police, as of 2014 there were at least 3,500 women from former Soviet states employed as sex workers in Delhi (Femen 2012).

13. A select group of people were able to take part in the tightly regulated travel from the Soviet Union to countries outside the socialist bloc. However, travel between socialist bloc countries was widespread and ranged from student work brigades to conference attendance to organized tours; in addition, mobility from socialist bloc countries into the Soviet Union, especially for the purpose of education, was extensive (Matusevich 2007). Travel within the Soviet Union was very popular and frequently features in nostalgic accounts; see Gorsuch and Koenker 2006 on the subject of travel within Soviet republics, as well as beyond the borders of the Soviet Union, and the role of this travel in shaping Soviet perceptions of mobility, identity, and social stature.

14. Throughout the text I use "shuttle trader" and "trader" interchangeably.

15. After the brief window of virtually unregulated trade (1991–1993), Russian government restrictions on shuttle traders, limiting the amount of untaxed goods that could be brought into Russia to $1,000 and 50 kilograms, or roughly two suitcases (Nikitina 1996), along with the Russian economic crisis of 1998, caused a sharp downturn in trade. However, by 2013 Russia was one of Turkey's largest sources of export revenue overall, at nearly 7 billion dollars annually, or 4.6 percent of total export revenue. Only Germany, Iraq, and Great Britain provided more revenue, with exports making up about 13.7, 11.9, and 8.8 billion dollars (or 9 percent, 7.9 percent, and 5.8 percent), respectively (Turkstat 2016). From 2006 to 2014 Turkey also relied on Russia more than any other country for imports, with 10–16 percent of all imports coming from Russia annually; Germany and China were the next most significant sources for imports.

16. According to Nicholas Barr, the proportion of registered unemployed women shifted somewhat as women dropped out of the official labor market in large numbers

and stopped being counted in employment data (1994, 167–68). However, Sarah Ashwin and Elaine Bowers argue that women may simply have registered more often, and that there is a significant difference between data on the "registered unemployed" and survey data, as well as significant variation by region and levels of white-collar employment (1997, 23–24, 35).

17. Cooper provides a productive critique of how the term "modernity" has been deployed, and he advocates for "a historical practice sensitive to the different ways people frame the relationship of past, present, and future, an understanding of the situations and conjunctures that enable and disable particular representations, and a focus on process and causation in the past and on choice, political organization, responsibility and accountability in the future" (1999, 149).

18. Douglas Rogers and Katherine Verdery also helpfully demarcate "postsocialist" to mean: "those countries that had been dominated by Communist parties and 'command economies' with socialized property forms, but that after 1989–1991 saw these forms decentralized and pluralized" (2013, 439).

19. Taking into account critical perspectives on the term "postsocialism" (or "post-socialism"), throughout the book I use "postsocialist" and "post-Soviet" to refer to a similar set of social relations, with "post-Soviet" as a subset of "postsocialist." I have chosen to use the spelling of "postsocialist/postsocialism" over a hyphenated variant to underscore this set of social relations as distinctive, and not just another in a long line of "post-" eras. Nevertheless, I am cognizant of the critique of some scholars that patterns which may appear "socialist" are not really; they could be "direct *responses* to the new market initiatives, produced *by* them, rather than remnants of an older mentality . . . people's responses . . . may appear as holdovers precisely because they employ a language and symbols adapted from previous orders" (Burawoy and Verdery 1999, 2).

20. I define former socialist or "emergent capitalist" or neocapitalist regions of the world—such as Vietnam, China, and the former Soviet Union—as places where under socialism labor was valued as something that produced an end product of use to the broader society. As Elizabeth Dunn writes about a Polish factory undergoing privatization, the employees viewed the firm as "more than an engine to make profit or even to make products. It was the heart of a social community. . . . Under socialism it was the vehicle through which the state carried out its moral obligation to care for its citizens" (2004, 46).

21. Here and elsewhere I borrow from Nancy Ries's formulation "newly capitalist" (2002, 283) to avoid a static, binary portrayal of socialist and postsocialist Russia and to suggest the distinct experience of recent capitalist processes in Russia. This analysis is also inspired by Aihwa Ong's (1999) important discussion of multiple capitalisms.

22. There is a vast literature on affect and, increasingly, a vibrant feminist critique of distinctions made between "affect" and "emotion," the possibility for a productive tension between the two, and the pitfalls of attempting an analysis that combines both. Carolyn Pedwell and Anne Whitehead helpfully analyze these terms and their use in feminist theorizing, also tracing how the "affective turn" emerged in response to the 1980s "textual turn" and its overemphasis on the discursive (2012, 116). Pedwell and Whitehead pose a key question: Does affect theory's aim to direct attention to forces *beyond* emotion that unconsciously work on people ultimately become a depoliticized project? In other words, if people are not aware of the forces that are working on them, what are the possibilities for social transformation?

23. Research revolving around discourse and forms of oral tradition has defined this scholarship, with work on expressions of anger in Papua New Guinea (Rosaldo 1980), honor among the Bedouin in Egypt (Abu-Lughod 1986), and love in Sri Lanka (Trawick 1990). For a review of the anthropological literature on emotion prior to the early 2000s, see Wilce 2004.

24. The definition of trafficking has evolved over the years, but the UN Protocol, in fact, emphasizes how a wide range of people—not excluding men, not limited to those involved in sex work, and including those who are legally located in a country—could be considered trafficked. As the Protocol states, to be trafficked hinges on "the act of recruiting, harbouring, transporting, providing, or obtaining a person for compelled labor or commercial sex acts through the use of force, fraud, or coercion" (see Madhavi 2011, 16–7). However, while the United Nations Palermo Protocol and the United States' Victims of Trafficking and Violence Protection Act (TVPA), passed in 2000—two of the most important anti-trafficking measures to be forged—claim to have an explicitly broad definition of trafficking, the assessment of anti-trafficking measures continues to focus heavily on women sex workers (see Vance 2011; US Department of State 2012a).

25. For instance, one long-established anti-trafficking organization, the Coalition Against Trafficking in Women (CATW), lumps prostitution with trafficking and notes that "prostitution and trafficking . . . [are] major human rights violations of women." In situating its work, CATW (2011) writes, "Our challenge, in opposition to the enormous power and resources of the sex industry that portrays prostitution as sexual liberation, work or even glamorous, has been to make the harm of prostitution visible."

26. For instance, without any clear means of substantiating the claim, in the late 1990s and early 2000s one figure repeatedly occurred in sources indicating that two-thirds of an estimated five hundred thousand women annually trafficked for prostitution to forty to fifty countries across the world came from Eastern Europe and the former Soviet Union (see Hughes 2002, 5).

27. A number of documentary and docudrama films were produced in the 2000s on the subject of trafficking. These include *Trafficking Cinderella* (2001), made in Canada with funds from the Open Society Institute, and *The Price of Sex* (2011), first aired as *Trafficking in Women* in October 2005 by the Canadian Broadcasting Corporation. The feature film *Lilya 4-Ever* (2002), a Swedish/Danish joint production, also had a wide viewership.

28. One source indicates that law agencies globally reported trafficking as affecting over forty-one thousand individuals in 2011 (USAID 2012a).

29. The constellation of feminism that Elizabeth Bernstein (2012) calls "carceral feminism" focuses on anti-prostitution and is staunchly in support of anti-trafficking measures that expand the powers of the state; adherents support intensifying policing to control trafficking in women, something they equate with prostitution/sex work.

30. As Donna Guy writes, "For many Europeans it was inconceivable that their female compatriots would willingly submit to sexual intercourse with foreign, racially varied men . . . so European women in foreign bordellos were construed as 'white slaves' . . . and the campaign to rescue them became a glorious battle pitting civilization at home against barbarism beyond" (2000, 74).

31. In writing about the history of prostitution and its regulation in Argentina, Guy (1991, 7) describes how European women fled poverty and sometimes religious persecution to seek a means of survival abroad; these women "filled Buenos Aires bordellos" at the peak of outmigration from Europe, from the 1870s to the beginning of the First World War.

32. The United States Trafficking Victims Protection Act (TVPA) of 2000 and subsequent Reauthorization Acts (2003, 2008, and 2013) were passed with the intention of combatting trafficking in persons worldwide, with the annual Trafficking in Persons reports (TIP) assessing each country's anti-trafficking efforts as a central component (see Mahdavi 2011, 16–21; Cheng and Kim 2014). The TIP reports, issued by the US Department of State, rate each country on a scale from Tier 1 to Tier 3. Tier 1 countries (consistently relatively wealthy countries, such as Sweden and the United Kingdom) are deemed to have adequate counter-trafficking measures in place, while Tier 3 countries (consistently less wealthy countries) are deemed to be inadequately addressing the issue of trafficking. A Tier 2 "provisional" rating

is meant to signal that a country needs to apply more effort to address concerns about trafficking. Countries identified as Tier 3 are then subject to US sanctions in the form of losing favored trade status and/or nonhumanitarian aid. Scholars have suggested that these ratings could have more to do with US foreign policy than any actual reflection of degrees of trafficking in a given location (Mahdavi 2011, 19; Cheng 2010, 201–2).

33. By 2014 the TIP report continued to classify Turkey as a "Tier 2" country, noting that Turkey "does not fully comply with the minimum standards for the elimination of trafficking" (US Department of State 2014, 383).

34. As a reflection of its growing mandate, as staff at the IOM office in Istanbul told me in 2007, in just two years, between 2004 and 2006, the IOM offices in Turkey expanded from two to twenty people, located in both Istanbul and Ankara. The IOM has also been instrumental in identifying (and partially financing) several Turkish NGO partners to provide police training in how to identify trafficking victims, to create and administer shelters for women identified as trafficked, and to provide assistance in returning those identified as victims of trafficking to their home countries. See Keough 2015 for a thorough discussion of discourses on trafficking in Moldova.

35. Each purchase of clothing was made in batches of five or seven sizes, so for instance a batch of pants would be in small (S), medium (M), Large (L), Extra Large (XL), and Extra Extra Large (XXL); shuttle traders would ask for a specific number of batches. For instance, two batches would result in ten shirts being purchased. As a reflection of the ways in which the shuttle traders acquired specialized knowledge, Olga and other shuttle traders would incorporate the English inflected labels and ask shopkeepers for a shirt in size "S-ka" or "L-ka" instead of "small" or "large" in Russian (*malen'kii* or *bol'shoi*). The goods, which were destined for a global market, including Russia but also Europe and North America, were most often labeled in English, or sometimes by number (e.g., 4, 6, 8, 10, etc. for women's clothing destined for North America, or 36, 38, 40, 42, etc. for clothing destined for Europe).

36. Ruzhena and Udara were adamant that they wanted me to use their real names, a request I am honoring here.

37. See Scheper-Hughes 2005 on how disenfranchised people in Europe are linked to a global traffic in human organs, including kidneys.

38. Among Russian speakers from the FSU the term "svoi," meaning "our own" or "one of us," is most often invoked to indicate that a person is in one's social circle or that a thing is particular to a specific circle of connection. Margaret Paxson translates "svoi" as "one's own," and points to the possible concentric circles the term can reference, including extended family, co-villager, or compatriot (2005, 53).

39. In part as an effort to attract less attention, in summer I wore loose tunics and trousers with sensible sandals, a look Russian speakers I came to know well sometimes chided me for, suggesting that I was too young to forgo wearing more revealing clothing and stylish footwear. Likewise, some Turkish friends who comfortably dressed in miniskirts or light strappy sundresses poked fun at me, saying that my attire implicitly lent support to Islamist factions and their preference for women to dress modestly.

40. Ahmet İçduygu notes that in Turkey in 2005 there were 132,000 people with residency permits, the document issued for those legally living in Turkey for more than three months, and nearly one-third of the permit holders were from Bulgaria (2009, 288). Only 17 percent of the permits were issued for people employed in Turkey, with 19 percent for students and the remaining permits for dependents of the primary permit holders.

CHAPTER 1. MAGNIFICENT CENTURIES AND ECONOMIES OF DESIRE

1. While *The Magnificent Century* has been the most popular of the transnationally broadcast Turkish television dramas, more than a hundred other shows are also internationally broadcast in either dubbed or subtitled form throughout the Balkans, Latin

America, the Middle East, and Asia (Soap Opera Diplomacy 2013). As of 2016 *The Magnificent Century* was distinctive as the only television drama that featured a woman historical figure who hails from a region of the former Soviet Union.

2. The earliest export of Turkish soap operas dates to 2001, when they were first sent to Central Asian countries, particularly Kazakhstan and Uzbekistan (Balli et al. 2013, 181). Viewership of Turkey's telenovelas expanded significantly in the early 2000s, in particular in Arab countries. Some reflect that this "media flow" may be explained by a number of factors, including widespread linguistic affinities, a common Muslim value system in at least twenty countries, the use of alluring Turkish locations for filming, such as the Bosphorus, and the common inclusion of libidinous and/or professional women in the series (Buccianti 2010). In 2014 *The Magnificent Century* also premiered in the United States via MundoFox Broadcasting (Global Agency 2014).

3. Outside Turkey some who see the telenovela as celebrating Turkish dominance in the region have also contested it. For instance, in one Internet forum revolving around things Slavic, in September 2012 the string for "Bulgaria" had a substring of "Turkish Neo-Ottoman TV Series," and the posts were dominated by a sentiment of alarm about the widespread fascination with the television series. As one person writes, "It's all part of the same plan, to make south Slavs more opened towards Turks. TV stations in Bosnia, Serbia and Croatia are full of Turkish soap-operas. This show about sultan Süleyman is just another in line but certainly the worst one in terms of Turkish propaganda.... I am especially mad at south Slavs which approve this show in our areas and thus take a **** on all the suffering our peoples had during the Turkish occupation" (Slavorum 2012).

4. Hürrem is most often referred to as "Roxelana" by Russian speakers, but depending on the source, she is also sometimes referred to as "Anastasia" or "la Russa," in reference to her origins (Freely 1996, 194).

5. Hürrem may have originally come from Rohatyn, Ukraine, but this is difficult to confirm given the paucity of sources (Peirce 1993, 59). Few documents exist on Hürrem's life, with the exception of some references gleaned from Venetian and French diplomats' correspondence, comments made by prisoners escaped from Ottoman prisons, merchants' records, and letters composed by Hürrem and addressed to Süleyman, although there are no known surviving letters written by Süleyman to Hürrem (Peirce 2015).

6. Alexandra Lisowska was known as "Roxelana" perhaps because of the Medieval Latin name for Rus'-Ukraine or due to a Polish term meaning "Ruthenian maiden," a reference to Alexandra's possible origins in a part of Poland (present-day Ukraine) where Ruthenians have been historically concentrated, even as the region has witnessed the expansion and contraction of more than one empire over nearly six hundred years (Peirce 1993, 58). The group most often known as "Ruthenian" in English is also referred to as "Rusyn." Since the Middle Ages the Rusyns have recognized a homeland in what some call the heart of Europe, in territory ruled at different points by many different governments and empires (Magosci 1995). Interestingly, this homeland is also seen by some as the site of a significant divide between the Catholic West and the Orthodox East (Picchio 1984). The Rusyns have never had their own state, but at different points in history they have mobilized for their own political representation and even distinct nationhood. According to Paul Magosci (1995), most often they allied themselves strategically as Russian or Ukrainian. Linguistically, Rusyns are Eastern Slavs, but whether they should be seen as closer to Russians or Ukrainians is much debated.

7. In Byzantine times, as well, women of humble origins sometimes rose to celebrated positions of power. One of the most famous women with a courtesan past was Empress Theodora, married to Byzantine Emperor Justinian once he ascended the throne in 527AD (Dauphin 1996, 5).

8. Circassia came to be widely known as the homeland of "Circassian beauties." At least since the seventeenth century the Orientalist idea of a "Circassian beauty," or an

idealization of Circassian women as embodying the pinnacle of aesthetic beauty, appeared in European art; in the eighteenth century with the growing encroachment of the Russian Empire on the area of Circassia, the notion of a "Circassian beauty" became even further entrenched in European art and literature, as well as in the popular Turkish imagination (Doğan 2011, 84). For further reflection on the links between gender, nation, and the Circassian diaspora, see Doğan 2011.

9. The woman known as "Roxelana" and "La Russa" in Western sources is referred to officially as Haseki Hürrem Sultan in Turkish sources, or more popularly as just Hürrem. Supposedly Alexandra was given the name of "Hürrem" because of her sunny demeanor; in Turkish, Hürrem means "the cheerful one." Leslie Peirce provides a fascinating discussion of the term *haseki*, meaning the "sultan's favorite," and describes it as a "candidly political role" that shifted over time (1993, 104–12). Peirce also lucidly traces how *sultan* emerged as a title carried by both male and female Ottomans, and at times favorite concubines, in a growing "legitimating discourse as the Ottoman dynasty advanced ever-greater claims to prominence in the Islamic world" (1993, 18). Hürrem Sultan died in April 1558, and although in her lifetime she wielded enormous power, surprisingly little is known about her (Peirce 2015).

10. A second monument to Hürrem, a large public bath, was also built at a prominent axis of the imperial city. It was located near the royal palace, the Aya Sofya (the church-turned-mosque then mosque-turned-museum, then, in 2016, museum-turned-mosque), and the Hippodrome (Peirce 1993, 203; First Call 2016).

11. The renowned Ottoman architect Mimar Sinan was commissioned to design the mosque complex, which included a mosque, school, college, soup kitchen, hospital, and fountain. In 2010 there were plans to allocate a portion of the complex for a museum dedicated to Mimar Sinan (Demır and Gamm 2010).

12. In one analysis that pivots around desire as a commodity but shortchanges relevant historical context, performance, or polyvalent meanings that might be brought to intimate encounters, Anna Agathangelou argues that "white but not quite" men in Cyprus in the 1990s and early 2000s looked to "white but not quite" women, who were predominantly from the former Soviet Union and Eastern Europe, as a means of gaining status for themselves and for their states (2004, 71).

13. Pelkmans (2006) describes the measures people would go to in trying to communicate across the closed border and provides a fascinating ethnographic account of the history of transborder connections between Georgia and Turkey, including the paradoxical post-Soviet slowing down of flows and cross-border connections for some, and the increased opportunities for others.

14. This concept of *kul'tura*, sometimes translated as "culture" and other times as "civilization," circulated widely in the Soviet Union and connoted a particular cultural hierarchy, including a high regard for literature, liberal ideals of gender equality, and a respect for education. The concept was also often implicitly linked to an understanding of different cultural groups as being at different points on an evolutionary scale where an urban, industrialized Europe was seen as the pinnacle. There is a large volume of writing on this concept as it emerged in Soviet society (see Grant 1995). In her *Mastering the Art of Soviet Cooking: A Memoir of Food and Longing*, Anya Von Bremzen (2013) discusses how by the 1930s acquiring *kul'turnost'* or "becoming cultured" came to revolve around trappings of "high" culture in the form of attending the theater or opera and being well versed in the classics of European literature.

15. Michael Reynolds (2011, 6) argues that interstate competition in the early twentieth century complicated political allegiances in eastern Anatolia, with Kurds and Armenians especially caught between struggles for Ottoman and Russian empire building.

16. As Vera Tolz vividly recounts, by the late nineteenth century a lively scholarly debate emerged, especially in Russia and Germany, around the geographic, political, and

cultural constructs of "East" and "West" (2011, 47–68). Following the horrors of the First World War, when the superiority of "Western" societies was widely questioned, Russian scholars fundamentally repositioned how they thought about "East," "West," "Europe" and "Asia"; for instance, one school of thought in Russia emerged holding that Russia was uniquely positioned at the "convergence" of East and West, and yet another group denied the existence of any meaningful differences between European and Asian traditions (Tolz 2011, 56–57).

17. The first time the Rus' sailed down the River Dnieper and across the Black Sea to threaten Constantinople, their appearance apparently terrified the Byzantines, whose reaction was to send out a missionary tasked with converting them to Christianity (Herrin 2007, 137).

18. In the most significant treaty, signed following the Rus' attack on Constantinople in 987, Vladimir of Kiev secured a promise of betrothal to Anna Porphyrogenita, the sister of Eastern Roman Emperors Basil II and Constantine VIII. The treaty also stipulated that the Rus' would send six thousand mercenaries to be incorporated into the Byzantine defense forces, including into the Varangian Guard, an elite group of non-Byzantine warriors safeguarding the emperor. While betrothal to an "authentically imperial" bride, or a *porphyrogenita*, solidified Vladimir's status in his nascent state, and the contribution of warriors meant that Byzantium became at least in part dependent on military reinforcements from the Rus', for Byzantium the treaty was crucial because it secured stability in the face of civil war (Herrin 2007, 16, 213; Bréhier 1977, 149). This was not the last time an arrangement combining marital and military solutions for brokering peace and commercial interests was to bring the Rus' and Byzantium together, but the 987 treaty portended fundamental transformations for Rus' society.

19. Vladimir also ordered the Rus' adoption of an early version of Cyrillic script, a system derived by the Bulgarian missionaries Cyril and Methodius, and probably the earliest form of writing known to the Rus'.

20. In 1473 Tsar Ivan III married Sophia, the niece of the last Byzantine emperor, and Russia increasingly adopted ritual practices borrowed from Byzantium, as well as the Byzantine double-headed eagle as the state symbol. By the middle of the sixteenth century, when Ivan IV (Ivan the Terrible) was crowned as tsar (in 1547), Muscovite Russia is said to have fashioned itself as the seat of the last authentic Orthodoxy, and Moscow as the "Third Rome." However, Marshall Poe (2001) argues that this "modern historical myth" was propagated in the second half of the nineteenth century. In 1589 the patriarch of Constantinople did establish Moscow as a patriarchate, making it the fifth of the Oriental sees, after the patriarchates of Constantinople, Alexandria, Antioch, and Jerusalem (Ware 1993, 112–16).

21. When in 1783 the Crimean Khanate in Russia was officially dissolved by Catherine the Great, a significant part of the Crimean Tatars moved to the Ottoman Empire. Although, as Reynolds cogently shows in his discussion of the rise of a "national idea" in the late nineteenth and early twentieth centuries, Tatars were drawn back to settle in Russia (2011, 47).

22. In the second half of the nineteenth century the thousands of Greeks and other non-Muslims who arrived to work in the city were mostly men. These new non-Muslim immigrants could often be identified by their *kepele*, a special European brimmed hat that distinguished them from the locals who wore a fur hat (Karpat 1985, 103).

23. Kemal Karpat traces a steady increase in the percentage of Istanbul's population that was Muslim from 1880 to 1900. He writes how "by the end of the century the colonization process was reversed, and Istanbul had become once more Islamic and Turkish in character, just as it had been from the fifteenth through the early nineteenth century" (1985, 86). Between 1844 and 1880, roughly 50 percent, and very likely much less, of the

population was Muslim; as Karpat notes, the 1844 census was conducted right after a large inflow of non-Muslims into Istanbul. However, these people would not have been registered, and therefore were not paying taxes, so would not have been included in the census (1985, 103).

24. Accordingly, whereas in 1913 one in five citizens in the territory that is today Turkey was Christian, by 1923 just one in forty citizens in the same territory was Christian (Keyder 2005, 5–6). This trend continued throughout the twentieth century, and as of the mid-2000s, 99 percent of Turks identified as Muslim (İçduygu et al. 2010, 360).

25. When General Wrangel, or Pyotr Nikolaevich Wrangel, evacuated Crimea in November 1920, 126 boats with 145,693 Russians on board arrived in Istanbul (Mansel 1995, 398).

26. A building in the popular present-day Beyoğlu, the "Flower Passage" (*çiçek passaj*), received its name in reference to the Russian women who sold flowers there in the 1920s (Mansel 1995, 399).

27. Charles King notes that there were 175 brothels operating throughout Istanbul in the early years following the First World War, and as many as 4,500 women employed in these; while Greek and Armenian women were the majority, Russian women were estimated to make up a quarter of those employed in the brothels (2014, 148–49).

28. According to one source the Modern Women's Club called press conferences in 1922 where it demanded that "Russian" women be deported (Deleon 1995, 35).

29. Not all literary treatments of this lively nightlife cast it as simply dissolute. Paul Haurigot's *Acide russique*, published in French (1929) and later in Turkish, portrays the love of a Frenchman for a Russian woman working in an Istanbul nightclub.

30. Those Russians (and others) who received Turkish citizenship as a result of Law 1312 adopted a Turkish surname. Those 986 Russians who were granted citizenship in 1934, according to the May 29 decree, were not required to take up a Turkish surname or convert to Islam, terms that were not enjoyed by any other ethnic community in the country at the time (Çağaptay 2006, 75–77).

31. The November 2, 1937, government order refused refugees from the USSR entry, but it also stipulated that in cases of those who had managed to enter the country, they were to be "resettled at least 50 kilometers away from the Soviet border." A 1933 government order sent to the Turkish provinces along the Soviet border demanded that those of "non-Turkish race . . . ought to be denied asylum and returned to their places of origin" (Çağaptay 2006, 97–98). The early Republican Turkish government also distinguished between Muslims, in particular Kurds; depending on perceived nationalist sentiments among these groups, as well as shifting political strategy, the government treated them differently, a practice Reynolds (2011, 52–70) links to the emergence of the nationalist ideas growing throughout the region in the late nineteenth and early twentieth centuries.

32. At the same time all twelve NATO countries combined spent an average of 6.6 percent of their national budgets on defense (Machado 2007, 94).

33. Cevat Tosun argues that Turkey expanded its tourism sector primarily as a means of acquiring foreign currency, and this pressing need compelled planners to privilege profit over considerations for sustainable development (2001, 291). Tosun also points out that the 1982 "Tourism Encouragement Law No. 2634" accelerated mass tourism development in a number of ways, including by allowing appropriation of state land for hotel development, by facilitating the employment of foreigners, and by encouraging vocational education related to tourism (2001, 291).

34. In 2011 Turkey ranked as the sixth most visited country in the world, with 29 million tourists; 4.8 million of these tourists were German (UNWTO 2012, 6–7). In the same year Russian citizens made up the second most numerous group of tourists visiting

Turkey, with 3.5 million Russians arriving as tourists (Russian Tourists 2012). In 2011 Russia also became the seventh highest ranked country in the world for tourism dollars being expended; Russians spent 33 billion dollars on tourism, up from 27 billion in 2010 (UNWTO 2012, 13).

35. While in 2007 the service sector made up 59.3 percent of the gross domestic product (GDP), by 2011 the service sector, including tourism, accounted for 65 percent of the GDP (CIA World Fact Book 2009).

36. Turkish government enthusiasm for the economic prospects associated with faith tourism does not necessarily insure that all churches will be preserved in the same way, however, and a particular tension around designations as "church" vs. "museum" continue to determine whether Christian pilgrims are permitted to pray at some sites (St. Nicholas Center 2012; Pravoslavie.RU 2012; First Call 2016).

37. In 2011 the only year-round residents of the Monastery of St. George were the caretaker, a Greek-Turkish Christian man, and his Turkish wife, and forty-eight Alevi Sh'ia Muslim families who were working the land (Lewis 2011).

38. Aya Yorgi Garibi, or the Monastery of St. George, is one of the sites currently under the control of the Turkish government that the Greek Orthodox Church is requesting be returned to it (Orthodox Church 2010). In the aftermath of the First World War and the breakup of the Ottoman Empire, leading to Turkey and Greece carrying out massive population exchanges, the Turkish authorities seized control of properties, ultimately placing twenty-four Greek Orthodox properties under the control of the Foundations General Directorate, a state organization dealing with confiscated properties owned by 147 foundations originally run by minorities. On the Foundations General Directorate, see Kurban and Tsitselikis 2010.

39. St. Pantaleimon, and one other small Russian Orthodox Church, St. Andrew's, was originally built as a chapel to serve Russian pilgrims staying in the attached dormitories as they were en route to Mt. Athos; the churches were most visited in the early 1920s when the dormitories housed Russians fleeing the Russian Revolution. For one literary treatment of the handful of Russian families that remained in Istanbul from the 1920s onward, see Barbara Nadel's detective thriller *Belshazzar's Daughter* (1999). For an eclectic, popular history of this community, see Deleon's *The White Russians in Istanbul* (1995).

40. From 2003 to 2006 Turkey's reliance on Russian sources of gas nearly doubled (Kınıklıoğlu and Morkva 2007, 540). However, Turkey also sought to avoid dependence on Russia, and Turkey has entertained a number of large-scale pipeline projects that would move Caspian gas via Georgia (bypassing Russia) and via Turkey to Central Europe (Weitz 2010, 66–67; EuroActiv 2012).

41. Although in 2010 there was substantial bilateral investment, with Russian investments in Turkey at $6 billion and Turkish investments in Russia at $4 billion, there was still a substantial trade imbalance. In the mid-2000s Turkey was $7 billion in debt to Russia (Kınıklıoğlu and Morkva 2007, 538), and for a number of years Russia was Turkey's largest trade partner; by 2010 Turkey ranked as the seventh largest trade partner for Russia (Weitz 2010, 71).

42. Among other changes, as of 2013 a number of countries were granted visa-free entry into Turkey with the following terms: citizens of Moldova could remain up to 90 days, "within 180 days, starting from the date of the first entry"; citizens of Russia and Ukraine could remain up to 60 days; and citizens of Central Asian countries such as Tajikistan, Uzbekistan, and Kazakhstan could remain up to 30 days. Although this is an important change making it easier for migrants to remain legally in Turkey, these tourist visas do not allow migrants to work (Turkish Ministry of Foreign Affairs 2016).

43. Other organizations have also played roles in these policies, including a Prime Ministry, President of Turks Abroad and Related Communities established in 2010, and the Black Sea Economic Cooperation Organization (BSECO) established in 1999.

44. As of 2008 the Fethullah Gulen movement had created a network of more than 800 elementary to college-level educational institutions in 160 countries. The Gulen movement, headed up by a Turkish Muslim preacher and political figure who has been based in the United States since 1999, claims to promote "moderate Islam rooted in modern life" (Hudson 2008; Putz 2016). In July 2016, in retaliation for a failed coup attempt that the Turkish government suspected the Gulen movement of orchestrating, more than three hundred Gulen-supported schools within Turkey were immediately closed, and tens of thousands of civic employees in fields ranging from education to media to social services were fired because they were perceived to be sympathetic to the Gulen movement.

45. For comparison, the International Labor Organization (ILO) reports that in 2002 in the United States women comprised 54 percent of professionals, and in Switzerland, 42 percent (Countries 2002). The Turkish Statistical Institute notes that in 2011 while the fertility rate was as high as 3.4 in some regions (eastern Anatolia), in Istanbul it was 1.7 per 1,000 women; also, for 15–19 year-olds, the rate was 20 per 1,000 in Istanbul, and 45 per 1,000 in eastern Anatolia (Turkstat 2012). The Human Development Index shows that overall for 2015 in Turkey 30.9 per 1,000 women in the 15–19 year-old age group had given birth, and this number dropped from 44.8 in 2005. By comparison, Moldova's rates were at 39.3 per 1,000 in 2015, up from 37.4 per 1,000 in 2005, while Russia's were 25.7 per 1,000 in 2015, down from 27.6 per 1,000 in 2005 (UNDP 2016).

46. The Human Development Index (HDI), produced by the United Nations Development Programme (UNDP), regularly assesses countries globally on a number of metrics, including gender equality. The Gender Inequality Indicator (GII) measures the "loss to achievements in reproductive health, empowerment, and access to the formal labor market due to gender inequalities." In 2014 Turkey ranked 72 out of the 188 countries rated, alongside such countries as Mexico, Venezuela, and Sri Lanka (UNDP 2016).

47. The World Economic Forum employs what it calls a "Gender Gap Index" measured on the basis of four categories where women's situation is analyzed: health, education, economic participation, and political empowerment. In 2015 Turkey placed 130 out of 145 countries ranked; with a score of .62 on a scale of 0 to 1, Turkey had one of the worst gender gaps recorded in the world (World Economic Forum 2015). Benin and Guinea also had similar scores, ranking at 129 and 131, respectively.

48. Thomas Naylor suggests that the military coup in Turkey in 1981 was, in part, brought about by the austerity measures imposed by the IMF. Naylor also traces an astounding set of links between drug circuits, weapon supplies, and Turkey as a strategic country for US political aims in the region (2004, 92–105).

49. These rural enclaves located at urban peripheries, known as *gecekondu,* burgeoned since the 1960s and have significantly shaped urban politics in Turkey. See Karpat 2004 on the phenomenon of these rural migrant settlements and the extensive scholarship dedicated to studying them. Also see İçduygu et al. 2013 for a cogent analysis examining Turkish rural to urban migration, emigration, and return migration.

50. Ayşe Akalin (2007) notes that in contrast to migrant women from the former Soviet Union, in part due to widespread cultural expectations for women to remain close to home, Turkish migrant women are rarely employed in positions that take them far away from home or require them to live at an employer's house. Furthermore, the $700–$800 per month demanded by Turkish women employed as domestic workers in the mid-2000s contributed to the demand for the more flexible, non-Turkish domestic

workers who would work longer hours, agree to be employed as live-ins, and work for $450–500 per month (Akalin 2007, 224).

51. In the mid-2000s, 22.8 percent of women were employed outside the household (Müftüler-Baç 2012).

52. In 2011 one Turkish NGO reported that 42 percent of women in Turkey had experienced domestic abuse or sexual harassment, and between 2002 and 2007 the number of women murdered increased from 66 to 953 per year (Jones 2011). In an essay critiquing the category of so-called "honor killings" and the "tradition effect," Dicle Koğacıoğlu notes that between 1994 and 1996 fifty-three women were targets of such murders (2004, 118); Koğacıoğlu argues for avoiding the idea of "honor killings" since this locates the causes of violence against women in "tradition," allowing a critique of the political and economic causes of such violence to go unexamined.

53. A vibrant women's movement, including a political party committed to women's rights, the Women's People's Party (Kadinlar Halk Firkasi), emerged in this era but was short-lived. As the only political organization founded by women in early Republican Turkey, it was disbanded in 1934 because it was seen as superfluous to the primary aims of the new nation (Parla 2001, 73). This mirrors the fate of the Soviet Union's Women's Commissariat (*Zhenskii sovet* or *Zhenotdel*), which was disbanded in 1930 with the retrenchment of revolutionary gender ideals (Goldman 1993, 338).

54. One of the forms of gender inequality that is enshrined in law involves the Penal Code. Until 2005, in the Penal Code, all assaults against women fell under a section of law that was particular only to women. Assaults generally fell under the category of "Felonies against Individuals," except in the case of women, when assaults were charged under the section of "Felonies against Public Decency and Family Order" (Parla 2001, 77; Miller 2007). With the 2005 Penal Code, crimes committed against women were classified along with crimes committed against any individual instead of being classed with crimes related to "public decency" or "family" (Müftüler-Baç 2012).

55. Sentiments about virginity, however, vary widely depending on urban and rural locations, but especially by age, class trajectory, and gender. In her survey of 360 upwardly mobile youth at Boğaziçi University in Istanbul, Gul Ozyegin found that 61 percent of all students whose mothers had only completed elementary school said they wanted to marry a "virgin," whereas 18 percent of those with mothers who had gone to university sought a virgin as a spouse. Fifty-one percent of male students responded affirmatively to the statement "I want to marry a virgin," but only 15 percent of female students said they preferred to marry a virgin (2015, 40, 43). Likewise, in a survey of university students in Diyarbakir (southeastern Turkey), male students found premarital sex less acceptable than female students did; men generally expected their future wives to be virgins, while female students largely said it did not matter to them if their future husbands were virgins (Eşsizoğlu et al. 2011, 146). See also Göksel 2009.

56. These exams have a historical precedent dating from the system of regulated brothels introduced under Abdulhamid II in 1884, when brothels came to be operated with a government-issued license, and regular inspections were conducted by police and health officials. After this system fell apart during the First World War, the French contingent of Allied occupation forces in Istanbul was tasked with overseeing and licensing brothels. In 1933, following international pressure, including a 1927 series of reports by the League of Nations that framed Istanbul as a prime center of "trafficking" in women, the Turkish government created a new state bureaucracy, the Ministry of Health and Social Assistance, to oversee the licensing and inspection of brothels and the regulation of sex workers (King 2014, 147–49). As of 2013 the ministry continued to carry out this mandate in designated neighborhoods (Evered and Evered 2013).

57. Drawing an extreme comparison, he equated both abortions and caesareans to a then recent massacre of Kurds at the Turkish-Iraqi border (Sehlikoğlu 2013).

CHAPTER 2: GENDER, LABOR, AND EMOTION IN A GLOBAL ECONOMY

1. There is a discrete literature focused on women engaged in small-scale trade, many of whom sell their wares in open-air market stalls, but all of whom deal in relatively small amounts of wares, frequently acting as supplier, stocker, bookkeeper, and salesperson in their businesses. Scholarship on such traders does not employ a uniform set of terminology. For instance, Hill Gates describes the "petty capitalist" women entrepreneurs in Taiwan (1991), Gracia Clark writes about Asante women in Ghana as "market women" (1999), and Florence Babb (2001) describes small-scale trader women as working in the "informal economy." Maria Quiñones (1997) writes about Barbadian "suitcase traders" and "higglers," a term Carla Freeman (2002) also uses in her discussion of Barbadian women moving apparel between New York and home communities. Michel Peraldi (2005) writes that male Algerian suitcase traders who travel to a wide range of destinations, including Istanbul, are referred to as *trabendistes* in Algeria. Konstantinov (1996) writes of "trader-tourists" to refer to those small-scale traders moving goods between Istanbul and Bulgaria. Humphrey (2002, 88) notes that in China, Mongolian shuttle traders are known as *gahaichin*, or "pig keeper," a pejorative term referring to pastoralists of the steppes but also the huge bales of goods that traders transport; she also indicates that at one point Russian traders in China were known as "vacuum cleaners," since they were thought to buy everything within sight.

2. I am borrowing this terminology from Roger Rouse (1992) who employs the idea of "transnational circuits" to describe the way in which Mexican migrants and negotiated ideals around masculinity, class, and citizenship circulate between southern California and northern Mexico.

3. These three women identified as ethnically Russian, although one of them also had family in Ukraine. However, the women traders I came to know in Istanbul and in a small city located about 60 miles south of Moscow identified with a range of ethnic identities—including Russian, Ukrainian, Belorussian, Moldovan, Gagauz, and Kazakh—and often referred to themselves collectively as "Soviet" (*sovetskie*).

4. Like many anthropologists studying this region, Humphrey resists the tendency to assume that Russia and other countries in the region are in "transition" to a Western-defined form of capitalism. She calls for ethnography to focus on the "nontheorized and most various frameworks and values through which people understand the world . . . they both inform economic action and create reactions to that action" (1999a, 21).

5. Likewise, for the Russian Federation, the shuttle trade was also crucial; in 1996, for instance, the shuttle trade from all countries to Russia was estimated to account for one-quarter of Russia's total imports, or about $21.5 billion (Yenal 2000, 3). In the case of Ukraine, in the mid-1990s the shuttle trade accounted for as much as 20 percent of the shadow economy, which in turn was estimated as being equivalent to as much as 50 percent of Ukraine's formal economy (Ivanova and Buslayeva 1999, 637).

6. Cognac is a type of brandy, named after the town of Cognac, France, and is produced from grapes grown in the region surrounding this town, but "cognac" (*koniak*) is a type of brandy that was considered a luxury good in the Soviet Union. For brandy to be considered Cognac it must be produced from specific grapes and processed according to legally defined international standards. Several domestically distilled "cognacs" are available in the former Soviet Union, most typically from Moldova and Armenia (Russian Market 2002). Although traders spoke of selling "cognac" in the early days of their travels, they most likely sold Armenian or Moldovan "cognac"/brandy, not the signature French

Cognac, which, as in other locations globally, in former Soviet locations today is a sign of distinction (Jarrard 2007).

7. For a film portraying women traders in Central Asia, see *Ballad of a Trader* (2005). I am grateful to Manduhai Buyandelgeriyn for sharing this source.

8. According to other estimates, by 2002, 12 percent of urban Russian households were involved in cross-border trade or labor migration (Badishtova 2002, 83).

9. There are a number of spheres related to shuttle trade; on classifications of trade and trade related work in Russia, see Humphrey 2002, 88–90. As Pernille Hohnen describes for Lithuania (2003, 20), in the early 1990s in Russia men and women entered into trade at open-air markets with gender-specific expertise—men sold shoes, tools, and sometimes vehicles, and women concentrated on selling food and clothing that was most often shuttled from Turkey.

10. Like Endre Sik and Claire Wallace (1999), I have translated *otkrytye* as "open-air" in reference to these markets. Although they could also be thought of as "community street markets," traders and vendors often emphasized that the markets were "open" (*otkrytye*), not "closed" (*zakrytye*), in direct reference to being outdoors in the "open," without a roof. This was in contrast to the "closed" markets, or what have since come to be referred to as "shopping centers" (*torgovye tsentry*), located in large enclosed complexes.

11. According to the Turkish Ministry of Tourism, in 1996 about 60 percent of arrivals (5.2 million) came from OECD countries, while about 26 percent (2.2 million) came from East European countries and countries of the former Soviet Union (Tosun 2001, 299).

12. In addition to selling several popular newspapers and tabloids published in Russia (e.g., *Moskovskii Komsomolets*, *SPEED-Info*), in the early 2000s kiosks sold the Istanbul-based Russian-language bimonthly newspaper *TurPressPanorama*; by 2012 kiosks in the neighborhood sold an Istanbul-based bilingual Russian-Turkish bimonthly newspaper, *Bosfor*.

13. Beginning in the early 1990s Russian-speaking customers were the most visible foreigners in the neighborhood, and Russian served as a lingua franca among most buyers and shop assistants, wholesalers, restauranteurs, and taxi drivers. However, as this garment district attracts a wide range of transnational traders, including from the Middle East, North Africa, and Eastern Europe, it is also common to see businesses, like tour agencies, appealing to clients in signs written in languages other than Russian. In 2013 with the Syrian civil war extending into its fifth year, and nearly three million people seeking refuge in Turkey, Arabic script was increasingly visible in Laleli and Aksaray. On Syrians in Istanbul, see Genç and Özdemirkıran 2015.

14. In fact, post-Soviet traders' assessments were often ahistorical and localized. They homogenized diverse realities, especially for urban Turkish women, and assumed all Istanbullu women to be defined by gender structures framing the lives of many working-class Islamist women's lives (White 2004, 212–41).

15. This woman emphasized that when she herself had to fill out paperwork, she never wrote affirmatively that her mother had a criminal record.

16. There are wide differences between how private entrepreneurship was viewed across Eastern and Central Europe (ECE) and the former Soviet Union prior to 1989. Hungary was the first country to introduce market reforms in the late socialist period, and by the late 1970s select consumer goods were permitted for sale in the private sector, including in open-air markets (Williams and Baláž 2002, 325). Polish and Czechoslovak shoppers were attracted to these markets, and a thriving cross-border trade developed; by 1995 an estimated five hundred thousand people annually were crossing as small-scale traders out of Poland (Williams and Baláž 2002, 327). Given the tightly controlled borders of the Soviet Union, with passport controls in place until the early 1990s even for travel to

the ECE, small-scale trade and informal markets were slower to develop there than in the ECE (Jerczynski 1999; Krassinets and Tiuriukanova 2001, 5).

17. In Dale Pesmen's account of sentiments about money in a post-Soviet Siberian city she quotes Jeffrey Brooks who writes of the Russian middle classes of the nineteenth century and their view of money: "Money [gained from business or commerce] . . . although clearly sought after . . . was regarded with ambivalence or hostility by much of Russian society, both because it was not old . . . and because commerce and industry were associated with the exploitation of others" (Brooks 1985, 278; Pesman 2000, 126).

18. With the onset of perestroika in the late 1980s fleeting trade was allowed to operate throughout Eastern Europe with fewer restrictions, and as it expanded, vendors often spilled over from the vacant lots and historic town centers into city streets (Sik and Wallace 1999). In Russia in the early 1990s, these market areas, as well as other public spaces, were rapidly "privatized" as local governments sold off government property to the highest bidder, a process noted in the formation of market spaces across the former Soviet Union (Hohnen 2003). The degree of legality of trade has shifted depending on the political climate, those trading, what is being traded, and local deals being made between the new investors and city government officials. Today open-air marketplaces are generally legal in Russia, although close monitoring of market spaces persists, especially in relation to irregular migration into Russia (Humphrey 1999a, 90–95; Rabina 2000; Kramer 2007; Bloch 2014). For more on the history of shuttle trade and entrepreneurship in Russia, see Mukhina 2014.

19. For instance, Jennifer Patico writes of St. Petersburg teachers' discourses about "morally upright persons" as linked to the social usefulness of a given profession (2008, 140). Others have examined how private trade in late socialism was viewed as implicitly revealing the failure of the state provisioning system and reflecting bourgeois tendencies to desire consumer goods and accumulate capital (Verdery 1996; Kaneff 2002; Dunn 2004).

20. Marta Bruno argues that women's "need to provide material and emotional support" for their families is linked to their success as entrepreneurs and originates in the Brezhnev era when difficulties in obtaining basic goods "turned women into able managers and specialists of market operations" (1997, 62). Similarly, in her study of shuttle traders moving between Belarus and Latvia, Olga Sasunkevich points to material concerns as one of the key reasons for women being involved in trade, but she also highlights the different "'female' resources" women are uniquely able to draw on, including social networks and socially acceptable expressions of emotion at key moments, such as when officials demand customs duties at the border (2016, 165–66).

21. This period of "late socialism" and a "backlash" against Soviet policies officially promoting gender equality has been the subject of a vibrant feminist scholarship since the late Soviet era. For instance, in the late 1980s the LOTOS group (the League for Emancipation from Social Stereotypes), from which the Moscow Center for Gender Studies grew, analyzed four major forces in Russia (socialism, perestroika, democracy, and the emergence of market forms of exchange) from the perspective of gender equality and identified perestroika as a "period of postsocialist patriarchal renaissance" (Posadskaia 1994, 4).

22. While "shame," and its twin, "honor," have been the focus of a wide range of anthropological literature for nearly fifty years (for instance, see Pitt-Rivers 1965; Herzfeld 1980; and Wikan 1984), here I turn attention to how these ideas are socially and historically produced in the context of postsocialism.

23. This wide range of professional backgrounds among traders is consistent with Irina Badishtova's findings (2002, 84). Her survey on temporary labor migration (including shuttle trading) among households in five major Russian cities found that adult household

members' past professions included teacher, lawyer, medical personnel, accountant, engineer, driver, and academic researcher.

24. Contrary to Badishtova's findings, where fewer than 10 percent of Russian households involved in labor migration had children under eighteen, the women in my sample were typically at a point in their life cycles where they had school-age children. Of the fifteen traders formally interviewed, all had children; two had grown children, and thirteen had children aged eight to eighteen. In fact, clothing and educating children are the primary reasons cited for becoming involved in trade.

25. In 2000 Olga had begun making weekly buying trips to Istanbul to fill out her inventory, including with chic silk blouses for $45 and knit sweaters for more than $100. In an economy where average monthly incomes at the time were $300–400 per month in urban Russia, these clothes were within the reach of only a small segment of the population.

26. This phrase is borrowed from Anne Marie Leshkowich's work (2006) on textile traders in postsocialist Vietnam.

27. Through such institutions as museums, schools, and work units, state discourses on undesirable behaviors, and conversely on what it meant to be an upstanding citizen, indelibly shaped moral frameworks (Grant 1995; Bloch 2003a; Bloch and Kendall 2004), thus illustrating Foucault's much cited point that "discourses . . . [are] . . . practices that systematically form the objects of which they speak" (1972, 49).

28. According to opinion polls conducted in Russia in 2005 and published in the *Moscow News*, more than 60 percent of those over sixty years old thought Russia "needs a new Stalin," while 40 percent of all those polled agreed with this view; see Over 40% of Russians 2005. In another public opinion poll commissioned by the Carnegie Endowment nearly a decade later in Russia, Azerbaijan, Armenia, and Georgia, the results were somewhat more nuanced, but still the authors concluded, "deStalinization has not succeeded in the former Soviet Union and most post-Soviet citizens have not come to grips with their history" (Lipman et al. 2013, 1).

CHAPTER 3. "WE ARE LIKE SLAVES—WHO NEEDS CAPITALISM?"

1. *Troitsa*, or Pentecost, considered by the Eastern Orthodox Church to be one of the Orthodox "Great Feasts," second only to Easter, is celebrated seven weeks (or fifty days) after Easter. Troitsa is recognized widely in the former Soviet Union in regions with historically Christian populations as a holiday when one should spend time with family and possibly attend church. Sonja Luehrmann notes that in the Russian Volga Republic of Mari El, Christians were anxious about how their membership in a church community competed with the time required for their gardens (2011, 201). Perhaps in part due to similar demands on their time, many people I met in Gagauzia did not necessarily attend church services. However, even those who did not attend church services did gather with relatives and attend to family graves on Pentecost. In the early 1990s in the Evenk District in central Siberia I observed similar ritual practices related to Pentecost (2003a).

2. These farms occupied about 17 million hectares of cultivated land (34 million acres) and employed nearly 570,000 people. In 1993 Moldova had 600 collective farms (*kolkhozy*) that covered 16.2 million hectares of land and employed over 401,000 people, and 389 state farms (*sovkhozy*) on 600,500 hectares of land employing over 168,000 people (Fedor 1995). The main distinction between collective and state farms was that, with the former the workers collectively owned the land and equipment, relying on a redistribution of farm earnings, whereas with the latter workers were employed by the state and received regular salaries. In reality, except for those who continue to work on land reform, few people in the region today make a distinction.

3. The average family was entitled to plots of land of 1.5 to 2.5 hectares, or about 3.3 to 6.8 acres (FAO 2001).

4. In 1996 remittances sent to Moldova via formal channels constituted just over 5 percent of the GDP, but by 2004 the International Monetary Fund (IMF) noted that 27 percent of Moldova's GDP consisted of remittances (Cuc et al. 2006, 2); in 2004 estimated remittances, including unofficially transferred sums, had reached $1 billion (Ghençea and Gudumac 2004, 75). In 2009, 23.1 percent of Moldova's GDP was based on official remittances, giving Moldova the dubious distinction of occupying fourth place in the world for the level remittances played in the national economy, just behind Tajikistan, Tonga, and Lesotho with 35.1, 27.7, and 24.8 percent, respectively (UNDP 2011, 129). Significantly, unofficial transfers do not factor into these figures, and in 2005 the IMF estimated that as much as half of the remittances transferred were done so informally (Ratha 2005). Likewise, a study of remittances in Moldova based on a sample of 4,500 households, 715 of which had at least one family member abroad from January to September 2003, found that 56 percent of remittances were received through "informal" channels, meaning not wired into bank accounts or via Western Union money transfers (Ghençea and Gudumac 2004, 11, 74).

5. In 2004 the official population of Moldova was 4,439,000 people, and by 2010 it was down to 3,600,000; in 2016 the population had dropped further to 3,553,056 (National Bureau of Statistics of the Republic of Moldova 2016). Numbers of those absent in labor migration have ranged from scholarly estimates of roughly 234,000 working-age adults in 2004 (Ghençea and Gudumac 2004, 41) to press accounts of as many as 1,600,000 people. There is a great lack of clarity in the statistics, with length of absence, circular migration, and age of those absent just some of the factors that demand close scrutiny.

6. The highest levels of outmigration are found in smaller towns and rural areas. In 2004, of the official population of about seventeen thousand people in Vulcănești, nearly one-quarter of the active working-age population was documented as absent (Primeriia Vulkaneshty 2004). This was similar to other regional town centers across the country where, on average, in 2003, 22 percent of the active working-age population was absent in labor migration, in contrast to just over 9 percent of the working-age population absent from the capital city of Chișinău (Ghençea and Gudumac 2004, 41).

7. For a classic ethnography about two collective farms in Buriatiia, see Humphrey 1999b.

8. Even by 2000, 83 percent of small farms and 60 percent of households with just subsistence plots were selling between one-third and one-half of their agricultural output. Farm households selling agricultural products made an average of $250 per year more than those without surplus products to sell (Lerman 2004, 463, 467).

9. As a settlement for winning the Russo-Ottoman War, the Russian Empire demanded the creation of a large, autonomous Bulgaria; independent states of Serbia, Romania, and Montenegro; and the Russian takeover of Ottoman territory in the Caucasus and the Balkans (Reynolds 2011, 14). Ultimately, however, Great Britain, Germany, and Austria-Hungary insisted on new peace accords (the Congress of Berlin), where a new settlement was forged. The 1878 Treaty of Berlin set out a transfer of Kars, Ardahan, and Batumi to Russia in place of the Ottomans paying reparations to Russia, and a smaller autonomous Bulgaria. Moreover, Russia was awarded only southern Bessarabia, a term Romania only agreed to as a price for having its independence recognized. For more on the negotiations around control of Bessarabia, see Anderson 1966, 202–12.

10. There is no consensus on the origins of the Gagauz. One theory traces Gagauz ancestors to the time of Genghiz Khan, linking them to the "Guz" or, according to the ancient Russian historical source of the *letopis*, to the Torks, a union of tribes that had ties to the Turkish Khanate (Ianyshev-Voloshin 1993, 5–12). Ianyshev-Voloshin argues

that the Gagauz as a distinct group first appeared in the seventh century C.E. when they occupied the northern part of the steppe near the Aral Sea; along with other Torks, they presided over an immense territory with its center at Tuva. They thrived, in part, by virtue of their knowledge of metalworking, which gave them an advantage in defending and conquering territory, in cooperating with the Khazars, and in their location along the Silk Route (1993, 13, 27–29). According to this theory, by the tenth century the Guz moved westward and played a part in defending the outer reaches of the increasingly powerful Kievan Rus', a connection which Ianyshev-Voloshin credits with forging the first union between "Turkic-speaking nomads and Russian-speaking Slavs" (1993, 31–33). King, however, points to another predominant theory that the Gagauz originated with the Turkic Oğuz tribes inhabiting the area of Dobrogea (the western Black Sea coastal area of Dobrudja in present-day Romania and Bulgaria) in the early thirteenth century, when as subjects of Byzantium they converted to Orthodox Christianity (2000, 211).

11. Irina Subbotina found that 43 percent of the urban/town dwelling Gagauz she surveyed indicated that they spoke Russian better than Gagauz, while 36 percent of urban/town dwellers said they spoke Gagauz better, and 17 percent said that they spoke each equally well. For urban Gagauz aged twenty to twenty-nine, however, nearly 50 percent indicated Russian as their better language, and for sixteen- to nineteen-year-olds about 60 percent indicated Russian as the language in which they had the greatest fluency (Subbotina 2007, 146). In contrast, rural Gagauz were more comfortable with the Gagauz language, with only 23 percent indicating they were more fluent in Russian than Gagauz, and 7 percent attesting that they spoke each language equally well. Generally, in 2007 the younger the person, the more fluently they tended to speak Russian, and the less comfortable they were in Gagauz (Subbotina 2007, 146–47).

12. Stepan Kuroglo and Maria Filimonova point to the lack of access to schooling and lack of voting rights for women under the Union of Bessarabia under Romania (1976, 22–23).

13. Transnistria, or the Prednestrovian Moldavian Republic, is located on the easternmost edge of Moldova, to the east of the Dniester River and bordering Ukraine. At a time between the two world wars, when most of the present-day Moldovan territory was part of Romania, Transnistria was part of the Soviet Union; in 1924 the Soviet Union designated the region as the Moldavian Autonomous Soviet Socialist Republic and governed it until 1990. In 1991 the majority of the population, which predominantly speaks Russian as a native language, voted in favor of independence and supported succession from the newly independent Moldova. Between 1991 and 1992 the state of Moldova asserted military force in its attempt to assert authority over the region, and Russia became involved in the conflict, threatening further military action if Moldova insisted on political control of the region. As of a July 1992 ceasefire Transnistria continues to be de facto autonomous from Moldova. However, internationally Transnistria is recognized as Moldovan territory. For more on this history, see King 2000 and Safonov 2014.

14. For an extensive treatment of the history of the Gagauz struggle for autonomy, and especially regarding language, see Demirdirek 2008.

15. As of January 2015 the Gagauz Autonomous Territory Administration reported the population of Gagauzia to be 155,656 people, with Gagauz accounting for 120,800 (82.1 percent) of the total population of the region. The remaining 18 percent of Gagauzian residents were Bulgarian (5.1 percent), ethnic Moldovan (4.8 percent), Russian (3.8 percent), or Ukrainian (3.2 percent) (Gagauz Autonomous Territory Administration 2015). This data was based on the 2004 census and with the extensive outmigration in the region over the past decade, including to Bulgaria and Romania, the percentage of Gagauz relative to other groups very likely increased.

16. Of the 123,800 Gagauz counted in the All-Soviet Census in 1959, 96.4 percent were living in southern Moldova and bordering areas of Ukraine, but by 1989 of the 153,500 Gagauz, only 93 percent were concentrated in these regions (Subbotina 2005, 4, 6). Subbotina writes that by 2002, 22 percent of all those identifying as Gagauz within the areas of the former Soviet Union were living in Russia, mostly in the central parts of the country and in the Ural regions (Subbotina 2005, 10). The Gagauz Autonomous Territory Administration (2015) indicates that in addition to the Gagauz residing in Moldova, in 2004 there were over 40,000 Gagauz living just across the border in Ukraine, as well as sizeable populations living in other parts of Ukraine, Kazakhstan, Russia, Romania, Greece, Bulgaria, and Turkey (Gagauz Autonomous Territory Administration 2015).

17. In 2005 two-thirds of the population surveyed in Gagauzia indicated that they survived on less than $42.70 per month; Subbotina reports that 6.8 percent of the population lived on less than $1.00 per day (2005, 14).

18. Based on a sample of 715 households, Ghençea and Gudumac (2004, 49) found that the "very poor" (9.9 percent of their sample) who migrated had incomes increase over thirteen times what they were prior to migration, while the households with relatively "good" material circumstances (12.6 percent of their sample) had incomes increase just over four times what they were prior to migration.

19. Subbotina reported that 53 percent of all Gagauz she surveyed in Moldova aimed to depart for Russia (2005, 21–22).

20. In 2003 Ghençea and Gudumac found that of those Moldovans engaged in labor migration, 63 percent were men and 37 percent were women (2004, 44). Subbotina also writes that more men than women were leaving Moldova, specifically noting that two-thirds of the "guest workers" (*gastarbaitery*) leaving Moldova were men (2007, 136).

21. For examples of typical media treatments of trafficking in women in Moldova, see Bell 2003 and Kirby 2004. Of the many journalistic accounts of trafficking in women from Moldova, William Finnegan's (2008) article provides useful context for understanding the situation.

22. The House of Culture was a fixture on the Soviet landscape and persists today in many communities in the former Soviet Union. As Joachim Habeck (2011) demonstrates, in Soviet times these organizations were central places for community events, recreation and artistic performances, and political meetings (see also Grant 1995).

23. According to Subbotina, in 2004 one in three Gagauz families had at least one household member abroad (2007, 136). In 2007, 50 percent of migrants from Gagauzia were in Russia, of which 23 percent were in Moscow. Just over one-third of Gagauz migrants (34 percent) were in Turkey, and 3 percent were in Ukraine. Another 1–2 percent of total Gagauz migrants were also in each of the following four countries: Italy, Germany, Spain, and Portugal. There were also Gagauz in the United States (3 percent of the migrants recorded in 2007) (Subbotina 2007, 138). There is a significant difference in the location of migrants depending on whether they originated in urban or more rural communities and whether they were men or women; 60 percent of the more urban Gagauz were in Russia and 32 percent in Turkey, while 53 percent of rural migrants were in Russia and 35 percent in Turkey (Subbotina 2007, 138). In all cases women overwhelmingly sought work in Turkey, and men in Russia.

24. I encountered two people who had won the right to immigrate to the United States via the Green Card Lottery; however, this was not a route widely discussed or one that affected many people in the town of Vulcaneşti. According to the US Department of State, each year the number of Moldovan citizens receiving visas through the Diversity Immigrant Visa Program, or "Green Card Lottery," grew steadily from 152 people in 2006 to 1,566 people in 2015 (US Department of State 2015).

25. Following Russia's military intervention in Ukraine beginning in the spring of 2014, Eva and Andrei told me via Skype that southern Moldovans had become more tentative about crossing this border. Although people still traveled for twenty-four hours by minibus (*rafik*) via Ukraine to reach Moscow for work, stories circulated of some migrants having passports ripped in two by border guards and bribes required for crossing into Russia. The more unpredictable nature of the border regime meant that transnational shopping for foodstuffs became less common, and migrants often postponed travel between Russia and Moldova until they saved enough money to make the trip by air.

26. Of the fifty-three members of the governing coalition in power in Moldova in July 2010, nine of them had a second passport that was Romanian, and eleven more members had applied for a Romanian passport (Bidder 2010).

27. The number of Moldovans who identified as having Bulgarian heritage may have more than quadrupled through the 2000s; Bulgaria's Diaspora Minister Bozhidar Dimitrov claimed there were about 250,000 such people (Dimitrov Eager 2010), but according to the 2004 Moldovan census, there were just 65,662 Moldovan citizens who identified as having Bulgarian heritage (National Bureau of Statistics of the Republic of Moldova 2004). In 2010 one news source indicated that as many as 4.7 million people from Moldova, Macedonia, Serbia, Turkey, and Ukraine could apply for Bulgarian or Romanian citizenship by virtue of their claim to ethnic ties to one of these countries (Mutler and Jahn 2010).

28. Graham Camfield notes that by 1878 the "Stundists," a generic term that emerged in Russia to denote those dissenting from dominant religious practices, had divided into two primary groups: the evangelical Stundobaptists and the Neostundists, who did not adhere to the Baptist focus on organization and dogma and had more in common with either the rationalist or mystical directions found among Spiritual Christians (1990, 693).

29. The fluidity of religious belief in the area is reflected in the fact that the 2004 Moldovan census noted 33,000 people identifying as Evangelical, although the number cited in 2012 by the Union of Evangelical Christian Baptists of Moldova was 19,578 (Sprinchana 2011; EBF 2012).

30. Non-Evangelicals in town casually referred to this secondhand store as the *gumanitarka*, or "humanitarian" store, often with a sense of dismissal. In 2011 the sign, in fact, featured a transliteration into Russian from the English term "secondhand" (*sekond khend*), and someone had also scribbled *gumanitarka* in Russian on the door.

31. In 2004 these plants together employed nearly 600 people, with one of the three plants employing nearly 450 of the total; all three had very high turnover (Gorodskoi otdel statistiki 2004).

32. The school principal noted that in 2004 it was common for children to be raised without one or both parents present; in the school's fifth grade class in 2004 nine of the twenty-four children were living with a grandparent or close family relative other than their parents.

33. Minibuses traveling between Vulcaneşti and Istanbul, via Bulgaria and Romania, departed several times each week, arriving at the minibus lot in Laleli. First-time migrants most often traveled by minibus or minibus and ferry. More-established migrants who could not afford to lose workdays and were taking short trips home from Istanbul usually flew. In 2013 a one-way ticket on the minibus cost about $75, while one-way flights from Chişinău were about $150, and a seat on the ferry from Ukraine to Istanbul was about $80. Until 2004, as Romania and Bulgaria restricted border crossing in preparation for their eventual EU accession, migrants were able to cross those countries' borders without any special visas and so most often traveled by minibus from Moldova through Romania and Bulgaria to Turkey.

34. A number of scholars have pointed out the slippery nature of the term "household" (Stack 1974, 31; Yanagisako 1979). Here I likewise understand the idea of "household" to include not just those living under one roof but also extended ties between grown siblings, parents and children, grandparents and grandchildren, et cetera. The key is, as Carol Stack (1974) suggests, "those you can count on," not the specific people living under one roof.

35. It is not uncommon for households to include a married couple with ties to more than one ethnic community; however, since the end of the Soviet Union ethnic lines are increasingly demarcated and households I encountered tended to choose to ally, at least in narratives they shared with me, with one or another ethnic group's interests in the region.

36. Pensions are significant for household incomes in the former Soviet Union and Eastern Europe, including for households where children are being raised. For instance, of households with children six years old and under being raised in Albania, 39 percent included recipients of pensions, and in Moldova 29 percent of such households included a person receiving a pension (Stewart and Huerta 2009, 168).

37. Historically Gagauz practiced ultimogeniture, where the last born son inherited land and other property from the father, in addition to taking on the responsibility of caring for elderly parents. As Elizaveta Kvilinkova points out, while ultimogeniture was the ideal form of inheritance among Gagauz, at least until the 1950s, in reality it was not always practiced (2007, 209).

38. There were some apartment dwellers who had significant ties to farming. In some cases the offspring of those in single family dwellings lived in such apartments, and so sometimes took part in homestead production in their natal family's homesteads. For instance, Zina's daughter in the Kaloglo household told me that on completing her technical degree, she was given one such apartment. In the early 1990s the apartment was privatized for barely $50. By 2005 this same apartment sold for $10,000. (Zina's daughter quoted US dollar sums, rather than the Moldovan lei, a currency that was relatively unstable at the time.)

39. According to one study, remittances in Moldova made up 75 percent of the household budget for 27 percent of households that were caring for children and receiving remittances (Salah 2008, 5).

40. Keough also writes of washing machines as a new way for households to signify status in southern Moldova (Keough 2015, 61).

41. Staff at the regional hospital in southern Gagauzia told me how even with the privatization of medical care in Moldova in recent years it was still more affordable than it would be for foreigners seeking care in Turkey. With few people's employment in Moldova including adequate health insurance (*strakhovoi polis*), some people individually purchased a standard insurance plan that in 2004 cost about $40/year (400 lei); only those who could afford more costly policies found the insurance really covered all their health care needs. See Rivkin-Fish 2011 on the privatization of health care and moral economies in Russia.

42. There was an especially sharp increase in divorce between 1990 and 2002, with only 77 divorces for the greater region in 1990, and 164 for the same region in 2002 (Raionnyi ZAGS 2002).

43. Although it was not impossible for men to take their mother's maiden name, or to take on their wife's surname, this was unusual. Cultural practice tended to mitigate against it. For instance, Zina's son was disgusted that his father had abandoned the family years earlier, and he did not want to have his father's surname. For months prior to actually submitting the necessary documents for receiving his identity papers at age sixteen, Zina's son told her he would not take his father's last name and would instead take his mother's maiden name. Ultimately, the social pressure and the hassle of having to gather

all essential documents (birth certificate, school diploma, etc.) for reassessment meant that Zina's son kept his father's surname as his own.

CHAPTER 4. STRATEGIC INTIMACY, "REAL LOVE," AND MARRIAGE

1. The educational and professional backgrounds of women I came to know were generationally defined. Women under thirty had all completed high school and sought out work in an emerging service sector; among them, just one had graduated from university, with a law degree. Women in their thirties, forties, and fifties had all obtained postsecondary training—for instance, in electronics or nursing; three women had also completed university (and been working in their professions) prior to the end of the Soviet Union, one woman was a teacher, one an architect, and one an engineer.

2. As of 2009 the Province of Istanbul, synonymous with the Municipality of Istanbul, comprised thirty-nine districts, including Beyoğlu, Fatih, Şişli, Eminönü, and Zetinburnu (Genç and Özdemirkıran 2015, 109). Migrants' conversations were interspersed with reference to districts, for instance, when discussing travel for work in relatively distant destinations (e.g., Beykoz), as well as reference to neighborhoods, such as when they exchanged information about the geography of a handful of areas of the city (e.g., Taksim, Zetinburnu, Aksaray, or Laleli) that were familiar to most other long-term migrants I met.

3. According to one news source, in 2002 alone more than fifty thousand marriages took place between Turkish men and "Russian" women (Türkiye ve Rusya 2003), although this number is difficult to substantiate and seems inflated. Another news source cites a Turkish think tank, indicating that in 2016 there were as many as three hundred thousand "Turkish-Russian" married couples in Turkey (Nemtsova 2016).

4. Based in part on data from the Turkish Office of Population and Citizenship, Ministry of the Interior, İçduygu (2009, 289) calculates that between 2001 and 2005 nine hundred people gained citizenship by being naturalized, and almost all of them, presumably able to demonstrate ties to Turkish descent or culture, came from Balkan countries (Macedonia, Serbia and Montenegro, Bulgaria, and the Former Yugoslavia) and just three from Romania. As with many countries globally, Turkey strongly favors the *jus sanguinus* principle for granting citizenship, with an emphasis on "proving Turkish descent or culture" for citizenship to be granted (İçduygu 2009, 288).

5. A total of 56,449 people were granted Turkish citizenship between 1995 and 2000 (İçduygu 2009, 289), and those being granted citizenship came predominantly from seven countries (Bulgaria, Iran, Iraq, Romania, Russia, Azerbaijan, and Moldova).

6. As a stateless ethnic group Kurds are concentrated in a mountainous area stretching among Turkey, Armenia, Syria, Iraq, and Iran. As the fourth largest ethnic group identifying as Muslim in the Middle East, in 2016 they made up as much as 20 percent of the overall population of Turkey and Iraq, and as much as 10 percent of the Syrian and of the Iranian populations (BBC 2016b).

7. In tracing the histories of interaction between the Ottoman and Russian empires from just before and just after the world wars, Michael Reynolds (2011) also examines the intricacies of Russia's history of conflict and diplomacy with various groups of Kurds.

8. The novel *Interdevushka* or *Intergirl* (Kunin 1991), featuring a struggling nurse in late 1980s Leningrad who turns to prostitution with foreigners, is perhaps the most iconic portrayal of radically shifting gender terrain in the late Soviet Union. In 1989 the film based on the novel was by far the most popular film of that year in the Soviet Union. The book was translated into English in 1991.

9. For a compelling documentary on Russian women's use of matchmaking agencies in their efforts to find husbands from North America, see *In the Name of Love* (2002).

10. The apartment I subleted in Istanbul during fieldwork in spring 2007 was no exception. A photograph of Kemal Atatürk posed in his swim suit hung by the apartment entrance.

11. Reynolds refers to "militant secularism" as a key element of the founding of the Turkish Republic in 1923 but notes "the Turkish Republic never dared turn its campaign against religion into an outright assault as the Soviet Union did" (2011, 260).

12. The AKP steadily increased its support over its first four terms in power, with nearly 34 percent of the vote in 2001, 47 percent in 2007, 50 percent in 2011, and 50 percent in 2015 (Taşpınar 2012; Henley et al. 2015). Notably, Prime Minister Erdoğan sought to signal the AKP's tempered association with Islam in describing his party's aims to establish "conservative democracy"; others have referred to the AKP's aims as "political Islam" (Taşpınar 2012). In an April 2017 referendum Prime Minister Erdoğan further consolidated power when just over 51 percent of voters affirmed their support for a constitutional change that would end the parliamentary system currently in place in Turkey and give a future president full control of the government (Kingsley 2017).

13. However, it would be a mistake to assume this as a fixed binary of ideational systems or a set of totalizing ideals. Feyda Sayan-Chengiz laments that women in headscarves get associated with a "fixed and reified identity" (2016, 3), and in her work among lower-middle-class women wearing headscarves and working in the retail sector in Turkey, she aims to show the various forms of negotiation women in fact engage in as they weigh when to wear headscarves.

14. Though Natasha is a relatively common Russian name, beginning in the early 1990s in Turkey the name became a term widely synonymous with "prostitute." One explanation for the widespread use of the epithet "Natasha" links it to a song popularized in the early 1990s (Béller-Hann 1995, 231–32).

15. Polina saw this man again after twenty years when he decided to marry and discovered that his divorce from Polina had not been properly processed. He and Polina had to hire lawyers and spend time in legal proceedings to affirm that they were, in fact, divorced.

16. There is a long tradition within the social sciences of examining the practices and meanings around marriage and intimacy (e.g., Giddens 1992; Kendall 1996; Hirsch 2003; Jankowiak 2008). This scholarship has shown that marriage practices are anything but static and instead are shaped by global economic flows, as well as new flows in media, people, and ideas about intimacy.

17. A number of scholars have written about contemporary marriage practices in Turkey. For instance, Kimberly Hart (2007) shows how arranged marriage and discourses on romance coexist in communities in eastern Turkey. For a challenge to modernization theories about the development of family forms and a brief historical review of urban and rural family forms in Turkey, see Vergin 1985.

18. Scholars have noted similar practices for other societies in the region at the time. For instance, see Manning 2015 on forms of "anti-marriage" that were historically practiced in Georgia, where until the mid-twentieth century mountain dwellers practiced forms of sexuality and romance that could never lead to marriage. Also see Haeri 2014 on the practice in Iran of "temporary marriage," an arrangement between a man and an unmarried woman in which they agree to be married for as long, or as short, as they wish the contract to last. Shahla Haeri also notes that Shi'a doctrine distinguishes between temporary marriage (*mutt's*), which is meant for sexual enjoyment, and "permanent marriage" (*nice*), meant for procreation (2014, 2).

19. Alan Duben and Cem Behar indicate that about 10 percent of high-ranking government officials in the late nineteenth and early twentieth centuries were polygynously

married, although no more than 2.3 percent of Istanbul marriages overall were polygynous (1991, 156).

20. It was unusual that the case even went to court. During my fieldwork undocumented workers from the former Soviet Union were normally deported within twenty-four hours, following a brief period in the Istanbul detention center for foreigners (*"yabancı şube"*).

21. Legislation passed in 2003 made employers liable for a fine of one billion Turkish lira for each undocumented worker they hired and subject to having their business license revoked (Narlı 2003, 34). In 2003 this was approximately $716.

22. Ali paid the student $500 a year to keep the marriage contract.

23. Like most of the women I met during the research who were working as shop assistants, Maria was paid in US dollars.

24. The amount migrants were required to pay in "exit fines" for overstaying tourist visas was regularly published in a bimonthly Russian- and Turkish-language newspaper distributed in Istanbul from 2004 to 2007. In 2007 the fines totaled 118 Turkish lira (about $89) for overstaying by one month and 840 Turkish lira (about $632) for overstaying by twelve months (Ugolok iurista 2007, 11). The fines for overstaying a work visa or for being employed without a work permit continued to change throughout the 2000s (Kocaoğlu 2012; Turkish Labor Law 2015).

CHAPTER 5. INTIMATE CURRENCIES

1. In 2002 as a newly arrived entertainer Kara earned $18/day.

2. Kara used this term even though gambling was not a component of the nightclub's activities. However, Julie Scott (1995) writes of post-Soviet women working as croupiers in casinos in northern Cyprus, and I met one woman who had worked there, so it is possible that the reference to the Istanbul club as a "casino" has its origins in this migration trajectory.

3. A representative of the Istanbul based Human Resource Development Foundation (HRDF), an NGO focused on reproductive health and family planning education that also assisted in anti-trafficking training among Istanbul law enforcement, pointed out that the anti-trafficking measures policed women but were an inexact means of identifying who might be a victim of trafficking (Interview, June 2005).

4. Local regulations required regular tests for AIDS and other STIs in order to work as an entertainer in a club, but these requirements did not apply just to foreign entertainers. Turkish law also requires all Turkish women registered as sex workers and working in government-run brothels to receive regular screenings for gonorrhea, syphilis, AIDS, and Hepatitis-B. According to Şükran Şimşek et al., in 2003 Turkish sex workers were required to be screened for gonorrhea twice a week, and for syphilis and AIDS every three months, with each set of test results sent to the local police (2004, 58).

5. See Shankland 2003 on the strong presence of left-leaning political sentiments among the Alevi, a historically Shi'ite group and the largest religious minority in Turkey, a predominantly Sunni country. Alevi and Kurdish communities and their politics significantly overlap, although they are not synonymous (Mandel 2008, 271–87).

6. These themes resonated through visual culture as well as through official discourse. For a vivid portrayal of these ideals, see *Bed and Sofa* (1927). The groundbreaking film traces the lives of a Soviet worker and his wife in the rapidly industrializing center of Moscow and the challenge to gender paradigms as the couple is caught up in a ménage à trois, leading to questions about sexual propriety, abortion, and the purposes and implications of the institution of marriage.

7. Although a wide cross-section of the population did take part in these protests, undocumented workers I know from the former Soviet Union did not take part because they generally avoided spaces that could make them vulnerable to police. Taksim Square

and the adjacent Gezi Park gained international visibility in summer 2013 when images of protesters clashing for weeks with police over plans to build a shopping complex in place of the park went viral on social media. As a popular leisure area for a wide cross-section of the Turkish public, protests in Gezi Park also came to catalyze protests across Turkey that called for political reform. See Yıldırım and Navaro-Yashin 2013; Zengin 2013.

8. Entertainers explained that they were given a chit (*fishka*) for each drink a customer bought, and for each chit they received 2 lira. They complained that instead they should receive a percentage of the total a customer spent, since men's drinks could cost as much as 20–30 lira and women's 30–40 lira. (In the spring of 2007 one Turkish lira was equivalent to about 75 cents US.) In some clubs entertainers were also expected to reach a set number of total drink sales; if they did not reach this, they were fined.

9. In 2002 dancers in one Ukrainian group paid their manager a fee of about $10 of each week's pay, and the Turkish manager $5. After paying about $10/night for their hotel room, women had just $18/night take home pay. Although dancers paid fees in Turkey in lira, they calculated their expenses in both lira and US dollars.

10. By 2007 dancers were making about $27/night plus tips, and the nightclub paid the majority of their hotel expenses. Dancers were still required to work six days a week and were expected not to take on any other jobs. The intermediaries continued to arrange employment for dance troupes. One manager described to me how he had teamed up with a former dancer to recruit women to dance in his club; over eight months they brought thirty women from Russia, and each woman paid a fee of $150 for the assistance in arranging visas and job placement.

11. Aside from the fact that many of the young women I met had studied some ballet, it is worth noting how erotic dance and classical dance forms might intersect. Patricia Demers identifies a certain commonality, if not tension, between erotic dance and ballet. As she says, "Admittedly there are recognizable differences between working at a horizontal barre and a vertical pole, between wearing toe shoes and five-inch stilettos. But what connections exist between glissade, pas de chat, grand plié, and demi-plié and . . . the smooth circular swivel of the hips of grind, and the various walks, leaps and struts of striptease? . . . Are there parallels—or parodies—of pirouette, deboulé, relevé and arabesque in the preening, snake moves, jumps, cartwheels and arched torsos of striptease?" (2004, 92).

12. One 2003 IOM-commissioned report on irregular migration and trafficking in women indicates that the Ministry of Tourism was issuing six-month "ballerina" visas at the time of publication (Erder and Kaşka 2003, 66). By 2005 these six-month visas were no longer available. Notably, other countries like Japan and Canada also had a visa category "entertainer" in place for at least a decade, until the late 2000s. On the Japanese entertainer visa, see Faier 2009 and on the Canadian entertainer visa, which was curtailed in 2012, see McDonald et al. 2000; Citizenship and Immigration Canada 2014.

13. Given the lost wages due to intermediaries, it is not surprising that in 2002 one of the dancers decided to join with several others to arrange her next contract independently, without the cost of managers.

14. In 2016 a number of provisions were put into place in the first widespread revision to legislation since 2003 regarding the employment of foreigners in Turkey. A series of laws spells out the conditions under which employers may hire temporary workers (e.g., for seasonal labor, in the case of an employee's extended absence, etc.), the required terms of employment, and in International Workforce Law no. 6735, the fines payable for unlawfully employing a foreign worker (Turkish Labor Law 2016; Turkish Parliament 2016). Also, this legislation made it easier to hire highly educated and specialized foreign workers, although not in the intimate services sector. This legislation was on the heels of the Law on Foreigners and International Protection (Turkish Ministry of the Interior 2014).

15. Hotels advertise on a wide array of websites, including "educational" ones like Learn4good.com, where positions are posted with descriptions that minimize the adult entertainment aspect of the job while retaining job titles that suggest duties with ambiguity around "entertainment." For instance, in 2013 the MTM Animation and Organization indicated in its company profile that it was "looking for animators, dancers with or without experience." However, the actual job description linked to this company profile noted that the "animator" would be: "organizing daily sport activities and games with hotel guest [sic] and their children and take part in the evening entertainment as well (mini disco, show time, guest relation) [sic]." The description also noted that the position required the "animator" (event coordinator) to work eight to ten hours a day, six days a week (Learn4good 2013a).

16. Interestingly, the very visible sex work and erotic entertainment that is part of tourism is almost completely elided in the growing literature on tourism (e.g., İçöz et al. 1998; Göymen 2000; Tucker 2007). See, however, Scott 1995 on sex work in northern Cyprus; and Agathangelou 2004 on sex work in Cyprus and the Mediterranean more generally.

17. Advertisements spell out many key terms of the potential position, and some are careful to position the status of the place of work. For instance, the advertisement placed by Marmaris Recruitment in 2013 indicated that their client was a "5* nightclub" and that the position would include accommodation in Izmir, pay "$1,000 to $1,500 per month, with bonus up to $400 per month on drink sales," and provide work permits paid for via deductions from the monthly wages. The advertisement also noted twice that applicants must be "attractive with good physic [sic]" (Learn4Good 2013c).

18. Some advertisements in 2016 stipulated that a permit could be applied for after a "trial period" of work, with no specific number of weeks or months indicated, while a few also attested that positions would come with a work permit. The divergence around work permit availability suggests that many positions assume employees will work on tourist visas.

19. In 2007 Belarus continued to have one of the more restrictive border regimes of formerly Soviet countries, with exit visas periodically required for citizens to leave the country, and police registration required of most noncitizens within three days of arrival in the country, although citizens from most countries of the former Soviet Union were able to travel to Belarus without visas. As an indication of the frequency of illegal exchanges of money with officials at the Belarus border, the Belarus Customs and Immigration website notes that it is forbidden to "leave money in the documents presented for checking" (Ministry of Foreign Affairs of the Republic of Belarus 2016).

20. This dominant discourse was exemplified by the IOM and British Council sponsored workshop "Trafficking in Women" held in Istanbul, June 20, 2002, and attended by representatives of international NGOs and Turkish law enforcement.

21. The word "muzhateer" is not Russian but Turkish, or more specifically Ottoman Turkish, in origin. It seems that entertainers modified a word that may have a long history of use dating back to the Ottoman era in reference to relationships and locations of sexualized labor. The word "muzhateer" derives from the Ottoman Turkish word musaytır, which has three separate definitions (Osmanlıca 2017). The first definition is "an overseer or protector," possibly implying "in place of" (kaim olmak) a male relative. The second definition is a synonym of musallat, a noun used for someone who is "imposing oneself on or obsessed with someone" (as in musallat olmak). The third definition is "someone who is commanding or governing another and insuring they act appropriately." When entertainers invoked the word "muzhateer" they appeared to be referencing the first definition and placing an emphasis on finding men who could "sponsor" them financially. I am thankful to Eda Cakmakci for her assistance in researching this issue.

22. While few Turkish women frequented the clubs, tourist women sometimes did, so it was conceivable that lesbian liaisons could have formed between them and entertainers. However, among the women I came to know I heard of no such instances.

23. Pioneer camps, or summer camps run by the Soviet government and sometimes trade unions, were widely attended by young people in the late Soviet Union, and one of the most famous ones was Artek, located in Gurzuf, Ukraine, and operating from 1925 until 1990 (World of Children 2007). Sonia would have been too young to attend Artek, but she might have attended the international children's center that was established in its place with substantial subsidies provided by the Ukrainian government.

24. Women were the most visible actors among post-Soviet sex workers, but I also encountered a vibrant economy of masseurs. In at least one case, the masseur was hired to both do "body work" and be a kept man for the gay man who hired him.

CHAPTER 6. "OTHER MOTHERS," GRANDMOTHERS, AND THE STATE

1. I coined this phrase partly in contrast to Elspeth Graham et al.'s (2012) framework of a "transnational family nexus," which I see as focusing too narrowly on a single institution as key to caregiving for children. I was also inspired by Barry Hewlett's extensive research on father-infant bonding among the Aka, a community of hunter-gatherers living in the rain forests of the southern Central African Republic and northern Congo-Brazzaville. Hewlett argues that father-infant bonding "is embedded within a cultural nexus—it influences and is influenced by a complex cultural system" (2013, 46), and he draws comparisons to North American and European models of father-infant bonding. Hewlett notes that while in the 1980s North American and European fathers typically held their infants ten to twenty minutes a day, Aka fathers held their infants about one hour during the day, as well as at least a quarter of the time once the sun went down (2013, 46), a practice Hewlett links to the high value Aka placed on egalitarianism and cooperation.

2. The number of women migrating into cities in the Soviet Union especially increased from the late 1920s to the early 1940s. Whereas in 1928 women constituted just 24 percent of the urban workforce, by 1940 women made up nearly 40 percent of the urban workforce (Lapidus 1978, 166). Still, in the tumultuous years of the early 1920s to the late 1930s—defined by famine, war, urbanization, and collectivization—men, and not women, predominantly left rural areas. Liubov Denisova indicates that in this period 30 percent of rural men left villages for urban areas, while only 9 percent of women left (2010, 74).

3. The Office for the Protection of Motherhood and Infancy, the OMM or OkhMat-Mlad (Okhrana materinstva i mladenchestva), which was intended to have divisions across the country, was one of the key proponents of creating new forms of mothercraft. The first head of the OMM, Alexandra Kollontai, widely known for her radical views on family and society, sought to establish an array of state provisions for child care that would make it possible for women to fully engage as worker-mothers (Waters 1992, 128).

4. According to a 1918 survey, of the provinces (*gubernii*) that responded 104 counties had set up preschools, and an equal number had not. Moscow Province was at the forefront of these efforts, with twenty-three kindergartens, eight day-care centers, and thirteen "summer playgrounds," or loosely supervised spaces where children would gather (Kirschenbaum 2001, 38). In Moscow alone in 1918 there were 5 kindergartens, 13 "colonies" and 51 playgrounds, and by 1919 the city had a combined total of 203 such organizations.

5. Even though in 1931 less than 8 percent of urban children and less than 2 percent of all children in the Soviet Union attended some sort of preschool institution, Kirschenbaum also cites Commissariat of Enlightenment statistics indicating an increase of more than 80 percent in the number of preschool institutions in place across the Soviet Union

between 1929 and 1931 (2001, 138). Nevertheless, the overall number of institutions and child attendees in 1931 was actually lower than in 1921; in 1921 there were 4,785 preschool institutions and 247,701 attendees, whereas in 1931 there were 3,769 institutions and 222,216 attendees (Kirschenbaum 2001, 91, 138).

6. See Kirschenbaum for a sense of the tensions that existed between educators and official curriculum in the 1920s, including as they played out in specific kindergarten settings in Russia (2001, 113). Kirschenbaum shows how ideals around caring for and educating preschool children shifted both structurally and philosophically. She traces the emphasis on "free upbringing," meant to "liberate" children from the authority of teachers and inculcate creativity that had defined the first years of Bolshevik efforts to promote preschool education. She also shows how "socialist upbringing," which would focus on "'the development in the child of a materialist world-view and collective habits," prevailed in the second half of the 1920s (2001, 106–7). If free expression was central to preschool curricula in the first years after the revolution, by the late 1920s, structure and state ideology around "labor" and "society" mattered more.

7. Jean Ipsa also indicates that by 1940 there were 46,041 child-care centers in the Soviet Union (Ipsa 1994, 12), although it is unclear if "child care" refers to only preschool programs for three- to seven-year-olds, or to care for all children, infants to seven-year-olds, at which time children entered school.

8. During the Second World War a tax was even introduced for those households that were childless. At first, a tax of 5 percent of household income applied to all childless adults, and then, in 1957, this was revised so that just twenty- to fifty-year-old childless men paid the tax, as well as twenty- to forty-five-year-old childless women (*Vedomosti* 1957, 531–32; Denisova 2010, 75).

9. As part of this massive investment in rural areas, by the late 1980s nearly fifty thousand medical facilities offered rural women in Russia neonatal care, as well as pre- and postpartum care (Rossiiskii statisticheskii ezhegodnik 2002, 245).

10. The number of children in residential schools and facilities went from fewer than thirty thousand in 1917 to four hundred thousand in 1920 and to more than five hundred thousand in 1922 (Waters 1992, 128).

11. In countries such as Poland, Hungary, and Czechoslovakia with discourses and policies around mothercraft also inflected by a socialist past, debates continue about the ways in which the state should support mothers and children. Predominant maternalist thinking supports looking after the needs of mothers and children both as a social good and as a pronatalist measure in an era of falling birth rates, but as critics point out these policies also serve government interests as a safety valve for rising unemployment, and they contribute to growing gender inequality (Saxonberg and Szelewa 2007; Szelewa and Polakowski 2008; Glass and Fodor 2011).

12. In 2009 these payments were credited with producing the 7.7 percent increase in births from the previous year (Denisova 2010, 174–75; Rivkin-Fish 2010), and by 2013 Russia's birth rates surpassed those of the European Union (Nechepurenko 2014). Russia's birthrate was 1.7 in 2013, while the EU's was 1.6.

13. Unlike women remaining in Moldova, women who were absent as labor migrants were also not eligible to take advantage of the Moldovan government's maternity policy provision allowing for the benefit to be paid to a caregiver, such as a grandmother or aunt, in lieu of the mother (US Social Security Administration 2014, 212).

14. In 1992 25 percent of households surveyed in urban Russia consisted of a mother, children, and grandmother, and by 1996, 32 percent did; correspondingly, the portion of single mothers living alone with children fell from 56 percent in 1992 to 45 percent by 1996 (Lokshin et al. 2000, 2186–87).

15. In 2004 there were six day-care centers with 688 children attending (Primeriia Vulkaneshty 2004).

16. As Irina Subbotina describes, the history of seasonal Gagauz labor migration from the 1950s onward, along with the deportation of nearly fourteen hundred Gagauz from southern Moldova during the Second World War, has led to Gagauz living dispersed across the former Soviet Union (2005, 9–12). In Maria's case, her mother migrated to Latvia in the 1950s for work and Maria was raised moving between family in Latvia and Gagauzia.

17. Bella's grandmother most likely arrived a little later than 1880, during the Turkish-Russian War. As described by Ianyshev-Voloshin (1993, 37–38), this was a time when refugees fled from Bulgaria, then occupied by the Ottoman Empire, to arrive in Bessarabia, then a part of the Russian Empire's territory. Ianyshev-Voloshin describes how these refugees were Gagauz and Bolgars but also Greeks, Germans, Jews, Albanians, and others.

18. Kvilinkova describes a number of types of adoption that Gagauz, and possibly others in the region, have historically practiced and have specific terms for, including when children are adopted out to relatives or nonrelatives, informally or legally (2007, 217–22).

19. Given the timing featured in Bella's account, her mother's family could also have been deported to Central Asia, along with more than 1,376 Gagauz (Subbotina 2005, 9–12), as well as members of other ethnic groups suspected of collaborating with Germany during the Second World War. Reynolds notes that between 1935 and 1938, anxieties about state security drove the Soviet Union to carry out "ethnic cleansing operations" of deportation, arrest, or execution of about 800,000 people (2011, 261).

20. Among formerly socialist states, as of the mid-2000s Bulgaria had the most extensive social benefits for mothers and children. For instance, in 2009 nearly 80 percent of households with children six years old and under received either economic assistance or child benefits (Stewart and Huerta 2009, 165). In the same year a small fraction (15 percent) of households in Moldova with two- to six-year-olds received child benefits, and nearly 50 percent of households with children under eighteen months received universal child benefit payments. Significantly, however, the share that child benefits played in household incomes steadily diminished to a minuscule level with the contribution to overall average household income decreasing from 1.7 percent in 1995 to 0.3 percent in 2002 (Stewart and Huerta 2009, 164).

21. For a comprehensive analysis of how maternity and paternity leaves and benefits are paid globally, see Heymann and McNeill 2013.

22. Kvilinkova goes on to describe how in the past the Gagauz term *buuk* (older) would also be added to "mother" to distinguish the biological mother from the relative caring for the child (2007, 221).

CONCLUSION

1. The Turkish government accused supporters of Fetullah Gulen, an Islamic cleric and former political ally of Prime Minister Erdoğan's, whose followers number as many as five million, of orchestrating the coup attempt. As of May 2017 more than 130,000 people in government, the military, the police, the media, and educational institutions had been removed from their positions, with 45,000 already jailed and many prosecutions still pending (Akınerdem 2016; Kingsley 2017). The Turkish government considered a number of apparently innocuous acts as evidence that could link someone to the Gulenist movement, including: having an account with Asya Bank, which was founded by the Gulenists; sending your children to a school associated with Gulen; being employed by

a Gulen-affiliated organization or institution, such as a hospital or university; subscribing to the Gulen newspaper Zaman; or even having Gulen's books in your possession (Hansen 2017).

2. Turkey's March 2016 agreement with the EU to step up policing of refugee flows seeking to enter Europe in exchange for improved prospects of EU accession, and Erdoğan's November 2016 retaliation against the EU vote to curtail accession talks with Turkey due to Turkey's response to the failed coup, exemplify how this plays out in Eurasia (BBC 2016a).

3. In 2015 Russia began stepping up deportations, as well as demanding high fees for monthly registration of migrants and a language proficiency exam even for temporary labor migrants (Andreeva 2015).

Bibliography

Abashin, Sergei. 2012. Sredneaziatskaia migratsia: Praktiki, local'nye soobshchestva, transnatsionalizm. [Central Asian migration: Practices, local communities, and transnationalism]. *Etnograficheskoe obozrenie*, no. 4: 3–13.

Abu-Lughod, Lila. 1997. Introduction: Feminist Longings and Postcolonial Conditions. In *Remaking Women: Feminism and Modernity in the Middle East*, edited by Lila Abu-Lughod, 3–33. Princeton, NJ: Princeton University Press.

———. 1991. Writing against Culture. In *Recapturing Anthropology: Working in the Present*, edited by Richard G. Fox, 137–62. Santa Fe, NM: School of American Research Press.

———. 1986. *Veiled Sentiments: Honor and Poetry in a Bedouin Society*. Berkeley: University of California Press.

Abu-Lughod, Lila, and Catherine Lutz. 1990. Introduction: Emotion, Discourse, and the Politics of Everyday Life. In *Language and the Politics of Emotion*, edited by Lila Abu-Lughod and Catherine Lutz, 1–23. Cambridge: University of Cambridge Press.

Agathangelou, Anna M. 2004. *The Global Political Economy of Sex: Desire, Violence, and Insecurity in Mediterranean States*. New York: Palgrave Macmillan.

Agustín, Laura. 2006. The Disappearing of a Migration Category: Migrants Who Sell Sex. *Journal of Ethnic and Migration Studies* 32(1): 29–47.

Ahearn, Laura. 2001. *Invitations to Love: Literacy, Love Letters, and Social Change in Nepal*. Ann Arbor: University of Michigan Press.

Ahmed, Sara. 2004. *The Cultural Politics of Emotion*. Edinburgh: Edinburgh University Press.

Akalin, Ayşe. 2007. Hired as Caregiver, Demanded as a Housewife: Becoming a Migrant Domestic Worker in Turkey. *European Journal of Women's Studies* 14(3): 209–25.

Åkesson, Lisa. 2011. Remittances and Relationships: Exchange in Cape Verdean Transnational Families. *Ethnos* 76(3): 326–47.

Akınerdem, Feyza. 2016. Are There Women Out There? Democracy Vigils and the Politics of Representation after the Failed Coup Attempt in Turkey. *Journal of Middle East Women's Studies* 13(1): 21–26.

Aktar, Cengiz, and Nedim Ögelman. 1994. Recent Developments in East-West Migration: Turkey and the Petty Traders. *International Migration* 32(2): 343–54.

Akyol, Mustafa. 2012. Ottomans, Soap Operas, and Erdoğan. *Hürriyet Daily News*. November 28. http://www.hurriyetdailynews.com/ottomans-soap-operas-and-erdogan.aspx?pageID=238&nid=35614.

Alexandrov, Vladimir. 2013. *The Black Russian*. New York: Atlantic Monthly Press.

Ambler, Effie. 1961. The Soviet Boarding School. *American Slavic and East European Review* 20(2): 237–52.

Anderson, Matthew Smith 1966. *The Eastern Question, 1774–1923: A Study in International Relations*. New York: Macmillan.

Andreeva, Nadezhda. 2015. Novaia metla [New broom]. *Novaia gazeta*. February 4. http://www.novayagazeta.ru/society/67102.html.

Angel Coalition Trafficking Victim Assistance Center. 2009. *Angel Coalition Report* 2009. Moscow. http://www.miramed.org/pdf/AngelCoalition2009.pdf.

Angey-Sentuc, Gabrielle, and Jérémie Molho. 2015. A Critical Approach to Soft Power: Grasping Contemporary Turkey's Influence in the World. *European Journal of Turkish Studies*, no. 15. http://ejts.revues.org/5287.

Appadurai, Arjun. 1996. *Modernity at Large: Cultural Dimensions of Globalization.* Minneapolis: University of Minnesota Press.

Arat, Zehra. 1994. Turkish Women and the Republican Reconstruction of Tradition. In *Reconstructing Gender in the Middle East,* edited by Fatma Müge Göçek and Shiva Balaghi, 100–112. New York: Columbia University Press.

Ashwin, Sarah. 2000. Introduction: Gender, State, and Society in Soviet and Post-Soviet Russia. In *Gender, State and Society in Soviet and Post-Soviet Russia,* edited by Sarah Ashwin, 1–29. London: Routledge.

Ashwin, Sarah, and Elaine Bowers. 1997. Do Women Want to Work? In *Post-Soviet Women from the Baltic to Central Asia,* edited by Mary Buckley, 21–37. Cambridge: Cambridge University Press.

Attwood, Lynne. 1990. *The New Soviet Man and Woman: Sex Role Socialization in the USSR.* London: Macmillan.

Aydos, Serpil. 2013. Muhafazakâr Milliyetçi Muhayyilede Kanunî: Muhteşem Yüzyıl'a Yönelik Tepkilere Dair Bir Okuma (Süleyman the Magnificent in the Imagination of Conservative Nationalists: A Reading on Reactions to Muhteşem Yüzyıl). *History Journal: International Journal of History* 5(1): 1–16.

Babb, Florence. 2001. *After Revolution: Mapping Gender and Cultural Politics in Neoliberal Nicaragua.* Austin: University of Texas Press.

Badishtova, Irina Mikhailovna. 2002. Specific Features of Migrant Worker Households in Russia. *Sotsiologicheskie issledovaniia* 28(9): 83–90.

Ballad of a Trader. 2005. Produced and directed by Gaëlle Lacaze. 59 min. Video recording.

Balli, Faruk, Hatice Ozer Balli, and Kemal Cebeci. 2013. Impacts of Exported Turkish Soap Operas and Visa-free Entry on Inbound Tourism. *Tourism Management* 37: 186–92.

Baptist World Alliance. 2011. Statistics. http://www.bwanet.org/about-us2/statistics#e.

Barr, Nicholas. 1994. Labor Markets: Unemployment. In *Labor Markets and Social Policy in Central and Eastern Europe: A World Bank Book,* edited by Nicholas Barr, 160–91. New York: Oxford University Press.

Barrera-González, Andrés, Melissa L. Caldwell, Monica Heintz, and Anna Horolets. 2013. Europe. In *The Handbook of Sociocultural Anthropology,* edited by James G. Carrier and Deborah B. Gewertz, 506–22. London: Bloomsbury.

Basch, Linda, Nina Glick Schiller, and Christina Szanton Blanc, eds. 1994. *Nations Unbound: Transnational Projects, Postcolonial Predicaments, and Deterritorialized Nation States.* Langhorne, PA: Gordon and Breach.

Başcı, Pelin. 2003. Love, Marriage, and Motherhood: Changing Expectations of Women in Late Ottoman Istanbul. *Turkish Studies* 4(3): 145–77.

Batuman, Elif. 2014. Ottomania: A Hit TV Show Reimagines Turkey's Imperial Past. *New Yorker.* February 17 and 24. http://www.newyorker.com/magazine/2014/02/17/ottomania.

Bed and Sofa. 1927. Directed by Avram Room. 88 min. Sovfilm Productions.

Behar, Ruth, and Deborah A. Gordon, eds. 1996. *Women Writing Culture.* Berkeley: University of California Press.

Bell, Bethany. 2003. Europe's Human Trafficking Hub. BBC. May 23. http://news.bbc.co.uk/2/hi/europe/2931646.stm.

Béller-Hann, Ildikó. 1995. Prostitution and Its Effects in Northeast Turkey. *European Journal of Women's Studies* 2(2): 219–35.

Berdahl, Daphne. 1999. *Where the World Ended: Re-unification and Identity in a German Bordertown.* Berkeley: University of California Press.

Berlant, Lauren. 2010. Cruel Optimism. In *The Affect Theory Reader,* edited by Melissa Greg and Gregory J. Seigworth, 93–117. Durham, NC: Duke University Press.

Berlinski, Mischa. 2007. *Fieldwork: A Novel.* New York: Farrar, Strauss, and Giroux.

Bernstein, Elizabeth. 2012. Carceral Politics as Gender Justice? The "Traffic in Women" and Neoliberal Circuits of Crime, Sex, and Rights. *Theory and Society* 41(3): 233–59.

——. 2007a. *Temporarily Yours: Intimacy, Authenticity, and the Commerce of Sex.* Chicago: University of Chicago Press.

——. 2007b. Buying and Selling the "Girlfriend Experience": The Social and Subjective Contours of Market Intimacy. In *Love and Globalization: Transformations of Intimacy in the Contemporary World,* edited by Mark B. Padilla, Jennifer S. Hirsch, Miguel Munoz-Laboy, Robert E. Sember, and Richard G. Parker, 186–202. Nashville, TN: Vanderbilt University Press.

Bidder, Benjamin. 2010. Entering the EU through the Back Door: Romanian Passports for Moldovans. *Spiegel Online.* July 13. http://www.spiegel.de/international/europe/0,1518,706338,00.html.

Bishop, Ryan, and Lillian S. Robinson. 1998. *Night Market: Sexual Cultures and the Thai Economic Miracle.* New York: Routledge.

Bledsoe, Caroline, and Sow Papa. 2011. Back to Africa: Second Chances for the Children of West African Immigrants. *Journal of Marriage and Family* 73(4): 747–62.

Bloch, Alexia. 2014. "Citizenship, Belonging, and Moldovan Migrants in Post-Soviet Russia," *Ethnos* 79(4): 445–72.

——. 2009. Discourses on Danger and Dreams of Prosperity: Confounding US Government Positions on "Trafficking" from the Context of the Former Soviet Union. In *International Migration and Human Rights: The Global Repercussions of US Policy,* edited by Samuel Martinez, 165–83. Berkeley: University of California Press.

——. 2003a. *Red Ties and Residential Schools: Indigenous Siberians in a Post-Soviet State.* Philadelphia: University of Pennsylvania Press.

——. 2003b. Victims of Trafficking or Entrepreneurial Women? Narratives of Post-Soviet Entertainers in Turkey. *Journal of Canadian Woman Studies* 22(3/4): 152–58.

Bloch, Alexia, and Laurel Kendall 2004. *The Museum at the End of the World: Encounters in the Russian Far East.* Philadelphia: University of Pennsylvania Press.

Bollywood's 'Raj' in Russia Continues. 2013. *The Times of India.* September 22. http://timesofindia.indiatimes.com/nri/Bollywoods-Raj-in-Russia-continues/articleshow/22887005.cms.

Bréhier, Louis. 1977. *The Life and Death of Byzantium,* translated by Margaret Vaughan. New York: Elsevier North-Holland.

Brennan, Denise. 2004. *What's Love Got to Do with it? Transnational Desires and Sex Tourism in the Dominican Republic.* Durham, NC: Duke University Press.

Brettell, Caroline. 2015. Theorizing Migration in Anthropology. In *Migration Theory: Talking Across Disciplines,* edited by Caroline B. Brettell and James F. Hollifield, 148–97. London: Routledge.

British Broadcasting Corporation (BBC). 2016a. Migrant Crisis: Turkey Threatens EU with New Surge. November 25. http://www.bbc.com/news/world-europe-38103375.

——. 2016b. Who Are the Kurds? March 14. http://www.bbc.co.uk/news/world-middle-east-29702440.

Brooks, Jeffrey. 1985. *When Russia Learned to Read: Literacy and Popular Literature, 1861–1917*. Princeton, NJ: Princeton University Press.

Browning, Robert. 1992. *The Byzantine Empire*, revised edition. Washington, DC: Catholic University of America Press.

Bruno, Marta. 1997. Women and the Culture of Entrepreneurship. In *Post-Soviet Women: From the Baltic to Central Asia*, edited by Mary Buckley, 56–74. Cambridge: Cambridge University Press.

Buccianti, Alexandra. 2010. Dubbed Turkish Soap Operas Conquering the Arab World: Social Liberation or Cultural Alienation? *Arab Media and Society*, no. 10. http://www.arabmediasociety.com/?article=735.

Buck-Morss, Susan 2000. *Dreamworld and Catastrophe: The Passing of Mass Utopia in East and West*. Cambridge, MA: MIT Press.

Burawoy, Michael, and Katherine Verdery. 1999. Introduction. In *Uncertain Transition: Ethnographies of Change in a Postsocialist World*, edited by Michael Burawoy and Katherine Verdery, 1–18. New York: Rowman and Littlefield.

Buyandelgeriyn, Manduhai. 2008. Post-Post-Transition Theories: Walking on Multiple Paths. *Annual Review of Anthropology* 37: 235–50.

Cabot, Heath. 2014. *On the Doorstep of Europe: Asylum and Citizenship in Greece*. Philadelphia: University of Pennsylvania Press.

Camfield, Graham. 1990. The Pavlovtsy of Khar'kov Province, 1886–1905: Harmless Sectarians or Dangerous Rebels? *Slavonic and East European Review* 68(4): 692–717.

Carling, Jørgen, Cecilia Menjívar, and Leah Schmalzbauer. 2012. Central Themes in the Study of Transnational Parenthood. *Journal of Ethnic and Migration Studies* 38(2): 191–217.

Carrier-Moisan, Marie-Eve. 2012. Gringo Love: Affect, Power, and Mobility in Sex Tourism, Northeast Brazil. PhD diss., University of British Columbia.

Carsten, Janet. 1995. The Substance of Kinship and the Heat of the Hearth: Feeding, Personhood, and Relatedness among Malays in Pulaulangkawi. *American Ethnologist* 22(2): 223–41.

Cash, Jennifer R. 2011. *Villages on Stage: Folklore and Nationalism in the Republic of Moldova*. Berlin: Lit-Verlag.

Chamberlain, Mary. 2013. Rethinking Caribbean Families: Extending the Links. In *Gender in Cross-Cultural Perspective*, 6th ed., edited by Caroline B. Brettell and Carolyn F. Sargent, 303–10. Upper Saddle River, NJ: Pearson.

Cheng, Sealing. 2010. *On the Move for Love: Migrant Entertainers and the U.S. Military in South Korea*. Philadelphia: University of Pennsylvania Press.

——. 2007. Romancing the Club: Love Dynamics between Filipina Entertainers and GIs in US Military Camp Towns in South Korea. In *Love and Globalization: Transformations of Intimacy in the Contemporary World*, edited by Mark B. Padilla, Jennifer S. Hirsch, Miguel Munoz-Laboy, Robert E. Sember, and Richard G. Parker, 226–51. Nashville: Vanderbilt University Press.

Cheng, Sealing, and Eunjung Kim. 2014. The Paradoxes of Neoliberalism: Migrant Korean Sex Workers in the United States and "Sex Trafficking." *Social Politics: International Studies in Gender, State, and Society* 21(3): 355–81.

Chernozub, Veslevod. 2015. Russia without Migrants: The Departure of Migrants Shows That We Are Not the West. *Novaia gazeta*. January 26. http://www.novayagazeta.ru/comments/66981.html.

Chu, Julie. 2010. *Cosmologies of Credit: Transnational Mobility and the Politics of Destination in China*. Durham, NC: Duke University Press.

CIA World Fact Book. 2009. Turkey: Economy. https://www.cia.gov/library/publications/theworld-factbook/geos/TU.html.

Citizenship and Immigration Canada. 2014. Temporary Foreign Worker Program and International Mobility Program: Protecting Workers from Abuse and Exploitation. http://www.cic.gc.ca/english/resources/tools/temp/work/vulnerable.asp.

Clark, Gracia. 1999. Mothering, Work, and Gender in Urban Asante Ideology and Practice. *American Anthropologist* 101(4): 717–29.

Clifford, James. 1997. *Routes: Travel and Translation in the Late Twentieth Century.* Cambridge, MA: Harvard University Press.

Coalition against Trafficking in Women (CATW). 2011. http://www.catwinternational.org/WhoWeAre/History.

Colen, Shellee. 1995. "Like a Mother to Them": Stratified Reproduction and West Indian Childcare Workers and Employers in New York. In *Conceiving the New World Order: The Global Politics of Reproduction*, edited by Faye Ginsburg and Rayna Rapp, 73–103. Berkeley: University of California Press.

Collier, Jane F. 1997. *From Duty to Desire: Remaking Families in a Spanish Village.* Princeton, NJ: Princeton University Press.

Collier, Jane F., Michelle Z. Rosaldo, and Sylvia Yanagisako. 1982. Is There a Family?: New Anthropological Views. In *Rethinking the Family: Some Feminist Questions*, edited by Barrie Thorne and Marilyn Yalom, 25–39. Longman: New York.

Collins, Patricia Hill. 1994. Shifting the Center: Race, Class, and Feminist Theorizing about Motherhood. In *Mothering: Ideology, Experience, Agency*, edited by Evelyn Nakano Glenn, Grace Chang, and Linda Rennie Forcey, 45–65. New York: Routledge.

——. 1990. *Black Feminist Thought: Knowledge, Consciousness, and the Politics of Empowerment.* Boston: Unwin Hyman.

Constable, Nicole. 2014. *Born Out of Place: Migrant Mothers and the Politics of International Labor.* Berkeley: University of California Press.

——. 2009. The Commodification of Intimacy: Marriage, Sex, and Reproductive Labor. *Annual Review of Anthropology* 38: 49–64.

——. 2007. *Maid to Order in Hong Kong: Stories of Migrant Workers*, 2nd ed. Ithaca, NY: Cornell University Press.

——. 2005. Introduction. In *Cross-border Marriages: Gender and Mobility in Transnational Asia*, edited by Nicole Constable, 1–16. Philadelphia: University of Pennsylvania Press.

——. 2003. *Romance on a Global Stage: Pen Pals, Virtual Ethnography, and "Mail Order" Marriages.* Berkeley: University of California Press.

——. 1999. Ambivalent Returns: At Home but Not at Home. Filipina Narratives of Ambivalent Returns. *Cultural Anthropology* 14(2): 203–28.

Consulate General of Turkey. 2012. Mobile Phones Need to Be Registered for Use with SIM Cards Bought In Turkey. http://www.turkishconsulate.org.uk/en/other_services.asp?PageID=12.

Coomes, Phil. 2011. Moldova: The Children Left Behind. BBC. August 12. http://www.bbc.co.uk/news/in-pictures-14488086.

Cooper, Frederick. 2005. *Colonialism in Question: Theory, Culture, Knowledge.* Berkeley: University of California Press.

Coşar, Simten, and Funda Gençoğlu Onbaşı. 2008. Women's Movement in Turkey at a Crossroads: From Women's Rights Advocacy to Feminism. *South European Society and Politics* 13(3): 325–44.

Countries Compared by Labor: Female Professionals. 2002. International Statistics at NationMaster.com, calculated on the basis of occupational data from ILO (International Labour Organization). Laboursta Database. http://www.nationmaster.com/country-info/stats/Labor/Female-professionals.

Couroucli, Maria. 2010. Empire Dust: The Web of Relations in Saint George's Festival on Princes Island in Istanbul. In *Eastern Christians in Anthropological Perspective*, edited by Chris Hann and Hermann Goltz, 220–39. Berkeley: University of California Press.

Cuc, Milan, Erik Lundbäck, and Edgardo Ruggiero. 2006. *Migration and Remittances in Moldova*. Washington, DC: International Monetary Fund.

Çağaptay, Soner. 2006. *Islam, Secularism, and Nationalism in Modern Turkey*. New York: Routledge.

Dahinden, Janine. 2010. Cabaret Dancers: Settle Down in Order to Stay Mobile? Bridging Theoretical Orientations within Transnational Migration Studies. *Social Politics: International Studies in Gender, State, and Society* 17(3): 323–48.

Dauphin, Claudine. 1996. Brothels, Baths, and Babes: Prostitution in the Byzantine Holy Land. *Classics Ireland* 3: 47–72.

Dedeoğlu, Saniye. 2008. *Women Workers in Turkey: Global Industrial Production in Istanbul*. London: Tauris Academic Studies.

De Genova, Nicholas, and Nathalie Peutz, eds. 2010. *The Deportation Regime: Sovereignty, Space, and the Freedom of Movement*. Durham, NC: Duke University Press.

Deleon, Jak. 1995. *The White Russians in Istanbul*. Istanbul: Remzi Kitabevi.

Demers, Patricia. 2004. Working Girls in Print: A Growth Industry. *Topia: Canadian Journal of Cultural Studies*, no. 12: 83–98.

Demintseva, Ekaterina, and Daniel Kashnitsky. 2016. Contextualizing Migrants' Methods of Seeking Medical Care in Russia. *International Migration* 54(5): 29–42.

Demirdirek, Hülya. 2008. (Re-)claiming Nationhood through Re-nativisation of Language: The Gagauz in Moldova. In *Nationalism in Late and Post-Communist Europe*, edited by Egbert Jahn, 231–47. Baden-Baden: Nomos.

Demır, Gül, and Niki Gamm. 2010. From Mosque to Museum: The Haseki Complex. *Hürriyet Daily News*. November 5. http://www.hurriyetdailynews.com/from-mosque-to-museum-the-haseki-complex.aspx?pageID=438&n=from-mosque-complex-to-museum-the-haseki-complex-2010-11-03.

Denisova, Liubov. 2010. *Rural Women in the Soviet Union and Post-Soviet Russia*, edited and translated by Irina Mukhina. New York: Routledge.

Dimitrov Eager to Naturalize 500,000 Bessarabia Bulgarians. 2010. Novinite.com (Sofia News Agency). September 22. http://www.novinite.com/articles/120399/Dimitrov+Eager+to+Naturalize+500+000+Bessarabia+Bulgarians.

Dimulescu, Valentina, and Andrei Avram. 2011. All Quiet on the Eastern Front: The Romanian Policy of Regaining Citizenship Compared to Other EU Case Studies. Romanian Center for European Policies. Policy Brief, no. 22. http://www.ssrn.com/abstract=2720937.

Doezema, Jo. 1999. Loose Women or Lost Women? The Re-emergence of the Myth of White Slavery in Contemporary Discourses of Trafficking in Women. *Gender Issues* 18(1): 23–50.

Doğan, Setenay Nil. 2011. Circassian Beauty: A Myth in Turkey. In *Gender, Ethnicity and the Nation-State: Anatolia and Its Neighbouring Regions*. Hrant Dink Memorial Workshop 2009 Proceedings, edited by Leyla Keough, 83–87. Istanbul: Sabancı University.

Duben, Alan, and Cem Behar. 1991. *Istanbul Households: Marriage, Family, and Fertility, 1880–1940*. Cambridge: Cambridge University Press.

Dunn, Elizabeth. 2004. *Privatizing Poland: Baby Food, Big Business, and the Remaking of Labor*. Ithaca, NY: Cornell University Press.

——. 1999. Slick Salesmen and Simple People: Negotiating Capitalism in Privatizing Poland. In *Uncertain Transition: Ethnographies of Change in the Postsocialist World*, edited by Michael Burawoy and Katherine Verdery, 125–51. New York: Rowman and Littlefield.

Ediger, Volkan S., and Itır Bağdadi. 2010. Turkey-Russia Energy Relations: Same Old Story, New Actors. *Insight Turkey* 12(3): 221–36.

Ehrenreich, Barbara, and Arlie Russell Hochschild. 2002. Introduction. In *Global Woman: Nannies, Maids, and Sex Workers in the New Economy*, edited by Barbara Ehrenreich and Arlie R. Hochschild, 1–13. New York: Metropolitan Books.

Einhorn, Barbara. 1993. *Cinderella Goes to Market: Citizenship, Gender, and Women's Movements in East Central Europe*. New York: Verso.

Elrick, Eric. 2008. The Influence of Migration on Origin Communities: Insights from Polish Migrations to the West. *Europe-Asia Studies* 60(9): 1503–17.

Embassy of the United Arab Emirates (UAE). 2015. Non-US Citizens. http://www.uae-embassy.org/visas-passports/non-us-citizens.

Erdem, Hakan. 1996. *Slavery in the Ottoman Empire and Its Demise, 1800–1909*. New York: St. Martin's.

Erder, Sema, and Selmin Kaşka. 2003. *Irregular Migration and Trafficking in Women: The Case of Turkey*. Geneva, Switzerland: International Organization for Migration. http://www.iom.int/jahia/webdav/site/myjahiasite/shared/shared/mainsite/published_docs/covers/Irregular_mig_in_turkey.pdf.

Erokhina, Liudmila. 2000. *Mashtaby vyvoza zhenshchin v strany aziatsko-tikhookeanskogo regiona* [The scale of the export of women to countries of the Asia-Pacific Region]. In *Conference Proceedings for Koalitsia Angel, 2nd International Conference on Trafficking in Women*, 122–29. Moscow, Russia. October 23–November 3. Volume 2.

Eşsizoğlu, Altan, Aziz Yaşan, Ejder Akgun Yıldırım, Faruk Gürgen, and Mustafa Özkan. 2011. Double Standard for Traditional Value of Virginity and Premarital Sexuality in Turkey: A University Students' Case. *Women and Health* 51(2): 136–50.

EuroActiv. 2012. Gas Pipeline Deal Sidelines Original Nabucco Project. June 28. http://www.euractiv.com/energy/tanap-gas-pipeline-shelves-nabuc-news-513593.

European Baptist Federation (EBF). 2012. Moldova. http://www.ebf.org/moldova.

Evered, Emine Ö., and Kyle T. Evered. 2013. "Protecting the National Body": Regulating the Practice and the Place of Prostitution in Early Republican Turkey. *Gender, Place, and Culture: A Journal of Feminist Geography* 20(7): 839–57.

Faier, Leiba. 2009. *Intimate Encounters: Filipina Women and the Remaking of Rural Japan*. Berkeley: University of California Press.

Fanon, Franz. 1963. *Wretched of the Earth*. New York: Grove.

Fedor, Helen, ed. 1995. *Moldova: A Country Study*. Washington: GPO for the Library of Congress. http://countrystudies.us/moldova/26.htm.

Femen. 2012. India Seeks to Ban Sex Workers from Former Soviet States. http://femen.info/india-seeks-to-ban-sex-workers-from-former-soviet-states/.

Finkel, Andrew. 2012. Erdogan, the Not-so Magnificent. *New York Times*. Latitude. November 30. http://latitude.blogs.nytimes.com/2012/11/30/erdogan-the-not-so-magnificent/.

Finnegan, William. 2008. The Countertraffickers: Rescuing the Victims of the Global Sex Trade. *New Yorker*. May 5. http://www.newyorker.com/magazine/2008/05/05/the-countertraffickers.

First Call to Prayer inside Istanbul's Hagia Sophia in 85 Years. 2016. *Hürriyet Daily News*. July 2. http://www.hurriyetdailynews.com/first-call-to-prayer-inside-istanbuls-hagia-sophia-in-85-years.aspx?PageID=238&NID=101161&NewsCatID=341.

Fodor, Eva, and Erika Kispeter. 2014. Making the "Reserve Army" Invisible: Lengthy Parental Leave and Women's Economic Marginalisation in Hungary. *European Journal of Women's Studies* 21(4): 382–98.

Food and Agriculture Organization (FAO) (United Nations). 2001. Seed Policy and Programmes for the Central and Eastern European Countries, Commonwealth of Independent States and Other Countries in Transition. In *Proceedings of the Regional Technical Meeting on Seed Policy and Programmes for the Central and Eastern European Countries, Commonwealth of Independent States and Other Countries in Transition* held in Budapest, Hungary, March 6–10. http://www.fao.org/docrep/005/Y2722E/y2722e0x.htm.

Foucault, Michel. 1972. *The Archaeology of Knowledge and the Discourse on Language.* New York: Pantheon.

Frank, Martina W., Heidi M. Bauer, Nadir Arican, Sebnem Korur Fincanci, and Vincent Iacopino. 1999. Virginity Examinations in Turkey: Role of Forensic Physicians in Controlling Female Sexuality. *Journal of the American Medical Association* 282(5): 485–90.

Franzblau, Susan H. 2002. Deconstructing Attachment Theory: Naturalizing the Politics of Motherhood. In *Charting a New Course for Feminist Psychology*, edited by Lynn H. Collins, Michelle R. Dunlap, and Joan C. Chrisler, 93–110. Westport, CT: Praeger.

Freely, John. 1996. *Istanbul: The Imperial City.* London: Viking.

Freeman, Carla. 2007. Neoliberalism and the Marriage of Reputation and Respectability: Entrepreneurship and the Barbadian Middle Class. In *Love and Globalization: Transformations of Intimacy in the Contemporary World*, edited by Mark B. Padilla, Jennifer S. Hirsch, Miguel Muñoz-Laboy, Robert E. Sember, and Richard G. Parker, 3–37. Nashville: Vanderbilt University Press.

——. 2002. Mobility, Rootedness, and the Caribbean Higgler: Production, Consumption, and Transnational Livelihoods. In *Work and Migration: Life and Livelihoods in a Globalizing World*, edited by Ninna Nyberg Sørenson and Karen Fog Olwig, 61–81. New York: Routledge.

Fromkin, David. 1989. *A Peace to End All Peace: Creating the Modern Middle East, 1914–1922.* New York: Henry Holt and Company.

Gagauz Autonomous Territory Administration. 2015. Istoricheskaia spravka o Gagauzakh. [Historical Note on the Gagauz]. http://www.gagauzia.md/pageview.php?l=ru&idc=98&nod=1&.

Gal, Susan, and Gail Kligman 2000. *The Politics of Gender after Socialism.* Princeton, NJ: Princeton University Press.

Gamburd, M.R. 2000. *The Kitchen Spoon's Handle: Transnationalism and Sri Lanka's Migrant Housemaids.* Ithaca, NY: Cornell University Press.

Gates, Hill. 1991. "Narrow Hearts" and Petty Capitalism: Small Business Women in Chengdu, China. In *Marxist Approaches in Economic Anthropology*, edited by Alice Littlefield and Hill Gates, 13–36. Lanham, MD: University Press of America.

Genç, Deniz, and Merve Özdemirkıran. 2015. Local Perceptions of Syrian Migration to Turkey: A Case Study of Istanbul Neighborhoods. In *Turkish Migration Conference 2015: Selected Proceedings*, edited by Güven Şeker, Mustafa Ökmen, Ali Tilbe, Pınar Yazgan, Deniz Eroğlu, and Ibrahim Sirkeci, 106–17. London: Transnational Press London.

Gessen, Masha. 1995. Sex in the Media and the Birth of the Sex Media in Russia. In *Postcommunism and the Body Politic*, edited by Ellen Berry, 197–228. New York: New York University Press.

Ghençea, Boris, and Igor Gudumac. 2004. *Labor Migration and Remittances in the Republic of Moldova.* Chişinău: Moldova Microfinance Alliance and Soros Moldova.

Ghodsee, Kristin. 2009. *Muslim Lives in Eastern Europe: Gender, Ethnicity, and the Transformation of Islam in Postsocialist Bulgaria.* Princeton, NJ: Princeton University Press.

Ghosh, Amitav. 1992. *In an Antique Land*. London: Granta Books.

Giddens, Anthony. 1992. *The Transformation of Intimacy: Sexuality, Eroticism, and Love in Modern Societies*. Stanford, CA: Stanford University Press.

Glass, Christy, and Éva Fodor. 2011. Public Maternalism Goes to Market: Recruitment, Hiring and Promotion in Postsocialist Hungary. *Gender and Society* 25(1): 5–26.

Glenn, Evelyn Nakano. 1994. Social Constructions of Mothering: A Thematic Overview. In *Mothering: Ideology, Experience, and Agency*, edited by Evelyn Nakano Glenn, Grace Chang, and Linda Rennie Forcey, 1–29. New York: Routledge.

Glick Schiller, Nina. 1999. Citizens in Transnational Nation-states: The Asian Experience. In *Globalization and the Asia-Pacific: Contested Territories*, edited by Kris Olds, Peter Dicken, Philip F. Kelly, Lily Kong, and Henry Wai-chung Yeung, 202–18. New York: Routledge.

Glick Schiller, Nina, and Ayşe Çağlar. 2008. "And Ye Shall Possess It, and Dwell Therein": Social Citizenship, Global Christianity, and Non-Ethnic Immigrant Incorporation. In *Immigration and Citizenship in Europe and the United States: Anthropological Perspectives*, edited by Deborah Reed-Danahay and Caroline Brettell, 201–25. New Brunswick, NJ: Rutgers University Press.

Global Agency. 2014. Magnificent Century Premieres in the United States. www.theglobalagency.tv/magnificent-century-premieres-in-the-united-states.

Gökovali, Ummuhan. 2010. Contribution of Tourism to Economic Growth in Turkey. *Anatolia: An International Journal of Tourism and Hospitality Research* 21(1): 139–53.

Göksel, İklim. 2009. Rhetorics of Virginity in Turkish Modernity. PhD diss., University of Illinois at Chicago.

Golden, Deborah. 2003. A National Cautionary Tale: Russian Women Newcomers to Israel Portrayed. *Nations and Nationalism* 9(1): 83–104.

Goldman, Wendy. 1993. *Women, the State and Revolution: Soviet Family Policy and Social Life, 1917–1936*. Cambridge: Cambridge University Press.

Gorman, Daniel. 2008. Empire, Internationalism, and the Campaign against the Traffic in Women and Children in the 1920s. *Twentieth Century British History* 19(2): 186–216.

Gorodskoi otdel statistiki. 2004. Zaniatnost′ naseleniia, 2003 g./2004 g. [Employment of the population, 2003–2004]. Vulkaneshty.

Gorsuch, Anne, and Diane E. Koenker, eds. 2006. *Turizm: The Russian and East European Tourist under Capitalism and Socialism*. Ithaca, NY: Cornell University Press.

Goscilo, Helena. 1993. Domostroika or Perestroika? The Construction of Womanhood in Soviet Culture under Glasnost. In *Late Soviet Culture: From Perestroika to Novostroika*, edited by Thomas Lahusen, 233–55. Durham, NC: Duke University Press.

Goscilo, Helena, and Andrea Lanoux. 2006. Introduction: Lost in the Myths. In *Gender and National Identity in Twentieth-century Russian Culture*, edited by Helena Goscilo and Andrea Lanoux, 1–17. DeKalb: Northern Illinois University Press.

Göymen, Korel. 2000. Tourism and Governance in Turkey. *Annals of Tourism Research* 27(4): 1025–48.

Graham, Elspeth, and Lucy Jordan. 2011. Migrant Parents and the Psychological Well-Being of Left-behind Children in Southeast Asia. *Journal of Marriage and Family* 73(4): 763–87.

Graham, Elspeth, Lucy Jordan, Brenda Yeoh, Theodor Lam, Maruja Asis, and Su-kamdi. 2012. Transnational Families and the Family Nexus: Perspectives of Indonesian and Filipino Children Left Behind by Migrant Parent(s). *Environment and Planning A* 44(4). http://doi.org/10.1068/a4445.

Grant, Bruce. 1999. The Return of the Repressed: Conversations with Three Russian Entrepreneurs. In *Paranoia within Reason: A Casebook on Conspiracy as Explanation*, edited by George E. Marcus, 241–67. Chicago: University of Chicago Press.

——. 1995. *In the Soviet House of Culture: A Century of Perestroikas*. Princeton, NJ: Princeton University Press.

Guboglo, Mikhail N. 2006. *Imeni iazyka. Ocherki etnokul'turnoi i etnopoliticheskoi istorii gagauzov* [Names of language: An outline of ethnocultural and ethnopolitical history of the Gagauz]. Moscow: Nauka.

Guy, Donna. 2000. *White Slavery and Mothers Alive and Dead: The Troubled Meeting of Sex, Gender, Public Health, and Progress in Latin America*. Omaha: University of Nebraska Press.

——. 1991. *Sex and Danger in Buenos Aires: Prostitution, Family, and Nation in Argentina*. Omaha: University of Nebraska Press.

Gülçür, Leyla, and Pınar İlkkaracan. 2000. The "Natasha Experience": Migrant Sex Workers from the Former Soviet Union and Eastern Europe in Turkey. *Women Studies International Forum* 25(4): 411–21.

Güsten, Suzanne. 2011. Turkey Cultivates Sites of Its Christian Heritage. *New York Times*. May 4. http://www.nytimes.com/2011/05/05/world/middleeast/05iht-M05-TURKEY-CHRISTIANS.html?pagewanted=all&_r=0.

Habeck, Joachim Otto. 2011. Introduction: Cultivation, Collective, and the Self. In *Reconstructing the House of Culture: Community, Self, and the Makings of Culture in Russia and Beyond*, edited by Brian Donahoe and Joachim Otto Habeck, 1–28. New York: Berghahn Books.

Hacaoğlu, Selcan. 2002. Turkey Tries to Crack Down on "Evil" Foreign Prostitutes. *Turkish Daily News*. June 11, 1.

Haeri, Shahla. 2014. *Law of Desire: Temporary Marriage in Shi'i Iran*. Rev. ed. Syracuse, NY: Syracuse University Press.

Haney, Lynne. 2003. Welfare Reform with a Familial Face: Reconstituting State and Domestic Relations in Post-socialist Eastern Europe. In *Families of a New World*, edited by Lynne Haney and Lisa Pollard, 159–78. New York: Routledge.

Hann, Chris, and Ildikó Béller-Hann. 1998. Markets, Morality, and Modernity in North-East Turkey. In *Border Identities, Nation and State at International Frontiers*, edited by Thomas M. Wilson and Hastings Donnan, 237–62. Cambridge: Cambridge University Press.

Hann, Chris, and Ildikó Hann. 1992. Samovars and Sex on Turkey's Russian Markets. *Anthropology Today* 8(4): 3–6.

Hann, Chris, Caroline Humphrey, and Katherine Verdery. 2002. Introduction: Postsocialism as a Topic of Anthropological Investigation. In *Postsocialism: Ideals, Ideologies, and Practices in Eurasia*, edited by Chris Hann, 1–11. New York: Routledge.

Hannerz, Ulf. 1996. *Transnational Connections: Culture, People, Places*. New York: Routledge.

Hansen, Suzy. 2017. Inside Turkey's Purge. *New York Times*. April 13. https://www.nytimes.com/2017/04/13/magazine/inside-turkeys-purge.html

Hardwick, Susan Wiley. 1993. *Russian Refuge: Religion, Migration, and Settlement on the North American Continent*. Chicago: University of Chicago Press.

Harrell, Stevan. 1985. Why Do the Chinese Work so Hard? Reflections on an Entrepreneurial Ethic. *Modern China* 11(2): 203–26.

Hart, Kimberly. 2007. Love by Arrangement: The Ambiguity of "Spousal Choice" in a Turkish Village. *Journal of the Royal Anthropological Institute* 13(2): 345–62.

Haurigot, Paul. 1929. *Acide Russique*. Paris: Emile-Paul frères.

Harvey, David. 1989. *The Condition of Postmodernity: An Inquiry into the Origins of Cultural Change.* Oxford: Blackwell.

Hausmann, Ricardo, Laura D. Tyson, Yasmina Bekhouche, and Saadia Zahidi. 2012. *The Global Gender Gap Index 2012.* Geneva, Switzerland: World Economic Forum. http://www3.weforum.org/docs/GGGR12/MainChapter_GGGR12.pdf.

Hemment, Julie. 2007. *Empowering Women in Russia: Activism, Aid, and NGOs.* Bloomington: Indiana University Press.

Henley, Jon, Kareem Shaheen, and Constanze Letsch. 2015. Respect Turkey Election Result, Says Victorious Erdoğan. *The Guardian.* November 2. https://www.the guardian.com/world/2015/nov/02/respect-turkey-election-result-says-victorious-erdogan.

Herrin, Judith. 2007. *Byzantium: The Surprising Life of a Medieval Empire.* London: Penguin.

Herzfeld, Michael. 1980. Honor and Shame: Problems in the Comparative Analysis of Moral Systems. *Man* 15(2): 339–51.

Hewlett, Barry S. 2013. The Cultural Nexus of Aka Father-Infant Bonding. In *Gender in Cross-Cultural Perspective*, 6th ed., edited by Caroline B. Brettell and Carolyn F. Sargent, 37–50. New York: Pearson.

Heymann, Jody, and Kristin McNeill. 2013. *Children's Chances: How Countries Can Move from Surviving to Thriving.* Cambridge, MA: Harvard University Press.

Hirsch, Jennifer S. 2003. *A Courtship after Marriage: Sexuality and Love in Mexican Transnational Families.* Berkeley: University of California Press.

Hirsch, Jennifer S., and Holly Wardlow. 2006. Introduction: Of Modernity/Modernities, Gender and Ethnography. In *Modern Loves: The Anthropology of Romantic Courtship and Companionate Marriage*, edited by Jennifer Hirsch and Holly Wardlow, 1–31. Ann Arbor: University of Michigan Press.

Hochschild, Arlie R. 1983. *The Managed Heart: Commercialization of Human Feeling.* Berkeley: University of California Press.

Hohnen, Pernille. 2003. *A Market out of Place? Remaking Economic, Social, and Symbolic Boundaries in Post-Communist Lithuania.* Oxford: Oxford University Press.

Holland, Dorothy, and Margaret Eisenhart. 1990. *Educated in Romance: Women, Achievement and College Culture.* Chicago: University of Chicago Press.

Hudson, Alexandra. 2008. Turkish Islamic Preacher—Threat or Benefactor? Reuters. May 14. http://uk.reuters.com/article/uk-turkey-religion-idUKL09390339200805 14?pageNumber=3&virtualBrandChannel=0.

Hughes, Donna M. 2002. *Trafficking for Sexual Exploitation: The Case of the Russian Federation.* Geneva: International Organization of Migration.

——. 2000. The "Natasha" Trade: The Transnational Shadow Market of Trafficking in Women. *Journal of International Affairs* 53(2): 625–51.

Hugo, Graeme. 2003. Asian Experiences in Remittances. In *Beyond Small Change: Migrants, Remittances and Economic Development*, edited by Donald F. Terry and Steven R. Wilson, 341–73. Baltimore: Inter-American Development Bank and Johns Hopkins University Press.

Humphrey, Caroline. 2002. *The Unmaking of Soviet Life.* Ithaca, NY: Cornell University Press.

——. 1999a. Traders, "Disorder," and Citizenship Regimes in Provincial Russia. In *Uncertain Transition: Ethnographies of Change in a Postsocialist World*, edited by Michael Burawoy and Katherine Verdery, 19–52. New York: Rowman and Littlefield.

——. 1999b. *Marx Went Away–But Karl Stayed Behind.* Ann Arbor: University of Michigan Press.

Humphrey, Caroline, and Ruth Mandel. 2002. The Market in Everyday Life: Ethnographies of Postsocialism. In *Markets and Moralities: Ethnographies of Postsocialism*, edited by Ruth Mandel and Caroline Humphrey, 1–18. Oxford: Berg.

Huntington, Samuel P. 1996. *The Clash of Civilizations and the Remaking of the World Order*. New York: Simon and Schuster.

Ianyshev-Voloshin, Aleksandr Ivanovich. 1993. *Gagauzy* [The Gagauz]. Moscow: Znanie.

İçduygu, Ahmet. 2009. Turkey. In *Statistics and Reality: Concepts and Measurements of Migration in Europe*, edited by Heinz Fassmann, Ursula Reeger, and Wiebke Sievers, 281–96. Amsterdam: University of Amsterdam Press.

——. 2007. *Turkey and International Migration, 2006/2007*. Report for the Continuous Reporting System on Migration (SOPEMI) of the Organization for Economic Cooperation and Development (OECD).

İçduygu, Ahmet, and Ayşem Biriz Karaçay. 2012. The International Migration System between Turkey and Russia: Project-Tied Migrant Workers in Moscow. *International Migration* 50(1): 55–74.

İçduygu, Ahmet, Şule Toktaş, and B. Ali Soner. 2010. The Politics of Population in a Nation-building Process: Emigration of Non-Muslims from Turkey. *Journal of Ethnic and Racial Studies* 31(2): 358–89.

İçduygu, Ahmet, and Deniz Yükseker. 2012. Rethinking Transit Migration in Turkey: Reality and Representation in the Creation of a Migratory Phenomenon. *Population, Space, and Place* 18(4): 441–56.

İçduygu, Ahmet, Deniz Yükseker, and Damla B. Aksel. 2013. *Migration around Turkey: Old Phenomena, New Research*. Istanbul: Isis.

İçöz, Orhan, Turgut Var, and Metin Kozak. 1998. Tourism Demand in Turkey. *Annals of Tourism Research* 25(1): 236–40.

İlkkaracan, Pınar. 2012. The Turkish Model: for Whom? *Open Democracy*. April 15. http://www.opendemocracy.net/5050/pinar-ilkkaracan/turkish-model-for-whom.

In the Name of Love. 2002. Directed by Shannon O'Rourke. 58 min. SOR Productions.

Interdevochka. 1989. Directed by Pyotr Todorovsky. 143 min. Mosfilm.

International Organization for Migration (IOM). 2002. *Migration Trends in Eastern Europe and Central Asia: 2001–2002 Review*. Geneva: International Organization for Migration.

Ipsa, Jean. 1994. *Childcare in Russia: In Transition*. Westport, CT: Bergin and Garvey.

Ivanova, Natalya, and Olga Buslayeva. 1999. The Dark Side of the Moon: Shadow Economy in Ukraine. *Ekonomický časopis* 47(4): 630–48.

Jankowiak, William. 2008. *Intimacies: Love and Sex across Cultures*. New York: Columbia University Press.

Jarrard, Kyle. 2007. With Cognac, a Taste of the Good Life for Russian Drinkers. *New York Times*. November 27. http://www.nytimes.com/2007/11/27/style/27iht-rcognac.1.8498627.html.

Jerczynski, Marek. 1999. Patterns of Spatial Mobility of Citizens of the Former Soviet Union. In *The Challenge of the East-West Migration for Poland*, edited by Keith Iglicka and Krystyna Sword, 105–19. London: Macmillan.

Johnson, Ericka. 2007. *Dreaming of a Mail-Order Husband: Russian-American Internet Romance*. Durham, NC: Duke University Press.

Jones, Dorian. 2011. Turkey's Murder Rate of Women Skyrockets. *Voice of America News*. February 27. http://www.voanews.com/content/turkeys-murder-rate-of-women-skyrockets-117093538/170517.html.

Kanbolat, Hasan. 2012. Are Russian Tourists Being Discouraged from Visiting Turkey? *Today's Zaman*. May 25. http://www.todayszaman.com/columnist-281509-are-russian-tourists-being-discouraged-from-visiting-turkey.html.

Kandiyoti, Deniz. 2011. A Tangled Web: The Politics of Gender in Turkey. *Open Democracy*. January 5. http://www.opendemocracy.net/5050/deniz-kandiyoti/tangled-web-politics-of-gender-in-turkey.

———. 1997. Gendering the Modern: On Missing Dimensions in the Study of Turkish Modernity. In *Rethinking Modernity and National Identity in Turkey*, edited by Sibel Bozdogan and Resat Kasaba, 111–32. Seattle: University of Washington Press.

———. 1988a. Slave Girls, Temptresses, and Comrades: Images of Women in the Turkish Novel. *Feminist Issues* 8(2): 35–50.

———. 1988b. Bargaining with Patriarchy. *Gender and Society* 12(3): 274–90.

———. 1987. Emancipated but Unliberated? Reflections on the Turkish Case. *Feminist Studies* 13(2): 317–38.

Kaneff, Deema. 2002. The Shame and Pride of Market Activity. In *Markets and Moralities: Ethnographies of Post-Socialism*, edited by Ruth Mandel and Caroline Humphrey, 33–52. Oxford: Berg.

Kapchan, Deborah. 1996. *Gender on the Market: Moroccan Women and the Revoicing of Tradition*. Philadelphia: University of Pennsylvania Press.

Karpat, Kemal. 2004. The Genesis of the Gecekondu: Rural Migration and Urbanization (1976). *European Journal of Turkish Studies*, no. 1. http://ejts.revues.org/54.

———. 1985. *Ottoman Population, 1830–1914: Demographic and Social Characteristics*. Madison: University of Wisconsin Press.

Kaufman, Nils Joseph. 2009. Empty Pedestals: Creating a National School System in an Era of Globalization. PhD diss., Michigan State University.

Kay, Rebecca. 2006. *Men in Contemporary Russia: The Fallen Heroes of Post-Soviet Change?* Aldershot: Ashgate.

Kaya, Ayhan. 2013. *Europeanization and Tolerance in Turkey: The Myth of Toleration*. London: Palgrave Macmillan.

Kaya, Ayhan, and Ayşe Tecmen. 2011. The Role of Common Cultural Heritage in External Promotion of Modern Turkey: Yunus Emre Cultural Centers. European Institute Working Paper, no. 4. Istanbul Bilgi University, European Institute and International Relations Department. http://eu.bilgi.edu.tr/media/uploads/2014/05/22/working-paper4_2.pdf.

Kearney, Michael. 1995. The Local and the Global: The Anthropology of Globalization and Transnationalism. *Annual Review of Anthropology* 24: 547–65.

Kempadoo, Kemala. 2005 *Trafficking and Prostitution Reconsidered: New Perspectives on Migration, Sex Work, and Human Rights*. Boulder, CO: Paradigm.

Kendall, Laurel. 1996. *Getting Married in Korea: Of Gender, Morality, and Modernity*. Berkeley: University of California Press.

Kenyon, Peter. 2013. Prime Minister Finds Soap Opera's Turkish Delights in Bad Taste. National Public Radio. January 3. http://www.npr.org/2013/01/03/167981036/prime-minister-finds-soap-operas-turkish-delights-in-bad-taste.

Keough, Leyla J. 2015. *Worker-Mothers on the Margins of Europe: Gender and Migration between Moldova and Istanbul*. Bloomington: Indiana University Press.

———. 2006. Globalizing "Postsocialism": Mobile Mothers and Neoliberalism on the Margins of Europe. *Anthropological Quarterly* 79(3): 431–61.

Keyder, Çağlar. 2005. A History and Geography of Turkish Nationalism. In *Citizenship and the Nation-State in Greece and Turkey*, edited by Faruk Birtek and Thalia Dragonas, 3–17. New York: Routledge.

———. 1999. The Setting. In *Istanbul: Between the Global and the Local*, edited by Keyder Çağlar, 3–28. Lanham, MD: Rowman and Littlefield.

Kınıklıoğlu, Suat, and Valeriy Morkva. 2007. An Anatomy of Turkish–Russian Relations. *Southeast European and Black Sea Studies* 7(4): 533–53.

King, Charles. 2014. *Midnight at the Pera Palace: The Birth of Modern Istanbul*. New York: W. W. Norton.

——. 2000. *The Moldovans: Romania, Russia, and the Politics of Culture*. Stanford, CA: Hoover Institution Press.

Kingsley, Patrick. 2017. Erdogan Claims Vast Powers in Turkey after Narrow Victory in Referendum. *New York Times*. April 16. https://www.nytimes.com/2017/04/16/world/europe/turkey-referendum-polls-erdogan.html?_r=0.

Kirby, Emma Jane. 2004. Poor Moldovans Lured into Sex Trade. BBC. July 10. http://news.bbc.co.uk/2/hi/programmes/from_our_own_correspondent/3878503.stm.

Kirschenbaum, Lisa A. 2001. *Small Comrades: Revolutionizing Childhood in Soviet Russia, 1917–1932*. New York: Routledge.

Kocaoğlu, Elif. 2012. Laws and Regulations Applicable to Foreigners in Turkey: A Practical Overview of the Legal Requirements for Visa, Residence, and Work Permit. *Ankara Bar Review*, no. 2: 15–36.

Koğacıoğlu, Dicle. 2004. The Tradition Effect: Framing Honor Crimes in Turkey. *Differences: A Journal of Feminist Cultural Studies* 15(2): 118–51.

Kollontai, Alexandra. 2008. *The Essential Alexandra Kollontai*. Chicago: Haymarket Books.

Kon, Igor. 1995. *The Sexual Revolution in Russia: From the Age of the Czars to Today*. New York: Free Press.

——. 1993. Sexuality and Culture. In *Sex and Russian Society*, edited by Igor Kon and James Riordan, 15–44. London: Pluto.

Konstantinov, Yulian. 1996. Patterns of Reinterpretation: Trader-Tourism in the Balkans (Bulgaria) as a Picaresque Metaphorical Enactment of Post-Totalitarianism. *American Ethnologist* 23(4): 762–82.

Konstantinov, Yulian, Gideon M. Kressel, and Trond Thuen. 1998. Outclassed by Former Outcasts: Petty Trading in Varna. *American Ethnologist* 25(4): 729–45.

Kramer, Andrew. 2007. Markets Suffer after Russia Bans Immigrant Vendors. *New York Times*. April 14. http://www.nytimes.com/2007/04/14/world/europe/14market.html?ref=world.

Krassinets, Eugene, and Elena Tiuriukanova. 2001. Potentials of Labor Out-migration from Russia: 2 Surveys. *Tijdschrift voor economische en sociale geografie/Journal of Social and Economic Geography* 92(1): 5–17.

Kukhterin, Sergei. 2000. Fathers and Patriarchs in Communist and Post-communist Russia. In *Gender, State and Society in Soviet and Post-Soviet Russia*, edited by Sarah Ashwin, 71–89. New York: Routledge.

Kunin, Vladimir. 1991 [1989]. *Intergirl: A Hard Currency Hooker*. Translated by Antonina Bouis. New York: Berg.

Kurban, Dilek, and Konstantinos Tsitselikis. 2010. A Tale of Reciprocity: Minority Foundations in Greece and Turkey. Istanbul, Turkey: Türkiye Ekonomik ve Sosyal Etüdler Vakfı (Turkish Economic and Social Studies Foundation). http://tesev.org.tr/wp-content/uploads/2015/11/A_Tale_Of_Reciprocity_Minority_Foundations_In_Greece_And_Turkey.pdf.

Kuroglo, Stepan Stepanovich. 1980. *Semeinaia obriadnost' gagauzov v XIX–nachale XX v.* [Gagauz family ritual practices in the 19th to 20th centuries]. Kishinev: Shtiintza.

Kuroglo, Stepan Stepanovich, and Maria Fedorovna Filimonova. 1976. *Proshloe i nastoiashchee gagauzskoi zhenshchiny* [Gagauz women's past and present]. Kishinev: Karta Moldoveniaskei.

Kuznetsov, Evgeny. 1995. Is Russia Becoming a Developing Country? Brain Drain and Allocation of Talent in a Post-Soviet Transition. *Communist Economies and Economic Transformation* 7(4): 485–97.

Kvilinkova, Elizaveta Nikolaevna. 2007. *Traditsionnaia dukhovnaia kul'tura gagauzov: etnoregional'nye osobennosti* [Traditional spiritual cultural of the Gagauz: Ethnoregional characteristics]. Kishinev: Biznes-Elita.

Lapidus, Gail Warshofsky. 1978. *Women in Soviet Society: Equality, Development, and Social Change.* Berkeley: University of California Press.

Larkin, Brian. 1998. Indian Films and Nigerian Lovers: Media and the Creation of Parallel Modernities. *Africa* 67(3): 406–40.

Learn4Good. 2016. Host/Hostess/Entertainer. http://www.learn4good.com/jobs/entertainment/e/142161/search/kusadasi/.

——. Animators/Dancers. 2013a. http://www.learn4good.com/jobs/e/90878/employer/search/.

——. 2013b. Entertainer/Animator. http://www.learn4good.com/jobs/entertainment/e/170852/search/antalya/.

——. 2013c. Host/Hostess/Entertainer. http://www.learn4good.com/jobs/entertainment/e/111547/search/izmir/.

Leifsen, Esben, and Alexander Tymczuk. 2012. Care at a Distance: Ukrainian and Ecuadoran Transnational Parenthood from Spain. *Journal of Ethnic and Migration Studies* 38(3): 219–36.

Leinaweaver, Jessaca. 2010. Outsourcing Care: How Peruvian Migrants Meet Transnational Family Obligations. *Latin American Perspectives* 37(5): 67–87.

Lerman, Zvi. 2004. Policies and Institutions for Commercialization of Subsistence Farms in Transition Countries. *Journal of Asian Economics* 15(3): 461–79.

Leshkowich, Ann Marie. 2006. Woman, Buddhist, Entrepreneur: Gender, Moral Values, and Class Anxiety in Late Socialist Vietnam. *Journal of Vietnamese Studies* 1(1–2): 277–313.

Lévi-Strauss, Claude. 1969. *Elementary Structures of Kinship.* Translated by James Hark Bell, John Richard von Stunner, and Rodney Needham. Boston: Beacon.

Lewin, Ellen, and Leni M. Silverstein. 2016. Introduction: Anthropologies and Feminisms: Mapping Our Intellectual Journey. In *Mapping Feminist Anthropology in the Twentieth Century,* edited by Ellen Lewin and Leni M. Silverstein, 6–37. New Brunswick: Rutgers University Press.

Lewis, Jonathan. 2011. Turkey: Christian Monastery Fights for Muslim Tenants. *Eurasia. net.* August 17. http://www.eurasianet.org/node/64057.

Lilya 4-Ever. 2002. 109 min. Sonet Films (Sweden)/Newmarket Films (US).

Lim, Sungsook. 2016. The Politics of Transnational Welfare Citizenship: Kin, State, and Personhood among Older Sakhalin Koreans. PhD diss., University of British Columbia.

Lipman, Maria, Lev Gudkov, and Lasha Bakradze, with Thomas de Waal, eds. 2013. The Stalin Puzzle: Deciphering Post-Soviet Public Opinion. Washington, DC: Carnegie Endowment for International Peace. http://carnegieendowment.org/files/stalin_puzzle.pdf.

Lokshin Michael, Kathleen Mullan Harris, and Barry M. Popkin. 2000. Single Mothers in Russia: Household Strategies for Coping with Poverty. *World Development* 28(12): 2183–98.

Lucas, Robert E. B. 2005. *International Migration and Economic Development: Lessons from Low-Income Countries.* Northampton, MA: Edward Elgar.

Luehrmann, Sonja. 2011. *Secularism Soviet Style: Teaching Atheism and Religion in a Volga Republic.* Bloomington: Indiana University Press.

——. 2004. Mediated Marriage: Internet Matchmaking in Provincial Russia. *Europe-Asia Studies* 56(6): 857–75.

Machado, Barry. 2007. *In Search of a Usable Past: The Marshall Plan and Postwar Reconstruction Today*. Lexington, VA: George C. Marshall Foundation.

Madison, Bernice. 1972. Social Services for Families and Children in the Soviet Union Since 1967. *Slavic Review* 31(4): 831–52.

Magosci, Paul Robert. 1995. The Rusyn Question. *Izbornik*. http://www.litopys.org.ua/rizne/magocie.htm.

Mahdavi, Pardis. 2011. *Gridlock: Labor, Migration, and Human Trafficking in Dubai*. Stanford, CA: Stanford University Press.

Makarenko, Anton. 1973. *The Road to Life: An Epic in Education*. New York: Oriole Editions.

Malarek, Victor. 2003. *The Natashas: The New Global Sex Trade*. Toronto: Viking.

Malysheva, Marina M., and Elena V. Tiuriukanova. 2000. *Zhenshchiny v mezhdunarodnoi trudovoi migratsii* [Women in international labor migration]. *Narodonaselenie*, no. 2: 91–101.

Mandel, Ruth. 2008. *Cosmopolitan Anxieties: Turkish Challenges to Citizenship and Belonging in Germany*. Durham, NC: Duke University Press.

Manderson, Lenore, and Margaret Jolly. 1997. Introduction: Sites of Desire/Economies of Pleasure in Asia and the Pacific. In *Sites of Desire, Economies of Pleasure: Sexualities in Asia and the Pacific*, edited by Lenore Manderson and Margaret Jolly, 1–26. Chicago: University of Chicago Press.

Manning, Paul. 2015. *Love Stories: Language, Private Love, and Public Romance in Georgia*. Toronto: University of Toronto Press.

Mansel, Philip. 1995. *Constantinople: City of the World's Desire, 1453–1924*. London: John Murray.

Marcus, George. 1995. Ethnography in/of the World System: The Emergence of Multi-sited Ethnography. *Annual Review of Anthropology* 24: 95–117.

Marsden, Magnus, and Diana Ibanez-Tirado. 2015. Repertoires of Family Life and the Anchoring of Afghan Trading Networks in Ukraine. *History and Anthropology* 26(2): 145–64.

Massey, Doreen. 1994. *Space, Place, and Gender*. Minneapolis: University of Minnesota Press.

Matusevich, Maxim, ed. 2007. *Africa in Russia, Russia in Africa: Three Centuries of Encounters*. Trenton, NJ: Africa World Press.

Mazzucato, Valentina, and Djamilla Schans. 2011. Transnational Families and the Well-Being of Children: Conceptual and Methodological Challenges. *Journal of Marriage and the Family* 73(4): 704–12.

McDonald, Lynn, Brooke Moore, and Natalya Timoshkina. 2000. *Migrant Sex Workers from Eastern Europe and the Former Soviet Union: The Canadian Case*. Ottawa: Status of Women in Canada.

Metaxa, Maia. 2006. Moldova Kids Get Old before Their Time. BBC. December 6. http://news.bbc.co.uk/2/hi/europe/6211444.stm.

Miller, Ruth A. 2007. Rights, Reproduction, Sexuality, and Citizenship in the Ottoman Empire and Turkey. *Signs: Journal of Women and Culture in Society* 32(2): 347–75.

Mills, Mary Beth. 1999. *Thai Women in the Global Labor Force: Consuming Desires, Contested Selves*. New Brunswick, NJ: Rutgers University Press.

Ministry of Foreign Affairs of the Republic of Belarus. 2016. "Rules of Border Crossing for Foreign Citizens. http://gpk.gov.by/en/informatsiya-dlya-peresekayushhih-granitsu/pravila-peresecheniya-granitsy-dlya-inostrantsev.php.

Mintz, Stanley W. 1998. The Localization of Anthropological Practice: From Area Studies to Transnationalism. *Critique of Anthropology* 18(2): 117–33.

Moore, Henrietta. 1988. *Feminism and Anthropology*. Minneapolis: University of Minnesota Press.

Morokvasic, Mirjana. 1984. Birds of Passage Are Also Women. *International Migration Review* 18(4): 886–907.

Moshkov, Valentine A. 1904. Turetskie plemena na Balkanskom poluostrove. [Turkic tribes on the Balkan peninsula]. *Izvestiia russkogo geograficheskogo obshchestva* 40(3): 29–32.

Müftüler-Baç, Meltem. 2012. Gender Equality in Turkey. Directorate General for Internal Policies, Policy Department C: Citizens' Rights and Constitutional Affairs. Brussels: European Parliament. http://www.europarl.europa.eu/document/activities/cont/201202/20120207ATT37506/20120207ATT37506EN.pdf.

Mukhina, Irina. 2014. *Women and the Birth of Russian Capitalism: A History of the Shuttle Trade.* DeKalb: Northern Illinois University Press.

Murakami, Haruki, 1997. *The Wind-up Bird Chronicle.* Translated by Jay Rubin. London: Harvill.

Mutler, Alison, and George Jahn. 2010. Millions of Outsiders Eligible for EU Passports: Citizens of Moldova, Macedonia, Serbia, Ukraine and Turkey May Benefit. NBC News. August 5. http://www.nbcnews.com/id/38580772/ns/world_news-europe/t/millions-outsiders-eligible-eu-passports/#.VRiUHWR4rB1.

Nadel, Barbara. 1999. *Belshazzar's Daughter.* London: Macmillan.

Nandy, Ashis. 1983. *The Intimate Enemy: Loss and Recovery of Self under Colonialism.* New Delhi: Oxford University Press.

Narlı, Nilüfer. 2003. Illegal Migrant Labor Force in Turkey. *Turkish Review of Middle East Studies* 14: 27–43.

National Bureau of Statistics of the Republic of Moldova. 2016. Population. Chişinău, Moldova. http://www.statistica.md/index.php?l=en.

——. 2004. Population Census 2004. Chişinău, Moldova. http://www.statistica.md/pageview.php?l=en&idc=295&id=2234.

Navaro-Yashin, Yael. 2002. The Market for Identities: Secularism, Islamism, Commodities. In *Fragments of Culture: The Everyday of Modern Turkey*, edited by Deniz Kandiyoti and A. Saktanber, 221–53. London: I. B. Tauris.

Naylor, Robin Thomas. 2004. *Hot Money and the Politics of Debt.* Montreal: McGill-Queens University Press.

Nazpary, Joma. 2001. *Post-Soviet Chaos, Violence, and Dispossession in Kazakhstan.* London: Pluto.

Nechepurenko, Oleg. 2014. Russia Reverses Birth Decline—But for How Long? *Moscow Times.* June 22. http://www.themoscowtimes.com/news/article/russia-reverses-birth-decline-but-for-how-long/502325.html.

Nemtsova, Anna. 2016. From Russia with Love: Thousands of Wives for Turkish Husbands. *Daily Beast.* January 1. http://www.thedailybeast.com/articles/2016/01/02/from-russia-with-love-thousands-of-wives-for-turkish-husbands.html.

Nikitina, E. 1996. "Chelnoki" tonut v more poshlin [Shuttle traders drown in a sea of import duties]. *Argumenty i Fakty*, no. 32: 7.

Öncü, Ayşe. 2002. Global Consumerism, Sexuality as Public Spectacle, and the Cultural Remapping of Istanbul in the 1990s. In *Fragments of Culture: The Everyday of Modern Turkey*, edited by Deniz Kandiyoti and Ayşe Saktanber, 171–90. London: I. B. Tauris.

——. 1999. Istanbulites and Others: The Cultural Cosmology of Being Middle Class in the Era of Globalism. In *Istanbul: Between the Global and the Local*, edited by Çağlar Keyder, 95–119. New York: Rowman and Littlefield.

Ong, Aihwa. 1999. *Flexible Citizenship: The Cultural Logics of Transnationality.* Durham, NC: Duke University Press.

Orthodox Church. 2010. Greek Orthodox Patriarchate Gears up to Ask Ankara for Return of More Properties. http://theorthodoxchurch.info/blog/news/2010/12/greek-orthodox-patriarchate-gears-up-to-ask-ankara-for-return-of-more-properties/.

Osmanlıca Türkçe sözlük. 2017. http://www.osmanlicaturkce.com/?k=Musayt%C4%B1r&t=@.

Over 40% of Russians Want New Stalin. 2005. *Moscow News.* March 4. www.mosnews.com/news/2005/03/04/wishedstalin.shtml.

Oxfeld, Ellen 1999. *Blood, Sweat, and Mahjong: Family and Enterprise in an Overseas Chinese Community.* Ithaca, NY: Cornell University Press.

Ozyegin, Gul. 2015. *New Desires, New Selves: Sex, Love, and Piety among Turkish Youth.* New York: New York University Press.

Padilla, Mark B., Jennifer S. Hirsch, Miguel Munoz-Laboy, Robert E. Sember, and Richard G. Parker, eds. 2007. *Love and Globalization: Transformations of Intimacy in the Contemporary World.* Nashville: Vanderbilt University Press.

Parla, Ayşe. 2009. Remembering across the Border: Postsocialist Nostalgia among Turkish Immigrants from Bulgaria. *American Ethnologist* 36(4): 750–67.

——. 2001. The "Honor" of the State: Virginity Examinations in Turkey. *Feminist Studies* 27(1): 65–88.

Parreñas, Rhacel Salazar. 2005. *Children of Global Migration: Transnational Families and Gendered Woes.* Stanford, CA: Stanford University Press.

——. 2001a. Mothering from a Distance: Emotions, Gender, and Intergenerational Relations in Filipino Transnational Families. *Feminist Studies* 27(2): 361–90.

——. 2001b. *Servants of Globalization: Women, Migration, and Domestic Work.* Stanford, CA: Stanford University Press.

Patico, Jennifer. 2010. Kinship and Crisis: Embedded Economic Pressures and Gender Ideals in Postsocialist International Matchmaking. *Slavic Review* 69(1): 16–39.

——. 2008. *Consumption and Social Change in the Post-Soviet Middle Class.* Stanford, CA: Stanford University Press.

Paxson, Margaret. 2005. *Solovyovo: The Story of Memory in a Russian Village.* Bloomington: Indiana University Press.

Pedwell, Carolyn, and Anne Whitehead. 2012. Affecting Feminism: Questions of Feeling in Feminist Theory. *Feminist Theory* 13(2): 115–29.

Peirce, Leslie. 2015. Writing Popular Biography: Hurrem Sultan, the Slave Who Became Ottoman Sultan. Presented in Simon Fraser University's Centre for the Comparative Study of Muslim Societies and Cultures Annual Lecture Series. March 12.

——. 1993. *The Imperial Harem: Women and Sovereignty in the Ottoman Empire.* New York: Oxford University Press.

Pelkmans, Mathijs. 2009. Introduction: Post-Soviet Space and the Unexpected Turns of Religious Life. In *Conversion after Socialism: Disruptions, Modernisms, and Technologies of Faith in the Former Soviet Union,* edited by Mathijs Pelkmans, 1–16. London: Berghahn Books.

——. 2006. *Defending the Border: Identity, Religion, and Modernity in the Republic of Georgia.* Ithaca, NY: Cornell University Press.

Peraldi, Michel. 2005. Algerian Routes: Emancipation, Deterritorialisation, and Transnationalism through Suitcase Trade. *Anthropology and History* 16(1): 47–61.

Pesmen, Dale. 2000. *Russia and Soul: An Exploration.* Ithaca, NY: Cornell University Press.

Pessar, Patricia R., and Sarah J. Mahler. 2003. Transnational Migration: Bringing Gender In. *International Migration Review* 37(3): 812–46.

Picchio, Ricardo. 1984. Guidelines for the Comparison of the Language Question among the Slavs. In *Aspects of the Slavic Language Question*, vol. 1, edited by Ricardo Picchio and Harvey Goldblatt, 1–42. New Haven: Yale University Press.

Pickard, Michael. 2012. Magnificent Quarter for CTC. C21Media. May 5. http://www. c21media.net/archives/81251.

Pine, Frances. 2002a. Dealing with Money: Zlotys, Dollars, and Other Currencies in the Polish Highlands. In *Markets and Moralities: Ethnographies of Post-Socialism*, edited by Ruth Mandel and Caroline Humphrey, 75–100. Oxford: Berg.

——. 2002b. Retreat to the Household? Gendered Domains in Postsocialist Poland. In *Postsocialism: Ideals, Ideologies, and Practices in Eurasia*, edited by Chris M. Hann, 95–113. New York: Routledge.

Pitt-Rivers, Julian. 1965. Honour and Social Status. In *Honour and Shame: The Values of Mediterranean Society*, edited by Jean G. Peristiany, 19–77. London: Weidenfeld and Nicholson.

Plešinger, Jan. 2014. Conference 20 Years of Gagauz Yeri. OSCE Mission to Moldova. Comrat. December 12. http://www.osce.org/moldova/131676?download=true.

Poe, Marshall. 2001. Moscow, the Third Rome: The Origins and Transformation of a "Pivotal Moment." *Jahrbücher für Geschichte Osteuropas* 49(3): 412–29.

Posadskaia, Anastasia. 1994. *Women in Russia: A New Era in Russian Feminism*. New York: Verso.

Potuoğlu-Cook, Öykü. 2008. Night Shifts: Moral, Economic, and Cultural Politics of Turkish Belly Dance across the Fins-de-Siècle. PhD diss., Northwestern University.

——. 2006. Beyond the Glitter: Bellydance and Neoliberal Gentrification in Istanbul. *Cultural Anthropology* 21(4): 633–60.

Pravoslavie.Ru. 2012. Return to Byzantium: An Interview with Bishop Tikhon (Zaitsev) of Podolsk. http://www.pravoslavie.ru/english/49781.htm.

The Price of Sex: An Investigation of Sex Trafficking. 2011. Produced and directed by Mimi Chakarova. 73 min. Violeu Films and A Moment in Time Productions.

Primeriia Vulkaneshty. 2004. Osnovnye pokazateli ekonomicheskogo razvitiia Vulkaneshty. January 1, 2004. [Primary indicators of economic development for Vulkaneshty]. Vulkaneshty.

Putz, Catherine. 2016. Turkish Targeting of Gulen Movement Reaches into Central Asia. *The Diplomat*. July 26. http://thediplomat.com/2016/07/turkish-targeting-of-gulen-movement-reaches-into-central-asia/.

Quiñones, María I. 1997. Looking Smart: Consumption, Cultural History, and Identity among Barbadian "Suitcase Traders." *Research in Economic Anthropology* 18: 167–82.

Rabina, Anna. 2000. "Gorbushka" pod ugrozoi. *Den'gi* 8 (261) (March 1): 7.

Raionnyi otdel zapisei grazhdanskogo sostoianiia (ZAGS). 2002. Brachnost' i razvody, s 2000-ogo g. po 2002 g. [Marriage and divorces, 2000–2002]. Vulkaneshty.

Rajagopalan, Sudha. 2008. *Indian Films in Soviet Cinemas: The Culture of Movie-going after Stalin*. Bloomington: Indiana University Press.

Ransel, David. 2000. *Village Mothers: Three Generations of Change in Russia and Tataria*. Bloomington: Indiana University Press.

Ratha, Dilip. 2005. Sending Money Home: Trends in Migrant Remittances. *Finance and Development* 42 (4). http://www.imf.org/external/pubs/ft/fandd/2005/12/picture. htm.

Rebhun, Linda-Anne. 1999. *The Heart Is an Unknown Country: Love in the Changing Economy of Northeast Brazil*. Stanford, CA: Stanford University Press.

Reddy, William M. 1999. Emotional Liberty: Politics and History in the Anthropology of Emotions. *Cultural Anthropology* 14(2): 256–88.

Reeves, Madeleine. 2014. *Border Work: Culture and Society after Socialism*. Ithaca, NY: Cornell University Press.

———. 2013. Clean Fake: Authenticating Documents and Persons in Migrant Moscow. *American Ethnologist* 40(3): 508–24.

Reynolds, Michael A. 2011. *Shattering Empires: The Clash and Collapse of the Ottoman and Russian Empires, 1908–1918*. Cambridge: Cambridge University Press.

Ries, Nancy. 2002. "Honest Bandits" and "Warped People": Russian Narratives about Money, Corruption, and Moral Decay. In *Ethnography in Unstable Places: Everyday Lives in Contexts of Dramatic Political Change*, edited by Carol J. Greenhouse, Elizabeth Mertz, and Kay B. Warren, 276–315. Durham, NC: Duke University Press.

Rivkin-Fish, Michelle. 2011. Learning the Moral Economy of Commodified Health Care: Community Education, Failed Consumers, and the Making of Ethical Clinical-Citizens. *Culture, Medicine, and Psychiatry* 35(2): 183–208.

———. 2010. Pronatalism, Gender Politics, and the Renewal of Family Support in Russia: Towards a Feminist Anthropology of "Maternity Capital." *Slavic Review* 69(3): 701–24.

Rofel, Lisa. 1999. *Other Modernities: Gendered Yearnings in China after Socialism*. Berkeley: University of California Press.

Rogers, Douglas. 2009. *The Old Faith and the Russian Land: A Historical Ethnography of Ethics in the Urals*. Ithaca, NY: Cornell University Press.

Rogers, Douglas, and Katherine Verdery. 2013. Postsocialist Societies: Eastern Europe and the Former Soviet Union. In *The Handbook of Sociocultural Anthropology*, edited by James G. Carrier and Deborah B. Gewertz, 438–55. London: Bloomsbury.

Rohde, David. 2012a. Inside Islam's Culture War. Reuters. March 8. http://blogs.reuters.com/david-rohde/2012/03/08/inside-islams-culture-war/.

———. 2012b. Why Turkey's Prime Minister Can't Stand His Country's Top Soap Opera. *The Atlantic*. December 14. http://www.theatlantic.com/international/archive/2012/12/why-turkeys-prime-minister-cant-stand-his-countrys-top-soap-opera/266274/.

Rosaldo, Michelle Z. 1980. *Knowledge and Passion: Ilongot Notions of Self and Social Life*. Cambridge: Cambridge University Press.

Rossiiskii statisticheskii ezhegodnik. 2002. *Statisticheskii sbornik*. [Digest of Statistics]. Moscow: Roskomstat. http://istmat.info/node/43527.

Rotkirch, Anna. 2004a. What Kind of Sex Can You Talk About? Acquiring Sexual Knowledge in Three Soviet Generations. In *On Living through Soviet Russia*, edited by Daniel Bertaux, Paul Thompson, and Anna Rotkirch, 90–117. New York: Routledge.

———. 2004b. "Coming to Stand on Firm Ground": The Making of a Soviet Working Mother. In *On Living through Soviet Russia*, edited by Daniel Bertaux, Paul Thompson, and Anna Rotkirch, 146–75. New York: Routledge.

Rotkirch, Anna, Anna Temkina, and Elena Zdravomyslova. 2007. Who Helps the Degraded Housewife? Comments on Vladimir Putin's Demographic Speech. *European Journal of Women's Studies* 14(4): 349–57.

Rouse, Roger. 1992. Making Sense of Settlement: Class Transformation, Cultural Struggle, and Transnationalism among Mexican Migrants in the United States. In *Towards a Transnational Perspective on Migration*, edited by Nina Glick Schiller, Linda Basch, and Cristina Blanc-Szanton. Annals of the New York Academy of Sciences 645: 25–52. New York: New York Academy of Sciences.

———. 1991. Mexican Migration and the Social Space of Postmodernism. *Diaspora* 1(1): 8–23.

Rubin, Gayle. 1975. The Sex/Gender System: Notes on the Political Economy of Sex. In *Toward an Anthropology of Women*, edited by Rayna Rapp, 157–210. New York: Monthly Review Press.

The Russian Market of Cognac and Brandy. 2002. *The Food Market*, no. 6. http://www.foodmarket.spb.ru/eng/archive.php?year=2014&number=7&article=74.

Russian Tourists to Surpass Germans in Turkey. 2012. *Hürriyet Daily News*. May 2. http://www.hurriyetdailynews.com/russian-tourists-to-surpass-germans-in-turkey-figures.aspx?pageID=238&nID=19728&NewsCatID=349.

Ruthven, Malise. 2012. *Islam: A Very Short Introduction*. Oxford: Oxford University Press.

Safonov, Andrey. 2014. Transnistria: A Policy of Denial, Containment, and Separation from Moldova. In *Moldova: Arena of International Influences*, edited by Marcin Kosienkowski and William Schreiber, 267–72. Lanham, MD: Lexington Books.

Salah, Mohamed Azzedine. 2008. The Impacts of Migration on Children in Moldova. New York: UNICEF. http://www.unicef.org/The_Impacts_of_Migration_on_Children_in_Moldova(1).pdf.

Sampson, Stevan. 1987. The Second Economy of the Soviet Union and Eastern Europe. *Annals of the American Academy of Political and Social Science* 493(1): 120–36.

Sanger, Carol. 1996. Separating from Children. *Columbia Law Review* 96(2): 375–517.

Sassen, Saskia. 2013. *The Global City: New York, London, Tokyo*. Rev. ed. Princeton, NJ: Princeton University Press.

Sasunkevich, Olga. 2016. *Informal Trade, Gender, and the Border Experience: From Political Borders to Social Boundaries*. New York: Routledge.

Sawatsky, Walter. 1981. *Soviet Evangelicals since World War II*. Kitchener, Ontario: Herald Press.

Saxonberg, Steven, and Dorota Szelewa. 2007. The Continuing Legacy of the Communist Legacy? The Development of Family Policies in Poland and the Czech Republic. *Social Politics: International Studies in Gender, State, and Society* 14(3): 351–79.

Sayan-Chengiz, Feyda. 2016. *Beyond Headscarf Culture in Turkey's Retail Sector*. New York: Palgrave-Macmillan.

Scheper-Hughes, Nancy. 2005. The Last Commodity: Post-Human Ethics and the Global Traffic in "Fresh" Organs. In *Global Assemblages: Technology, Politics, and Ethics as Anthropological Problems*, edited by Aihwa Ong and Stephen J. Collier, 145–67. Oxford: Blackwell.

———. 1989. Lifeboat Ethics: Mother Love and Child Death in Northeast Brazil. *Natural History* 98(10): 8–16.

Schillinger, Liesl. 2011. A Turkish Idyll Lost in Time. *New York Times*. July 10. TR1.

Schmalzbauer, Leah. 2004. Searching for Wages and Mothering from Afar: The Case of Honduran Transnational Families. *Journal of Marriage and Family* 66(5): 1317–31.

Scott, Julie. 1995. Sexual and National Boundaries in Tourism. *Annals of Tourism Research* 22(2): 385–403.

Sehlikoğlu, Sertaç. 2013. Vaginal Obsessions in Turkey: An Islamic Perspective. *Open Democracy*. February 18. https://www.opendemocracy.net/5050/serta%C3%A7-sehliko%C4%9Flu/vaginal-obsessions-in-turkey-islamic-perspective.

Semenova, Victoria, and Paul Thompson. 2004. Family Models and Intergenerational Influences: Grandparents, Parents and Children in Moscow and Leningrad from the Soviet to the Market Era. In *On Living through Soviet Russia*, edited by Daniel Bertaux, Paul Thompson, and Anna Rotkirch, 118–43. New York: Routledge.

Shah, Nasra, and Indu Menon. 1997. Violence against Women Migrant Workers: Issues, Data, and Partial Solutions. *Asian and Pacific Migration* 6(1): 5–30.

Shankland, David. 2003. *The Alevis in Modern Turkey: The Emergence of a Secular Islamic Tradition*. Routledge: Curzon.

Shlapentokh, Dmitry. 2003. Making Love in Yeltsin's Russia: A Case of "De-medicalization" and "De-normalization." *Crime, Law & Social Change* 39(2): 117–62.

Shlapentokh, Vladimir. 1989. *Public and Private Life of the Soviet People: Changing Values in Post-Stalin Russia*. Oxford: Oxford University Press.

Sik, Endre, and Claire Wallace. 1999. The Development of Open-Air Markets in East-Central Europe. *International Journal of Urban and Regional Research* 23(4): 697–714.

Sirman, Nükhet. 1989. Feminism in Turkey: A Short History. *New Perspectives on Turkey* 3(1): 1–34.

Slavorum. 2012. Turkish Neo-Ottoman TV Series. September 12. http://www.slavorum.org/forum/.

Soap Opera Diplomacy: Turkish TV in Greece. 2013. *The Record*. February 12. https://www.newsrecord.co/soap-opera-diplomacy-turkish-tv-in-greece/.

Soderlund, Gretchen. 2005. Running from the Rescuers: New U.S. Crusades against Sex Trafficking and the Rhetoric of Abolition. *NWSA Journal* 17(3): 64–87.

Solari, Cinzia. 2014. "Prostitutes" and "Defectors": How the Ukrainian State Constructs Women Emigrants to Italy and the USA. *Journal of Ethnic and Migration Studies* 40(11): 1817–35.

Sprinchana, Vitaly. 2011. Unsecularizing the World: Moldovan Baptists as Global Citizens. *Kristiianskii megapolis*, no. 11. http://www.christianmegapolis.com/unsecularizing-the-world-moldovan-baptists-as-global-citizens/.

Stack, Carol B. 1974. *All Our Kin: Strategies for Survival in a Black Community*. New York: Harper and Row.

Stanley, Alessandra. 1996. Russian Traders Go Abroad for Some Serious Shopping. *New York Times*. November 9, 1, 6.

Stewart, Kitty, and Maria Carmen Huerta. 2009. A Share of New Growth for Children? Policies for the Very Young in Non-EU Europe and the CIS. *Journal of European Social Policy* 19(2): 160–73.

St. Nicholas Center. 2012. Turkey. http://www.stnicholascenter.org/pages/turkey/.

Stoler, Anne. 2002. *Carnal Knowledge and Imperial Power: Race and the Intimate in Colonial Rule*. Berkeley: University of California Press.

Subbotina, Irina A. 2007. *Gagauzy: Rasselenie, migratsiia, adaptatsiia (vtoraia polovina XX–nachalo XXI vv.)* [Gagauzy: Settlement, migration, and adaptation (second half of the 20th and beginning of the 21st centuries]. Moscow: Institut etnologii i antropologii RAN.

——. 2005. *Gagauzy: Transformatsiia rasseleniia i sovremennye migratsionye protsessy* [Gagauz: Transformations of their settlement patterns and contemporary migration processes]. Moscow: Institut etnologii i antropologii RAN.

Suchland, Jennifer. 2011. Is Post-socialism Transnational? *Signs* 36(4): 837–62.

Svanberg, Ingmar. 2011. Gagauz. In *Ethnic Groups of Europe: An Encyclopedia*, edited by Jeffrey E. Cole, 159–62. Santa Barbara, CA: Greenwood.

Szelewa, Dorota, and Michal Polakowski. 2008. Who Cares: Changing Patterns of Childcare in Central and Eastern Europe. *Journal of European Social Policy* 18(2): 115–31.

Şenyuva, Özgehan. 2012. Turkey: Politics of Balance and Caution toward Moldova. In *Moldova: Arena of International Influences*, edited by Marcin Kosienkowski and William Schreiber, 205–18. Lanham, MD: Lexington Books.

Şimşek, Şükran, Adnan Kısa, and Sophia F. Dziegielewski. 2004. Sex Workers and the Issues Surrounding Registration in Turkey. *Journal of Health and Social Policy* 17(3): 58–69.

Taşpınar, Ömer. 2012. Turkey: The New Model? Brookings Institution. April 25. http://www.brookings.edu/research/papers/2012/04/24-turkey-new-model-taspinar.

Temkina, Anna, and Anna Rotkirch. 1997. Soviet Gender Contracts and Their Shifts in Contemporary Russia. In *Russia in Transition: The Case of New Collective Actors and New Collective Actions*, edited by Anna Temkina, 195–203. Helsinki: Kikimora.

Thelen, Tatjana. 2003. The New Power of Old Men: Privatization and Family Relations in Mesterszallas (Hungary). *Anthropology of East Europe Review* 21(2): 15–21.

Tianynen-Qadir, Tatiana. 2016. Transnational Grandmothers Making Their Multi-sited Homes between Finland and Russia. In *Transnational Migration and Home in Older Age*, edited by Katie Walsh and Lena Näre, 25–37. New York: Routledge.

Ticktin, Miriam. 2011. *Casualities of Care: Immigration and the Politics of Humanitarianism in France*. Berkeley: University of California Press.

Tiuriukanova, Elena. 2003. Zashchita prav trudiashchikhsia-migrantov v Rossii i perspektivy prisoedineniia k konventsii OON 1990 g. [Defending the rights of labor migrants in Russia and prospects for abiding by the 1990 UN convention]. In *Trudovaia migratsiia i zashchita prav gastarbaiterov: Praktika postkommunisticheskikh stran* [Labor migration and defending the rights of guestworkers: the experience of post-communist countries], edited by Zhanna Zaionchkovskaia and Valerii Moshniaga, 177–89. Chişinău: Moldavskii gosudarstvennyi universitet.

Toksabay, Ece, and Ibon Villelabeitia. 2011. Sultan's TV Drama Opens Turkish Divide on Religion. Reuters. February 8. http://www.reuters.com/article/us-turkey-ottoman-drama-idUSTRE7173GA20110208.

Tosun, Cevat. 2001. Challenges of Sustainable Tourism Development in the Developing World: The Case of Turkey. *Tourism Management* 22(3): 289–303.

Tolz, Vera. 2011. *Russia's Own Orient: The Politics of Identity and Oriental Studies in the Late Imperial and Early Soviet Periods*. New York: Oxford University Press.

Trafficking Cinderella. 2001. Produced and directed by Mira Niaglova. 48 min. Miran Productions.

Trawick, Margaret. 1990. The Ideology of Love in a Tamil Family. In *Divine Passions: The Social Construction of Emotion in India*, edited by Owen M. Lynch, 37–63. Berkeley: University of California Press.

Tsing, Anna Lowenhaupt. 2004. *Friction: An Ethnography of Global Connection*. Princeton, NJ: Princeton University Press.

Tucker, Hazel. 2007. Undoing Shame: Tourism and Women's Work in Turkey. *Journal of Tourism and Cultural Change* 5(2): 87–105.

Türkiye ve Rusya akraba oluyor [Turkey and Russia are becoming relatives]. 2003. *Hürriyet*. April 19. http://webarsiv.hurriyet.com.tr/2003/04/19/277193.asp.

Turkey Allows Female Police Officers to Wear Headscarf. 2016. *Daily Sabah*. August 27. http://www.dailysabah.com/legislation/2016/08/27/turkey-allows-female-police-officers-to-wear-headscarf.

Turkish Labor Law. 2016. New Fines for Illegal Employment of Foreigners in Turkey. September 21. http://turkishlaborlaw.com/news/legal-news/418-new-fines-for-illegal-employment-of-foreigners-in-turkey.

——. 2015. Obtaining a Work Permit in Turkey. April 21. http://turkishlaborlaw.com/work-permits-in-turkey/work-permit-process.

Turkish Ministry of Foreign Affairs. 2016. Visa Information for Foreigners. http://www.mfa.gov.tr/consular-info.en.mfa.

Turkish Ministry of Interior. 2014. Law on Foreigners and International Protection. http://www.goc.gov.tr/files/files/eng_minikanun_5_son.pdf.

Turkish Parliament Passes New Labor Law on Foreigners. 2016. *Hürriyet Daily News.* July 29. http://www.hurriyetdailynews.com/turkish-parliament-passes-new-labor-law-on-foreigners--.aspx?PageID=238&NID=102241&NewsCatID=341.

Turkish Statistical Institute (Turkstat). 2016. Foreign Trade. Imports and Exports by Country and Year. http://www.turkstat.gov.tr/PreTablo.do?alt_id=1046.

———. 2012. Birth Statistics, 2011. General Directorate of Civil Registration and Nationality. http://www.turkstat.gov.tr/PreHaberBultenleri.do?id=10923.

Tyner, James A. 1996. Constructions of Filipina Migrant Entertainers. *Gender, Place, and Culture* 3(1): 77–93.

Ugolok iurista [Lawyer's corner]. 2007. *TurPressPanorama.* May 11. 56: 16–31.

United Nations Development Programme (UNDP). 2016. Human Development Data (1980–2015). www.hdr.undp.org/en/data.

———. 2011. Towards Human Resilience: Sustaining MDG Progress in an Age of Economic Uncertainty. New York, NY: UNDP. http://www.undp.org/content/dam/undp/library/Poverty%20Reduction/Towards_SustainingMDG_Web1005.pdf.

United Nations High Commission on Refugees (UNHCR). 2017. Syria Regional Refugee Response. http://data.unhcr.org/syrianrefugees/regional.php.

United Nations International Children's Emergency Fund (UNICEF). 2009. Assessment of the Childcare System in Moldova. http://www.ceecis.org/ccc/publications/Raport_Eng_PDF.pdf.

United Nations Population Fund (UNFPA). 2015. Migration. http://www.unfpa.org/migration.

United Nations World Tourism Organization (UNWTO). 2012. UNWTO World Tourism Highlights. Madrid, Spain: UNWTO. http://mkt.unwto.org/sites/all/files/docpdf/unwtohighlights12enhr.pdf.

US Agency for International Development (USAID). 2012. Global Law Enforcement Data. http://www.state.gov/j/tip/rls/tiprpt/2012/192361.htm.

US Department of State. 2016. Trafficking in Persons Report 2016. https://www.state.gov/j/tip/rls/tiprpt/countries/2016/258723.htm.

———. 2015. Immigrant Number Used for Visa Issuances and Adjustments of Status in the Diversity Immigrant Category: Fiscal Years 2006–2015. https://travel.state.gov/content/dam/visas/Statistics/AnnualReports/FY2015AnnualReport/FY15AnnualReport-TableVII.pdf.

———. 2014. Trafficking in Persons Report 2014. https://www.state.gov/documents/organization/226849.pdf.

———. 2012a. Trafficking in Persons Report. "Definitions and Methodology." http://www.state.gov/j/tip/rls/tiprpt/2012/192352.htm.

———. 2012b. 2011 Report on International Religious Freedom—Moldova. http://www.unhcr.org/refworld/docid/5021059f2d.html.

———. 2010. International Religious Freedom Report. November 17. http://www.state.gov/j/drl/rls/irf/2010/148963.htm.

———. 2003. Trafficking in Persons Report. https://www.state.gov/j/tip/rls/tiprpt/2003/21277.htm.

———. 2002. Trafficking in Persons Report. https://www.state.gov/j/tip/rls/tiprpt/2002/10682.htm.

US Social Security Administration. 2014. Social Security Programs Throughout the World. Pp.208–212. http://www.ssa.gov/policy/docs/progdesc/ssptw/2014–2015/europe/moldova.pdf.

Utrata, Jennifer. 2011. Youth Privilege: Doing Age and Gender in Russia's Single-Mother Families. *Gender and Society* 25(5): 216–41.

Uygun, Banu Nilgün. 2004. Post-socialist Scapes of Economy and Desire: The Case of Turkey. *Focaal: European Journal of Anthropology* 43: 27–45.

Vance, Carol S. 2011. Thinking Trafficking, Thinking Sex. *GLQ: A Journal of Lesbian and Gay Studies* 17(1): 135–43.

———. 1982. Pleasure and Danger: Toward a Politics of Sexuality. In *Pleasure and Danger: Exploring Female Sexuality*, edited by Carole S. Vance, 1–27. Boston: Routledge and Kegan Paul.

Vanore, Michaella, Valentina Mazzucato, and Melissa Siegel. 2015. "Left Behind" but Not Left Alone: Parental Migration and the Psychosocial Health of Children in Moldova. *Social Science and Medicine* 132: 252–60.

Vedomosti verkhovnogo soveta SSSR. 1957. O naloge na kholstiakov, odinokikh, i bezdetnykh grazhdan SSSR [Taxation of bachelors, single people, and childless citizens of the Russian Republic]. August 29. 17(884): 531–32.

Verdery, Katherine. 2004. The Obligations of Ownership: Restoring Rights to Land in Postsocialist Transylvania. In *Property in Question: Value Transformation in the Global Economy*, edited by Katherine Verdery and Caroline Humphrey, 139–59. Oxford: Berg.

———. 2003. *The Vanishing Hectare: Property and Value in Postsocialist Transylvania*. Ithaca, NY: Cornell University Press.

———. 1996. *What Was Socialism and What Comes Next?* Princeton, NJ: Princeton University Press.

Vergin, N. 1985. Social Change and the Family in Turkey. *Current Anthropology* 26(5): 571–74.

Vertovec, Steven. 1999. Conceiving and Researching Transnationalism. *Ethnic and Racial Studies* 22(2): 447–62.

Vojdik, Valerie K. 2010. Politics of the Headscarf in Turkey: Masculinities, Feminism, and the Construction of Collective Identities. *Harvard Journal of Law and Gender* 33: 661–85.

Von Bremzen, Anya. 2013. *Mastering the Art of Soviet Cooking: A Memoir of Food and Longing*. New York: Crown.

Von Hagen, Mark. 2004. Empires, Borderlands, and Diasporas: Eurasia as Anti-paradigm for the Post-Soviet Era. *American Historical Review* 109(2): 445–68.

Wanner, Catherine. 2005. Money, Morality, and the New Forms of Exchange in Postsocialist Ukraine. *Ethnos* 70(4): 515–37.

Ware, Kallistos. 1993. *The Orthodox Church*. New ed. Harmondsworth: Penguin.

Waters, Elizabeth. 1992. The Modernization of Russian Motherhood: 1917–1937. *Soviet Studies* 44(1): 123–35.

Watson, Rubie S. 1986. The Named and the Nameless: Gender and Person in Chinese Society. *American Ethnologist* 13(4): 619–31.

Weber, Gerard A. 2014. After a Lifetime of Labor: Informal Work among the Retired in Romania. *Anthropology Now* 6(1): 15–24.

Weber, Max. 1958. Social Psychology of World Religions. In *From Max Weber: Essays in Sociology*, edited, translated, and introduced by H. H. Gerth and C. W. Mills, 267–301. New York: Oxford University Press.

Weitz, Richard. 2010. Russian-Turkish Relations: Steadfast and Changing. *Mediterranean Quarterly* 21(3): 61–85.

Werbner, Pnina, and Nira Yuval-Davis. 1999. Introduction: Women and the New Discourse of Citizenship. In *Women, Citizenship, and Difference*, edited by Pnina Werbner and Nira Yuval-Davis, 1–38. London: Zed.

Werner, Cynthia. 2004. Feminizing the New Silk Road: Women Traders in Rural Kazakhstan. In *Post-Soviet Women Encountering Transition: Nation-building, Economic Survival, and Civic Activism*, edited by Kathleen Kuehnast and Carol Nechemias, 105–26. Baltimore, MD: Johns Hopkins University Press.

White, Jenny B. 2004. *Money Makes Us Relatives: Women's Labor in Urban Turkey*. New York: Routledge.

——. 2002. *Islamist Mobilization in Turkey: A Study in Vernacular Politics*. Seattle: University of Washington Press.

——. 1999. Islamic Chic. In *Istanbul: Between the Global and the Local*, edited by Çağlar Keyder, 77–91. Lanham, MD: Rowman and Littlefield.

Wikan, Unni. 1984. Shame and Honor: A Contestable Pair. *Man* 19(4): 635–52.

Wilce, James M. 2004. Passionate Scholarship: Recent Anthropologies of Emotion. *Reviews in Anthropology* 33(1): 1–17.

Willen, Sarah S. 2005. Birthing "Invisible" Children: State Power, NGO Activism, and Reproductive Health Among Undocumented Migrant Workers in Tel Aviv, Israel. *Journal of Middle East Women's Studies* 1(2): 55–88.

Williams, Allan M., and Vladimir Baláž. 2002. International Petty Trading: Changing Practices in Trans-Carpathian Ukraine. *International Journal of Urban and Regional Research* 26(2): 323–42.

Williams, Raymond. 1977. *Marxism and Literature*. Oxford: Oxford University Press.

Wilson, Ara. 2012. Intimacy: A Useful Category of Transnational Analysis. In *The Global and the Intimate: Feminism in Our Time*, edited by Geraldine Pratt and Victoria Rosner, 31–57. New York: Columbia University Press.

——. 2004. *Intimate Economies of Bangkok: Tomboys, Tycoons, and Avon Ladies in the Global City*. Berkeley: University of California Press.

Woodall, Carole G. 2015. Decadent Nights: A Cocaine-Filled Reading of 1920s Post-Ottoman Istanbul. In *Mediterranean Encounters in the City: Frameworks of Mediation between East and West, North and South*, edited by Michela Ardizzoni and Valerio Ferme, 17–36. Lanham, MD: Lexington Books.

World Economic Forum. 2015. Global Gender Gap Report. https://www.weforum.org/reports/global-gender-gap-report-2015/.

World of Children—Artek Pioneer Camp Archives, 1944–1967 Online. 2007. Leiden and Boston: Brill. http://primarysources.brillonline.com/browse/world-of-children-in-the-ussr-camp-archives.

Wrangel, Peter N. 1930. *The Memoirs of General Wrangel*. London: Duffield and Company.

Yanagisako, Sylvia J. 1979. Family and Household: The Analysis of Domestic Groups. *Annual Review of Anthropology* 8: 161–205.

Yang, Yunxiang. 2003. *Private Lives under Socialism: Love, Intimacy, and Family Change in a Chinese Village, 1949–1999*. Stanford, CA: Stanford University Press.

Yenal, Deniz. 2000. Weaving a Market: The Informal Economy and Gender in a Transnational Trade Network between Turkey and the Former Soviet Union. PhD diss. Binghamton University, State University of New York.

Yıldırım, Umut, and Yael Navaro-Yashin. 2013. An Impromptu Uprising: Ethnographic Reflections on the Gezi Park Protests in Turkey. Hot Spots, *Cultural Anthropology*, October 31. https://culanth.org/fieldsights/391-an-impromptu-uprising-ethnographic-reflections-on-the-gezi-park-protests-in-turkey.

Yükseker, Deniz. 2007. Shuttling Goods, Weaving Consumer Tastes: Informal Trade between Turkey and Russia. *International Journal of Urban and Regional Research* 31(1): 60–72.

——. 2004. Trust and Gender in a Transnational Market: The Public Culture of Laleli, Istanbul. *Public Culture* 16(1): 47–65.

Yurchak, Alexei. 2003. Soviet Hegemony of Form: Everything Was Forever until It Was No More. *Comparative Studies in Society and History* 45(3): 480–510.

Zabusky, Stacia E. 2007. Ethnography in/of Transnational Processes: Following Gyres in the Worlds of Big Science and European Integration. In *Ethnographic Fieldwork: An Anthropological Reader*, edited by Antonius C. G. M. Robben and Jeffrey A. Sluka, 368–84. Malden, MA: Blackwell.

Zengin, Aslı. 2016. Violent Intimacies: Tactile State Power, Sex/Gender Transgression, and the Politics of Touch in Contemporary Turkey. *Journal of Middle Eastern Women's Studies* 12(2): 225–45.

——. 2013. What Is Queer about Gezi? Hot Spots, *Cultural Anthropology* website. October 31. https://cultanth.org/fieldsights/407-what-is-queer-about-gezi.

Zhao, Xinluo. 1994. Barter Tourism along the China-Russia Border. *Annals of Tourism Research* 21(2): 401–3.

Zhurzhenko, Tat'iana. 1999. Gender and Identity Formation in Post-Socialist Ukraine: The Case of Women in the Shuttle Business. In *Feminist Fields: Ethnographic Insights*, edited by Rae Bridgeman, Sally Cole, and Heather Howard-Bobiwash, 243–63. Peterborough, ON: Broadview.

Zigon, Jarrett. 2011. *HIV Is God's Blessing: Rehabilitation Morality in Neoliberal Russia.* Berkeley: University of California Press.

Index

Abu-Lughod, Lila, 169
affect. *See* emotion work; structures of feeling
agriculture. *See* Vulcăneşti (Vulkaneshty): collective farms (*kolkhozy*)
Ahmed, Sara, 69
Åkesson, Lisa, 105
Aksaray, 23, 32, 61, 208n13. *See also* Laleli
anthropology: anthropologist, perceptions of, 28, 31–33, 199n39; ethnography of the particular, 169. *See also* fieldwork
Appadurai, Arjun, 10
Atatürk, Mustafa Kemal. *See* Kemalist secularism

Belarus, 42, 122, 150, 155–56, 209n20, 220n19
Béller-Hann, Ildikó, 127
Berdahl, Daphne, 52, 65, 165, 189
Bernstein, Elizabeth, 158, 162, 198n29
Bessarabia, 79–81, 181, 211n9, 212n12, 223n17
Beyoğlu, 44, 46, 203n26. *See also* Taksim Square
Bulgaria, 61, 89, 200n3, 214n27
Byzantium, 41–42, 202nn17–18, 202n20. *See also* Constantinople

care work, 49–50, 73, 88, 102, 105–6, 111
Carrier-Moisan, Marie-Eve, 155
cartographies of desire. *See* sites of desire
Central Asia, 3, 8, 26, 36, 49, 82, 91, 208n7, 211n4, 223n19
Chamberlain, Mary, 166–67, 185
Cheng, Sealing, 152, 161
Chişinău (Kishinev), 13, 76–77, 163, 182, 211n6
Christianity: Baptists, 84, 90–92, 94; born again, 92; Eastern Orthodoxy, 42, 48, 143, 200n6, 204n38, 210n1, 211–12n10; Evangelism, 81, 90–92, 214n28; Moldovan Orthodoxy, 90; Seventh Day Adventists, 91; Spiritual Christianity, 90, 214n28; transnational networks of, 90–92. *See also* Russian Orthodox Church
Chu, Julie, 83
citizenship, 89, 117, 216nn4–5. *See also* passports

Clark, Gracia, 165, 207n1
Cold War, 41, 46–47
Collins, Patricia Hill, 165–67, 179, 184, 187
conspicuous consumption, 106–7
Constable, Nicole, 127–28, 139, 150, 155
Constantinople, 42–46, 126–27, 202nn17–18, 202n20. *See also* Byzantium
coups, Turkish, 188, 205n44, 205n48, 223–24nn1–2

Demirel, Süleyman, 49
deportations, 50, 109–10, 150, 177, 203n28, 218n20, 223n16, 223n19, 224n3
domestic labor, 51, 100–101, 119–20, 143, 146, 155, 205n51

Edib, Halide, 127
emotion work, 20, 58–59, 63, 67, 69, 74–75; affective labor, 69–70, 75; emotion regimes, 57, 70. *See also* shame
emotional labor, 20, 63, 74. *See also* emotion work
entertainers, 119, 135, 138, 151, 160–61; aspirations of, 146, 151–52, 155–58, 161–62; learning to labor as, 158–59; medical exams of, 148, 218n4; as "Natashas", 125, 217n14; and nightclubs, 135, 143, 145, 147, 218n2; photo albums of, 137, 151, 153; policing and detentions of, 148–50, 161–62; visas, 148–49, 219n12; work arrangements of, 145–49, 219nn8–10, 219n13. *See also* sex work
entrepreneurship. *See* shuttle trading
Erdoğan, Recep Tayyip, 35–36, 52–53, 124, 188, 217n12, 224n2
Eurasia, concept of, 16–17; map of 7
Evangelism. *See* Christianity
exotic dancers. *See* entertainers

Faier, Leiba, 119, 138, 219n12
faith tourism, 48, 204n37
Fethullah Gulen movement, 49, 205n45, 223–24n1
fieldwork, 23–26, 30–33, 153; with post-Soviet women, 6, 8; with young child, 29–31, 145, 163, 175

CPSIA information can be obtained
at www.ICGtesting.com
Printed in the USA
BVOW03*0022101117
499363BV00003B/13/P